BIOCITIZENSHIP

# BIOPOLITICS: MEDICINE, TECHNOSCIENCE, AND HEALTH IN THE 21ST CENTURY

General Editors: Monica J. Casper and Lisa Jean Moore

# Biocitizenship

*The Politics of Bodies, Governance, and Power*

*Edited by*

Kelly E. Happe, Jenell Johnson, and Marina Levina

NEW YORK UNIVERSITY PRESS

New York

NEW YORK UNIVERSITY PRESS
New York
www.nyupress.org

References to Internet websites (URLs) were accurate at the time of writing. Neither the author nor New York University Press is responsible for URLs that may have expired or changed since the manuscript was prepared.

Library of Congress Cataloging-in-Publication Data
Names: Happe, Kelly E., editor. | Johnson, Jenell M., 1978–
editor. | Levina, Marina, 1975–  editor.
Title: Biocitizenship : the politics of bodies, governance, and power /
edited by Kelly E. Happe, Jenell Johnson and Marina Levina.
Description: New York : New York University Press, 2018. |
Includes bibliographical references and index.
Identifiers: LCCN 2017045031| ISBN 978-1-4798-4519-4 (cl : alk. paper) |
ISBN 978-1-4798-6053-1 (pb : alk. paper)
Subjects: LCSH: Biopolitics | Citizenship. | Citizenship—Social aspects.
Classification: LCC JA80 .B498 2018 | DDC 323.601—dc23
LC record available at https://lccn.loc.gov/2017045031

New York University Press books are printed on acid-free paper, and their binding materials are chosen for strength and durability. We strive to use environmentally responsible suppliers and materials to the greatest extent possible in publishing our books.

Manufactured in the United States of America

10 9 8 7 6 5 4 3 2 1

Also available as an ebook

# CONTENTS

# Introduction

JENELL JOHNSON, KELLY E. HAPPE, AND MARINA LEVINA

Citizenship has a long, complex relationship with the body. One need only consider the intersection of medicine and immigration policy, antisuffrage arguments regarding the physical and mental "fitness" of women and people of color, or policies based on eugenics to see how bodies become subject to political recognition and political regulation—some more than others. In recent years, however, a number of developments in biomedicine and biotechnology, as well as a number of political initiatives, grassroots efforts, and public policies have given rise to new ways in which bodies shape—and are shaped by—ideas of citizenship, what has become known as "biological citizenship" or, simply, "biocitizenship."

Biocitizenship, according to sociologist Nikolas Rose in a foundational definition, comprises "all those citizenship projects that have linked their conceptions of citizens to beliefs about the biological existence of human beings, as individuals, as men and women, as families and lineages, as communities, as populations and as species."[1] This definition holds that the material body and its health, vitality, and natural and social environments not only create and discipline the citizen-subject but also provide the conditions necessary for its recognition and political agency within biopolitical modes of governance, broadly construed. Biocitizenship is thus a complex and generative concept that allows scholars to delve deeply into the intersections of bodies with issues of agency, politics, and resistance in a variety of contexts.

This edited collection expands the work of Rose and others in its three primary goals: to serve as the first multidisciplinary forum on biocitizenship, bringing together a variety of voices from different fields (including voices from outside the academy); to redefine biocitizenship as a broad mode of political action linked to health, bodies, and life, thus extending beyond the narrow confines of biomedicine and the privileged liberal subject often at its center; and to critically interrogate both the "bio" and the "citizenship" of biocitizenship. The chapters that follow examine the role of science, medicine, the state, and capital as means of enabling and restraining the exercise of biocitizenship in social, cultural, political, activist, aesthetic, and technical spheres. Importantly, one of the primary contributions of the volume is to expand the meaning of biocitizenship in response to ongoing scholarly conversations regarding the intersection of bodies and gender, disability, race, class, sexuality, nation, and the boundaries of humanhood.

Like any scholarly concept, the origins of biocitizenship are distributed, and depending on one's critical orientation and political commitments, the term can have substantially different meanings. In this introductory essay, we first outline a brief critical genealogy of biocitizenship and distill three primary meanings it has developed in the scholarly literature: as redress for collective bodily injury by the state; as a mode of biopolitical governance; and as a form of health advocacy and activism. We then turn to criticism of biocitizenship, which helps to sketch out the important relationships between biocitizenship and the state, biocitizenship and the market, biocitizenship and biomedicine, and—particularly salient in the contemporary moment—the combinations thereof.

## Biocitizenship Defined

The term "biological citizenship" first appeared in *Life Exposed*, anthropologist Adriana Petryna's 2002 study of political action in Ukraine after the Chernobyl disaster. In this groundbreaking work, Petryna investigates how the deleterious health effects of radiation exposure led citizens to petition the state for reparations, and also served as the "grounds for social membership and the basis for staking citizenship claims." Biological citizenship, as Petryna defines it, is "massive demand for but selective access to a form of social welfare based on medical, scientific, and legal criteria that both acknowledge biological injury and compensate for it."[2] Since the Chernobyl disaster took place only three years before the collapse of the Soviet Union, the emergence of the biological citizen went hand in glove with the emergence of democracy. The "biological" and "citizenship" of Petryna's analysis are thus equally weighted:

The collective and individual survival strategy called biological citizenship represents a tangle of social institutions and the deep vulnerabilities of persons; it is also part of a broader story of democratizing processes and structures of governance in the postsocialist states. Here the experience of health is irreducible to a set of norms of physiological and mental activity, or to a set of cultural differences. Only through concrete understandings of particular worlds of knowledge, reason, and suffering, and the way they are mediated and shaped by local histories and political economies, can we possibly come to terms with the intricate human dimensions that protect or undermine health. Seen this way, health is a construction as well as a contested way of being and evolving in the world.[3]

As her terminology suggests, Petryna's biological citizen is grounded in a democratic society in which the citizen is tied to the state in a relationship of rights and obligations. The political impetus that drives her study is thus found in that relationship's failure, particularly when it results in harm to the body.[4] For example, one might find this type of biological citizen-subject emerging in Flint, Michigan, after the community—which is 57 percent black—discovered that its water supply was contaminated with lead. After a 2014 state decision to begin drawing Flint's water from the Flint River instead of Detroit's municipal water system rendered the water toxic, harming (sometimes fatally) its citizens, enraged Flint residents took action, petitioned for their grievances, and spoke in the language of democracy. As Melissa Mays, one of Flint's leading water activists explains:

> [The recent] changes were actually forced by the citizens. We not only brought awareness to this crime by doing research, protesting, holding rallies, and doing social media blitzes . . . we banded together to form the Coalition for Clean Water and hired Attorney Trachelle Young to file injunctions starting in April of 2015. . . . Without the citizen focus, dedication and sacrifice, no one would have looked into the lead problem and helped us validate what the citizens were suffering through. We proved that everyday parents and citizens who never met before can team up and force change.[5]

The crime Mays describes is a crime not so much against individuals but against the community. Petryna's biological citizen emerges from an embodied, injured *citizenry* created by collective political action. In other words, Petryna's biological citizen is not an individual passively interpellated by biopolitical modes of governance but part of an active citizenry that takes shape through the injured biological body politic's challenge to the state.

In 2004, a more generalized theory of biological citizenship emerged in the work of sociologists Nikolas Rose and Carlos Novas, who have become the scholars most closely associated with the term.[6] As Rose and Novas point out, biological citizenship is not necessarily a new idea or practice. At the turn of the century, for example, monitoring migrants to the United States for signs of physical or mental disability—features inextricably tied to assumptions about the norms of race, ethnicity, and sexuality—was motivated by judgment about their capacity to work and also buttressed by eugenic visions of the present and future body of the nation.[7] Here biocitizenship might be thought of as a direct outgrowth of the concepts of biopower and biopolitics so famously articulated by Michel Foucault. If "biopower" describes "the numerous and diverse techniques for achieving the subjugations of bodies and the control of populations,"[8] and "biopolitics" names the expansion and intensification of biopower via a "set of mechanisms through which the basic biological features of the human species became the object of a political strategy,"[9] then biocitizenship might be described as the instrumentalization of biopower, authorized by the force of biopolitics to legitimate certain subjects of the state. One might thus classify actions such as compulsory vaccination, quarantines, and fitness programs for schoolchildren as examples of state biocitizenship practices designed to construct a normative national body.[10]

Expanding Foucault's work on biopower, Rose and Novas argue that biocitizenship projects and practices have expanded far beyond state programs and policies that discipline and govern the bodies of its subjects. In part, this reach is tied to a particular way of thinking about the relationship between bodies and selfhood they call "somatic individuality." Somatic individuality names a way of thinking about humans as "beings whose individuality is in part at least, grounded within our fleshly, corporeal existence, and who experience, articulate, judge, and act upon themselves in part in the language of biomedicine."[11] Somatic individuality describes the ascendance of a biomedicalized understanding of the body and its role in shaping both personal and political senses of identity. As somatic individuals, people think of themselves as collections of genes, tables of risks and probabilities, habits of neural impulses, and percentages of body fat. This approach to the self extends beyond personal understanding into the public sphere and political arena. To be fat in the United States today, for example, entails not only a private relationship to the body's desires for pleasure, its needs for nourishment, and its presence in space. It also involves the politicization of those relationships insofar as that body, or rather, that body imagined in the aggregate, is imagined as a "burden" that the taxpayer must bear or, worse yet, depicted as a threat to the nation. This is not an academic abstraction: in 2015, Dame Sally Davies, chief medical officer of the United Kingdom, declared obesity—and obesity in women in particular, pointing to relationships between maternal weight and pregnancy outcomes—to be a threat to the British people as grave as terrorism or climate change.[12]

As Foucault repeated again and again, where there is power, there is resistance, which gives power its legibility, authority, and force.[13] And so where there is biopower, there is also what we might think of as bioresistance, which operates on a tactical level, to use de Certeau's military metaphor. That is to say, tactics of bioresistance take place within the "field of vision" of institutional science and medicine, and necessarily operate upon its epistemological, material, and rhetorical terrain.[14] Consider, for example, the critics of "obesity epidemic" discourse who challenge the assumption that fat bodies are unhealthy, and who use scientific and medical research to do so.[15] Consider, further, the use of neurological research to support a kind of biological kinship in some autistic social movements and political organizing,[16] the use of genetic research to establish and politically mobilize an African diaspora,[17] or vaccine opponents' use of scientific studies (though most now discredited) to challenge the administration of vaccines to young children. These examples reflect an enactment of biocitizenship in which political agency is enabled and activated by the very state-sponsored programs that articulate normative health and/as civic responsibility.

On this point, we turn back to Rose, who has described these kinds of active, "ground-up" biocitizenship practices in detail, which he develops, in part, from Paul Rabinow's writing on biosociality.[18] To illustrate how the biological provides resources for new forms of sociality, Rabinow points to organizing by patient advocacy groups that sought to intervene in science or policy, or the gathering of somatic individuals into what we might call "somatic collectives." The citizenship projects enacted by these somatic collectives vary in goal and method, and Rose organizes them accordingly in *The Politics of Life Itself*. He describes the seeking out of technical scientific or medical knowledge as "informational biocitizenship." Collective action on behalf of new research, better treatment, or access to health or public services or to fight stigma might be thought of as "rights biocitizenship." Joining together with others with the same medical condition via e-mail lists and websites could be gathered under the name of "digital biocitizenship."[19] These types of biocitizenship practices by somatic collectives, driven by hope and optimism,[20] make demands on science and the state for biomedical goods and services and on behalf of cures and treatments.[21]

These approaches to biocitizenship have proved immensely fruitful to scholars from a wide variety of disciplines, who have used Petryna's, Rose's, and Novas's concepts to build compelling studies of the meaning of citizenship, belonging, political action, and resistance in a time of intensifying biomedicalization[22] and biopolitical governance. However, although biocitizenship has proved to be a powerful descriptive term, when it takes on a normative cast—that is, when the biocitizen becomes something we ought to be—things become more complicated. Underlying this affirmative discourse is an image of the model biocitizen, who is assumed to be a rational, autonomous actor, healthy, and able-bodied (or, importantly, wants to be), and has some measure of class privilege. When yoked to biomedicine, and when biomedicine is tied to state and corporate interests, the biological citizen thus becomes a much more troubling figure.

## Biocitizenship Critiqued

Thinking about citizens and citizenship in biomedical terms "help[s] to understand how it is that medical treatment should be a site of, rather than an alternative to, social and political contestations," Anne Pollock argues.[23] In that light, it might be tempting to think of the models of biocitizenship described earlier as a teleological movement, as citizen-bodies "take their power back" from science, doctors, and the state and use it to act and advocate on behalf of their own health. However, Pollock continues, it is important to consider that "if we are to grapple with biological citizenship in the United States, both our famously consumerist medicine and our infamously unequal access to it are fundamental. The diverse forms of biological citizenship overlap and coexist."[24]

Even further, the forms of biological citizenship we have described here "overlap and coexist" at a global cultural moment when what it means to be a good citizen has become subsumed by a market rationality. Wendy Brown argues that neoliberalism "normatively . . . figures individuals as rational, calculating creatures whose moral autonomy is measured by their capacity for 'self-care'—the ability to provide for their own needs and service their own ambitions."[25] This self-care extends to the body, of course, making the biological citizen in some aspects the quintessential neoliberal subject. As Ruha Benjamin defines them, biological citizens

> are those who make demands upon the state for biomedical goods and articulate their agenda as a nonpolitical, consumer-based movement seeking scientific research that is unencumbered by social justice concerns that might slow or thwart their quest for cures.[26] Reciprocally, these citizens are expected to take responsibility for their own health as a matter of civic duty, so that people and populations that are deemed "irresponsible" in this respect are what we might call "defectors," insofar as they do not perceive or engage their biological "defects" within the neoliberal frame of reference defined by the primacy of autonomy and self-enhancement, thereby also rejecting the terms of biological citizenship.[27]

Importantly, then, *who* fleshes out the biological citizen-subject matters a great deal. However, scholarship on biocitizenship often neglects issues of social location, such as race, class, gender, and disability, and in so doing tends to "promot[e] individual health as a way of ignoring larger social inequalities," argues Dorothy Roberts.[28] As Benjamin puts it, most of the critical literature on activist biocitizenship tends to focus on "a more elite strata of people who have the resources and influence to organize around their shared interests," and the "empowerment" in this model of biocitizenship is chiefly the power to consume.[29] Understood as part of a larger neoliberal social and political milieu, the action of the somatic individual—emphasis on *individual*—at the heart of biocitizenship "threatens to replace active, collective engagement to create a better society with providing information to the biotech industry and consuming its goods and services."[30]

The key point in these critiques is *not* that there is something necessarily wrong with health, individual or otherwise, or its promotion by state or nonstate entities. The point is that discussions of biocitizenship tend to coalesce around particular issues (individual health and/as civic responsibility), assume particular social locations of its subjects, and operate according to a neoliberal rationality that champions the private over the public and the individual over the collective—all while being underwritten by the pharmaceutical and biotechnology industries.[31]

For example, in an essay exploring the rise of personalized medicine and the emergence of the "quantified self movement," Melanie Swan uses the term "biocitizen" to positively describe a person who gathers information on their body, shares that information with others, and engages in "proactive health self-management and responsibility-taking."[32] DIYGenomics, a research organization founded by Swan, uses crowdsourced, self-gathered data as the basis of research trials and promotes itself as a form of decentralized citizen science.[33] Despite the empowerment rhetoric that saturates nonprofit organizations like DIYGenomics, for-profit companies like 23andMe, or state-funded initiatives like the American Gut Project (which seeks to map the U.S. gut microbiome through voluntary donation of data), the common language of self-management, responsibility, and individualism sites these projects squarely within a neoliberal approach to health that "has encouraged obsessive attention to individual embodiment, especially in the forms of self-surveillance and self-maximization" and the consumption of goods and services to support them.[34]

The rhetoric of improvement, enhancement, and optimization brings up another major issue that haunts the literature of biocitizenship: disability. We use "haunt" here deliberately, since the disabled subject serves as both the past and the future specter against which biological citizens are defined. The model biocitizen is rational, autonomous, healthy, able-bodied, or *endeavors to be so*. The model biocitizen thus maps closely onto the model liberal subject of classical democratic theory, and in many ways the liberal subject—which by its very definition excludes many disabled people—is the biocitizen's telos.[35]

To extend this point: What does disability activism look like through a lens of biocitizenship, and particularly those forms of activism that explicitly counter medical models of disability?[36] While there are certainly disability groups that mobilize around discourses of cure, the majority of disability rights and justice activism centers on access to education, employment, and the creation of a social world free of stigma and a physical world designed with a variety of bodies in mind.[37] Measured against the model biocitizen, activist biocitizenship practices are limited to the pursuit of treatment and cure (rather than, say, to distribution of resources or universal accessibility).[38] Even worse, in some of these discourses of biocitizenship, Ruha Benjamin argues, disability is deployed rhetorically through a narrative of tragedy—a narrative, we will add, that buttresses the claims of injured biological citizens, the fears of social engineers, and the urgency of activists alike. Haunting this discourse are the hundreds of thousands of disabled people murdered as "useless eaters" in Nazi Germany or sterilized in the United States in the pursuit of a healthy nation—perhaps the nightmarish perfection of biocitizenship. Unless they are actively moving toward the goal of a fit, healthy, normative body, disabled and chronically ill people, particularly those who actively challenge medical models of embodiment, at best find themselves sidelined from the biocitizenship literature; at worst, they are seen as "pathological citizens" who threaten the national body.[39]

As we have argued earlier, "biocitizenship" has taken on a number of meanings in the scholarly literature. However, although each of these meanings reflects a slightly different approach to the body and political action on its behalf, there is one point that unites nearly all scholarship on biocitizenship: no matter the mechanism by which it emerges or the purposes it serves, the biological citizen is a subjectivity made legible by biomedicine. Biocitizenship is a way of thinking about political belonging, recognition, and action "mediated by biomedical categories."[40] As a critical concept, biocitizenship is thoroughly anchored in a privileged, liberal subject, for whom norms of embodiment, livelihood, and affect are both intelligible and accessible. While biomedicine is certainly a rich place to look for manifestations of biocitizenship and its critics, as do

many of the essays in this volume, limiting our understanding of biocitizenship to a subject position constitutively tied to science, medicine, or
biomedical technology needlessly limits the critical reach and political
utility of this rich concept and may also reproduce the very norms that
can and must be questioned.[41] To that end, the essays that follow expand
and rethink both the "bio" and the "citizenship" of biocitizenship, and
some imagine biocitizenship not just beyond biomedicine but also beyond the human at its center.

## Organization of the Volume

The first part, "Categorical Understandings," theorizes biocitizenship in
case studies dealing with sexual health, incarceration, and epigenetics.
These essays challenge the uncritical valorization of biocitizenship
while also expanding the categories and methodologies of its analysis.
In chapter 1, "Governing Sexual Health," Steven Epstein shows how governmental interest in sexual health created the conditions for "biosexual
citizenship."[42] In so doing, he expands the notion of biocitizenship to
encompass embodied pleasure and risk and also broadens the concept
of sexual citizenship to include the institution of public health. Looking at historical case studies of two moments when U.S. public health
programs targeted sexual practices, Epstein reveals tensions between
competing approaches to biosexual citizenship. In chapter 2, "Carceral
Biocitizenship," Sarah Burgess and Stuart J. Murray further complicate a relationship between biocitizenship and sovereignty through an
analysis of the case of nineteen-year-old Ashley Smith, who, in 2007,
died of self-inflicted strangulation while on suicide watch at the Grand
Valley Institution for Women in Kitchener, Ontario, Canada. Their
essay examines how various institutions constituted Smith as a *carceral
biocitizen*—a subject caught between biopolitical practices and scenes
of legal sovereignty. By treating Smith as a dead subject, Burgess and
Murray argue, carceral institutions repudiate the traditional forms of
biocitizenship as a form of agency. And in chapter 3, "Epigenetics and
the Biocitizen," Kelly Happe argues that epigenetics, with its theories
of environmentally induced changes in the organism (including the
human) and the transmission of those changes intergenerationally, is
calling into question the temporality and materiality of biocitizenship

in profound ways. Examining one instantiation of epigenetic biocitizenship, the call to ground antiracism politics in evidence showing the biological damage of white racism, Happe shows how this temporality and materiality ultimately traffics in the dangerous proposition that biological evidence is more politically actionable than ethics or need. Happe asks whether other materialist gestures, such as historical materialism and affect-informed theories of materialization, might offer more ethically charged modes of biocitizenship grounded in bodily need, as well as queer temporality and relationality.

The second part, "Modes of Governance," examines how citizenship is enacted in what we might think of as the biopolitical public sphere. As a consequence, the authors imagine biocitizenship as a category of identity that can be constrained, enacted, or expanded for social, cultural, political, and economic purposes. In chapter 4, "Chronic Citizenship," Jeffrey Bennett introduces readers to the notion of "chronic citizenship," which he describes as a "performative mode of belonging" that privileges queer kinship and desire. Looking closely at public discourses around HIV prevention, in particular, the drug Truvada, and the rhetoric of respectability it threatens to unravel, Bennett shows how a theory of chronic citizenship avoids the otherwise problematic risk/risk-free binary—a binary that inevitably secures normative sexuality. In contrast, chronic citizenship is enacted by the always already risky body, thus opening up the space to reconfigure the relationship between risk, power, and sexuality. In chapter 5, "The Necropolitical Functions of Biocitizenship," Karma Chávez explores how biocitizenship might be thought of as a boundary-making project. Looking at controversies surrounding the International AIDS Conference in 1990 and its tacit support of the United States' travel ban on HIV-positive immigrants, Chávez demonstrates how the "life" at the heart of biocitizenship projects also entails death for those who fall outside the protection of national belonging. Finally, in chapter 6, "Exploiting Vulnerable Citizens," Carl Elliott and Emma Bedor Hiland extend our understanding of the necropolitical logic of biocitizenship even further by throwing light on the status of the "clinical laborer": the human subjects on whose bodies biomedical research is constructed. Far from relics from an unethical past, Elliot and Bedor Hiland show how these clinical laborers—specifically, people with mental illness—are stripped of the rights of citizenship and treated merely as raw, living material that enables the life and flourishing of others.

The third part, "Activism and Resistance," features essays that explore particular instances and practices of biocitizenship. The authors in this part explore how individuals and collectivities perform biocitizenship for purposes of reproduction, advocacy, and/or political resistance. In chapter 7, "Feeding Hunger-Striking Prisoners," Nayan Shah explores the ways in which hunger strikes may be considered a form of biocitizenship that positions bodily precarity and the willingness to sacrifice one's livelihood—one's life, even—as the ground of politics' very possibility. Yet it is a biocitizenship that remains largely unintelligible given a biopolitics insistent on "making live." It is this mode of biopolitical power, manifested in the practice of force-feeding, that is enforced upon the bodies of hunger strikers, as the interests of the state and of biomedicine collide. In chapter 8, "Biocitizenship on the Ground," Merlin Chowkwanyun documents the history of American medical student activism in the 1960s and 1970s, a remarkable time during which medical interests were linked to demands for community health and social justice. Describing these events as a revolution of medical governance—a revolution that was short-lived but nonetheless influential on the institutional practices that followed—Chowkwanyun examines how biocitizenship can take as its object micro-level practices in which expert knowledge is less contested than taken up in unconventional ways. This kind of biocitizenship, Chowkwanyun concludes, may be a sobering reminder of the limits of social movements organized around narrow conceptions of community insofar as social and economic forces external to it will, more often than not, render it unsustainable. In chapter 9, "The Rise of Health Activism," Celia Roberts and Richard Tutton explore how class structures the embodiment and enactment of biocitizenship—a crucial component of biocitizenship that has been overlooked and undertheorized by health scholars. Building on research showing that class positionality plays a role in observed health disparities, Roberts and Tutton examine how different modes of health activism are enabled by the otherwise unremarked privilege and interests of advocates, such as special access to knowledge networks or access to a public audience. Nevertheless, class alone may prove insufficient for describing both health disparities and the modes of biocitizenship enacted as a result. Roberts and Tutton conclude by presenting "biosectionality" as one concept that can provide the empirical and methodological means to understand the role of multiple positionalities on health outcomes and health activism. Finally, in chapter 10, "Patient Activists," Heather Aspell, Julie Cerrone, and Kirsten Schultz—health activists with long records of public engagement—detail their experiences with chronic illnesses and the institutions of science and medicine in relationship to biocitizenship. First, Aspell narrates how she uses art and digital media to challenge the preconceived notions of the disabled body. She draws our attention to biocitizenship as a status not available to many. In her section within this chapter, Cerrone explains how social media has helped her to understand and manage chronic disease and also reach out to others. She expresses hope about the potential of social media to extend biocitizenship practices across geographic and socioeconomic boundaries. Finally, Schultz describes her optimism about the potential of patient activists to transform the often-patriarchal institutions of science and medicine to better address the needs of disease communities. She urges us to think of biocitizenship as a form of advocacy for proper health care as a human right available to all.

The final part, "Beyond the Biocitizen," applies the concept of biocitizenship to nonhuman entities not traditionally considered in the literature on biocitizenship and helps us to think broadly about who and *what* we mean by the "bio" of biocitizenship. The authors consider lab animals, incubators, cyborgs, and corporations as sites for the expansion of biocitizenship as a category of analysis. In chapter 11, "Nonhuman Biocitizens," Marina Levina analyzes advertising images, research photos, and editorial content in *Lab Animal*, a monthly peer-reviewed journal for professionals in animal research, to consider lab animals as biocitizens in the network of laboratory scientific research. She contends that the journal integrates the tensions between stylized pictures of animals and the bloody work of surgery and experimentation through the affective unification of animals and scientists in the search for the cure. Levina argues that the condition of hopefulness traditionally associated with biocitizenship may be understood as a function of cruel optimism and necropolitics in which the gruesome death of some is necessary for participation in the "good life" of scientific research. In chapter 12, "The Citizens of Incubators," the renowned bioartists Oron Catts and Ionat

Zurr examine their own work with neolife—technologically created and fragmented life-forms—through the theoretical lens of biocitizenship. Catts and Zurr argue that the incubator functions not only as a conceptual and biopolitical apparatus, but also as a literal place where biocitizenship takes shape. In the final chapter, "The Super-Cyborg," Celeste Condit extends the concept even further by imagining the limits of the biological in our networked global society. Building from Donna Haraway's foundational work on the cyborg, Condit develops the concept of the supra-cyborg to name a phenomenon in which multiple human bodies and minds have become integrated with technologies and other forms of matter, which are themselves imbricated in the interests of nation-states and flows of global capital. How, Condit asks, might we live well—or live at all—in such a world? How do we conceive of justice or care in an era of the supra-cyborg?

The essays in this collection demonstrate that the intersection of bodies and citizenship is complex and variable, undergirded by history, power, and social forces, and also how this intersection may enable modes of agency and praxis not reducible to a set of fixed political practices or biological materialities. As global capital continues to blur the boundaries between states and their interests, as migration patterns change the composition of national bodies politic, as (bio)technology and environmental crises demand a rethinking of the human and non-human, the "bio" of biocitizenship must be subject to ongoing negotiation and critique. And perhaps most important, the book suggests that we must always be mindful of who occupies the position of biocitizen—model and otherwise—and for what reasons. We hope that this volume will start an important and ongoing discussion, both theoretical and practice-driven, of the notion of biocitizenship as unavoidable but no less differential in its effects, as normative yet also potentially disruptive of the very norms on which it often relies for its intelligibility, and as a mode of agency and governance with great promise and peril, reacting to and reflecting the always and already changing social worlds we inhabit.

NOTES

1 Nikolas Rose, *The Politics of Life Itself: Biomedicine, Power, and Subjectivity in the Twenty-First Century* (Princeton, NJ: Princeton University Press, 2007), 132.

2   Adriana Petryna, *Life Exposed: Biological Citizens after Chernobyl* (Princeton, NJ: Princeton University Press, 2002), 5–6.

3   Ibid., 33.

4   See the following literature on health activism and citizenship: Rajiv N. Rimal, Scott C. Ratzan, Paul Arnston, and Vicki S. Freimuth, "Reconceptualizing the 'Patient': Health Care Promotion as Increasing Citizens' Decision-Making Competencies," *Health Communication* 9 (1997): 61–74; and, especially, Heather M. Zoller, "Health Activism: Communication Theory and Action for Social Change," *Communication Theory* 15, no. 4 (2005): 341–64. See also the related concept of "therapeutic citizenship" as developed in Vinh-Kim Nguyen, *The Republic of Therapy: Triage and Sovereignty in West Africa's Time of AIDS* (Durham, NC: Duke University Press, 2010), 109. Nguyen sees therapeutic citizenship as more narrow than biological citizenship, which he defines as "an understanding of the role of the state and other large, stable institutions as guarantors of health care and social security." Therapeutic citizenship, in contrast, is tied to a single disease (like HIV/AIDS) and political mobilizations for access to resources.

5   Stacy Parker Lemelle, "'We're Not Victims, We're Fighters': Interview with Flint Water Activist Melissa Mays," *Huffington Post*, January 27, 2016, accessed June 1, 2016, www.huffingtonpost.com.

6   Nikolas Rose and Carlos Novas, "Biological Citizenship," in *Global Assemblages: Technology, Politics, and Ethics as Anthropological Problems*, ed. Aihwa Ong and Stephen J. Collier (Malden, MA: Blackwell, 2005), 439–63.

7   See, for example, Jay Dolmage, "Disabled upon Arrival: The Rhetorical Construction of Disability and Race at Ellis Island," *Cultural Critique* 77, no. 1 (2011): 24–69; and Nancy Ordover, *American Eugenics: Race, Queer Anatomy, and the Science of Nationalism* (Minneapolis: University of Minnesota Press, 2003).

8   Michel Foucault, *History of Sexuality, Vol. I: An Introduction*, trans. Robert Hurley (New York: Vintage, 1980), 140.

9   Michel Foucault: *Security, Territory, Population: Lectures at the Collège de France 1977–1978*, ed. Michael Senellart, trans. Graham Burchell (New York: Palgrave Macmillan, 2007), 1.

10  Rose, *The Politics of Life Itself*, 131.

11  Carlos Novas and Nikolas Rose, "Genetic Risk and the Birth of the Somatic Individual," *Economy and Society* 29, no. 4 (2000): 485–513.

12  Sophie Boreland, "Obesity in Women 'As Dangerous as Terror Threat,'" *Daily Mail*, December 11, 2015, accessed May 15, 2017, www.dailymail.co.uk.

13  Foucault, *History of Sexuality*, 95; *Foucault Live: Collected Interviews*, trans. Sylvère Lotringer (Cambridge, MA: Semiotexte, 1996), 386.

14  Michel de Certeau, *The Practice of Everyday Life*, trans. Steven Randall (Berkeley: University of California Press, 1988), 37.

15  Irmgard Tischner, and Helen Malson, "Deconstructing Health and the Un/healthy Fat Woman," *Journal of Community and Applied Social Psychology* 22, no. 1 (2012): 50–62.

16 See Chloe Silverman, *Understanding Autism: Parents, Doctors, and the History of a Disorder* (Princeton, NJ: Princeton University Press, 2011), especially 141–66; and Steve Silberman, *Neurotribes: The Legacy of Autism and the Future of Neurodiversity* (New York: Penguin Books, 2015).

17 Alondra Nelson, "DNA Ethnicity as Black Social Action?," *Cultural Anthropology* 28, no. 3 (2013): 527–36. See also Kelly Happe, *The Material Gene: Gender, Race, and Heredity after the Human Genome Project* (New York: NYU Press, 2013).

18 Paul Rabinow, "Artificiality and Enlightenment: From Sociobiology to Biosociality," in *Anthropologies of Modernity: Foucault, Governmentality, and Life Politics*, ed. Jonathan Xavier Inda (Oxford: Blackwell, 2005), 181–93.

19 Rose, *The Politics of Life Itself*, 133–34.

20 Carlos Novas, "Political Economy of Hope: Patients' Organizations, Science, and Biovalue," *BioSocieties* 1, no. 3 (2006): 289–305. Although Novas names hope as the dominant emotion driving biological citizenship, there are clearly other emotions at play as well. On this point, see Ole Andreas Brekke and Thorvald Sirnes, "Biosociality, Biocitizenship and the New Regime of Hope and Despair: Interpreting 'Portraits of Hope' and the 'Mehmet Case,'" *New Genetics and Society* 30, no. 4 (2011): 347–74.

21 For more on this kind of activism, see Steven Epstein, *Impure Science: AIDS, Activism, and the Politics of Knowledge* (Berkeley: University of California Press, 1996); and Paula A. Treichler, *How to Have Theory in an Epidemic: Cultural Chronicles of AIDS* (Durham, NC: Duke University Press, 1999).

22 See Adele E. Clarke, *Biomedicalization* (New York: Wiley, 2010).

23 Anne Pollock, *Medicating Race: Heart Disease and Durable Preoccupations with Difference* (Durham, NC: Duke University Press, 2012), 144.

24 Ibid., 7.

25 Wendy Brown, "Neo-liberalism and the End of Liberal Democracy," *Theory and Event* 7, no. 1 (2003): n.p.

26 On the demand and desire for cures, see Eli Clare, *Brilliant Imperfection: Grappling with Cure* (Durham, NC: Duke University Press, 2017).

27 Ruha Benjamin, *People's Science: Bodies and Rights on the Stem Cell Frontier* (Palo Alto, CA: Stanford University Press, 2013), 191n47.

28 Dorothy Roberts, "The Social Immorality of Health in the Gene Age: Race, Disability, and Inequality," in *Against Health: How Health Became the New Morality*, ed. Jonathan M. Metzl and Anna Kirkland (New York: NYU Press, 2010), 61.

29 Benjamin, *People's Science*, 17. See also Roger Cooter and Claudia Stein, "Cracking Biopower," *History of the Human Sciences* 23, no. 2 (2010): 109–28.

30 Dorothy Roberts, *Fatal Invention: How Science, Politics, and Big Business Re-create Race in the Twenty-First Century* (New York: New Press, 2011), 224–25.

31 Pollock, *Medicating Race*, 144. Rose and Novas also note that "not all have equal citizenship in this new biological age" ("Biological Citizenship," 442). See also Alexandra Plows and Paula Boddington, "Troubles with Biocitizenship?," *Genomics, Society, and Policy* 2, no. 3 (2006): 115–35.

32 Melanie Swan, "Health 2050: The Realization of Personalized Medicine through Crowdsourcing, the Quantified Self, and the Participatory Biocitizen," *Journal of Personalized Medicine* 2, no. 3 (2012): 93–118.

33 Elie Dolgin, "Personalized Investigation," *Nature Medicine* 16 (2010): 953–55.

34 Mara Mills, "Bio-X: Review," *WSQ: Women's Studies Quarterly* 40, no. 1 (2012): 257–65.

35 See Stacy Clifford Simplican, *The Capacity Contract: Intellectual Disability and the Question of Citizenship* (Minneapolis: University of Minnesota Press, 2015).

36 On this point, see Benjamin, *People's Science*, 55–78.

37 For more on the complex discussions of cure in disability studies and activism, see Eunjung Kim, *Curative Violence: Rehabilitating Disability, Gender, and Sexuality in Modern Korea* (Durham, NC: Duke University Press, 2016); and Clare, *Brilliant Imperfection*.

38 On the problem of uncritical medicalization in the biocitizenship literature, particularly around issues of mental health, see Plows and Boddington, "Troubles with Biocitizenship?," 120–21.

39 On the relationship between disability and biocitizenship, see the excellent discussion in Bill Hughes, "Disability Activisms: Social Model Stalwarts and Biological Citizens," *Disability and Society* 24, no. 6 (2009): 677–88. See also Anne Kerr, "Genetics and Citizenship," in *Biotechnology between Commerce and Civil Society*, ed. Nico Stehr (New Brunswick, NJ: Transaction Press, 2004), 159–74; Bruce Braun, "Biopolitics and the Molecularization of Life," *Cultural Geographies* 14, no. 1 (2007): 6–28; and Sujatha Raman and Richard Tutton, "Life, Science, and Biopower," *Science, Technology and Human Values* 35, no. 5 (2010): 711–34.

40 Nguyen, *The Republic of Therapy*, 108.

41 Plows and Boddington explore this idea in "Troubles with Biocitizenship?"

42 Epstein draws this term from Aaron T. Norton, "Cutting the Risk: The Emergence of Male Circumcision Status as an HIV-Risk Reduction Strategy" (PhD diss., University of California, Davis, 2014).

PART I

Categorical Understandings

1

# Governing Sexual Health

*Bridging Biocitizenship and Sexual Citizenship*

STEVEN EPSTEIN

For two days in April 2010, staff employees at the U.S. Centers for Disease Control and Prevention (CDC) sat down with sixty-seven invited experts and stakeholders to hash out an agenda for the nation's sexual health. Dr. Kevin Fenton, the director of the CDC's National Center for HIV/AIDS, Viral Hepatitis, STD, and TB Prevention, told those assembled: "Sexual health is a state of physical, emotional, mental, and social well-being in relation to sexuality and is not merely the absence of disease, dysfunction, or infirmity."[1] Noting that the U.S. Department of Health and Human Services (HHS) had recently designated sexual health and responsible sexual behavior as one of ten leading health indicators, Fenton called for a "radically inclusive" public health approach to promoting sexual health, one that would "bring new partners to the table."[2] The group of attendees was, in fact, diverse and included leaders from the National Coalition of STD Directors, the National Coalition for LGBT Health, and the National Alliance of State and Territorial AIDS Directors, along with representatives of the Ford Foundation's Sexuality, Reproductive Health and Rights Program, the Navy and Marine Corps' Sexual Health and Responsibility Program, and the Metropolitan Interdenominational Church.

While this meeting was distinctive, it was neither the first nor the last occasion on which something specifically called sexual health has been made the object of governmental scrutiny and policy making in the United States, or deemed a key linkage point between individual conduct and social membership. Nine year earlier, at the dawn of the new millennium, Surgeon General David Satcher issued the landmark "Call to Action to Promote Sexual Health and Responsible Sexual Behavior." Sexual health has also been featured as a chief goal in important federal planning documents, including HHS's National Prevention Strategy and HHS's most recent decennial health promotion agenda for the nation, "Healthy People 2020."[3]

These efforts have sought to make sexual health an object of governance—and to link governing efforts with the self-governance of individuals.[4] Such developments raise questions that are both practical and theoretical. What is the place of the *sexual* in a well-developed conception of biocitizenship? What is the place of the *biomedical* in our understandings of sexual citizenship? In this chapter I seek to show how a focus on the social management of the sexual health of citizens prompts a dual expansion of view: on one hand, an enlargement of *biocitizenship* to encompass the embodied nature of sexual pleasure and risk, and on the other hand, an enhanced understanding of *sexual citizenship* to highlight the roles of public health officials, in engagement with ordinary citizens, in defining sexual meanings, practices, rights, responsibilities, and identities. I begin by locating my project in relation to the literature on citizenship, biocitizenship, and sexual citizenship, building an intersectional concept that Aaron Norton has termed "biosexual citizenship."[5] Then, I describe two historical moments in which state regulation of sexual conduct has emphasized health and medical concerns: the "social hygiene" era in the turn-of-the-twentieth-century United States, and the "sexual health" era, which dates to the mid-1970s but became a formal feature of governance with the surgeon general's "Call to Action" in 2001.[6]

Examining these two moments helps me to call attention to important continuities in how notions of "sexual responsibility" have been made central to conceptions of the good citizen. Yet the juxtaposition of these historical episodes also points to certain relatively distinct characteristics of biocitizenship and governance in the recent era of sexual health. I emphasize several points of divergence that I suggest are loosely linked, including the knitting together of ideas of rights and responsibilities in relation to sexuality, the kinds of science and forms of evidence that undergird sexual health governance, the political openings afforded by a policy emphasis on reducing health disparities, and the salience of a practical emphasis on consensus formation and inclusiveness. I conclude by suggesting that these characteristics of modern sexual health governance provide openings for, but also impose constraints on, the active exercise of biosexual citizenship "from below." Individuals and groups confronting sexual health challenges such as the HIV/AIDS epidemic must negotiate their way around these terms of citizenship—or else find themselves positioned as standing "against health." The case therefore highlights the tensions between the top-down and bottom-up dimensions of biosexual citizenship.

## Fleshing out "Biosexual Citizenship"

By "citizenship," I refer to differentiated modes of incorporation of individuals or groups fully or partially into a polity through the articulation of notions of rights and responsibilities.[7] Citizenship is not an "either/or": in place of a static notion of citizenship as something one either fully possesses or fully lacks, it makes sense to understand the boundaries of citizenship as the outcome of ongoing struggles that reflect "constantly shifting relationships of power."[8] According to Lauren Berlant, citizenship "is continually being produced out of a political, rhetorical, and economic struggle over who will count as 'the people' and how social membership will be measured and valued."[9] Hence, as many scholars have described, the history of citizenship as a category of universal membership is simultaneously a history of exclusion, and citizenship has been defined in practice by means of the creation or dismantling of a wide range of social divisions and hierarchies.[10]

As Christian Joppke has observed, citizenship should be thought of simultaneously as a *status* (membership governed by rules of access), as *rights* that attach to that status, and as an *identity* articulated in relation to a political collectivity.[11] While some discussions of citizenship—for example, some writings on cultural citizenship[12]—veer in the direction of including within its ambit nearly any form of belonging or affinity, I prefer to reserve the term for cases where the reference point includes some sort of political community (though in the broadest sense of "political") associated with a state, government, or polity (whether national, transnational, local, or translocal).

### Biocitizenship

As the essays in this volume attest, biocitizenship (and its various cousins, including biological citizenship, biopolitical citizenship, genetic citizenship, therapeutic citizenship, etc.) is an evocative label that has been used in many ways.[13] Just as I believe that not every form of belonging should be called citizenship, I would similarly distinguish between "biosociality" and biocitizenship. As described by Paul Rabinow in an influential formulation, biosociality refers to the bases for affiliation provided by various sorts of classifications created, or given a transformed meaning, by the life sciences—for example, all those who share a disease, a treatment, a genetic risk factor, an exposure, or even a sex or a race.[14] As suggested earlier, I would prefer to reserve "biocitizenship" for those moments when biosociality references a political community. However, it is important to say that this can happen in many different ways.

In an early usage, Adriana Petryna described how, in the Ukraine after the nuclear accident at Chernobyl, "the damaged body of a population [became] the grounds for social memberships and the basis for staking citizenship claims."[15] Others have pointed to patient activism or other political organizing around disease states or genetic risk factors as quintessential examples of biocitizenship.[16] In a somewhat different register, in my own earlier work I used the term "biopolitical citizenship" to describe how biomedical classification of social groups (according to race, gender, sexuality, etc.) has proceeded hand in hand with political struggles to direct medical attention and public resources to such groups—and how the question of numerical representation in clinical trials became joined to that of political representation in U.S. society.[17] Still others refer to the biotechnologies used to police membership in a nation-state as mechanisms of biometric or biopolitical citizenship.[18] Finally, Nikolas Rose and Carlos Novas, while referencing many of the aspects of biocitizenship described here, also call attention to processes of self-formation—"the creation of persons with a certain kind of relation to themselves [who] use biologically colored languages to describe aspects of themselves or their identities, and to articulate their feelings of unhappiness, ailments, or predicaments."[19]

As Nicole Charles has observed in a critical commentary on Rose and Novas's emphasis on self-formation, such processes of constructing biocitizens in practice are often "prompted 'from above'" in ways that may be coercive and damaging.[20] Yet her own example of human papillomavirus (HPV) vaccination can be turned against her: while she correctly points to how public health campaigns to promote HPV vaccination call forth a gendered responsible citizen,[21] she misses the contrary example of groups such as gay health advocates who have used the issue of HPV strategically and in a sex-positive way to demand biomedical inclusion and state attention.[22] Thus biocitizenship is often double-sided, as several scholars have noted, and it may become manifest in ways that are either "top-down" and imposed, or "bottom-up" and achieved, or some complex combination of the two.[23]

Drawing on these various shades of meaning in recent discourse on biocitizenship, I now seek to extend the focus of biocitizenship studies by signaling the importance of sexuality. Put another way, I want to emphasize the place of the sexual in an expanded conception of biocitizenship, but also the place of health and biology in an expanded conception of sexual citizenship.

### From Sexual Citizenship to "Biosexual Citizenship"

Much like biocitizenship, the term "sexual citizenship" has proved productive despite—or perhaps because of—the lack of agreement about either its definition or its practical implications.[24] The concept has been used widely and variously to describe sexual rights claimed by citizens that may or may not be recognized by the state; the claims to equal treatment of groups such as sexual minorities; the heteronormative presumptions and functions of citizenship more generally; policing by state agencies of the boundaries between "good" and "bad" sexuality; and state-sponsored projects of subject formation via the inculcation of specific norms related to sexuality.[25]

At the greatest level of generality, we can describe sexual citizenship as the claim to rights and assumption of responsibilities associated with the multiple dimensions of exclusion or incorporation that stem from sexual practices, identities, norms, and attributions. Yet despite the long history of medical involvement in categorizing and evaluating sexualities, only occasionally has the sexual citizenship literature trained its attention on matters of health and biomedicine—most notably, in relation to the HIV/AIDS epidemic. For example, Carlos Decena has explored questions of "ethical sexual citizenship" in relation to federal health officials' exhortations to non-gay-identified men who have sex with men to "come out" as gay, while Jeffrey Bennett, in his book *Banning Queer*

*Blood*, has examined how a policy of the Food and Drug Administration that has been in place since the early years of the epidemic separates gay men from civic participation while "constructing queer identity through representations of diseased and undisciplined sexuality."[26] In relation to a different health threat, I have addressed the intertwining of the sexual and the biomedical dimensions of citizenship by characterizing the case of gay men's advocacy around anal cancer and its causal agent, HPV, as a fight "waged simultaneously on two fronts—as one of many present-day struggles against health inequalities, and as one of many present-day struggles for full equality on the basis of sexual identity"—and hence as an example of the junction of biopolitical and sexual citizenship.[27]

Following Aaron Norton, I propose to bring the concerns of biocitizenship and sexual citizenship into closer connection.[28] As Norton described in his study of male circumcision as an HIV prevention approach, the rise of circumcision as a proposed ethical imperative for men in sub-Saharan Africa (and perhaps elsewhere) "enacts new forms of responsibility and obligation based on *sexual anatomy* and one's willingness to alter it . . . for the sake of oneself and one's community, a form of biological citizenship I call 'biosexual citizenship.'"[29] Norton's analysis hints at the more general applicability of the term. I will define biosexual citizenship as differentiated modes of incorporation of individuals or groups fully or partially into a polity through the articulation of notions of rights and responsibilities, in cases where biological and health-related processes are brought into some relation with sexual meanings or identities. This conceptual intersection of biocitizenship and sexual citizenship calls attention to how embodied pleasures and risks associated with sexuality figure in the worlds of biomedicine and public health, as well as how public health officials, in engagement with others, participate in defining sexual rights and responsibilities.

While my broader claim is that the concept of biosexual citizenship could be usefully applied in many contexts, my emphasis here is on how this framework proves helpful in describing certain key features of recent discourses and practices that have emerged under the sign of "sexual health"—but also for an earlier era of "social hygiene." Comparing the social hygiene and sexual health eras makes sense because both were periods when the connections between sexuality, health, and disease were highlighted in government policies, and when the implications of sexuality for health became of concern to a broad array of government officials, physicians, and social reformers. Examining these two moments will help me call attention to important continuities in how notions of "sexual responsibility" and health promotion have been made central to conceptions of the good citizen. Yet juxtaposing these historical episodes will also highlight certain relatively distinct characteristics of governance and citizenship in the recent era of sexual health.

## Biosexual Citizenship in the Era of Social Hygiene

As Theo Sandfort and Anke Ehrhardt have also observed, "the recent emergence of the concept of sexual health does not mean that a completely new field of practice and research has materialized," and they point to the social hygiene movement as a relevant historical predecessor.[30] Visible in the United States from the latter years of the nineteenth century through the First World War, social hygiene united the efforts and interests of physicians, social workers, public health officials, military leaders, and other government bureaucrats with those of "predominantly female moral reformers, heirs to the tradition of the 'purity crusade.'"[31] As Kristin Luker has noted: "Together, the two traditions created the quintessentially Progressive blend of moral zeal and technical expertise."[32] The name of this movement is revealing. While "social" functioned as much as a euphemism for "sexual" as a reference to social issues, "hygiene," according to Luker, "was a magical word": it "encompassed health in all its dimensions: social, mental, spiritual, and physical."[33] But in particular, as Allan Brandt has emphasized, social hygiene was the imagined solution both to the moral contamination of modern urban society and to the "venereal diseases" that seemed to be the physical embodiment of a fraying moral fabric.[34] In line with the eugenic discourses that were ubiquitous at the time, reformers associated this moral decay with the infusion of immigrants to U.S. urban centers at the same time as those of Anglo-Saxon descent were committing "race suicide" through their failure to reproduce at the same rates as newcomers.[35]

Social hygienists focused on diverse strategies of sex education, disease prevention, and social regulation to carry out their moral campaigns, assert a normative vision of social order, and draw boundaries around proper biosexual citizenship. According to Dr. Prince Morrow, the founder in 1905 of the American Society for Sanitary and Moral Prophylaxis (a group that consisted mostly of physicians), "Venereal disease seeks no man . . . ; it must be sought in order to be acquired."[36] Surgeon General W. C. Gorgas, like the movement generally, placed the blame for venereal disease on the looser morals of men and argued against the sexual double standard; yet in practice it was female sex workers who bore the brunt of reformers' energies.[37] In addition, a concern with "male perversion" prompted new scrutiny of male same-sex activity in urban areas.[38]

Legislation promoted by reformers created a new category of laws against "morality crimes" that focused particularly on penalizing commercial sex workers, including, in some jurisdictions, the detention of prostitutes found to be infected with a venereal disease.[39] The campaign against venereal disease took on new urgency with the entry of the United States into the First World War, for, as secretary of the navy Josephus Daniels observed, "Men must live straight if they would shoot straight."[40] Or, as one reformer claimed: "It is generally recognized that a bad and diseased woman can do more harm than any German fleet of airplanes that has yet passed over London."[41] Of course, concerns about the moral fiber of soldiers coincided with more prosaic worries about manpower: government officials characterized syphilis as the primary cause of lost workdays within the U.S. military during the war.[42]

The twin impetuses of moralism and science existed in some state of tension within the social hygiene movement; and especially with the advent, by midcentury, of antibiotic treatment for sexually transmitted infections (STIs), moral campaigners and health professionals pushed toward different practical solutions.[43] While some of the discourse of social hygiene continued to find expression through the Second World War and beyond, the energy of the reform wave subsided. Meanwhile, the language of "hygiene" came to sound both quaint and unduly moralistic, and too closely associated with ideas of purity and cleanliness. Interestingly, the most important organization to be formed during the social hygiene era, the American Social Hygiene Association (founded in 1914), changed its name to the American Social *Health* association in 1959 and then to the American *Sexual* Health Association in 2012.[44] In other words, as "hygiene" fell out of favor, "health" became available as a more all-encompassing substitute, paving the way for this organization to adopt the sexual health mantle once the latter term had become ubiquitous. This shift in nomenclature is not altogether surprising: just as "hygiene" was then a "magical word" with particular salience and utility in connoting a fusion of medical and moral concerns, so "health" nowadays is the likely term of choice when one seeks to describe how bodies, selves, and societies are best meant to be.[45] Yet it is important to say that social hygiene did not "become" sexual health. While both eras are marked by the emergence of new forms of activism, social regulation, and normalization with regard to sexuality and health, the differences between these two historical formations are significant.

## The Rise, Proliferation, and Governmentalization of Sexual Health

Scholars have located sexual health in its modern sense as an invention of the late 1960s that achieved its first moment of stabilization in the form of a World Health Organization (WHO) definition in 1975.[46] This modern wave of sexual health discourse emerged at the juncture of a set of significant historical developments and issues, centrally including the sexual revolution, birth control, and population control. In the late 1960s and early 1970s, these various concerns came together with the professionalizing project of the academic field of sexology, as practitioners sought to establish the field on a firmer scientific footing on an international basis.[47]

A "technical consultation meeting" held in Geneva in 1974 that was devoted to solidifying and reinvigorating the field of sexology led to the promulgation of the first of several official WHO definitions of sexual health the following year, written by sexologists (including mostly physicians but also some psychologists and sociologists).[48] Consistent with WHO's avowed emphasis, since midcentury, on defining health as more than simply the absence of disease, the authors of the report defined sexual health as "the integration of the somatic, emotional, intellectual, and social aspects of sexual being, in ways that are positively enriching and that enhance personality, communication, and love." They went on to clarify that this "notion of sexual health implies a positive approach to human sexuality, and the purposes of sexual health care should be the enhancement of life and personal relationships and not merely counseling and care related to procreation or sexually transmitted diseases."[49] This discussion presaged, in its expansiveness, the polyvalent discourse that sexual health has since come to represent.[50]

Once the term "sexual health" began to circulate, it became available for a wide range of strategic appropriations—indeed, the term began to seem both useful and inescapable as a way of conferring legitimacy on sexual matters.[51] By the 1990s, usage of the term increased sharply in health and medical domains and elsewhere.[52] A pivotal factor here was the global HIV/AIDS epidemic, which functioned as a relay to move the concept and term "sexual health" into broader circulation. In the context of a stigmatized disease that affected stigmatized populations, "sexual health" was mobilized as a respectable and, often, euphemistic way of addressing a host of issues that were often difficult to name directly, particularly including gay sexuality, and the term began to enjoy wide use among professionals and activists alike.[53] However, as Laura Mamo and I have documented and analyzed elsewhere,[54] this quantitative explosion of sexual health discourse was paralleled by a qualitative expansion of meanings and a dispersion of the term across social space. While there seemed to be a convergence around the specific phrase, this apparent consolidation masked a remarkable diversity of scientific, political, economic, and practical agendas, as abstract conceptions of sexual health increasingly took concrete shape in a bewildering variety of forms and in many different geographic locations. Whether advocates characterized the problem as the risk of STIs, the difficulties caused by sexual dysfunction, the injustices linked to the absence of sexual rights, the need to control population growth or promote reproductive control, the threat of sexual irresponsibility, or the need for sexual self-expression, key actors invested in these problems all promoted solutions under the banner of something they called sexual health.[55]

By the close of the twentieth century, sexual health was also becoming more fully integrated into projects of governance. Appointed in 1998 by President Bill Clinton to serve as surgeon general and assistant secretary for health, Dr. David Satcher turned his attention to a variety of social problems, and he proceeded to issue reports on mental health, youth violence, smoking, and suicide prevention. By 1999, Satcher had trained his gaze on sexuality. In December of that year, he convened a "dialogue conference" of more than 100 people, described by one participant as being "from a wide range of disciplines, opinions and value systems," to discuss the feasibility of a national strategy. A second conference the following July brought together 130 individuals representing ninety organizations to draft a set of recommendations.[56]

According to John Bancroft, the director of the Kinsey Institute, who was an insider to the process, the report was originally scheduled to be released in late 2000 or early 2001 in the waning days of the Clinton administration. However, upon the election of Republican president George W. Bush—whose administration seemed far less disposed to open discussion of sexuality[57]—the project was put temporarily on hold. "To our pleasant surprise," wrote Bancroft afterward, "David Satcher held firm to his commitment, albeit a little delayed." On June 28, 2001, Satcher declared sexual health a national health priority in his "Call to Action to Promote Responsible Sexual Health and Responsible Sexual Behavior." In the face of criticism of the document from religious conservatives, Bancroft recalled, "the White House remained awkwardly silent."[58]

Yet the "Call to Action" was far from radical in its approach to sexual matters. Although he alluded briefly to "the many positive aspects of sexuality," Satcher quickly turned his attention to the "undesirable consequences." Pointing to "alarmingly high levels of sexually transmitted disease (STD) and HIV/AIDS infection, unintended pregnancy, abortion, sexual dysfunction, and sexual violence," he called for "a mature national dialogue on issues of sexuality, sexual health, and responsible sexual behavior."[59] As Alain Giami has observed in an analysis of this episode, Satcher's discourse diverged in important ways from that of the WHO definition: in place of WHO's capacious definition of sexual health that lauded the autonomous pursuit of sexual well-being, Satcher emphasized the key theme of "responsibility."[60] In fact, the words "(ir)responsible" and "responsibility" appeared forty-six times in the sixteen-page main text of the document. (By contrast, these terms do not appear at all in the thirty-three-page WHO report from 1975, except in quite different contexts.) To be sure, "responsibility" was a resonant watchword of the era, and not just for conservatives: in 1996, Clinton had signed into law the "Personal Responsibility and Work Opportunity Act," described as putting an end to "welfare as we have come to know it." Thus Satcher's discourse was broadly consistent with a neoliberal emphasis on self-management (and declining faith in the capacity of government to distribute resources effectively)—and invoking responsibility may have seemed a safe route to garnering broad support for the initiative across the political spectrum.[61]

Looking backward in 2013, Satcher would lament the limited progress in achieving sexual health in the United States and would point to his earlier agenda as "a dream deferred."[62] Displaying similar disappointment, academic commentators writing in the *Journal of the American Medical Association* in 2010 complained that "the United States lacks an integrated approach to sexual health" and observed critically that not a single reference to sexual health appeared in the 1,000 pages of the Affordable Care Act.[63] Such observations highlight not only the ever-precarious and "illegitimate" status of sexual matters but also the uneven character of attention to sexual health within the branches and agencies of the federal government: it is not surprising that legislators defending an already controversial health care overhaul would steer clear of sexual topics.

Yet the years following Satcher's "Call to Action" did see important steps to making a sexual health agenda central to public health governance within HHS, particularly during the Obama administration. Public health officials gave weight to Satcher's goals by incorporating "responsible sexual behavior" as one of ten leading health indicators in "Health People 2010," which laid out the nation's preventive health agenda for the first decade of the new century.[64] According to the document, these indicators "reflect the major public health concerns in the United States and were chosen based on their ability to motivate action, the availability of data to measure their progress, and their relevance as broad public health issues." A decade later, in "Healthy People 2020," a revised list of twelve leading health indicators included "reproductive and sexual health."[65]

In 2011, one of Satcher's successors, Surgeon General Regina Benjamin, launched the nation's first "National Prevention Strategy," which identified seven health priorities for the nation, of which one was reproductive and sexual health.[66] The strategy document called for increased preconception and prenatal care, greater support for reproductive and sexual health services, the provision of effective sexual health education, and enhanced early detection of HIV, viral hepatitis, and other STIs.[67] In a section titled "Partners Can," it identified a host of potential partners for these efforts, including include state, tribal, local, and territorial governments; businesses and employers; health care systems, insurers, and clinicians; schools, colleges, and universities; community, nonprofit, and faith-based organizations; and individuals and families.[68]

Of the various HHS component agencies in the Obama years, the CDC proved especially focused on the theme of sexual health. The CDC's two-day consultation on the topic in 2010 (described at the beginning of this chapter) reflected an explicit effort by the agency to build consensus on a science-driven sexual health agenda that would propel, but extend beyond, its efforts to prevent sexually transmitted disease. As Dr. Kevin Fenton, director of the CDC's National Center for HIV/AIDS, Viral Hepatitis, STD, and TB Prevention, affirmed in his presentation:

> The public health approach provides scientifically tested and proven interventions and engages communities in their own health. Advancing a sexual health framework can effectively shift the focus to a more positive, health-based approach from a disease-based focus, enhance the efficiency and effectiveness of prevention, and normalize conversations regarding contributions of sexuality to overall health.[69]

## Historical Continuities and Discontinuities

A comparison between the recent moves toward sexual health governance in the United States and the history of social hygiene in the Progressive Era is instructive and sheds further light on the particularities of the current concern with sexual health. In both cases, agendas that connect sexuality with health have bridged the public sphere and civil society and have addressed social problems by linking matters of state governance to the governance of the self. But it should be pointed out that sexual health governance to date is patchy, incomplete, and often more evident at the level of exhortations than accomplishments, and in that sense it differs in significance from social hygiene.[70]

There are interesting resonances that connect the two eras: certainly the consistent language of "responsibility" reflects an abiding interest in the forging of "good" biosexual citizens, and it is not hard to detect, in the prose of Satcher and other modern preachers of responsibility, distant echoes of the goals of "moral prophylaxis" of an earlier era. Yet sexual health governance ties responsibility to rights, thereby balancing the two sometimes opposing tugs of citizenship. This approach presumes not only the historical rise of rights discourses in relation to sexual expression and sexual identity but also the broader valorization of the individual that rights discourses themselves presuppose—a modern individual who is deemed capable of self-knowledge and who can be exhorted to make responsible choices.[71]

In addition, the nature of the interest in promoting biosexual citizenship has also changed since the social hygiene era, with the moral dimensions of the discourse transformed—at least up through the Obama administration—by a partial and tentative embrace of the virtues and benefits of sexuality, the endorsement of the idea of a right to sexual expression (within fairly well-demarcated bounds), a more straightforward repudiation of a sexual double standard between men and women, and a much greater openness than in the past to diversity with regard to sexual identity. For example, when it finalized its definition of sexual health in 2012, the CDC's Sexual Health Workgroup affirmed that "sexual health is an inextricable element of human health and is based on a positive, equitable and respectful approach to sexuality, relationships and reproduction that is free of coercion, fear, discrimination, stigma, shame and violence." The workgroup's definition also balanced the "risks and responsibilities" of sexual behavior with its "benefits," and likewise balanced "adverse outcomes" with "the possibility of fulfilling sexual relationships."[72] (The word "pleasure" did not appear, however, as one of those potential benefits.)

Of course, greater openness at the level of rhetoric is no guarantee of changed practice, and in any case it would be misleading to read these differences between social hygiene discourse and sexual health discourse as a simple tale of social progress. Still, the undeniable differences in moral and political valences between the two eras cannot be understood absent a consideration of how certain sensibilities of late twentieth-century and early twenty-first-century social movements—particularly feminism and LGBT rights—have percolated through government administrative agencies, especially though not exclusively during Democratic administrations.[73] (It is striking, for example, to see on the official National Institutes of Health [NIH] webpage a document titled "NIH Pride Celebration 2016," a set of activities organized by three NIH units: the Office of Equity, Diversity, and Inclusion; the Sexual and Gender Minority Research Office; and the National Institute on Minority Health and Health Disparities.)[74] Changed sensibilities are likewise apparent in the discourse around race and immigration. While these issues certainly remain hot-button concerns in the United States, and while xenophobic and anti-immigrant sentiments continue to be widespread in the broader society, in the era of social hygiene and eugenics they were part of the official discourse, while (again, at least up through the Obama years) they have been delinked from sexual health governance, at least in any overt fashion. Thus, while governance continues to involve the drawing of symbolic boundaries between "good" and "bad" sexual citizens, the precise location of those boundaries, not surprisingly, has shifted over the course of a century.[75]

Similarities and differences also surface when considering the pragmatic interests of military officials during the two eras. Much like the preoccupations of the military during the First World War, the Sexual Health and Responsibility Program (SHARP) of the U.S. Navy and Marine Corps (founded in 1998) directs its educational efforts at "the consequences of sexual risk-taking," not just for the individual sailor or marine but also for the efficiency of the organization. Writing in the journal *Public Health Reports* in 2013, the program manager, Michael R. (Bob) MacDonald, provided statistics to emphasize the burden placed on the military by health care costs and lost-duty days as a result of STIs and unplanned pregnancies. Yet the program's motto, "Chart a Safe Course" (symbolized by a lighthouse logo), is intended to affirm "that individuals have both the right and responsibility to make choices about their health, and that sexual health decision making is a lifelong and dynamic process because a person's life circumstances and relationships may change over time."[76] While the more blatant moral rhetoric of the social hygiene era is mostly absent here, it is replaced by a discourse of "responsibilization" that locates the individual moral actor as the person who has both the right and the responsibility to make health-promoting choices.

In a further indication of social change, MacDonald hailed the repeal of the military's "Don't Ask, Don't Tell" policy as "a new opportunity to more openly address issues of HIV risk among gay and bisexual men in uniform."[77] Here again, we see how certain tropes associated with recent social movement activism around gender equality, LGBT rights, and HIV/AIDS destigmatization have made their way into health governance and even military organizations, resulting in new emphases on inclusiveness, choice, and agency. Yet, at the same time, the exercise of choices and rights inevitably runs up against limits in the context of a military organization. Indeed, the careful balancing of rights with responsibilities in the discourse of SHARP suggests a perception that there may be only so many potential "safe courses" that might be charted while still ensuring that—so to speak—the sailor makes it safely back to port.

Three other, loosely linked points of partial contrast between the visions of citizenship and governance in the social hygiene and sexual health eras deserve attention. These involve changes in appeals to science, a policy emphasis on reducing health disparities, and a focus on consensus formation and inclusiveness. I address each of these briefly in turn.

### Science, Evidence, and Legitimacy

While "science" figures prominently in both eras as a rhetoric of legitimation, the Progressivist faith in technocratic rule and in the person of the expert has been supplemented by an emphasis on the evidentiary basis and methodological warrants for proper action to promote sexual health.[78] Government documents and articles have referred to "scientifically tested and proven interventions"; "scaling up evidence-based practices"; "the CDC-recommended, evidence-based, six-step model for working with patients to reduce sexual risk behavior"; and "formal government recognition of the need for an evidence-based public health approach to the promotion of sexual health to enhance population health in the U.S."[79] This emphasis on locating the government's sexual health advice within the framework of evidence-based medicine and policy[80] is accompanied by an interest in developing formal models—for example, "a social-ecological model that addresses the impact of individual characteristics, relationships, and the community and societal context on sexual health"—as well as in creating the nationally representative

surveys and the surveillance systems that will permit public health officials to track progress toward sexual health goals.[81]

In these ways and through these various means, the "good biosexual citizen" is imagined as someone who acts in accordance with the
best available evidence and divulges truthful information about his
or her sexuality. To be sure, public health officials' insistence on evidence is an important tactic in countering attempts to impose policies
that are driven, first and foremost, by narrowly political or ideological
concerns—always a particular risk when the topic is sexuality. Yet the
turn to evidence as the final arbiter of "responsible" sexual practice may
have the effect of demarcating the bounds of legitimate participation in
decision making about sexuality by delimiting the kinds of authorized
individuals who have the expertise, credentials, and experience deemed
necessary to produce and evaluate evidence.

While the original WHO discussion of sexual health made no mention of evidence, the current emphasis on evidence-based interventions
assumes that matters of sexuality should be addressed from the standpoint of outcomes, and more specifically that sexual health practices require validation of a particular sort, derived by testing an "intervention"
in a prospective manner using a control group.[82] However, the policy
emphasis on validating sexual health interventions and disseminating
those that are "evidence-based" is controversial insofar as it typically
imposes the model of the randomized clinical trial onto the domain of
sexual practice. Susan Kippax, a prominent social science researcher on
sexuality and HIV, has made the point forcefully that "most, if not all,
sexual health interventions are inherently unsuitable for experimental
evaluation."[83] Kippax has observed: "Social transformation is not ame-
nable to experiment because effectiveness is the *contingent* outcome of
the collective activity of a diverse range of actors both human and nonhuman, including the prevention technologies themselves; scientific
practices; clinical services; cultural, political and social environments;
and the norms, values, and discourses that animate human behaviour or
practice."[84] When community-based organizations that design innovative programs to promote sexual health are obliged to meet the requirements of evidence-based practice to be eligible for governmental support
and funding, then the effect may be to limit the possibilities for building
an active biosexual citizenship "from below." The burdens here may fall

particularly on those organizations less adept at deploying the desired framings and less capable of undertaking research projects—smaller and struggling nonprofit organizations, including those that represent less well funded constituencies or newly emerging health concerns.[85]

## Health Disparities and the Case of LGBT Health

A second point of contrast between the two eras concerns the kinds of political opportunities that emerge at a time when the reduction of health disparities is an important official goal of government health agencies as well as a guiding frame for health advocacy groups. In the 1980s and 1990s, through the efforts of a tacit coalition that encompassed advocacy groups, health professionals, and government health officials (importantly including Surgeon General Satcher), HHS agencies embraced the mandate of reducing and eliminating health disparities, especially by race, ethnicity, and gender This policy framework subsequently has provided important new possibilities for advancing biosexual citizenship claims under the banner of LGBT health (or, increasingly, "sexual and gender minority [SGM]" health), which has come to be understood as another domain where health disparities regularly surface.

In response to lobbying by LGBT organizations, federal health agencies began turning their attention to health concerns affecting sexual and gender minorities in the late 1990s, as LGBT people crossed the symbolic boundary from "outsider" to "citizen."[86] This new emphasis ebbed during the George W. Bush administration but picked up steam again with the publication in 2011 of a lengthy Institute of Medicine report on LGBT health (commissioned by the NIH), as well as by the establishment of the Internal LGBT Coordinating Committee within HHS.[87] In 2015, the NIH released its inaugural Strategic Plan for Sexual and Gender Minority Health Research and created a new Sexual and Gender Minority Research Office, located within the Office of the NIH Director and tasked with coordinating SGM research activities across the agency.[88] Then, in October 2016, the NIH formally designated sexual and gender minorities (or "SGM populations") as "a health disparity population for research purposes."[89] All these efforts came about through the interplay of health officials with LGBT advocacy organizations, particularly those focusing specifically on rights to medical care and rights to sexual freedom.[90]

To be sure, matters of LGBT health may often concern issues unrelated to sexual behavior and sexual health per se—focusing instead, for example, on health effects of social stigmatization or, in the case of transgender individuals, effects of hormones. Yet while earlier moves, in the final decade of the twentieth century and first decade of the twenty-first, toward promoting LGBT health often sought to bypass controversy by downplaying sexuality altogether,[91] more recent attention has treated sexual health as an intrinsic component of the overall health of sexual and gender minorities. (For example, the Institute of Medicine report specifically reviewed not just the impact of the HIV/AIDS epidemic but also, as a separate category, the sexual health concerns of LGBT individuals.)[92]

Thus, while the emphases of LGBT health advocacy extend beyond questions of sexuality, in practice the new attention to sexual and gender minorities reflects, in part, their incorporation within an inclusionary framework of biomedical and sexual governance and citizenship that targets health disparities while aligning with sexual health.[93] This framework may be both enabling and constraining for LGBT individuals and social movement organizations. While inclusion may be preferable to its opposite, a particular risk here is that of reifying gender and sexual identity categories—solidifying a sense of the biopsychological "naturalness" of these categories while eliding the many potential slippages between identity, desire, and behavior.[94]

*Inclusivity and Consensus Formation*

The final aspect of partial divergence between the eras of social hygiene and sexual health has to do with recent emphases on inclusivity and consensus in building bridges between government, civil society, and individual citizens. To be sure, in promoting projects such as sex education, moral reformers in the social hygiene era sought to enlist not only public schools but also "families, churches, [and] civic institutions," as John D'Emilio and Estelle Freedman have described.[95] But the aspirations of sexual health governance are even broader. Consistent with his assembling of a wide array of participants from academia, religious institutions, foundations, and public interest groups at the technical consultation in 2010, the CDC's Fenton called for "radical inclusivity" that brings "new, diverse, and dynamic partners" to the table in building a "holistic coalition."[96] Former surgeon general Satcher has particularly emphasized the need to "find common ground and reach consensus" in order to advance sexual health, and after leaving the government he organized the National Consensus Process on Sexual Health and Responsible Sexual Behavior, in which he tried to hammer out a common vision for sexual health among heads of more than two dozen nonprofit organizations across the political spectrum.[97]

While such consensus has been an elusive goal, and while inclusiveness in policy making may often have limited substantive impact, these emphases nonetheless reflect a political environment in which government health officials perceive the expectation that they reach out to advocacy groups and other so-called partners and stakeholders that may claim a right to participate in the process of addressing social problems. Like other "technologies of elicitation" analyzed by scholars of public participation in expert decision making, such mechanisms for including stakeholders "produce publics and topics of collective discussion."[98] Whether community-based organizations and social movements can substantially shape such discussion, or whether the basic parameters of sexual health governance are essentially set "from above," remains an open question.

## Conclusion

The institutional and political practices relating to sexual health, like those relating to social hygiene at an earlier historical moment, have multiple effects. These include prescribing (and sometimes challenging) what constitutes acceptable sexual practices, providing templates for the—often partial—incorporation of individuals and groups into U.S. society, and drawing boundaries between those who are deemed to "belong" and those deemed not. In both eras, these processes have unfolded through contestation and consensus, through consideration of responsibilities (and, more recently, rights), and precisely through the joining together of biomedical and sexual matters. I have called attention to some of the historical echoes, yet the differences between the eras of social hygiene and sexual health are as noteworthy as the similarities, and the virtues of comparison of modes and systems of biosexual governance and citizenship are therefore clear.

More generally, my analysis of these two historical moments in the social and biomedical regulation of sexuality suggests the importance of scrutinizing both the place of the sexual in biocitizenship and the place of the biomedical and the biopolitical in sexual citizenship. Future studies of the intersectional domain of biosexual citizenship can potentially shed light on a broader range of cases in which bodies and populations; sexual desires, beliefs, and practices; ideas about what it means to be risky or to live healthily; and biomedical and public health interventions become intertwined in ways that matter for the practices and rituals of political belonging.

My analysis has also suggested the potentially double-sided character of biosexual citizenship as both "top-down" and "bottom-up." Even while the recent era of sexual health governance is more formally inclusive than that of the earlier era of social hygiene and more respectful of the rights-bearing individual, nonetheless the kinds of biocitizenship offered in the name of sexual health frequently appear to involve the inculcation of authorized ways of behaving responsibly so as to be granted access to the status of the good citizen. Given new official emphases on inclusiveness and the participation of designated stakeholders, and following the diffusion into worlds of governance of rights-based language promoted by social movements, it appears that advocacy groups demanding sexual rights—including a right to sexuality as a form of pleasure—have become important and recognized voices in the public sphere. Moreover, the polyvalent discourse of sexual health often provides such groups with "cover" to raise taboo topics in a socially legitimate language. But advocacy groups rarely set the terms of discourse or policy in a domain increasingly governed by a fairly limited set of authoritative frameworks: biomedical risk, social responsibility, and evidence-based practice. As I have noted, these frameworks do not inhere necessarily in modern conceptions of sexual health and indeed were much less present in the original WHO definition, but they have become increasingly central to what I have termed "sexual health governance," at least in the U.S. context (though probably beyond).

The question, then, is whether and how those groups that seek, in the face of health crises like the AIDS epidemic, to articulate desires and promote alternative visions of sexual rights and responsibilities—what Kane Race has termed the practices of "counterpublic health"—can find room to negotiate.[99] Will they be obliged to accept the terms of sexual health governance to avoid otherwise being positioned as antievidence, irresponsible, and "against health"?[100] Or, like AIDS treatment activists of the 1980s and 1990s who reworked the science of drug trials and the politics of regulatory approval, will they be able to marshal the "lay expertise" that might permit them to tack back and forth between conventional and alternative definitions of science, evidence, ethics, pleasure, and health?[101] An interesting example is provided by recent gay community support for pre-exposure prophylaxis (PrEP) against HIV, insofar as it joins a pharmaceuticalization of HIV prevention with an affirmation of sexual pleasure and even "sexual revolution."[102] If hybrid forms of sexual health promotion of this sort are viable, then perhaps we can imagine models of biosexual citizenship that productively manage the tension between "bottom-up" and "top-down" approaches.

NOTES

1 Centers for Disease Control and Prevention, "A Public Health Approach for Advancing Sexual Health in the United States: Rationale and Options for Implementation" (Atlanta: U.S. Department of Health and Human Services, 2010), 10. Here Fenton was drawing on key aspects of the World Health Organization's definition of sexual health.

2 Ibid., 10, 33.

3 "The Surgeon General's Call to Action to Promote Responsible Sexual Health and Responsible Sexual Behavior" (Washington, DC: Office of the Surgeon General, U.S. Department of Health and Human Services, 2001); National Prevention Council, *National Prevention Strategy* (Washington, DC: Office of the Surgeon General, U.S. Department of Health and Human Services, 2011); "Healthy People 2020," accessed April 14, 2017, www.healthypeople.gov.

4 On governmentality and the "conduct of conduct," see Graham Burchell, Colin Gordon, and Peter Miller, eds., *The Foucault Effect: Studies in Governmentality* (Chicago: University of Chicago Press, 1991).

5 Aaron T. Norton, "Cutting the Risk: The Emergence of Male Circumcision Status as an HIV-Risk Reduction Strategy" (PhD diss., University of California, Davis, 2014).

6 While my focus in this essay is on the United States at the federal level, sexual health governance can also be studied in other countries, and it can also be observed in action both at the local level (e.g., in certain cities' sexual health

strategic plans) and at the transnational level (in the work of the WHO and other United Nations agencies).

7  Stuart Hall and David Held, "Citizens and Citizenship," in *New Times: The Changing Face of Politics in the 1990s*, ed. Stuart Hall and Martin Jacques (London: Verso, 1990), 173–88; Gershon Shafir, ed. *The Citizenship Debates: A Reader* (Minneapolis: University of Minnesota Press, 1998).

8  Claire Rasmussen and Michael Brown, "Radical Democratic Citizenship: Amidst Political Theory and Geography," in *Handbook of Citizenship Studies*, ed. Engin F. Isin and Bryan S. Turner (London: Sage, 2002), 179. See also Chantal Mouffe, *The Return of the Political* (London: Verso, 1993).

9  Lauren Berlant, *The Queen of America Goes to Washington City: Essays on Sex and Citizenship* (Durham, NC: Duke University Press, 1997), 20.

10  Carole Pateman, "Equality, Difference, Subordination: The Politics of Motherhood and Women's Citizenship," in *Beyond Equality and Difference: Citizenship, Feminist Politics, and Female Subjectivity*, ed. Gisela Bock and Susan James (New York: Routledge, 1992), 17–31; Melissa Nobles, *Shades of Citizenship: Race and the Census in Modern Politics* (Stanford, CA: Stanford University Press, 2000); Steven Epstein and Héctor Carrillo, "Immigrant Sexual Citizenship: Intersectional Templates among Mexican Gay Immigrants to the United States," *Citizenship Studies* 18, nos. 3/4 (2014): 259–76.

11  Christian Joppke, "Transformation of Citizenship: Status, Rights, Identity," *Citizenship Studies* 11, no. 1 (2007): 37–48.

12  For example, Renato Rosaldo, "Cultural Citizenship, Inequality, and Multiculturalism," in *Latino Cultural Citizenship: Claiming Identity, Space, and Rights*, ed. William V. Flores and Rina Benmayor (Boston: Beacon Press, 1997), 27–53.

13  Torsten Heinemann, "Biological Citizenship," in *Encyclopedia of Global Bioethics*, ed. Henk Ten Have (online: Springer, 2015), accessed April 16, 2017, https://link.springer.com.

14  Paul Rabinow, *Essays on the Anthropology of Reason* (Princeton, NJ: Princeton University Press, 1996), 91–111.

15  Adriana Petryna, *Life Exposed: Biological Citizens after Chernobyl* (Princeton, NJ: Princeton University Press, 2002), 5.

16  Deborah Heath, Rayna Rapp, and Karen-Sue Taussig, "Genetic Citizenship," in *A Companion to the Anthropology of Politics*, ed. David Nugent and Joan Vincent (London: Blackwell, 2004), 152–67; Vinh-Kim Nguyen, "Antiretroviral Globalism, Biopolitics, and Therapeutic Citizenship," in *Global Assemblages: Technology, Politics, and Ethics as Anthropological Problems*, ed. Aihwa Ong and Stephen J. Collier (Malden, MA: Blackwell, 2005), 124–44; Steven Epstein, "Patient Groups and Health Movements," in *The Handbook of Science and Technology Studies*, ed. Edward J. Hackett, Olga Amsterdamska, Michael Lynch, and Judy Wajcman (Cambridge, MA: MIT Press, 2008), 499–539; Steven Epstein, "The Politics of Health Mobilization in the United States: The Promise and Pitfalls of 'Disease Constituencies,'" *Social Science and Medicine* 165 (2016): 245–54.

17  Steven Epstein, *Inclusion: The Politics of Difference in Medical Research* (Chicago: University of Chicago Press, 2007), esp. p. 21.

18  Btihaj Ajana, "Biometric Citizenship," *Citizenship Studies* 16, no. 7 (2012): 851–70; Sarah Morando Lakhani and Stefan Timmermans, "Biopolitical Citizenship in the Immigration Adjudication Process," *Social Problems* 61, no. 3 (2014): 360–79; Torsten Heinemann, Ilpo Helén, Thomas Lemke, Ursula Naue, and Martin G. Weiss, eds., *Suspect Families: DNA Analysis, Family Reunification and Immigration Policies* (Surrey, UK: Ashgate, 2015).

19  Nikolas Rose and Carlos Novas, "Biological Citizenship," in *Global Assemblages: Technology, Politics, and Ethics as Anthropological Problems*, ed. Aihwa Ong and Stephen J. Collier (Malden, MA: Blackwell, 2005), 445–46. See also Adele E. Clarke, Janet K. Shim, Laura Mamo, Jennifer Ruth Fosket, and Jennifer R. Fishman, "Biomedicalization: Technoscientific Transformations of Health, Illness, and U.S. Biomedicine," *American Sociological Review* 68, no. 2 (2003): 161–94.

20  Nicole Charles, "Mobilizing the Self-Governance of Pre-damaged Bodies: Neoliberal Biological Citizenship and HPV Vaccination Promotion in Canada," *Citizenship Studies* 17, nos. 6–7 (2013): 773. For additional critique of Novas and Rose, see Dorothy E. Roberts, *Fatal Invention: How Science, Politics, and Big Business Re-create Race in the Twenty-First Century* (New York: New Press, 2011), 202–25.

21  On this point, see also Laura Mamo, Amber Nelson, and Aleia Clark, "Producing and Protecting Risky Girlhoods," in *Three Shots at Prevention: The HPV Vaccine and the Politics of Medicine's Simple Solutions*, ed. Keith Wailoo, Julie Livingston, Steven Epstein, and Robert Aronowitz (Baltimore: Johns Hopkins University Press, 2010), 121–45.

22  Steven Epstein, "The Great Undiscussable: Anal Cancer, HPV, and Gay Men's Health," in *Three Shots at Prevention: The HPV Vaccine and the Politics of Medicine's Simple Solutions*, ed. Keith Wailoo, Julie Livingston, Steven Epstein, and Robert Aronowitz (Baltimore: Johns Hopkins University Press, 2010), 61–90.

23  In Torsten Heinemann's terms, the duality of biocitizenship encompasses "the extension of rights, the emergence of new possibilities of participation, the empowerment of the individual, and the choice-enhancing options of the new genetics," but also "the potential for exclusion and restriction of citizenship rights based on biological traits." Heinemann, "Biological Citizenship." On the dualisms of biocitizenship in relation to both the state and the market, see Roberts, *Fatal Invention*, 202–25.

24  Epstein and Carrillo, "Immigrant Sexual Citizenship," 261.

25  On citizenship and sexual rights, see Jeffrey Weeks, "The Sexual Citizen," *Theory, Culture and Society* 15, nos. 3–4 (1998): 35; Diane Richardson, *Rethinking Sexuality* (London: Sage, 2000), 98–115. On citizenship and equal treatment, see Wendy Pearson, "Interrogating the Epistemology of the Bedroom: Same-Sex Marriage and Sexual Citizenship in Canada," *Discourse* 26, no. 3 (2004): 136–65. On the heteronormative dimensions of citizenship, see M. Jacqui Alexander, "Not Just (Any) Body Can Be a Citizen: The Politics of Law, Sexuality and Postcoloniality in

Trinidad and Tobago and the Bahamas," *Feminist Review* 48 (1994): 5–23; David Bell and Jon Binnie, *The Sexual Citizen: Queer Politics and Beyond* (Cambridge: Polity, 2000); Margot Canaday, *The Straight State: Sexuality and Citizenship in Twentieth-Century America* (Princeton, NJ: Princeton University Press, 2009). On the state's policing of sexual boundaries, see Carol Johnson, "Heteronormative Citizenship and the Politics of Passing," Sexualities 5 (2002): 317–36; Steven Seidman, "From Outsider to Citizen," in *Regulating Sex: The Politics of Intimacy and Identity*, ed. Elizabeth Bernstein and Laurie Schaffner (New York: Routledge, 2005), 225. And on citizenship in terms of state-sponsored projects of subject formation, see Barbara Cruikshank, *The Will to Empower: Democratic Citizens and Other Subjects* (Ithaca, NY: Cornell University Press, 1999); Carlos Ulises Decena, "Profiles, Compulsory Disclosure and Ethical Sexual Citizenship in the Contemporary USA," *Sexualities* 11, no. 4 (2008): 397–413.

26  Decena, "Profiles, Compulsory Disclosure," 397–413; Jeffrey A. Bennett, *Banning Queer Blood: Rhetorics of Citizenship, Contagion, and Resistance* (Tuscaloosa: University of Alabama Press, 2009), 2. Similarly, the ban on entry into the United States of HIV-positive immigrants (lifted in 2010) was an episode that demonstrated the juncture of biomedical and sexual (and legal/territorial) dimensions of citizenship; see Epstein and Carrillo, "Immigrant Sexual Citizenship," 269–70. On sexual citizenship in the context of HIV/AIDS, see also Jeffrey A. Bennett, chapter 4, this volume, on HIV and "chronic citizenship"; Karma R. Chávez, chapter 5, this volume, on the detention of HIV-positive Haitians.

27  Epstein, "The Great Undiscussable," 62, 83n5.

28  Norton, "Cutting the Risk," 193–237.

29  Ibid., 196 (emphasis in the original).

30  Theo Sandfort and Anke Ehrhardt, "Sexual Health: A Useful Public Health Paradigm or a Moral Imperative?," *Archives of Sexual Behavior* 33, no. 3 (2004): 182.

31  Kristin Luker, "Sex, Social Hygiene, and the State: The Double-Edged Sword of Social Reform," *Theory and Society* 27, no. 5 (1998): esp. 606. See also Allan M. Brandt, *No Magic Bullet: A Social History of Venereal Disease in the United States since 1880* (New York: Oxford University Press, 1985).

32  Luker, "Sex, Social Hygiene, and the State," 611. See also Brandt, *No Magic Bullet*, 46.

33  Kristin Luker, *When Sex Goes to School: Warring Views on Sex—and Sex Education—since the Sixties* (New York: Norton, 2006), 38–39.

34  Brandt, *No Magic Bullet*, 5. See also John D'Emilio and Estelle B. Freedman, *Intimate Matters: A History of Sexuality in America* (New York: Harper and Row, 1988), 203–8.

35  Brandt, *No Magic Bullet*, 7.

36  Ibid., 37; Luker, "Sex, Social Hygiene, and the State," 610.

37  Luker, "Sex, Social Hygiene, and the State," 612.

38  George Chauncey Jr., *Gay New York: Gender, Urban Culture, and the Making of the Gay Male World, 1890–1940* (New York: Basic Books, 1994), 143–45.

39  Luker, "Sex, Social Hygiene, and the State," 614, 624; Brandt, *No Magic Bullet*, 36.

40  Brandt, *No Magic Bullet*, 59.

41  Ibid., 73.

42  Luker, "Sex, Social Hygiene, and the State," 619.

43  Brandt, *No Magic Bullet*, 168–73.

44  See American Sexual Health Association, "Who We Are," accessed March 7, 2017, www.ashasexualhealth.org.

45  Robert Crawford, "Healthism and the Medicalization of Everyday Life," *International Journal of Health Services* 10, no. 3 (1980): 365–88; Peter Conrad, "Medicalization and Social Control," *Annual Review of Sociology* 18 (1992): 209–32; Clarke et al., "Biomedicalization"; Jonathan M. Metzl and Anna Kirland, eds., *Against Health: How Health Became the New Morality* (New York: NYU Press, 2010).

46  Alain Giami, "Sexual Health: The Emergence, Development, and Diversity of a Concept," *Annual Review of Sex Research* 13 (2002): 1–35; Weston M. Edwards and Eli Coleman, "Defining Sexual Health: A Descriptive Overview," *Archives of Sexual Behavior* 33, no. 3 (2004): 189–95.

47  Giami, "Sexual Health."

48  Edwards and Coleman, "Defining Sexual Health," 191; Giami, "Sexual Health"; World Health Organization, "Education and Treatment in Human Sexuality: The Training of Health Professionals, Report of a WHO Meeting [Held in Geneva from 6 to 12 February 1974]," in *World Health Organization Technical Report Series No. 572* (Geneva: World Health Organization, 1975).

49  World Health Organization, "Education and Treatment in Human Sexuality," 6–7.

50  On the longer history of the polyvalent functions of sexuality in the modern West, see Michel Foucault, *The History of Sexuality, Vol. 1: An Introduction*, trans. Robert Hurley (New York: Vintage, 1980).

51  Steven Epstein and Laura Mamo, "The Proliferation of Sexual Health: Diverse Social Problems and the Legitimation of Sexuality," *Social Science and Medicine* 188 (2017): 176–90.

52  Laura Mamo and I graph usage of the term over time in biomedical journals, NIH grants, and the mass media. See ibid. See also Sandfort and Ehrhardt, "Sexual Health," 182.

53  Richard Parker, Diane DiMauro, Beth Filiano, Jonathan Garcia, Miguel Muñoz Laboy, and Robert Sember, "Global Transformations and Intimate Relations in the 21st Century: Social Science Research on Sexuality and the Emergence of *Sexual Health* and *Sexual Rights* Frameworks," *Annual Review of Sex Research* 15 (2004): 3962–98; Sandfort and Ehrhardt, "Sexual Health," 182.

54  Epstein and Mamo, "The Proliferation of Sexual Health."

55  Ibid.

56  See the "Methodology" section in "The Surgeon General's Call to Action," 24–25. See also John Bancroft, "Promoting Responsible Sexual Behavior," *Sexual and Relationship Therapy* 17, no. 1 (2002): 9–12; Giami, "Sexual Health," 21.

57  See Steven Epstein, "The New Attack on Sexuality Research: Morality and the Politics of Knowledge Production," *Sexuality Research and Social Policy* 3, no. 1 (2006): 1–12.

58  Bancroft, "Promoting Responsible Sexual Behavior," 10.

59  "The Surgeon General's Call to Action," ii, 10, 15.

60  Giami, "Sexual Health," 23.

61  On neoliberalism as an economic, social, political, and cultural phenomenon, see Peter A. Hall and Michèle Lamont, "Introduction: Social Resilience in the Neoliberal Era," in *Social Resilience in the Neoliberal Era*, ed. Peter A. Hall and Michèle Lamont (Cambridge: Cambridge University Press, 2013), 1–31.

62  David Satcher, "Addressing Sexual Health: Looking Back, Looking Forward," *Public Health Reports* 128, suppl. 1 (2013): 111–14.

63  Andrea Swartzendruber and Jonathan M. Zenilman, "A National Strategy to Improve Sexual Health," *Journal of the American Medical Association* 304, no. 9 (2010): 1005.

64  See "Leading Health Indicators," *Healthy People 2010 Archive*, accessed March 7, 2017, www.healthypeople.gov.

65  Ibid.; "Reproductive and Sexual Health: Overview and Impact," *HealthyPeople.gov*, accessed April 16, 2017, www.healthypeople.gov.

66  National Prevention Council, *National Prevention Strategy*.

67  Ibid., 44.

68  Ibid., 46–47.

69  Centers for Disease Control and Prevention, "A Public Health Approach for Advancing Sexual Health," 10.

70  For example, the cause of sexual health has not been translated into formal legislation to the degree that social hygiene prompted.

71  On the historical rise of a concept of rights connected to sexual desires, practices, and identities, see Ilsa L. Lottes, "Sexual Rights: Meanings, Controversies, and Sexual Health Promotion," *Journal of Sex Research* 50, nos. 3–4 (2013): 367–91; Parker et al., "Global Transformations and Intimate Relations"; Rosalind P. Petchesky, "Sexual Rights: Inventing a Concept, Mapping an International Practice," in *Framing the Sexual Subject: The Politics of Gender, Sexuality, and Power*, ed. Richard Parker, Regina Maria Barbosa, and Peter Aggleton (Berkeley: University of California Press, 2000), 81–103.

72  "CDC/HRSA Advisory Committee on HIV, Viral Hepatitis and STD Prevention and Treatment: Record of the Proceedings" (Atlanta: U.S. Department of Health and Human Services, 2012).

73  Here I adopt the perspective of Mark Wolfson, who has noted that too often analysts of social movements tend to see the state simply as a movement's "target," "sponsor," or "facilitator" or as the provider or denier of "opportunities" for activism. But in many cases, "fractions of the state are . . . allied with the movement in efforts to change the policies of other fractions." In such cases—for which he has proposed the label "interpenetration"—"it is hard to know where the movement

ends and the state begins." Mark Wolfson, *The Fight against Big Tobacco: The Movement, the State, and the Public's Health* (New York: Aldine de Gruyter, 2001), 7, 144–45.

74 See National Institutes of Health, "Telling Our Stories," accessed April 14, 2017, www.edi.nih.gov. While the early days of the Trump administration saw reports of "liberal" content, including LGBT-related material, being deleted from federal websites such as those of the State Department, this page has remained active and available at least through the access date specified earlier in this note. See also note 93.

75 On symbolic boundaries, see Michèle Lamont and Virág Molnár, "The Study of Boundaries in the Social Sciences," *Annual Review of Sociology* 28, no. 1 (2002): 167–95.

76 Michael R. (Bob) MacDonald, "Sexual Health and Responsibility Program (SHARP): Preventing HIV, STIs, and Unplanned Pregnancies in the Navy and Marine Corps," *Public Health Reports* 128, suppl. 1 (2013): 82.

77 Ibid., 87.

78 More generally, on the historical shift toward the use of quantification and formal methods as a solution to the problem of distrust of experts in the United States, see Theodore M. Porter, *Trust in Numbers: The Pursuit of Objectivity in Science and Public Life* (Princeton, NJ: Princeton University Press, 1995).

79 Centers for Disease Control and Prevention, "A Public Health Approach for Advancing Sexual Health," 6, 10; MacDonald, "Sexual Health and Responsibility Program," 84; Megan B. Ivankovich, Kevin A. Fenton, and John M. Douglas, "Considerations for National Public Health Leadership in Advancing Sexual Health," *Public Health Reports* 128, suppl. 1 (2013): 105.

80 On the rise of evidence-based medicine more generally, see Stefan Timmermans and Marc Berg, *The Gold Standard: The Challenge of Evidence-Based Medicine and Standardization in Health Care* (Philadelphia: Temple University Press, 2003).

81 Ivankovich, Fenton, and Douglas, "Considerations for National Public Health Leadership," 104; Megan B. Ivankovich, Jami S. Leichliter, and John M. Douglas, "Measurement of Sexual Health in the U.S.: An Inventory of Nationally Representative Surveys and Surveillance Systems," *Public Health Reports* 128, suppl. 1 (2013): 62–72.

82 See, for example, Jeffrey S. Becasen, Jessie Ford, and Matthew Hogben, "Sexual Health Interventions: A Meta-analysis," *Journal of Sex Research* 52, no. 4 (2015): 433–43.

83 Susan Kippax, "Sexual Health Interventions Are Unsuitable for Experimental Evaluation," in *Effective Sexual Health Interventions: Issues in Experimental Evaluation*, ed. Judith M. Stephenson, John Imrie, and Chris Bonell (Oxford: Oxford University Press, 2003), 17.

84 Susan Kippax, "Effective HIV Prevention: The Indispensable Role of Social Science," *Journal of the International AIDS Society* 15 (2012): 5. See also Judith D. Auerbach, Juston O. Parkhurst, and Carlos F. Cáceres, "Addressing Social Drivers

of HIV/AIDS for the Longterm Response: Conceptual and Methodological Considerations," *Global Public Health* 6, suppl. 3 (2011): S302; Paul Van de Ven and Peter Aggleton, "What Constitutes Evidence in HIV/AIDS Education?," *Health Education Research* 14, no. 4 (1999): 461–71.

85 Examples might include organizations working on transgender health or hepatitis C.

86 Steven Epstein, "Sexualizing Governance and Medicalizing Identities: The Emergence of 'State-Centered' LGBT Health Politics in the United States," *Sexualities* 6, no. 2 (2003): 131–71; Kenneth H. Mayer, Judith B. Bradford, Harvey J. Makadon, Ron Stall, Hilary Goldhammer, and Stewart Landers, "Sexual and Gender Minority Health: What We Know and What Needs to Be Done," *American Journal of Public Health* 98, no. 6 (2008): 989–95. On the outsider/citizen distinction in LGBT politics, see Seidman, "From Outsider to Citizen."

87 Institute of Medicine, Committee on Lesbian, Gay, Bisexual, and Transgender Health Issues and Research Gaps and Opportunities, *The Health of Lesbian, Gay, Bisexual, and Transgender People: Building a Foundation for Better Understanding* (Washington, DC: National Academies Press, 2011); William Byne, "A New Era for LGBT Health," *LGBT Health* 1, no. 1 (2013): 1–3; Rashada Alexander, Karen Parker, and Tara Schwetz, "Sexual and Gender Minority Health Research at the National Institutes of Health," *LGBT Health* 3, no. 1 (2016): 7–10.

88 National Institutes of Health Sexual and Gender Minority Research Coordinating Committee, "NIH FY 2016–20 Strategic Plan to Advance Research on the Health and Well-Being of Sexual and Gender Minorities" (Bethesda, MD: National Institutes of Health, n.d. [ca. 2013]); Rashada Alexander, Karen Parker, and Tara Schwetz, "Appointment of Dr. Karen L. Parker as Director of the Sexual & Gender Minority Research Office, NIH" at Sexual and Gender Minority Health Research at the NIH, dpcpsi.nih.gov (accessed February 20, 2017).

89 Eliseo J. Pérez-Stable, "Director's Message: Sexual and Gender Minorities Formally Designated as a Health Disparity Population for Research Purposes," October 6, 2016, National Institute on Minority Health and Health Disparities, National Institutes of Health, accessed April 16, 2017, www.nimhd.nih.gov.

90 These include organizations such as the Gay and Lesbian Medical Association (GLMA) and advocacy and research projects organized by the Fenway Institute in Boston. The increasing attention to SGM health and health disparities has also been accompanied by the founding of a new journal, *LGBT Health*.

91 Epstein, "Sexualizing Governance."

92 Institute of Medicine, *The Health of Lesbian, Gay, Bisexual, and Transgender People*, chaps. 5–6.

93 It remains unclear whether LGBT health disparities will continue to receive the same degree of attention from the NIH and other HHS agencies under the Trump administration. One press report from shortly after the inauguration in January 2017 described how the CDC had postponed indefinitely an LGBT youth health summit that had been in the works for months. Allegra Kirkland, "The CDC

Abruptly Cancelled an LGBT Youth Health Summit after Trump Got Elected," *Talking Points Memo*, January 26, 2017, accessed April 16, 2017, www.businessinsider.com.

94  Epstein, "Sexualizing Governance."

95  D'Emilio and Freedman, *Intimate Matters*, 205.

96  Centers for Disease Control and Prevention, "A Public Health Approach for Advancing Sexual Health," 33.

97  "Surgeon General's Call to Action," n.p.; "Interim Report of the National Consensus Process on Sexual Health and Responsible Sexual Behavior" (Atlanta: Morehouse School of Medicine, 2006).

98  Brice Laurent, "Technologies of Democracy: Experiments and Demonstrations," *Science and Engineering Ethics* 17, no. 4 (2011): 650. See also Javier Lezaun and Linda Soneryd, "Consulting Citizens: Technologies of Elicitation and the Mobility of Publics," *Public Understanding of Science* 16, no. 3 (2007): 279–97.

99  Kane Race, *Pleasure Consuming Medicine: The Queer Politics of Drugs* (Durham, NC: Duke University Press, 2009).

100  Metzl and Kirland, *Against Health*.

101  Steven Epstein, *Impure Science: AIDS, Activism, and the Politics of Knowledge* (Berkeley: University of California Press, 1996).

102  On debates concerning PrEP and sexual pleasure, see Jeffrey A. Bennett, chapter 4, this volume; Tim Dean, "Mediated Intimacies: Raw Sex, Truvada, and the Biopolitics of Chemoprophylaxis," *Sexualities* 18, nos. 1/2 (2015): 224–46; Kane Race, "Reluctant Objects: Sexual Pleasure as a Problem for HIV Biomedical Prevention," *GLQ: A Journal of Lesbian and Gay Studies* 22, no. 1 (2016): 1–31. In an interesting example of the diffusion of the language of sexual revolution, a recent CDC-funded PrEP campaign in San Francisco (promoted by a public-private partnership that includes the city's Department of Public Health) targets gay men under the banner "Our Sexual Revolution." See San Francisco Department of Public Health, "Our Sexual Revolution," accessed April 16, 2017, oursexualrevolution.org.

2

Carceral Biocitizenship

*The Rhetorics of Sovereignty in Incarceration*

SARAH BURGESS AND STUART J. MURRAY

## Introduction

On October 19, 2007, nineteen-year-old Ashley Smith died of self-inflicted strangulation while on suicide watch at the Grand Valley Institution for Women in Kitchener, Ontario, Canada. As she tied a ligature around her neck, correctional officers, who had been instructed not to enter into her cell if she was still breathing, watched—and in compliance with Canadian regulations,[1] videorecorded—her death. As the video footage attests, they entered her cell only when she was nonresponsive and could not be resuscitated. Six days later, the three correctional officers who stood by and watched Smith's suicide were charged, along with one of their supervisors, with criminal negligence causing death, while the warden and deputy warden were fired. Criminal charges were later dropped. The case gained some attention following the June 2008 publication of a report by the Office of the Correctional Investigator of Canada titled *A Preventable Death*; and public outcry grew considerably when Canada's national CBC News Network's *The Fifth Estate* broadcast two special investigative reports in January and November 2010, titled "Out of Control" and "Behind the Wall," respectively. The latter broadcast included the video footage of Smith's death, and the Correctional Service of Canada (CSC) came under intense scrutiny for its treatment of prisoners with mental health problems.

What emerged over the course of the Coroner's Inquests (there were two, in 2011 and 2012) were the systemic yet oftentimes highly coordinated, seemingly intentional failures and abuses on the part of the CSC.

The 2008 Correctional Investigator's thirty-three-page report had already cataloged countless instances of "inhumane" treatment and intolerable living conditions: Smith was reportedly assaulted by correctional staff, subjected to excessive "use of force" (both physical and chemical), denied her right to physical exercise, and not permitted sufficient toilet paper or soap; according to the report, "while menstruating, she was not permitted underwear or sufficient sanitary products to meet her hygiene needs."[2] Initially arrested for assault, trespassing, and causing a disturbance at a mall, Smith entered the New Brunswick Youth Centre, where, because of behavioral problems, she was often held for twenty-three hours a day in the "Therapeutic Quiet Unit"—a 9-by-six-foot segregation cell that was only 7.5 feet high. She was allowed out for one hour a day to exercise, shower, and interact with staff. After being released from the youth center, she was again arrested on October 21, 2003, for throwing crab apples at a postal worker. Returned to the New Brunswick Youth Centre for a time, she was transferred to an adult facility after her eighteenth birthday, whereupon her violations as a juvenile while in custody were commuted to adult violations. During her final year of custody, spent almost entirely in solitary confinement, Smith was transferred seventeen times between nine different institutions across five provinces. Each transfer effectively reset the clock on her solitary confinement, circumventing legal limits on the length of time it can be used without a detailed psychiatric assessment and treatment plan. Indeed, it was in part because of these transfers that Smith never received a psychiatric assessment, nor was a comprehensive treatment plan put into place. Extended periods of seclusion and extralegal transfers without doubt were detrimental to Smith's mental and physical health.

The first Coroner's Inquest effectively ended in a mistrial, with legal challenges from the Smith family and controversy over the exclusion of video evidence, including footage of Smith's forced sedation at one institution, as well as the sudden replacement of the presiding coroner (ostensibly due to her impending retirement). At the close of the second Coroner's Inquest, the official report of the specially convened coroner's jury displayed the full extent of the miscarriage of justice in the life and death of Ashley Smith. Issued on December 19, 2013, this report, officially titled the "Coroner's Inquest Touching the Death of Ashley Smith," delivered a stunning verdict: "Cause of death: ligature strangulation and positional asphyxia. By what means: homicide."[3] As an act of administrative law lacking the full force of a criminal verdict, the finding of homicide symbolically recognized the ways that the carceral system was responsible for Smith's death, even if she died by her own hand. The report confirmed what many had suspected: Smith's rights guaranteed to her as a citizen—and as a human being—had been violated by the very system charged with protecting rights for all.

What does it mean to say that the carceral system, as an arm of law, is *in fact* responsible for Smith's death? And, what does such a pronouncement presume about the power of carceral institutions over life and death? In this essay, we explore these questions as a way to understand how various institutions constituted Smith as a *carceral biocitizen*—a subject caught between biopolitical practices and scenes of legal sovereignty. We argue, more specifically, that Smith's death was produced by a diffuse agency that cannot be definitively located or prosecuted—a neoliberal administration of law that presumed that Smith was already "socially dead" and was, thus, no citizen at all. Carceral institutions, however, steadfastly repudiate the *biopolitical* operations of law and corrections. They work to reinscribe a logic of *sovereignty*, and their sovereign repudiation shores up their own power as they affirm the citizenship rights of those incarcerated, claiming to safeguard the conditions under which life can continue. In this cover-up, incarcerated subjects, like Smith, have no place from which to make a claim to the very rights law claims to guarantee. This form of biocitizenship, we suggest, radically diverges from accounts that find in biocitizenship a form of agency through which one might lay claim to life in an affirmative biopolitics.

Our argument in this chapter develops through three sections. In the first, we draw on Michel Foucault's distinction between sovereign and biopolitical power to demonstrate how the carceral archipelago constitutes Smith as a socially dead subject, one who is stripped of her rights through the day-to-day administration of law's judgment. In the second section, we read the published response by the CSC to the Coroner's Inquest. That response, we demonstrate, tries to reinstate sovereignty, as law's prerogative, and yet the CSC finds itself in a difficult position, effectively outsourcing responsibility for Smith's death onto other agencies that should, in its opinion, be the rightful locus of mental health care. By crafting her mental illness as the agent or cause of her death and denying its own role in creating and addressing her illness, the CSC preserves not only its right to punish but also its sovereign jurisdiction over life. The concluding section outlines how this ruse, this cover-up, reveals a form of biocitizenship that is not capable of producing the potential forms of agency imagined by theorists of biocitizenship, such as Petryna, Rose, and Novas.

## Biocitizenship and Somatic Subjectivity

The verdict of the coroner's jury, which included 104 recommendations, suggests that the tragedy of Ashley Smith's case might be located in the scene of her death: "This case study can demonstrate how the correctional system and federal/provincial health care can collectively fail to provide an identified mentally ill, high risk, high needs inmate with the appropriate care, treatment and support."[4] There, with the guards watching as she takes her own life, is framed a perfect snapshot of the failures of correctional institutions to care for the subjects over whom they rule. We are told that, in this scene, carceral institutions—acting in the name of and as law—failed to protect life and to discipline appropriately. We claim here that this failure is a product of the ways Smith's life is constituted through the deployment of biopolitical logics that render her a nonsubject. Smith, we argue specifically, becomes a somatic subject, the body-subject of a biopolitical order. During her short life she was as faceless and as anonymous as the vast and coordinated system over which she was powerless in all but her final act of suicide. It is in this sense that we speak of her carceral biocitizenship: the biopolitical power wielded by the state and its institutions, a power to capture and to regulate, if not to "correct" and to care for, those it counts as members of a particular population to be managed. We are drawing here specifically on Foucault's understanding of biopolitics, a form of governance, he argues, that emerges at the beginning of the nineteenth century and comes to permeate, and in some sense to supplant, the classical right of the sovereign. Here, the sovereign's prerogative "to take life or let live" gradually yields to the state's power "to make live and let die."[5] In the shift from sovereign to biopolitical power, power is decentralized: it becomes diffuse, anonymous, no longer localized (even figuratively) in the body of the king. Instead, much like the vast and coordinated correctional system in which Smith found herself, it is driven by securitization, forecasts, statistics, overall measures, and a regime of "evidence" and "best practices" that address a population (or "mass") in aggregate form. Indeed, this efficiency matrix is one strategy of a neoliberalized penal system, which uses solitary confinement as one "management" strategy to control patient-inmates.[6] While both sovereign and biopolitical state power have as their point of application the body of the subject, the form of somatic subjectivity of each differs significantly. The mechanism of sovereign power is aligned with discipline and the spectacle of the scaffold: "Discipline tries to rule a multiplicity of men to the extent that their multiplicity can and must be dissolved into individual bodies that can be kept under surveillance, trained, used, and, if need be, punished."[7] In other words, discipline *individualizes*. Biopolitical power, on the other hand, *massifies*: it is power "addressed to a multiplicity of men, not to the extent that they are nothing more than their individual bodies, but to the extent that they form, on the contrary, a global mass that is affected by overall processes characteristic of birth, death, production, illness, and so on."[8] Biopolitics intervenes on the species-body, while the individual all but disappears.

Our understanding of biocitizenship, in the context of Ashley Smith's life and death, suggests a form of citizenship that is foremost biopolitical. And the distinction from citizenship under the sovereign must be emphasized. As a sovereign citizen, one is subject to the sovereign prerogative "to take life or let live"—in other words, to be killed or to be left to live. Here, one's livingness is presumed, as it were, and the sovereign enjoys the power to intervene in that life, either to take that life or not to take it. Sovereign killing is the limit of an individual's citizenship: as a citizen one is subject to being killed, and to be killed terminates one's citizenship. Biopolitical power, by contrast, is in Foucault's terms the power "to make live and let die." Here, one's livingness is *not* presumed, one must be *made* to live: power perpetually intervenes on the level of life itself, on a deindividuated and massified body—subjects who are said to demonstrate statistical risks, endemic deviance, and so forth. Significantly, unlike sovereign power, it is not an either/or proposition: being "made to live" is concomitant with "letting die." With biopolitical state power, then, it is death that is presumed, rather than life—death that is contained, social death, which is the covert condition, the cost and the consequence, of biopolitical life and the state itself.

We might, then, characterize Ashley Smith's life as a social death,[9] a form of necrocitizenship, properly speaking, neither quite living nor dead, but stripped of her right, a body that belongs to the state and as part of that state's aggregating technologies, administrative mechanisms, and institutions. Smith is part of the nonnormative population that we "let die" because she cannot be "made to live" in the terms that the state proffers; it is as if she constitutively refused to live by these terms, and her suicide retroactively "proves" this constitutive failure; finally, we might say, she is "allowed to die" in order to shore up—to protect—the normative biocitizenship of the rest of us, whose existence is threatened, as it were, by the continued existence of her nonnormative livingness. By focusing on Smith's death, we distinguish ourselves from the ways that the term "biocitizenship" has typically been deployed, and we seek to complicate the relationship between life and death that biocitizenship might otherwise suggest. Indeed, "biocitizenship" has been used in affirmative discourses on life—injured or damaged biological life, to be sure, but life nonetheless, life worthy of protection. One of the first uses of the term "biological citizenship" appears in Adriana Petryna's book *Life Exposed: Biological Citizens after Chernobyl.* In a fascinating anthropological study that addresses the aftermath of the Chernobyl nuclear disaster, Petryna characterizes biocitizenship as "a massive demand for but selective access to a form of social welfare based on medical, scientific, and legal criteria that both acknowledge biological injury and compensate for it."[10] Even though the "selective access" to social services operationalizes the biopolitics of making live and letting die, the "demand" of biocitizenship is nevertheless made by the living, for and on behalf of life. Likewise with Nikolas Rose and Carlos Novas's seminal text on biocitizenship appearing a few years later, which focuses on the democratic potential of biotechnologies, "biovalue," and the molecularization of life.[11]

By contrast, we are interested less in the strictly biological understanding of somatic subjects and their biological claims to citizenship, and turn instead to a wider moral understanding of the human *bios*—the somewhat abstract concept of a life worth living, abstract but nonetheless concrete in the ways that this concept organizes the body biopolitic through the "soft" power coordinated in and through state technologies, mechanisms, and institutions. This is what we might call "delinquent life": when the "offender" is not just subject to a legal judgment corresponding to individual criminal acts, but a delinquent subject in which it is "not so much his act as his life that is relevant in characterizing him."[12] More precisely, then, we are interested in the ways that such lives are already forfeited, endemically disqualified as lives worth living—or, said otherwise, the ways in which delinquent lives are already morally dead and socially dead. So while we undoubtedly see in the case of Ashley Smith the application of biopower on a biological body—assaults, physical and chemical "use of force," control over bodily movement and exercise, and the punitive regulation of defecation and menstruation— this application of biopower, on the biological body, is underwritten by *moral* terms in which the biological life of a somatic subject is already a life not worth living, a life already consigned to death, a dead life. And it is this death that has a strange afterlife in the case of Ashley Smith. It was, then, only in her ghostly apparition, across highly mediatized depictions of her life and death, that Smith became a "person" in the eyes of the law. The $5 million Coroner's Inquest into her death included eyewitness testimonies, thousands of pages of evidence, and many videos of her life—and death—that circulated widely. Through these, Smith was socially reembodied in the public imaginary. Several depict her extralegal transfers, hooded and being duct-taped into the seat of an airplane, surrounded by guards in full riot gear. The scene is reminiscent of Hollywood depictions of CIA counterinsurgency tactics. It became clear that to protect the content of normative citizenship, delinquent life needed to be contained and mortified. The CSC fought by legal injunction and other means—ultimately unsuccessfully—to ban the publication of the videos and to refuse them as evidence. The inquest also revealed that staff were instructed to lie and falsify reports about Smith, to lend the illusion of law and order.

In the jury's verdict of homicide, then, we have the specter of a murder with no clear murderer. Smith was not killed as the sovereign's prerogative to "take life"; she did not die at the hands of a particular person or persons; rather, the verdict clearly points to the subtle ways that a biopolitical system "lets die," and the jury did not hesitate to call this a homicide—killing. The verdict of homicide suggests that, somehow, an impersonal moral agency was at work in Smith's death, and suggests that the CSC—a vast and diffuse system—is "guilty" of homicide. Of course, this was not a criminal trial, but its symbolic force cannot be denied: the jury saw Smith, posthumously, not as someone who was disposable life, socially dead, but as a person whose right to life was systemically and systematically abrogated. The verdict exposes a system that kills, however obliquely or covertly—through neglect, exposure, indignity, and torture—and it exposes the necrotizing conditions of a biopolitics that ostensibly "makes live," but which "lets die" as the condition and consequence of this life. It exposes the terms of biocitizenship, today, as producing in order to contain, control, and regulate social death: those who are "made" to live will be protected, whereas those the system "lets die" are destined to perish. It regulates the threshold of life and death not from the perspective of life, as it was under sovereign power, but instead through the specter of mortification and death.

## Scenes of Legal Sovereignty and the Lively Politics of Law

In December 2014, the Correctional Service of Canada issued its formal response to the verdict and recommendations offered by the coroner's jury. The document details the changes made within women's (and sometimes men's) correctional facilities since the death of Ashley Smith and charts the ways that the CSC plans to incorporate the recommendations in the oversight and delivery of mental health services in the future. While the aim of this document might be to legitimize the work of the CSC in light of the Smith "tragedy" by demonstrating how it protects and even advances the rights of those who are incarcerated, the document's language reveals how Ashley Smith and others like her are positioned (in time and place) between a scene of legal sovereignty—anxiously reconstituted by the report itself—and the biopolitics of carceral citizenship in the quotidian. Here, we show how the CSC refuses to recognize and in fact repudiates the social deaths of persons such as Smith, biopolitically produced on the stage of an immense legal drama, and thus fails to account for the way the administration of law empties their ability to embody, enact, and express the rights and responsibilities of citizenship. Instead, the CSC claims that law authorizes and secures the rights of incarcerated subjects by securing life perpetually and in advance, as it were. It is here, we argue, that we begin to see that what is at stake in Smith's physical (biological) death is not only who is responsible for this "preventable death" but also how law performatively constitutes itself as sovereign through the scenes in which it operates, rather than only through the bodies over which it rules.

At the very beginning of the report, the CSC attempts to define and frame what the homicide ruling means for correctional services. The authors begin their "Response" by noting that "the jury classified Ashley Smith's death as a homicide. They identified ligature strangulation and positional asphyxiation as the cause of her death. This determination does not imply criminal responsibility. Rather, it means that through acts or omissions, a person or persons has or have contributed to an individual's death."[13] At first blush we might read this text as a confirmation of Giorgio Agamben's thesis in *Homo Sacer: Sovereign Power and Bare Life*.[14] In this sense, we have a homicide that does not imply criminal responsibility—a crime that is no crime, because it enacts the sovereign prerogative to take life and, in so doing, to revoke a subject's citizenship—the grounds for any criminal charge in the first place. But for the CSC, the homicide "classification" (as the report calls it) can be absorbed and reconciled in part by drawing a distinction between causation and contribution. The agents of the state—the employees—who watched (and videorecorded) as Smith took her own life, the multiple transfers between institutions, the time spent in administrative segregation all provide the background against which Smith's death must be understood. In the report's terms, these are the "acts or omissions" of "a person or persons," rather than anything that warrants a slightly more systemic or sociological investigation into correctional cultures; in other words, law reinstates its sovereignty by insisting on the "subjectivity" of personal agents, including Smith herself, "an individual," whose suicide is only "classified" a homicide because a person or persons "contributed" to it. The report deflects any claim that a diffuse and biopolitical moral agency was—and is still—at work in and through the carceral system itself, operating in and through the countless employees responsible for Smith's care and custody. According to the report, this set of ostensibly "individual" acts and the people responsible (by act or omission) constitute an environment that "contributes" to her death but that nevertheless remains sufficiently diffuse and abstract in such a way that no one or no thing can be pinpointed as the *causal* factor in her death, and as such cannot become the object of law's punitive force. The cause, it is implied, rests with Smith herself.

This distinction at first glance recalls Hannah Arendt's differentiation between guilt and responsibility. In her essay "Collective Responsibility," Arendt argues that guilt, a judgment produced in law and in moral systems, concerns what a person has done—what she has done, the extent of her involvement, and the degree of her participation.[15] Guilt takes the person—a figure who always already has a kind of intelligibility and agency through law—as the object of judgment. Collective responsibility, however, means for Arendt that a subject must take responsibility for that which she did not do and that her responsibility for what has happened is assigned to her by virtue of belonging to a group. One might certainly translate the jury's ruling of homicide into these terms. Smith's death is not an issue of guilt, where we hold the individual guards or prison administrators criminally liable for Smith's suicide. Instead, the ruling of homicide becomes an ethical demand—a demand that asks the CSC to account for the scene in which Smith took her own life or, in other words, to assume a collective responsibility. The CSC, however, refuses to see itself as the object of this ethical demand. In describing the purpose of the CSC, it figures itself self-reflexively—indeed, almost paranoically—as a passive actor within a larger scene managed by law: "The mandate of the federal correctional system, as defined in law, is to contribute to the maintenance of a just, peaceful and safe society by carrying out sentences imposed by courts through the safe and humane custody and supervision of offenders, and by assisting the rehabilitation of offenders and their reintegration into the community as law-abiding citizens through the provision of programs in penitentiaries and in the community."[16] By these lights, the correctional system, authorized and constituted by law, functions as a contributor and an assistant—a worker—in the project of rehabilitation that is determined and set out by law's judgment. Correctional institutions are thus figured both as the effect of law's ability to institute and institutionalize and as the mechanism through which law applies and inflicts its punitive (or corrective) power.

To put it simply, the CSC cannot be responsible for Smith's death because it consists simply of institutional actors who find themselves in a scene not of their own making. They—the person or persons involved—are victims of circumstance, as it were. Consider the way the CSC positions itself, in its introduction, as the *response* not to Smith's death in particular but to a national mental health crisis for which it cannot be responsible:

> The issue of mental illness in Canada is significant and has become a major societal issue affecting all Canadians. It is estimated that 20% of Canadians will experience difficulties with their own mental health at some point in life. More than 70% of adults living with mental illness have reported that the onset of their difficulties occurred before they were 18 years of age.
>
> Self-injury and suicide are among the most serious consequences of mental illness. In Canada, suicide is the leading cause of death for people between the ages of 10 and 24 years.
>
> [ . . . ]
>
> Across Canada, provincial and territorial health care systems are burdened by an increasing demand for mental health care. As a result, agencies like CSC have slowly emerged as a last resort for people with active mental health issues who have come into conflict with the law and received a term of imprisonment.[17]

This passage works rhetorically to figure correctional facilities as an almost accidental locus of mental health treatment and response. We are meant to believe that the CSC has "inherited" the problem of mental illness over time and as a result of the failures of other systems—systems, it is implied, that are rightfully responsible for the care of those with mental health issues. The CSC positions itself throughout its document as an institution that has been placed into a context of mental health involuntarily. Because it never asked for it, it can only be understood as a "last resort"—literally, a place to rest for those with mental illness; here the CSC rhetorically absolves itself of responsibility for a history of incarceration that exacerbates if it does not produce mental illness through its techniques.

As Robert Cover rightly observes, this ritualized refusal or dispersion of responsibility across institutions and actors defers and displaces the recognition that law is a system "designed to generate violence."[18] The ruling of a judge, then, is not an act in and through which "we talk our prisoners into jail,"[19] but instead a "routinization of violent behavior"[20] that depends on "others, occupying pre-existing roles, [who] can be expected to act, to implement, or otherwise to respond in a specified way to the judge's interpretation."[21] In the case at hand, the CSC is thus most certainly not a passive actor beholden to the law and its proclamations but a critical dimension of a wider system that works to morally legitimize the scene within which law operates—for Cover, the "field of pain and death."[22] Cover's point is that we must come to terms with the fact that law, whether located in the judge's interpretation of legal language or the baton of the prison guard, is an act of domination that takes place in a scene marked by violence and death. This is the scene for which the CSC must be accountable. And yet, it misses the importance of its own metaphor. Referring to Smith's death as a "tragedy," it dissociates the tragic "act" from the scene on which it takes place. If her death is tragic, this tragedy played out on the CSC's stage, with its actors, under its lights and direction. This mise-en-scène is perpetuated by a sovereign repudiation of responsibility, not simply the old sovereign right to "take life," but to refuse that life as one that is its responsibility, to refuse its claims to citizenship by figuring that life as already dead.

Refusing responsibility for this scene, we argue, creates a spectacle meant to hide the body, to strip it of its right to claim citizenship. The extra-legal transfers suffered by Smith amount to little more than the displacement of a corpse through a sovereign suspension of law. Foucault, in a short essay titled "Pompidou's Two Deaths," explains:

> Prison is not the alternative to death: it carries death along with it. The same red thread runs through the whole length of that penal institution which is supposed to apply the law but which, in reality, suspends it: once through the prison gates, one is in the realm of the arbitrary, of threats, of blackmail, of blows. Against the violence of the penitentiary personnel, the convicts no longer have anything but their bodies as a means for defending themselves and nothing but their bodies to defend. It is life or death, not "correction," that prisons are about.[23]

Correctional facilities usurp the sovereign power of law to discipline bodies in a scene that speaks to the very conditions of life and death. Against this power, the convict's resistance lies in her body. In the case of Ashley Smith, might this mean we can read her suicide as a refusal of the law's power to determine life and death? Can suicide be read, as

Foucault suggests, as a way to "risk death to save one's life, to risk one's very life at the possible cost of death"?[24]

The CSC response, however, forecloses any possibility of reading Smith's death as an act of resistance or refusal of law's sovereign power constituted in a scene of violence, domination, and death—the scene on which she takes her own life. Her death is only ever understood as a "tragedy," although one that is viewed as if through the disembodied lens of the camera that recorded it, obscuring or blocking from view the larger scene at play. And while this alone reveals the anxiety that marks law's use and application of violence, the report evidences a further disavowal of its own constitutive violence. The response from the CSC performs a sleight of hand in which, it is claimed, correctional facilities work to guarantee and enforce the citizenship rights of all who reside there *irrespective of the scene in which they find themselves.* That prisoners are citizens and enjoy the rights guaranteed to them should be trusted because, as the report contends, the CSC acts "to preserve life as the paramount consideration."[25] And, yet, the acts carried out in the name of and toward the ends of "preserving life" render the subject unrecognizable, in advance, as the one who might claim citizenship rights, and to have that claim heard or recognized. These persons not only are removed from the scene in which such a claim could receive an audience and garner a hearing but also are constituted as biopolitical subjects, "massified" and anonymous, predictable and symptomatic—subjects who have no place or voice to claim citizenship rights before the law. It is in this sense that the carceral biocitizen finds herself caught between a scene of legal sovereignty and a biopolitical scene in which she has already been "allowed to die," denying her the very conditions in which she might exercise her rights as a citizen.

This ruse appears most clearly in the CSC's quibble with some of the language employed by the coroner's jury around the issue of "solitary confinement." Noting that the term "is not accurate or applicable within the Canadian federal correctional system,"[26] the report argues that the use of "administrative segregation" is "not intended to be a form of punishment. It is an interim population management measure resulting from a carefully considered decision made by the Institutional Head to facilitate an investigation or to protect the safety and security of individuals and/or the institution."[27] The difference between "solitary confinement" and "administrative segregation" here is one of intent, object, and effect. Whereas the former means to bring the force of the law to bear on an individual as a punitive measure for some behavior or action, the latter is a management decision about *populations* meant to prevent force or violence and to enable safety. This description of administrative segregation betrays that the quotidian scene in which the CSC operates is not framed by a sovereign power of law. Instead, it acts biopolitically, focused on securitizing decisions applied at the level of the "population"— both in and out of prison—and, moreover, for *the institution itself.* The CSC's "management decisions" are designed and carried out in an effort to ensure that the institution is safeguarded over and against the population of prisoners, so that they might serve and protect them. The noble language of the CSC report contradicts actual practice. As the Standing Committee on Public Safety and National Security reported in 2010, "While administrative segregation is seen as an essential tool for crisis management, the Committee learned that CSC uses it too often to deal with offenders with mental health issues."[28] So, while administrative segregation is commonly used, and while it can serve to exacerbate mental health issues (or indeed cause them), it is well documented that those locked inside often experience it as punitive.[29]

According to the CSC, the focus on the security of the institution or the population as a whole does nothing to diminish the rights of the individual who is segregated. In fact, the report once again appeals to the law as that which legitimizes, authorizes, and reconciles the violence of the actions taken by correctional facilities. The report states, "Legislation and policies provide procedural safeguards to ensure that administrative segregation is a fair and humane process that follows the Canadian Charter of Rights and Freedoms, particularly Section 7 (*Everyone has the right to life, liberty and security of the person and the right not to be deprived thereof except in accordance with the principles of fundamental justice which focuses on procedural fairness*) and the duty to act fairly."[30] Administrative segregation is thus merely a "procedural" issue that does not, according to the report, infringe on the substantive rights of the prisoner—the right to life being the most important of these. If we follow this logic, administrative segregation allows prisoners to maintain their rights, or to regain the right to life and security that might otherwise have been threatened. The only difference for prisoners, apparently, is the place in which they might be able to lay claim to these rights. "Segregated inmates," the report emphasizes, "are entitled to all the rights and privileges of other inmates within the physical limitations of the segregation unit."[31] The logic here replicates itself: the location of the prisoner, her scene—both within the segregation unit and presumably within the prison itself—does nothing to compromise her ability to lay claim to her rights as a citizen. She is presumably free to act, and her acts are her own, they are just contained or performed against the background that the CSC provides, but for which it is not (entirely or causally) responsible.

This logic has paralyzing effects on the imprisoned subject who is ostensibly given full control over her actions, her body, and her rights within a place that defines and constitutes her, yet as one who is incapable of tendering such a claim in the first place. As a way of offering background to its argument about administrative segregation, the CSC characterizes women offenders by listing their shared characteristics: "low self-esteem, dependency, low levels of education and vocational achievement, parental death at an early age, frequent foster care placements, residential placement, and living on the street, participation in the sex trade, as well as suicide attempts and self-injurious behaviours."[32] Women offenders are, by this definition, constitutively unable to secure and practice their citizenship rights in appropriate ways and are thus in need of the measures provided by prisons *in order to* gain access to the places in which they might act as full citizens. Incarcerated women, on the one hand, are caught between the sovereign scene of the law in which they are individual actors who can consent (or not) to mental health treatment, determine who has access to their health records, and take their own lives, while, on the other hand, they are captive to the biopolitical logics of the prison and are part of a population to be managed by interdisciplinary teams of specialists, assessed and evaluated through mental health protocols, and made to live out a social death in service of the institution's established goals. The dizzying speed with which the CSC moves between these two positions reveals the precarious position of women inmates. They belong to the state, but their citizenship is an empty one, a biocitizenship that not only violates and effaces the biological body but also mortifies that body, figuring it as already dead, and therefore incapable of issuing a claim to rights.

## Conclusion: The Remains of Biocitizenship

The story of biocitizenship we tell here is not the story of biocitizenship that we have inherited from Petryna or Rose and Novas. For the latter, "biological citizenship" is a descriptive term meant "to encompass all those citizenship projects that have linked their conceptions of citizens to beliefs about the biological existence of human beings, as individuals, as families and lineages, as communities, as population and races, and as a species."[33] Interested in the ways that we are engaged in "making up citizens" (from above and below), they claim that contemporary forms of biological citizenship, generated from the ways we engage with biomedical technologies and come to understand the responsibilities for our own health and our own genetic makeup, enable a form of collective action—they draw on Paul Rabinow's idea of "biosociality"—that challenges the ways citizenship has long been tied to national identity. Biocitizenship in this understanding represents the possibility of new—assuredly neoliberalized—formations or discourses through which we might renegotiate our identities and forge alliances that become the foundation for forms of engaged citizenship. As Rose's subsequent work makes clear, this is an affirmative, if not hopeful, biopolitical project.[34] Our argument about biocitizenship counters this hopeful politics that finds possibilities for collective decision making and new political formations within a biopolitical regime. For us, the deployment of biopolitical logics in carceral settings works to foreclose the possibility of collective action and an exercise of citizenship. In the prison, biopolitical logics contain, manage, and assess populations in the name of preserving life. But what life is being preserved? We might argue that it is, in fact, the life of the institution itself, the life of the state, that is constituted by biocitizenship. And that those who are "allowed to die"—perversely, in the name of life itself—threaten to remain, and to expose these logics.

Ashley Smith's death—at once social and physical—reveals the remains of biocitizenship, remains that are no longer living in any biological sense but that haunt us—and the CSC—in their strange afterlife. She remains on the record as her remains are tied to the record. On September 24, 2007, a member of the Canadian Association of Elizabeth Fry Societies visited Ashley Smith while she was incarcerated. Smith requested that a complaint be filed on her behalf. She wished to be taken out of segregation and placed in the hospital. As well, she claimed that the staff's denials of her requests for mattresses, blankets, pens, and hygiene materials were violations of her human rights as well as her charter rights. In a timeline of events summarizing Ashley Smith's life and death, a CBC website commenting on this meeting simply notes: "The complaint is not read until after her death."[35]

It is only in death that Smith becomes a person in the eyes of the law, a ghostly presence demanding a response, we might say, though the CSC's "response," as its title makes clear, is not to Smith but a "Response to the Coroner's Inquest Touching the Death of Ashley Smith." The ambivalence of this language mimes the ambivalence of the CSC—and indeed, of its other inmates who, like Smith, are caught between a sovereign mise-en-scène and the diffuse logics of biopolitics: Does the Coroner's Inquest "touch" the death of Ashley Smith, does the CSC report "touch" her death, and what would it mean to "touch" the death of someone who, herself, was touched in many ways, violently, inhumanely, but who was ultimately deemed untouchable—seen but untouched—as she lay dying? Smith's death and her ghostly afterlife demonstrate the precarity of those who live in between the law's sovereign gaze and the machinations of biopolitical logics enacted in and by the day-to-day procedures of correctional facilities. She demonstrates how having rights by virtue of belonging to the law does not guarantee the conditions in which one might lay claim to these rights. She illustrates how the prison disavows the way it "carries death" with it even as it disavows its own violence.

NOTES

1 "Procedures: Video-Recording," Commissioner's Directive on "Use of Force," 18–25, Correctional Service Canada, last updated January 26, 2016, accessed March 15, 2016, www.csc-scc.gc.ca.

2 Howard Sapers, *A Preventable Death*, Office of the Correctional Investigator, Government of Canada, 11, last updated June 20, 2008, accessed March 15, 2016, www.oci-bec.gc.ca.

3 Correctional Service Canada, "Coroner's Inquest Touching the Death of Ashley Smith," December 19, 2013, last updated May 21, 2014, accessed July 6, 2016, www.csc-scc.gc.ca.

4 Ibid.

5 Michel Foucault, *"Society Must Be Defended": Lectures at the Collège de France, 1975–1976*, trans. David Macey (New York: Picador, 2003), 241.

6 See Lisa Guenther, *Solitary Confinement: Social Death and Its Afterlives* (Minneapolis: University of Minnesota Press, 2013). Also see Stuart J. Murray and Dave Holmes, "Seclusive Space: Crisis Confinement and Behavior Modification in Canadian Forensic Psychiatry Settings," in *Extreme Punishment: Comparative Studies in Detention, Incarceration and Solitary Confinement*, ed. Keramet Reiter and Alexa Koenig (New York: Palgrave Macmillan, 2015), 115–34.

7 Foucault, *"Society Must Be Defended,"* 242.

8 Ibid., 242–43.

9 See Guenther, *Solitary Confinement*. Also see Orlando Patterson, *Slavery and Social Death: A Comparative Study* (Cambridge, MA: Harvard University Press, 1985).

10 Adriana Petryna, *Life Exposed: Biological Citizens after Chernobyl* (Princeton, NJ: Princeton University Press, 2002), 6.

11 Nikolas Rose and Carlos Novas, "Biological Citizenship," in *Global Assemblages: Technology, Politics, and Ethics as Anthropological Problems*, ed. Aihwa Ong and Stephen J. Collier (Malden, MA: Blackwell, 2005), 439–63.

12 Michel Foucault, *Discipline and Punish: The Birth of the Prison* (New York: Vintage, 1977), 251; also see Stuart J. Murray and Sarah Burgess, "Delinquent Life: Forensic Psychiatry and Neoliberal Biopolitics," in *Power and the Psychiatric Apparatus: Repression, Transformation and Assistance*, ed. Dave Holmes, Jean-Daniel Jacob, and Amélie Perron (Farnham, UK: Ashgate, 2014), 135–45.

13 "Response to the Coroner's Inquest Touching the Death of Ashley Smith," Correctional Service Canada, Government of Canada, last updated December 11, 2014, accessed March 15, 2016, www.csc-scc.gc.ca.

14 Giorgio Agamben, *Homo Sacer: Sovereign Power and Bare Life*, trans. Daniel Heller-Roazen (Stanford, CA: Stanford University Press, 1998).

15 Hannah Arendt, "Collective Responsibility," in *Responsibility and Judgment*, ed. Jerome Kohn (New York: Shocken Books), 148.

16 Ibid.

17 "Response to the Coroner's Inquest," n.p.

18 Robert M. Cover, "Violence and the Word," *Yale Law Journal*, no. 95 (1986): 1613.

19 Ibid., 1608.

20 Ibid., 1614.

21 Ibid., 1611.

22 Ibid., 1601.

23 Michel Foucault, "Pompidou's Two Deaths," in *Power: Essential Works of Michel Foucault, 1954–1984*, ed. James D. Faubion, trans. Robert Hurley (New York: New Press, 2000), 419.

24 Ibid.

25 "Response to the Coroner's Inquest," n.p.

26 Ibid.

27 Ibid.

28 "Mental Health and Drug and Alcohol Addiction in the Federal Correctional System," Report of the Standing Committee on Public Safety and National Security,

Government of Canada, last updated December, 2010, accessed March 15, 2016, www.parl.gc.ca. Also see "Segregation in Canadian Federal Corrections: A Prison Ombudsman's Perspective," Office of the Correctional Investigator, Government of Canada, last updated March 22–23, 2013, accessed March 15, 2016, www.oci-bec.gc.ca.

29  Stuart Grassian, "Psychiatric Effects of Solitary Confinement," *Washington University Journal of Law and Policy* 22 (2006): 325–38.

30  "Response to the Coroner's Inquest," n.p.

31  Ibid.

32  Ibid.

33  Rose and Novas, "Biological Citizenship," 440.

34  See Nikolas Rose, *The Politics of Life Itself: Biomedicine, Power and Subjectivity in the Twenty-First Century* (Princeton, NJ: Princeton University Press, 2006).

35  "Timeline: The Life & Death of Ashley Smith," Canadian Broadcasting Corporation, The Fifth Estate blog, last updated November 12, 2010, accessed March 15, 2016, www.cbc.ca/fifth.

3

# Epigenetics and the Biocitizen

## *Body Temporality and Political Agency in the Postgenomic Age*

KELLY E. HAPPE

## Introduction

It is hard to overstate the degree to which epigenetics is growing in popu-
larity as an alternative model of biological development over and against
genomics.[1] A fast-growing area of research on cellular processes that
influence biological development not attributable to DNA sequences
(as when different traits are expressed across generations of corn plants
despite no change in DNA sequence), epigenetics is embraced by an
array of scholars as a paradigm-shifting understanding of biology. Epigenetics, it is claimed, has opened the door to considering the ways that
human bodies undergo environmentally induced change and, more
radical still, how those changes may be inherited. Described as a "neo-
Lamarckian" model of biology given its reworking of long-standing
understandings of heredity, what is "emerging is an entirely new, non-
determinist model of biological life as plastic, that is, changeable,"[2] one
that is described as "revolutionary."[3]

Researchers are especially interested in whether epigenetics can explain how physical and social environments influence health outcomes,
including those understood to be racially based. Epidemiologists have
for some time held that structural racism plays a significant role in differential rates of diagnosis and mortality for many chronic illnesses.
Epigenetics promises to contribute to health disparities research insofar
as it can putatively show evidence of transgenerational effects of racism, thereby broadening significantly the time frame through which
researchers trace patterns and effects. Beyond methodological innova-

tions, however, is the way in which epigenetics raises the stakes for those scholars concerned with the social justice implications of health disparities research. For example, Shannon Sullivan, a philosopher of race, turns to epigenetics to show a newfound degree of harm from racism that compels both an interdisciplinary approach to ethics and immediate, broad-based action, including social, economic, and environmental policy reforms.[4] To advocate for the redistribution of material resources on the basis of the lived experience of inequality resembles, then, a familiar model of biocitizenship insofar as the citizens in question are defined by shared yet differential embodied experiences of exposure, risk, and inequality, necessitating both recognition and distributive justice.

The turn to epigenetics as a more compelling, actionable type of evidence of racism over and against what is produced by other health sciences rests on a number of assumptions about the body, including its temporality and embodied becoming. These assumptions in turn necessitate an elaboration of what we mean by the "bio" of biocitizenship. Indeed, epigenetic biocitizenship rests on a materialist approach to the body and its history, one that has both explanatory and emancipatory potential. Its promise rests largely on the notion that a documentable "bodily memory" of past systemic abuses may overcome some of the conceptual and methodological limitations of other biological models such as those informing genomics or epidemiology. It is equally possible, however, that epigenetic methods for constituting evidence and translating it into action enact instead something more akin to a biologistic and deterministic racialism, one animated by a materialism more likely to sabotage than enable biocitizenship and its claims for redress.

## Environmental Epigenetics and Temporality: Collapsing the Diachronic/Synchronic Binary

There are several reasons why epigenetics is proving attractive to various scholars who wish to definitively link environments, broadly construed, to disparities in health, economic security, possibilities for advancement, and the like.[5] First, epigenetics holds the promise of displacing what has been long considered the undue influence that genomics plays in thwarting efforts to improve both physical and social environments. The much-celebrated genetic "revolution" initiated by Francis Crick's Central

Dogma hypothesis and culminating in the Human Genome Project brought much excitement and resources to the idea that we should change genes, not social and economic environments.[6] Despite the valiant attempts by social scientists and biologists alike to show the limits of a DNA-centric model of biological development, it has remained more or less triumphant.[7]

Second, epigenetics implicitly positions itself as a necessary supplement to epidemiology, specifically, health disparities research establishing linkages between institutional racism and specific biological effects. Epidemiology's limits extend largely from its inability to track effects over time and to draw compelling connections between societal-level causes of disease and individual symptoms. To take the specific example of chemical exposures and environmental health—exposures that constitute a crucial index of the impact of environmental racism on health—"body burden" measurements can detect the presence of chemical metabolites in particular bodies but do not necessarily tell the observer anything about the history of exposure over time. Even when geographic information system technologies can account for travel patterns of chemicals, some chemicals metabolize quickly or are expelled from the body. Indeed, the lag time between exposure and effect has been a vexing problem for environmental health advocates. Breastfeeding, for instance, is a powerful confounding variable in research attempting to show a relation between chemical exposure and increased risk for breast cancer. Simply put, a cause-and-effect relation is difficult to prove and so serve as the basis for managing, or eliminating entirely, the use of a chemical or class of chemicals. Environmental justice advocates, therefore, have no choice but to make the case for policy reform on the basis of risk—a difficult concept to ground advocacy if for no other reason than it is abstract, is the province of exclusionary kinds of expertise, and epistemologically, privileges uncertainty over actionable knowledge.[8]

Health disparities research is further hampered by its unavoidable translation of society-wide effects into proximate causes. Reflecting on such methodological limits, Merlin Chowkwanyun has argued that

> to the extent quantitative methodology—and its language of variables and associations—becomes predominant, its practitioners can unwit-

tingly narrow the scope of analysis. Questions and their explanations become constricted by quantitative categories that can reduce complex social processes into variables for models. Moreover, explanation can take on a rather mechanical cause-effect form. Such a form then focuses heavily on individual-level characteristics or behaviors and how much they predict life chances in the larger social structure—but far less attention is given to how transformations of the latter can alter the former.[9]

As Janet Shim has put it, "Adjusting at the individual level for an effect that occurs causally at the society level cannot logically produce a meaningful model of disease etiology, no matter how refined the measures."[10]

Epigenetics can possibly overcome these methodological limitations in part by connecting observed bodily damage to long-standing historical processes. For example, while other health science tools can detect trace amounts of chemicals in the body or levels of stress hormones in real time (therein making no claims about past events or possible effects on future generations), epigenetics shows how the observed damage can be traced to prior events and processes. Scholars have termed this "bodily memory," a materialization that epigenetics is uniquely suited to study.[11] For example, it is hypothesized that DNA methylation—the process by which methyl groups influence the activity of DNA segments without changing the sequence of nucleotides making up the genome—both influences gene expression and is a material change that may be transmitted intergenerationally, adding a potentially hereditary dimension to the process by which racism is embodied.

By privileging both environmental agents and their possible intergenerational effects, epigenetics can bolster our collective sense of political agency and social responsibility: environments can be changed much more readily than DNA, and the urgency with which we should enact broad-based social, health, economic, and environmental reform becomes all the more apparent.[12]

With its emphasis on bodily memory and heredity (effectively closing the gap between historical events and the moment of observation), epigenetics makes temporality as important as, if not more important than, spatiality in discourses about our shared social, economic, and physical environments.[13] Epigenetics provides what many consider compelling, actionable evidence not only of the body's exposure and permeability to environments but also of the biological traces of embodied experience—effects that can be seen and felt across generations. And it is evidence that rests on a complex temporality that brings the past to bear on the present and the future. To determine how it might enable particular forms or modes of biocitizenship requires, then, that we theorize the relationship between the body and its history. One approach to such an inquiry is distinguishing between diachronic and synchronic models of biological change.

Jacqueline Stevens, in her critique of genomics research that purports to contribute to an elucidation of health disparities, makes the distinction between diachronic and synchronic approaches to the study of racialization, racism, and health.[14] For Stevens, genomics is a diachronic model par excellence: evaluations of genomes tell a story of DNA over evolutionary time in the language of genetic stability and change. The limit of the diachronic model, however, is that it privileges one aspect of the human body—the genome—thereby positing a more fragmented, atomistic understanding of the body and its history. Moreover, when African ancestry is hypothesized as having something to do with disparities in health, researchers can unwittingly confuse two very different material realities: ancestry and the lived experience of racialization. While ancestry may be linked with certain diseases, research about it will have limited bearing on disparities such as differential rates of breast cancer diagnoses and mortality. While ancestry may be interesting from an evolutionary point of view, it is of limited use in understanding the multiple and interlocking variables behind disparities or in the treatment of patients in medical contexts for whom ancestry is unlikely to be a verified bodily attribute.

The synchronic model, by contrast, assumes that the relationship between health and race can be elucidated through an analysis of many intersecting social, cultural, and economic forces. Epidemiology can be said to embrace such a model, insofar as it tells a story of the human body as the materialization of multiple, converging events and processes in space and time. For example, elevated glucocorticoid levels, which are linked with heightened risk for particular kinds of breast cancers, are sometimes the outcome of one's experience with housing precarity, financial insecurity, and exposure to microaggression, experiences that can be traced back to a variety of policy decisions and institutional practices (that are themselves historically variable). The limit of the synchronic model, however, is that although it is more inclusive and comprehensive, it does not necessarily give us a sense of what has endured and what has changed over time. As I noted earlier, historians have challenged epidemiological studies of health disparities for unwittingly quantifying and individualizing what are in effect society-wide factors in these disparities. As they have argued, complex causes cannot be reduced to racial identity as happens in public discourse about this research—the discursive effect of repeatedly telling audiences that racially identified groups of persons are more likely to suffer from disease, poverty, and the like.[15]

Epigenetics would appear to encompass both diachronic and synchronic analyses—or even to collapse the distinction altogether. It is a diachronic narrative of the body insofar as it reads the epigenome as a storehouse of the body's memory, as when studies link methylation patterns to past famines. At the same time, there is a level of actionability that genomics alone does not seem to allow for. Since epigenetics shows that human practices may influence genomic function, it follows that human practice can reverse changes that society collectively determines are not desirable. Epigenetics thus temporalizes the body in a way that can enable, rather than short-circuit, the enactment of effective biocitizenship: the body's memory serves as a storehouse of information about past practices, which then mobilizes action to ameliorate the damage in the name of future generations. Over and against genomic narratives of the body in which one is marked indelibly by matter for which we have no control, epigenetics renarrates the genome as a substance inextricably linked with material practices. And over and against epidemiology's reductionist account whereby society-level causes are reduced to observable, fleeting bodily processes in real time, epigenetics provides material evidence of the work of complex historical events. What happens, however, when diachronic and synchronic models of the body are collapsed in the specific context of research about race and racism?

## Epigenetics as Ethical Ground

In terms of scientific method, epigenetics research produces evidence that appears to blur the distinction between diachronic and synchronic approaches to the body, with possibly paradigm-shifting consequences for the biological sciences.[16] Shifting our analysis to a different register, namely, to the enactment of epigenetic biocitizenship, raises questions as to how these temporalities translate into a politics. What kind of grounds does epigenetics provide for claims to ameliorate racial disparities? To put it another way, how does the "bio" of biocitizenship index not just the body of the citizen actor but also ethics, temporal relations with others, and materialist frameworks of interpretation?

To explore these questions, I will consider an essay by the philosopher Shannon Sullivan in which she admirably calls for a feminist politics grounded in epigenetic evidence of the long-lasting, damaging effects of what she terms "white racism." For Sullivan, the fact that racist abuses far exceed the temporal boundaries of the present—lasting across generations even—makes fighting racism an even more crucial and pressing project. Arguing that we need to understand the biological effects of racism, she writes that "the field of epigenetics can help philosophers and others understand the transgenerational biological impact of social forces, such as white racism. It reveals that the damage done by white racism is more extensive than critical philosophers of race might have realized, and also that interventions against white racism must address not just the economic, geographical, social, and psychological, but also the biological aspects of human existence."[17]

Bringing the past to bear on the present, Sullivan writes that epigenetics "means, for example, that the stress and trauma of Jim Crow continue to live even though Jim Crow formally ended in the 1960s."[18] The epigenetic turn is justified, she says, due to studies linking maternal and paternal experience of stress to long-term damage to mechanisms of stress response in their children.[19] Specifically, epigenetics adds a crucial hereditary component to current "weathering" research in epidemiology showing a connection between long-term stress from racially motivated discrimination and adverse health effects. Whereas epidemiology can scientifically explain the embodied experiences of blacks in the United States, epigenetics shows a vicious cyclical pattern: the way that a black woman responds to discrimination today is both evidence of her relatives' experience of white racism and a biological response that will undermine the ability of her own children to appropriately respond to stress in their lifetimes.

Here we see how epigenetics allows for the integration of both dia-chronic and synchronic narratives of the bodily memory of racism: Jim Crow retains analytic force insofar as its effects are felt over time, while the current configuration of structural racism further contributes to the bodily assaults felt and lived by African Americans (Sullivan is care-ful to clarify that "ongoing racism after Jim Crow also can be blamed for contributing to the high rates of infant mortality and cardiovascu-lar disease experienced by African Americans"). "Jim Crow" is no mere metaphor, as when Michelle Alexander describes the current carceral economy as the "new" Jim Crow—with epigenetics, it is an enduring biological reality.[20]

What is at stake, conceptually and politically, when "Jim Crow" and "Dutch famine"—otherwise complex sets of forces including laws, in-stitutional practices, and political economy—transform into epigenetic markers and effects over time? This question begs yet others: What do we mean by "history," and why is this an especially pressing question in the context of research about race and racism? To help answer these ques-tions, I turn to a critique of racial disparities research by Adolph Reed and Merlin Chowkwanyun. Taking as their point of departure observa-tions about the racial disparities of the 2008–9 economic crisis, in partic-ular, the ways in which blacks were hit harder by the dramatic downturn, Reed and Chowkwanyun pay close attention to the collection of studies that serve as founding narratives of racialized economic disparity. Some, they point out, do little more than advance the claim that white prejudice (a psychologizing discourse, they say) is to blame for structural, institu-tional racism. Other studies, such as Oliver and Shapiro's *Black Wealth/White Wealth*, though purporting to show the historical reasons for en-during disparities, nevertheless assumes that "history powerfully exerts its effects at all times, from the creation of racial wealth gaps through their persistence to the present."[21] Reed and Chowkwanyun argue that the book presumes a "sedimentation of racial inequality," the effect of "the cumulative effects of the past"[22]—much in the same way that epigenetics is touted as demonstrating, through bodily memory, the compounding effects of racism over time.[23] As Reed and Chowkwanyun write:

> Who could quarrel with this? The language of sedimentation, legacy, and history certainly separates *Black Wealth/White Wealth* from pedestrian

research that simply describes another disparity *du jour* with little else. But this may amount more to rhetorical genuflection than substantive historical analysis. Rigorous invocation of the past to shed light on present conditions (in this case, the racial wealth gap) must not only identify a persistent social mechanism in the past (in this case, unequal asset accumulation and later inheritance) but also carefully consider when it changes or even stops and to what degree.[24]

In terms of historiography, they claim:

> One interpretive goal should therefore be to think hard about whether mechanisms that have perpetuated racial wealth gaps in the past will take the same form in the future. This is the task, in other words, of concrete periodization and historicization rather than reliance on self-satisfying but overly elastic, transhistorical phrases like "America's racist legacy."[25]

Reed and Chowkwanyun's main point is that although injustices of the past are surely relevant to any historicization of disparity (of which race classifications matter), what is equally important is documenting precisely how the material conditions of the past may no longer be the historical conditions of the present. Racialization and its differential effects are the result of and, in turn, enable particular intersections of unemployment, uneven economic redevelopment, maldistribution of wealth, and the like. As in the case of economic disparity studies that Reed and Chowkwanyun carefully unpack, a "sedimented inequality" trades off with what they call a "dynamic historical materialist perspective," in which variables such as class, race, and gender are

> inflections within a unitary system of capitalist social hierarchy. . . . From this perspective insistence that race, or any other category of ascriptive differentiation, is somehow *sui generis* and transcendent of particular regimes of capitalist social relations appears to be, as we have suggested here, itself reflective of a class position tied programmatically to the articulation of a metric of social justice compatible with neoliberalism. That is a view that both obscures useful ways to understand the forces that are intensifying inequality and undermines the capacity to challenge them.[26]

Thus, central to the argument advanced by Reed and Chowkwanyun is that a sole focus on racial disparity (and the problem of white racism) does not have as much explanatory force as would appear given its inattention to political economy, class, stages of capitalism, and categories of difference such as gender. More significantly, the lack of explanatory force will then fail to realize policy reform that would attend to the role of state-sanctioned practices imbued with logics of neoliberalism and the contextually specific ways they materialize in housing development, economic revitalization, and workforce dislocation—to name just some of the ways in which disparities persist, albeit in historically unique and changing ways. As Reed and Chowkwanyun put it, implicitly neoliberal discourses "represent détente with rather than commitment to changing capitalist social relations, including those that contribute to intra- and inter-racial disparities in the first place."[27]

What we mean by "Jim Crow," then, is entirely dependent on an analysis of the intersection of multiple social and economic forces at a given time and place in history. To claim, as Sullivan does, that Jim Crow "lives on" in the bodies of African Americans today effects just the opposite: the particularities of material conditions of the past live on in bodily memory via durable biological effects, thereby transforming those particularities into abstract matter that endures over time. Historical conditions of racist practices, including capitalist-driven economic policy, become the rarefied matter of biological systems. The epigeneticization of Jim Crow suggests that what it means to embody racial positionality today is the same as it did during the actual Jim Crow era, thereby enabling an idea of race as a materiality capable of existing transhistorically—the epigenome becomes a kind of biological vector of equivalence and, more worrisome, is a racial form of biological matter at that. It is just this sort of confusion of the diachronic and the synchronic that Stevens says is so dangerous when genomics and health disparities research overlap (and why, she says, the National Institutes of Health would be entirely justified in denying funding for such research.[28] I note later that this kind of slippage is unique to discussions of *racial*, not other, disparities in Sullivan's essay, such as those associated with gender).

It is just these ontologizing effects of epigenetics science that ground Becky Mansfield and Julie Guthman's scholarship about key conceptual developments in this growing area of biological research. They pay particular attention to the privileging of the maternal body as the material site for the study of heritable environmental events—a site that paradoxically becomes unbounded temporally and spatially. They write:

> In epigenetics, the fetus becomes a crucial node in space-time, simultaneously archiving the past while becoming the future. Because of this, the "prenatal" temporality is not limited to conception and pregnancy but to everything prior to birth (e.g., grandparents' exposures). Similarly, the effects of the prenatal environment extend to future generations, as the epigenetic *outcomes* of exposures in one's own lifetime become *factors* for future generations—whether through direct inheritance or through what Szyf calls "the social environment." In epigenetics, what organisms "are" now constitutes the "environment" for future generations.[29]

Thus, when otherwise variable, historical "environments" transform into biomarkers of the body, they take on a transhistorical quality that collapses the being/becoming binary. But since this collapsing occurs within a context of still circulating ideas that race is "real," and therefore normative, the outcome is likely the belief that epigenomes perpetually mark the black body as pathological.

Even if we allow for the possibility that epigenetics will keep the idea of broad social and economic reform on the agenda (after all, interventions now may have positive effects on future generations), using epigenetics as the *grounds* for such changes substitutes a technocratic imagination for one animated by ethics and needs. Sullivan, for example, advocates for broadening the definition of prenatal care beyond biomedical frames.[30] Yet she opens up the troubling possibility that policy effectiveness could or should be measured by way of epigenetic (or more broadly biological/physiological) surveillance rather than on the egalitarian or distributive goals it serves. In a context in which the redistribution of wealth is becoming more and more unthinkable, deploying epigenetics as grounds could set up a possible scenario in which social and economic reforms are discredited in the face of epigenetic "proof" that their effectiveness is lacking. And this further begs the question that policy makers would act in the first place given the entirely likely outcome that uncertainty around epigenetic evidence of the effects of white racism will result in endless scientific study. (Nearly all scientific evidence of bodily harm can be subject to endless dispute, which is why environmental science is such a fraught basis for biocitizenship.) We may also witness a scenario wherein the proposed solution is epigenome editing, returning us to a genomics-inflected logic that we should change bodies, not policies.

Curiously, Sullivan distances herself from the very premise by which philosophers might ground their arguments about the ethical obligation to eliminate racism. Rather than embrace and bolster an ethical stance, Sullivan, by asserting that humanists need to incorporate scientific evidence into their claims, implicitly concedes that ethical arguments are not sufficient.

While Sullivan intends to enact a feminist antiracist stance, her turn to epigenetics is, ultimately, unnecessary, even counterproductive. We already know that lack of basic material resources is a large part of differential outcomes such as higher infant mortality and preterm birthrates among African Americans. It remains unclear why, in the case of race and race alone, the need for transgenerational biological proof is necessary. Beyond the fact that epigenetics may be unnecessary to ground arguments about the damaging effects of racism is the danger that the discursive shift that Sullivan enacts reduces the black body to a kind of bare life, or what Elizabeth Povinelli calls "ethical substance" that contains within itself no agency, no liveliness around which an ethical argument about racism can be articulated.[31] Sullivan's refusal to consider how epigenetics might offer biological explanations for the experience of embodied gender (e.g., by entertaining the possibility that the stress of sexism and misogyny can account for preterm birthrates) is telling. When she writes that her analysis is strictly about the relationship between racism and parenting style (and not mothering specifically), she betrays a long-standing logic whereby the behavior of blacks is reframed as biological defect while simultaneously allowing that the behavior of whites (in particular, white women) is a social pathology.[32] It is as if, to borrow from Mel Chen, black bodies do not so much absorb the toxic effects of racism as they themselves are toxic.[33]

How might we, then, theorize biocitizenship as enacted on ethical grounds while still maintaining a materialist approach to the body? If the ultimate lesson of epigenetics is that we cannot avoid what has long been posited by Marxists as the materialist view of history, how might it still be possible to translate this into a politics, namely, in the practices of biocitizenship?

## Historical Materialism and the Body: Needs, Affect, and the Political Subjectivity of the Biocitizen

In a review of historical materialist understandings of the body, Rebecca Orzeck attends to the question of whether there is a "natural" body in Marxist scholarship. This is an important question insofar as any theory of the body necessarily confronts the question of needs, even when understood as the outcome of historically contingent material forces. Epigenetics implicitly posits itself as a historical materialist theory of the body par excellence. That is to say, epigenetics holds that the material conditions of the body (e.g., the epigenome) are the drivers of development over and against an insular, unidirectional, outward-acting genome—the theory behind the Central Dogma and other deterministic theories of DNA and genes. If the epigenome is the agent of those material forces (racist acts of aggression, denial of basic health needs, environmental pollution), then we can say that epigenetics merely documents the ways in which the body is quite literally the outcome of material conditions.

While historical materialism provides a way of demonstrating how and why the forces of capitalist modes of production materially create bodies (e.g., in the ways in which assembly-line work produces disfigured bodies), it also holds that there are basic human needs that exceed cultural forces and therefore can provide the grounds, and means, for resistance. Orzeck writes, "Where I earlier suggested that needs, or rather the imperative of their satisfaction, implied bodies as perpetually produced through labour, it now seems that needs and aversions may suggest precisely what presupposes production and possibly what portends the destruction of a mode of a particular production."[34] What I want to add is that a turn to the "natural" body, insofar as the body has needs (and can perceive what is anathema to them),[35] enacts an oppositional stance on ethical, not biological, grounds. "Natural" is not synonymous with "biological," or at least it need not be. The body in pain, the sick body, the precarious body—all are felt and perceived and can be the grounds of oppositional politics without recourse to biological evidence. Angela Davis, writing more than thirty years ago, described the problem of black women's health not in terms of scientifically confirmed causes but of the lived experience of illness and death.[36] Her authority to make claims for recognition and redress is grounded in an agency and ethos of a racialized and gendered positionality—one that is subject to change over time but always in relation to a complex set of economic and social forces. She contextualizes black women's health against the backdrop of the militarization of the economy wherein cuts in health care were really *transfers* to a bloated and ever-growing military budget, which is to also contextualize black women's health within an expansion of geopolitical power and the globalization of economies. Davis cites infant mortality and preterm birth *not* as evidence that the black woman's body is the materialization of transhistorical forces but as evidence of historically specific circulations of capital.[37]

More recently, in the book *Animancies*, Mel Chen describes the experience of the condition known as multiple chemical sensitivity, one caused, it seems, by Chen's repeated exposure to mercury as a child. Chen experiences what can only be described as a complete physical and psychological breakdown when exposed to chemical fumes, to the extent that they must wear a mask a good deal of the time while in public—a prosthetic that seems only to further queer Chen's already queer body, living as both Asian American and transgender. Tellingly, Chen does not ever talk about medical theories of cause and effect, even though that language is certainly available. Rather, Chen talks of toxicity as a "condition," a state of immunity (not in the medical sense) with a political affect, one that then calls forth or animates a "toxic worlding." Toxicity is a condition that "is too complex to imagine as a property of one or another individual or group or something that could itself be so easily bounded."[38] Intoxification is understood (and lived) by Chen as a confrontation and inhabitation of cultural codings of queer as toxic while at the same time opening up the possibility of being otherwise. "What happens," Chen asks, "when queers become intoxicated?"[39]

For Chen, the experience of intoxification—in which time is suspended and the experience of subject-object relations breaks down—is, we might say, an otherworldly experience, or perhaps a hyperworldly experience insofar as it is hard to feel or identify the lines or boundaries between body, self, and objects. Chen's telling of the story in this way is important for the argument that the low status we impute upon matter—as inert, as blank surface, or as toxic invader of the otherwise bounded and normal (pure?) body—needs to be rethought, reanimated, re-worlded to confront our new embodied being as intoxicated (as biomonitoring data show, we are all toxic now). In part this is because Chen's narrative of intoxification also raises the question of relationality and care: Chen's partner "tolerates this because she understands very deeply how I am toxic. What is this relating? Distance in the home becomes the condition of these humans living together in this moment, humans who are geared not toward continuity or productivity or reproductivity but to stasis, to waiting, until it passes."[40]

In Chen's everyday experience of multiple chemical sensitivity, bodily memory of earlier exposures collides with particular configurations of matter—configurations that include consumer goods like perfume, the ubiquity of mercury pollution and the political economy of its production, and cultural codings of the queer body. Their narrative is a historical materialist account of the body insofar as the pain, disorientation, and isolation they experience, a combination of affect and need so frequent as to be a banal feature of lived experience, are possible because of a variety of interlocking human practices. But Chen's account is historically materialist in another way; that is to say, it takes seriously the ways in which bodily mattering is the very grounds of a political subjectivity. As Jason Edwards reminds us, historical materialism is a theory not only of the relationship between labor and the reproduction of relations of production and consumption but also of the relationship between everyday life and the reproduction of social relations key to sustaining—or resisting—a particular mode of production.[41]

## Conclusion

I began this essay with the question, what is the "bio" of biocitizenship? In particular, how might a consideration of the history and temporality of the body help elucidate the possibilities and limitations of biocitizenship organized and enacted on the grounds that the body is the materialization of environments? Exemplars of biocitizenship, such as activism around environmental contamination (e.g., post-Chernobyl articulations), enactments that served to ground the very idea of biocitizenship and its theorization by scholars of various disciplinary commitments, have assumed that the "bio" is simply the body of the citizen—otherwise healthy, now diseased or at risk. Biomedical evidence of disease may or may not be part and parcel of the demands for recognition or redress.

But what if the very idea of the body is at stake? Epigenetics not only holds that the body itself can provide evidence that far surpasses what the biocitizen even perceives as when epigenetic evidence is used to demonstrate that the harm one experiences in the present is in fact evidence of otherwise unknown harm suffered by one's ancestors; it also holds that the very idea of one's body, its materiality, does not exist prior to the exposure but is in fact the materialization of environments, both physical and social.

When advocates of epigenetics assert that it provides a kind of evidence that is more compelling, more actionable even, they are making a number of assumptions not only about other types of biomedical evidence but of what can animate effective calls for both public health intervention and more broad-based social reform. Inextricably bound with these claims are assumptions about history and temporality. I have argued here that claims about bodily memory rest on assumptions about diachronic and synchronic narratives of the body's history. The enthusiasm around epigenetics rests on unstated assumptions that it can collapse the diachronic/synchronic distinction insofar as evidence of bodily harm tells a story about a long history of exposure as well as the embodiment of environments in the present. It is not a history of atomistic genomes far removed from the social world of human practices but just the opposite: epigenomes are narratives of human social history in all its complexity. Unlike evolutionary narratives, epigenetics promises a historical materialist conception of the body, one that not only has explanatory function in describing the relationship between environment and embodiment but also provides the ethical grounds for biocitizenship's claims for redress.

We saw this in practice in the essay by Sullivan in which she proposes that epigenetics provides new urgency for ameliorating and preventing further harms experienced by African Americans as a result of white racism and its various institutional practices—environmental destruction, denial of care, discrimination, and stigmatization.

Upon closer examination, however, we find that Sullivan enacts what Reed and Chowkwanyun describe as an "interpretive pathology"—one that not only has little analytical force but that also displaces a comprehensive contextualization and understanding of disparity for a theory of race and racism as historically static, essentialized categories of human sociality. Epigenetics naturalizes what has until now been the rhetorical use of the past as a metaphor of the present, as when Jim Crow is used as a metaphor to evaluate mass incarceration today.[42] Epigenetics renders the body not just the materialization of the current configuration of material conditions but the aggregation of past practices. Its diachronic narrative is not one of the reproduction of the social relations necessary to reproduce capitalist modes of production and consumption (which must be part of any adequate understanding of racialization), but of the reproduction of bodily matter through time. This, then, short-circuits the possibility of the very agency needed for the enactment of biocitizenship. Historical materialist understandings of the body, by contrast, consider how it is made by the practices it engages in, not only in terms of labor but also in terms of the creation of social worlds. At the same time, these very conditions provide the grounds for political subjectivity, including the political subjectivity of particular instantiations of biocitizenship.

I ended with a gesture toward a different kind of historical materialist understanding of the body, political agency, and biocitizenship by briefly considering the work of Mel Chen, which uses both diachronic and synchronic models of bodily mattering. While not couched explicitly in the language of biocitizenship, Chen's work on ideologies and manifestations of bodily mattering offer an alternative to epigenetics while also allowing for a consideration of the body as such. Chen does not shy away from an engagement with matter, even understood at the molecular level (for, surely, they experience, in a profound way, the molecular, as when chemical particulates become part of the body's biological systems, utterly transforming one's being in the world). Nevertheless, it is an engagement with matter at the level of affect, not science, and animated by historically specific conditions of a collective, distributed agency and so not reducible to mere substance or bare life.

* * *

Paul Rabinow introduced the term "biosociality" to describe subjectivity and agency in the wake of human genome sequencing, in particular, a sociality that emerged when explicit ideological appeals to model culture on biology gave way to the micropractices of biopolitical governance.[43] Casting eugenics and sociobiology as social projects that, while animated by biological metaphors did not emerge directly from scientific practice, he wrote that "if sociobiology is culture constructed on the basis of a metaphor of nature, then in biosociality, nature will be modeled on culture understood as practice. Nature will be known and remade through technique and will finally become artificial, just as culture becomes natural. Were such a project to be brought to fruition, it would stand as the basis for overcoming the nature/culture split."[44]

Epigenetics is surely just this sort of project, ushering in a mode of biosociality that perhaps Rabinow could not have envisioned. But while such a theory of subjectivity and subjectification can tell us a lot about power and the mechanisms by which it is differentially distributed, it will fall short of the historical materialist analysis that scholars such as Reed and Chowkwanyun call for—displacing, in their words, a "commitment to changing capitalist social relations" for a "détente" with the current social and economic order.[45] Nevertheless, what biosociality—and biocitizenship in particular—requires is an embrace with the very material and discursive conditions of bodily mattering that will enable new possibilities for radical embodiment and politics. The "molecular biopolitics" enacted by Chen can, in their words, release the "organism from its biological underpinnings," all the while enacting a queer ontology of relationality and temporality. It is a biocitizenship that can demand environmental, social, and economic reform not on the grounds of a static identity and essentialist ontology but from the body's potentiality for needs and desires outside the reach of the normative.

NOTES

1  What is particularly startling is the sheer breadth of its appeal: not only are biologists examining the workings of epigenetic processes, but social scientists and humanities scholars are writing about the ways in which bodies do not interact with environments so much as they are emergent properties of different materialities that cannot be easily disentangled. Epigenetic theories are thus working their way

into what is called "new materialism" in philosophy, critical theory, and feminist studies.

2 Becky Mansfield and Julie Guthman, "Epigenetic Life: Bioplasticity, Abnormality, and New Configurations of Race and Reproduction," *Cultural Geographies* 22, no. 1 (2014): 3–20. I should note that there is debate within the scientific community as to whether epigenetics augurs a paradigm shift in how heredity is conceptualized. I only wish to point out that the prospect of such a shift is one factor in the attention epigenetics has garnered among various fields of inquiry, regardless of whether it is in fact "revolutionary" in its actual effects.

3 See Zaneta M. Thayer and Christopher W. Kuzawa, "Biological Memories of Past Environments: Epigenetic Pathways to Health Disparities," *Epigenetics* 6, no. 7 (2011): 1–6. Whether or not actual epigenetics research has lived or will live up to these claims is a topic for a different essay. The point here is that such claims are driving the uptake of epigenetic principles in a variety of discourses, including health disparities, which I address here. The "neo-Lamarckian" reference is to the work of Jean-Baptiste Lamarck, the early nineteenth-century researcher known to have advanced the notion that acquired characteristics can be inherited.

4 Thayer and Kuzawa, "Biological Memories"; Shannon Sullivan, "Inheriting Racist Disparities in Health: Epigenetics and the Transgenerational Effects of White Racism," *Critical Philosophy of Race* 1, no. 2 (2013): 190–218.

5 For example, the Breast Cancer Fund discusses epigenetics research in its science and advocacy work.

6 For an elaboration of this point, see chapter 2 of Kelly Happe, *The Material Gene: Race, Gender, and Heredity after the Human Genome Project* (New York: NYU Press, 2013).

7 Evelyn Fox Keller, "Nature, Nurture, and the Human Genome Project," in *The Code of Codes: Scientific and Social Issues in the Human Genome Project*, ed. Daniel Kevles and Leroy Hood (Cambridge, MA: Harvard University Press, 1993). For an elaboration of this point, see chapter 5 of Happe, *The Material Gene*. Crick's Central Dogma thesis held that DNA is the primary agent in gene expression and that certain "transfers" of coding (such as proteins activating the formation of other proteins) were impossible. For an explanation of epigenetics' rethinking of heredity and its implications for social theory, see Maurizio Meloni, "The Social Brain Meets the Reactive Genome: Neuroscience, Epigenetics, and the New Social Biology," *Frontiers in Human Neuroscience* 8 (2014): 1–12. Meloni writes that epigenetics has "opened the doors to a broader, extended view of heredity by which information is transferred from one generation to the next by the actions of multiple 'inheritance systems' including social and environmental" (3).

8 Ulrich Beck, *Risk Society: Towards a New Modernity* (London: Sage, 1992).

9 Merlin Chowkwanyun, "The Strange Disappearance of History from Racial Health Disparities Research," *Du Bois Review* 8, no. 1 (2011): 258–59.

10  Janet K. Shim, "Understanding the Routinized Inclusion of Race, Socioeconomic Status and Sex in Epidemiology: The Utility of Concepts from Technoscience Studies," *Sociology of Health and Illness* 24, no. 2 (2002): 132.

11  Moshe Szyf, "Implications of a Life-Long Dynamic Epigenome," *Epigenomics* 1, no. 1 (2009): 9–12.

12  Thayer and Kuzawa, "Biological Memories." Indeed, advocates are clear that epigenetics leaves open the possibility that damage can be reversed; so while they engage in a kind of crisis rhetoric, it is one that can theoretically enable agency rather than foreclose it (over and against older appeals, such as Rachel Carson's claim in *Silent Spring* that pollutants such as radiation were permanently altering the human germ line).

13  See Julie Guthman and Becky Mansfield, "The Implications of Environmental Epigenetics: A New Direction for Geographic Inquiry on Health, Space, and Nature-Society Relations," *Progress in Human Geography* 37, no. 4 (2012): 486–504. In their review essay discussing the implications of environmental epigenetics for geographic methodology, they write, "Epigenetic mechanisms may thus compound the difficulty in health geography of disaggregating what is an effect of space itself and what is an effect of the clustering of historically made bodies in space. . . . overall, environmental epigenetics suggests that health disparities are historical/temporal and not only spatial" (499). See also Mansfield and Guthman, "Epigenetic Life."

14  Jacquelyn Stevens, "Racial Meaning and Scientific Methods: Changing Policies for NIH-Sponsored Publications Reporting Human Variation, *Journal of Health Politics, Policy, and Law* 28, no. 6 (2003): 1033–87.

15  Adolph Reed Jr. and Merlin Chowkwanyun, "Race, Class, and Crisis: The Discourse of Racial Disparity and Its Analytical Discontents," *Socialist Register* 48 (2012): 149–75.

16  Rather than elevating the importance of environment over and above heredity, epigenetics promises to displace the nature-nurture binary entirely and with it the assumption of bounded, distinct entities interacting with one another. The current state of affairs arguably requires a new language of biology, one grounded in different ontological and epistemological assumptions. See Evelyn Fox Keller, *The Mirage of a Space between Nature and Nurture* (Durham, NC: Duke University Press, 2010).

17  Sullivan, "Inheriting Racist Disparities in Health," 194.

18  Ibid., 210.

19  Studies include those of pregnant women who survived the Holocaust and the World Trade Center attacks, experimental studies of laboratory mice, and studies of the long-term effects of famine. See, for example, Bastiaan T. Heijmans, Elmar W. Tobi, Aryeh D. Stein, Hein Putter, Gerard J. Blauw, Ezra S. Susser, P. Eline Slagboom, and L. H. Lumey, "The Persistent Epigenetic Differences Associated with Prenatal Exposure to Famine in Humans," *Proceedings of the National Academy of*

*Sciences* 105, no. 44 (2008): 17046–49. In this particular study, the famine in question is the Nazi-induced Dutch famine during World War II.

20 Sullivan, "Inheriting Racist Disparities in Health," 210; Michelle Alexander, *The New Jim Crow: Mass Incarceration in the Age of Colorblindness* (New York: New Press, 2012).

21 Reed and Chowkwanyun, "Race, Class, and Crisis," 161.

22 Ibid.

23 Sullivan, "Inheriting Racist Disparities in Health"; Thayer and Kuzawa, "Biological Memories."

24 Reed and Chowkwanyun, "Race, Class, and Crisis," 163.

25 Ibid., 164.

26 Ibid., 169.

27 Ibid., 165.

28 Jacqueline Stevens, "The Feasibility of Government Oversight of NIH-Funded Population Genetics," in *Revisiting Race in a Genomic Age*, ed. Barbara A. Koenig, Sandra Soo-Jin Lee, and Sarah S. Richardson (New Brunswick, NJ: Rutgers University Press, 2008), 320–41.

29 Mansfield and Guthman, "Epigenetic Life," 7.

30 Sullivan argues persuasively that prenatal care should include "community building and urban renewal, improved schools and educational opportunities, wage equality, and support for working mothers and families" ("Inheriting Racist Disparities in Health," 212).

31 Elizabeth A. Povinelli, *Economies of Abandonment: Social Belonging and Endurance in Late Liberalism* (Durham, NC: Duke University Press, 2011).

32 Rickie Solinger, *Wake Up Little Susie: Single Pregnancy and Race before Roe v. Wade* (New York: Routledge, 1992).

33 Mel Chen, *Animacies: Biopolitics, Racial Mattering, and Queer Affect* (Durham, NC: Duke University Press, 2012). For Chen, the hierarchies produced by naturalists wherein blackness is closer to objects and animals than whiteness emerge anew when lead risk is differentially articulated to racialized children's bodies in the contemporary moment. I have talked about the possible effects on policy when lead absorption is racialized in epidemiological research. See Happe, *The Material Gene.*

34 Rebecca Orzeck, "What Does Not Kill You: Historical Materialism and the Body," *Environment and Planning D: Society and Space* 25 (2007): 507.

35 "The continued relevance of these instinctual needs and the desire for survival that they assert constitutes, for Buck-Morss, the source of the body's political trustworthiness: even if the body does not know exactly what is good for it, it can be trusted to know what is anathema to it." Orzeck, "What Does Not Kill You," 505.

36 Angela Y. Davis, *Women, Race, and Class* (New York: Vintage, 1983).

37 Orzeck reminds us that capital both equalizes and differentiates—equalizes insofar as different persons occupy the position of exploited laborer and differentiates

insofar as not all persons will feel this positionality in the same way (e.g., in the production of health disparities like differential preterm birthrates). Thus, the importance of the kind of historical analysis Reed and Chowkwanyun call for.

38  Chen, *Animacies*, 196.

39  Ibid., 198.

40  Ibid., 202.

41  Jason Edwards, "The Materialism in Historical Materialism," in *New Materialisms: Ontology, Agency, and Politics*, ed. Diana Coole and Samantha Frost (Durham, NC: Duke University Press, 2010).

42  Alexander, *The New Jim Crow*. For a critique of her use of this metaphor, see Doug Henwood, "On the 'New Jim Crow': An Interview with Adolph Reed," *North Star*, March 22, 2013, www.thenorthstar.info.

43  Paul Rabinow, "Artificiality and Enlightenment: From Sociobiology to Biosociality," in *Incorporations*, ed. Jonathan Crary and Sanford Kwinter (New York: Zone Books, 1992), 234–52.

44  Ibid., 241–42.

45  Reed and Chowkwanyun, "Race, Class, and Crisis," 165.

PART II

Modes of Governance

# 4

## Chronic Citizenship

### *Community, Choice, and Queer Controversy*

JEFFREY A. BENNETT

Blue pills occupy an unusual space in our cultural medical imaginary. Abraham Lincoln famously took "blue mass," a pill composed of elemental mercury, and historians have long debated the reasons he used them and the imposing neurological effects they may have inaugurated.[1] Since the 1970s, medical researchers have consistently documented that participants who consume blue placebos report feeling less alert than counterparts who ingest inert red pills, indicating that the form of a capsule can be as significant as its content in affecting treatment outcomes.[2] Viagra metonymically became "the little blue pill" in the first decade of the millennium, promising men virility and the reclamation of masculinity in middle age. Far from being limited to the medical sphere, opting for the "the blue pill" signifies taking the easy way out and choosing, according to *Urban Dictionary*, to ignore reality and live in blissful ignorance. As the character Morpheus says in *The Matrix*, "You take the blue pill—the story ends, you wake up in your bed and believe whatever you want to believe."[3]

In 2012, a new blue pill, one that promised to prevent HIV infection in those who adhered to a daily regimen, made its way into our cultural lexicon. Truvada, a form of pre-exposure prophylaxis (PrEP), is an antiretroviral cocktail composed of the drugs tenofovir and emtricitabine.[4] The therapy has been used for over a decade to treat people who are HIV-positive, but it has also proved astoundingly effective in warding off HIV transmission among seronegative populations. Studies are finding that adherence to PrEP can reduce risk of infection by up to 99 percent.[5] However, despite promising results, the use of a pill to lower HIV infection rates has initiated controversy among queer publics about the variability of risk, the definition of safe sex, and the stigma of nonnormative sexual practices.[6] Although some opponents argue that people who take the blue pill are merely allowing themselves to wake up in their beds believing whatever they like, Truvada appears to be working. And while the science continues to evolve, the rhetoric stemming from Truvada's growing sphere of influence lends insight into shifting understandings of risk, the medicalization of queer bodies, and the biopolitical investment in techniques of pleasure.

The tenuous relationship between duty and pleasure has underwritten HIV/AIDS activism since the early 1980s. The sometimes competing responsibilities to one's self, one's communities, and one's sex partners have acted historically as sites of contestation in exchanges about safe-sex education, bareback porn, and the criminalization of people who are HIV-positive. Not surprisingly, then, Truvada's introduction as a preventative measure has summoned a predictable, if misguided, chorus of antagonisms about the dangers of sexual gratification and the conventions of AIDS activism.[7] Even as HIV has evolved from epidemic to endemic, disputes about PrEP are situated in a familiar narrative arc that fixates on the consequences of sexual pleasure, ethical obligations to the other, and the biopolitical tensions of embracing public health interventions. Using the debates about PrEP as a catalyst, I look to the implications this technology has for the civic identities of queers, the contingent nature of safe sex, and discordant approaches to HIV-awareness efforts.

Discussions of Truvada currently rest in a tragic frame underscored by a politics of respectability that demands monogamy, condom use, and fidelity to normative sexual mores.[8] That is, contrary to decades of empirical, theoretical, and activist work detailing the multiplicitous character of desires and sexualities, arguments about PrEP are frequently couched in a language that sets "dangerous limitations upon our capacity to know" why people have particular kinds of sex in distinct situations.[9] Imagining a world free of HIV requires us to resist tragic frames, embracing instead comic attitudes that recognize the partiality of identifications and desires, and in the process raising consciousness about how safer sex can be made intelligible for multiple publics.[10] This essay forwards one potentially generative approach to PrEP by giving presence to a micropolitics of collective participation that can eliminate HIV and foster bonds of intimate belonging among publics—what is being conceptualized here as a "chronic citizenship." This rendering of citizenship is a performative mode of belonging that gives preference to notions of queer kinship and desire, superseding biopolitical renderings of discipline and surveillance to acknowledge (sometimes contentious) quotidian sexual practices. Such an orientation accepts the ongoing reality of "risk," no matter how minuscule. It acknowledges that expanded opportunities for individual safer sex can gradually diminish HIV rates but also that the amalgamation of intimacies being accounted for in PrEP use cannot be easily charted by institutions. Widespread participation in daily prevention efforts, regardless of serostatus or sexuality, would also ideally lessen the stigma that continues to underwrite cultural discourses about HIV. PrEP can alleviate burdensome confessional expectations for people who are HIV-positive even as it energizes various ways of making pleasure intelligible.

Rhetorically the efforts to proselytize Truvada are more difficult than they may at first appear. Opponents of Truvada subtly suggest they can foresee an end to AIDS, offering narrative closure to a decades-long catastrophe that has morphed from a national trauma into a privatized "slow death." In their telling, if we stay the course with traditional safe-sex measures, that do not include PrEP, then the fight against HIV can at long last be won.[11] PrEP's detractors evacuate the contexts of sexual encounters among queers, in part by amplifying unrealistic presumptions about condom use, and in the process cloud the multitude of desires that motivate intimacy. Counterintuitively, and despite its promise, Truvada does not offer narrative closure in exchanges about sexually transmitted infections (STIs), the curious pleasure of risk, and ongoing bodily regulation. Indeed, proponents are situated to respond that some risk always remains, that pleasure may or may not be psychologically interrupted because of daily medication, and that some degree of bodily governance is always at play.

This essay investigates the decisive, blunt, and vitriolic interchanges about Truvada, often among queers, in numerous media outlets.[12] In some regards this rhetoric has been homogeneous, being told from the perspective of, or focusing on, white, gay, cisgender men. As a corrective, advocates have implored the Centers for Disease Control and Prevention (CDC) to more actively use black media outlets to reach more queers of color, who are disproportionately affected by HIV and who would benefit enormously from PrEP.[13] At other times the discourse tackles complicated variables that give attention to class, age, political commitments, and the messy realities of sex and desire. It is significant to note that both cis and trans women are a rapidly expanding percentage of Truvada consumers, but they remain underrepresented in dialogues about PrEP. Both biomedical research and vernacular sites dedicated to PrEP would benefit from a diversity of voices, bodies, and representations in order to best serve the sometimes different needs of women, queers of color, and trans people, among others. Although the particulars of individual cases are essential to initiating and maintaining proper care, that does not mean cultural commonalities are not evident across bodies. Those who oppose PrEP are strident in their attempts to demonize sex they construe as perverse and reiterate a dubious politics of respectability.

## The Politics of Respectability

As far back as 1986, Simon Watney proposed that AIDS complicated the idea of a "moral panic," insofar as the syndrome engendered perpetual alarm and was not an isolated crisis contained within a specific political moment.[14] Narratives about HIV and AIDS generally lack closure, denying the resolution typical of outbreak narratives and their accompanying lessons about social responsibility, containment, and the public good.[15] The paranoia underwriting fear of HIV/AIDS, Eve Sedgwick famously reminded us, has been a persistent element of the epidemic even after technologies allowed us to suppress viral loads and keep people alive.[16] Those suspicious of Truvada mobilize paranoid discourses, expressing angst about the blurred line between serostatuses among sex partners and the intimations of that fizzled border. One blogger captured this sentiment well in a post titled "Truthyness and Truvada," remarking that "unprotected sex is still Russian Roulette."[17] Despite the presumptions of this post, Truvada is a form of "protected sex," even if it may be condomless sex. The pill abrogates the criteria with which judgments are made about sexual practices deemed respectable, decent, and trustworthy and redefines the very notion of "safe sex."

The ceaseless anxiety that Watney described continues to beleaguer queer publics, with the specter of AIDS and its accompanying trauma still looming, even as HIV infection has largely morphed into a chronic condition for those with access to medical care. It is not an overstatement to say that the reactionary politics of respectability surrounding Truvada is depressingly moralistic. Gay men posting to the "PrEP Facts" Facebook page (which has more than 19,000 members as of this writing) frequently report that they have been shamed by medical practitioners when asking for a prescription and also disparaged by other gay men when they disclose using the drug. The widely circulated label "Truvada whore" has come to signify a point of pride among those who take the drug, and the hashtag of the same name is frequently employed on Twitter to mark conversations about its use. Ironically, the phrase "Truvada whore" was coined by an HIV-positive freelance journalist in the *Huffington Post*. In that piece, David Duran argued that PrEP is an invaluable invention for serodiscordant couples but questioned the extent to which the pill should be prescribed to just anyone. He wrote:

> I'm not a prude. I enjoy sex just as much as anyone else. I just personally enjoy sex more when I know that I am doing everything to prevent myself from ending up with a sexually transmitted infection. Having a "there's a pill for that" attitude is absolutely disgusting. Don't get me wrong: Thank goodness for the free clinic or the neighborhood pharmacy that will prescribe whatever lotion or pill or ointment you need to get rid of whatever you picked up from that random stranger, but HIV is not a "whatever." Instead, it's something that has lifelong consequences, and I sincerely hope that Truvada PrEP is not encouraging the "there's a pill for that" attitude.[18]

Duran's remarks, which he has since retracted, conjure the work of Mary Douglas, who reminds us that "arguments about risk are highly charged, morally and politically. Naming a risk amounts to an accusation."[19] Even with a generous read of Duran's statement, words such as "disgusting" and "free clinic" trigger images of dirt, contagion, and moral rebuke. "Free clinic" also animates classist and racist rhetorics popular in conservative political speech. Even on gay hookup apps such as Grindr there remains a discourse that seronegative men are "clean." Projections of the impure gay man act as a trope not only for disreputable practices but also for unacceptable identities, stratifying bodies and creating a sententious hierarchy of sex in the process. This is to say nothing of the image of the "stranger" Duran invokes, which has haunted public health since epidemiology's beginnings.[20] Such stigmatization has long hindered safer-sex efforts, and Duran's initial position perpetuates fears of people who are HIV-positive and rehearses needless sex shaming. When "sex is regarded as intrinsically dirty and degrading," Watney observed, "it will undoubtedly become dirty and degrading."[21]

Moralistic finger-wagging is especially prevalent when practices such as barebacking—in its broadest use, sex without a condom—is brought into the picture. In a "post-AIDS" era, the image of the good gay man has been tied directly to his conformity to condom use.[22] Yet, scholars such as Tim Dean argue that the risks of unsafe sex are exactly what make those practices so appealing. Dean reads barebacking as a treatise against normalized sexual paradigms that have structured public rhetorics about sex for the last several decades, especially among gay men. Suspending judgment about risk to further understand the politics and pleasures of sexuality, Dean contends that unregulated sex "defines nonrespectability precisely because it disrespects the boundaries that separate persons, classes, races, and generations from each other."[23] In this way, barebacking cannot be understood without giving serious attention to the "fantasies that animate it."[24] David Halperin has further speculated that changing norms around condom use may simply indicate an evolution in the techniques of pleasure among gay men.[25] Only one in six gay men use condoms consistently, and adherence is thought to be even less among heterosexuals.[26] In short, just because condom use is the imagined normativity of safe sex does not mean it is the norm.[27] Nor does adherence to Truvada necessarily mean that people are barebacking. It bears repeating that pleasure and desire are multifarious, not univocal.

The idea that condomless sex is universally shunned has drawn strong retort from proponents of PrEP, many of whom point to the ways unprotected heterosexual acts are lauded, if not celebrated. In a widely circulated passage, appearing on sites that include *Gawker* and the *Daily Dish*, Jim Pickett, the director of advocacy for the AIDS Foundation of Chicago, argued:

> You're here because people barebacked. Your grandmother was a bare-backer. That secretary in your office, when you're invited to her baby shower, she's a barebacker. You're bringing gifts for someone who engaged

in risky fucking behavior. What the fuck are you doing? She's a bad person. We would never [say] that. We're like, "Yay! You're pregnant! What is it? Woohoo!" With a gay man, it's like, "Oh my God. You're reckless, you're careless, you're insane, you're self-destructive, you want to hurt yourself and others." And we ignore the fact that gay men have the same needs to feel close and intimate and pleasure. For a lot of people, condoms get in the way. That just is. That's just a fact. And if you can use a condom yourself and that doesn't interfere, again, great for you. Hallelujah! Keep doing it. But if you can't, that's not a mark against you.[28]

Pickett's statement reminds us that procreative intercourse maintains its status in the "charmed circle" of culturally sanctioned sex practices while barebacking resides somewhere in the "outer limits."[29] In Pickett's formulation, procreative coitus makes sexual pleasure permissible, even as most sex between people is non-procreative. Barebacking in this configuration is one act among many that is not easily reducible to an identity. The particulars of sexual liaisons are juxtaposed to the universal appeal of intimacy and pleasure, repositioning the mundaneness (if not the sometimes accidental outcomes) of heterosexuality to demystify otherwise culturally taboo encounters. And while such universalism invites as much scrutiny as it does opportunity (women's bodies and sexualities are often situated as impure), it is also a stark reminder that there is nothing more public than sex.[30]

The politics of respectability is an especially prominent part of Truvada's public narrative, which had no shortage of critics when it hit the market in 2012. Skeptics blasted the drug for promoting promiscuity, its potential side effects, and the huge profits it stood to make from the anxieties of queer men.[31] Regan Hoffman, a former editor at *POZ*, called Truvada "a profit-driven sex toy for rich Westerners."[32] Actor Zachary Quinto took heat from LGBT advocates after he criticized Truvada as potentially lethal, a statement that he walked back numerous times in the following year.[33] AIDS activist Larry Kramer went so far as to call gay men on the pill "cowardly" for not using condoms and filling their bodies with "toxins." Like others before him, however, Kramer eventually came around to the utility and social significance of the pill.[34]

Whereas queer communities used to battle Christian conservatives and their charges of damnation, the most contentious and vitriolic critic of Truvada is not a cultish zealot from the heartland but Michael Weinstein, director of the AIDS Healthcare Foundation (AHF), one of the world's largest AIDS organizations. The AHF plays a significant role in the global fight against HIV/AIDS, claiming to reach 570,000 patients worldwide and acting as one of the largest providers of HIV/AIDS medical care in the United States.[35] The group was instrumental in passing Proposition B in Los Angeles, which required condoms for all penetrative pornography filmed in the city. It also compelled the manufacturer of Viagra to include language in its television advertisements about that little blue pill's inability to protect people from HIV.[36] It is one of the few HIV/AIDS organizations not to have embraced Truvada, but its dissent has drawn noticeable consideration in a media culture that exalts antagonistic public debate.[37]

Weinstein notoriously called Truvada a "party drug," repeatedly suggesting that it will prove ineffective in the struggle against AIDS because gay men will not adhere to daily regimens.[38] According to Weinstein, this lack of fidelity will lead to condomless sex, false reassurances among sex partners, and unbridled promiscuity. He has gone so far as insisting that the gay porn industry is leading the drive to push Truvada on gay men. Weinstein maintains that he is not opposed to individual use of PrEP, but he stands against it as a commonplace tool in public health planning.[39] This individualization has the effect of ignoring the collective potential of PrEP and usually leads to caricatures of queer men abating all control of their sexual discretion. Weinstein once contended, "A person who's taking crystal and is on a bender for three days isn't going to remember to take their" Truvada.[40] And he may be correct. However, a person on a "bender" for three days might not remember to use condoms, be of sound mind to communicate with a partner, or be in a position to consent to sex at all. More important, the analogy is meant to energize negative feelings about the respectability of those using PrEP, not engender productive deliberation about its utility.

Weinstein's is a loud and prominent voice, but his positions have little backing from cognate organizations that conduct HIV/AIDS outreach. Some, such as *Bay Area Reporter* columnist Race Barron, call the AHF "the climate change deniers of HIV prevention."[41] Scientific consensus about PrEP's effectiveness in blocking HIV transmission has manifested quickly, making opposition to its distribution bewildering. The *Advo-*

*cate* reports that more than 100 AIDS advocacy and LGBT groups have endorsed PrEP, including the Foundation for AIDS Research, the Gay Men's Health Crisis, and the National Minority AIDS Council.[42] Even the Human Rights Campaign, an organization that often draws the ire of progressive LGBT groups, has called for widespread adoption of PrEP and lobbied pharmaceutical manufacturer Gilead to lower the price of Truvada to ensure access for economically disadvantaged people at risk for HIV.

The politics of respectability hampering efforts to disseminate PrEP is unconscionable in an era when infection rates are skyrocketing. PrEP is an invaluable preventive tool for those most at risk for HIV infection, offering an additional form of protection that might help to eradicate AIDS. Equally significant, the politics of respectability outlined here demands personal surveillance and discipline, occluding political questions about corporate alliances, shared understandings of risk, and the varied nature of sexuality. These quandaries need to be addressed not simply as matters of personal choice but also engaged as public affairs deserving of collective deliberation. In the next section, I explore how intimate bonds can gradually eliminate HIV, situating those equipped with PrEP in preventative networks that are at once pleasurable and political.

## Chronic Citizenship and the Shared Ethics of Ending AIDS

Turning away from the dire and paranoid predisposition of a politics of respectability, I now look to the productive capacities of cultural membership fostered by PrEP. Far from a legal apparatus of conferred rights, the idea of chronic citizenship stresses the praxis of belonging and the serial relations of sexual communities.[43] I do not presume that taking a pill is a defining characteristic of identity, though the stigmatization accompanying PrEP hints at a socially precarious positionality. "Truvada whore" and "PrEP warrior" are signs to be rallied around in a collective context. Still, a skeptic might rightfully ask how taking a pill every day is entrée to the responsibilities of citizenship. I contend that the answer is quite simple: making PrEP routine and not salacious diminishes the communicability of HIV, body by body, crafting a network of stopgaps while acknowledging the realities of nonuse of condoms. Pleasure and duty are coconstitutive means *and* effects, accentuating how personal intimacies can revolutionize public life. In short, the individualistic benefits of the pill have cumulative effects on cultural identity by working to dissipate the panic embedded in sexual imaginaries. And, far from a utopic understanding of technologies and bodies, the denomination "chronic" functions to recognize the temporal nature of eventually expunging both the fear of HIV and the disease itself. If HIV is indeed a chronic condition (i.e., one marked by time), then chronic citizenship projects not the slow death of individual actors but the gradual dissolution of the epidemic through the micropractices enabled by PrEP. This heuristic also combats the ableism frequently imparted by vernacular sexual health narratives that unreflectively centralize the perspectives of seronegative people. The widespread use of PrEP instigates a more robust engagement with desire and pleasure, conceived in broad and multiplicitous forms.

Chronic citizenship is informed, in part, by Nikolas Rose's writings about "biocitizenship" and the increasingly variant ways medicine and bodies interrelate. Biocitizenship focuses on the uptake of biomedical knowledge in the service of community, often acting as a catalyst for awareness, research, and rights.[44] The concept can also proffer a cautionary warning against exploitation by institutions.[45] In *The Politics of Life Itself*, early AIDS activists are cited as an "exemplar" of biocitizenship and its possibilities.[46] Rose rightfully contends those activists performed myriad functions (disseminating information, advocating civil rights, combating stigma) but mainly captured his attention because of the alliances they forged with health officials to reach populations at risk for HIV infection.[47] Rose's account of AIDS activism is brief, but it underscores an aspect of citizenship useful for this analysis: biocitizenship in the twenty-first century is not imposed from above; rather, it is active, summoning the identifications and affiliations of people who are invested in the trajectory of individual and collective health.[48] Biocitizenship understands social actors as political, but Rose is not overly prescriptive about how politics might be activated. Seeking out information on the Internet, for example, marks a routine feature of biological citizenship, articulating information from official channels like government organizations and vernacular sources such as PrEP user narratives.

On the one hand, Rose warns that the moral economy in which biocitizenship is situated has the potential to inspire anxiety, fear, and dread about one's future because overcontemplation inevitably breeds doubt. On the other hand, he notes that resignation and misgivings about the future are frequently countered by discourses of expectation and anticipation, a trust of institutional innovation that will eventually save us. This oscillation between apprehension and faith subtly envelops discussions of Truvada, conjuring the past failures of scientific intervention, the promise of future developments, and both unease and hope about new sexual freedoms. The latitude to have sex with scant worry about AIDS can be overwhelming, even if welcome. Plenty of men on the PrEP Facebook page relay the psychological apprehensions they have confronted after adopting the pill. Even if one accepts the promise of possibilities lurking on PrEP's horizon, Rose cautions that the discourse of hope animating biocitizenship raises ethical questions about the relationship between identity, technology, and practice.[49] Truvada provides optimism, but to what extent should queers put their faith in a pharmaceutical corporation that rakes in billions of dollars in profits annually? If Watney was concerned with a politics of respectability that was cultural in its orientation, Rose suggests a weariness about the intermingling of corporations and citizens and the adoption of scripts that work in the service of consumerism, often over the interests of wider prevention efforts.

Even if we wish to resist the all-consuming heuristic of neoliberalism, technologies such as PrEP compel questions about access, affordability, and the individualistic focus given to pharmaceutical use. The CDC speculates that 1.2 million Americans, less than half of whom are gay men, could benefit from Truvada.[50] As of December 2015, Truvada costs between $13,000 and $17,000 annually (depending on the source) without insurance, placing it out of reach for countless people, though many insurers and some state Medicaid programs cover the drug. Gilead has been lobbied heavily to lower Truvada's price and be more generous with co-payment options. Counting on the benevolence of multinational corporations would be naive, especially in light of the fact that Gilead was investigated for price gouging hepatitis C drugs at a cost of $84,000 a year for treatment (about $1,000 per pill).[51] Despite this lackluster outlook, several municipalities are making efforts to expand the availability of PrEP. Los Angeles County and San Francisco are now distributing PrEP, and Fulton County, Georgia, home to Atlanta, is attempting to make PrEP widely accessible. PrEP Facebook members (especially those with insurance) often report paying nothing for the drug when pharmaceutical co-pays are applied, though an equal number continue to report barriers to care.

The tension between individual consumerism and communal responsibility is a stubbornly consistent facet of HIV's history, and resisting the profit-driven tendencies of multibillion-dollar corporations remains vital to eliminating AIDS. Still, there is little denying that this drug could save countless lives. Embracing technologies that prevent HIV need not be separate from the quest to obtain drugs for marginalized populations, produce generics, and distribute them globally. Marketers, Rose tells us, do not take advantage of passive audiences so much as they tap into the desires of those they are appealing to most.[52] And while we should be deliberate about who "they" may be among Truvada's clientele, medicine's sweeping reach has nonetheless "made us what we are" and will continue to shape subjectivities and cultural norms.[53] Like Rose, I believe we "relate to ourselves and others, individually and collectively, through an ethic and in a form of life that is inextricably associated with medicine in all its incarnations."[54] This ethic is ongoing, chronic in the sense that the road is long and the battle hard fought.

Michel Foucault persuasively suggested that in constituting agentic subjects who can always be more in control of their bodies, institutional and vernacular voices alike produce burdensome, if sometimes contradictory and always partial, narratives about disease. If he was correct that excess is read socially as an expression of deviancy, producing an exigency that obligates people to manage their desires, then people using Truvada are not simply captive to opaque disciplinary power structures.[55] Rather, they are confronted with crafting and performing moral and ethical identities as they engage in "self-forming activities."[56] Chronic citizenship acknowledges that queer sex is already imagined as excessive and deviant (and sometimes it is), often requiring resistance to heterosexual imaginaries and at other times reveling in the innovative prospects of a benign variant of sexuality. Such a disposition resists a politics of respectability that situates bodies positioned at the margins of culture, including people who are HIV-positive, as the moralizing fiction of normative kinship. These nonnormative practices, however, hold the very promise for reimagining identities. Sex and intimacy act as sites of invention to move us, in Judith Butler's words, "beyond patrilineality, compulsory heterosexuality, and the symbolic overdetermination of biology."[57]

In this way, PrEP might refashion not simply technologies of the self but also encounters with the other. Even as "stranger relationality" has enjoyed a renaissance in the humanities, the image of the stranger in public health rhetoric remains a source of apprehension and variability. PrEP has the potential to break through these discursive imaginaries, inspiring more inclusive attitudes about the sundry methods of safer sex. More than simply individual considerations of health and safety or biopolitical projections of collectives, the serial relations among partners can resituate practices stubbornly articulated to unease, shame, and suspicion into affinities of pleasure out of HIV's treacherous reach. In this sense, chronic citizenship functions on a capillary scale similar to Foucault's notion of resistance, recognizing the unusual ways individual rituals can produce cultural enclaves and eventually reshape social landscapes. It reimagines safer sex as more than just condom use to celebrate already existing sexual customs free of the suffocating politics of respectability.

## Risk, Rhetoric, and Narrative Remainders

Resistance to Truvada stems in part from the (sometimes hyperbolic) fear of HIV infection among people who are seronegative. These anxieties frequently erect psychological and physical barriers to embracing PrEP and the physical intimacy it seemingly authorizes. PrEP parlance tends to privilege the standpoint of seronegative men, and the apprehension evident in their narratives illustrates the ways the pill is still being negotiated as a viable technology for everyday use. PrEP's potential to refigure relations among sex partners was captured by a respondent to Andrew Sullivan's blog the *Daily Dish*, which addressed Truvada at length. The reader reflected:

> Taking a Truvada pill means, for some, the taking of an HIV pill. And being HIV-negative is sometimes defined as not having to take an HIV pill. So taking Truvada as a preventative means, for some, crossing the HIV divide, when they have spent an entire adult life-time keeping their

> distance from HIV culture. This makes no logical sense—taking Truvada
> as well as using safer sex helps you stay free of HIV more effectively than
> any other method. . . . But it does make psychological sense for the count-
> less who remain traumatized by the memory of the plague.[58]

Technologies like Truvada create liminal positions that are not easily
reconcilable among many seronegative people. Permissibility to engage
in condomless sex and keep HIV at bay generates both jubilation and
melancholic distress. Sullivan's respondent draws attention to the
genuine anxiety many people have about HIV exposure, even though
condoms have a lower success rate than PrEP. It is curious to see "HIV
culture" so easily isolated in this man's response, as though the history
of queer publics is not coterminous with the history of HIV. Clearly,
seropositive men are a part of queer sexual cultures, and the sentiment
(though meant to be instructive in this case) illuminates the fictive ways
sexual identities are sometimes imagined. What happens when the "constitutive outside" of safe sex—in this case seropositive men—is depleted,
demanding equitable undertakings among sex partners?

John Erni's work investigating the internal contradictions of "curing
AIDS" is instructive when contemplating the challenges of a reimag-
ined subjectivity less beholden to the hesitation perpetuated by enduring HIV narratives. Erni explores the long-standing tension in scientific
discourse that simultaneously trumpets medicine's innovative potential
and gives emphasis to the limitations of science.[59] There is no narrative closure about HIV in scientific discourses, and conversations about
PrEP occasionally further ambiguities instead of reconciling them. The
"bridging" effect outlined by the blog reader quoted earlier creates more
connections and possibilities across bodies, and until Truvada is proved
effective over long periods of time, some fears will be insurmountable.
Put another way, Truvada consistently alludes to an eventual end to HIV,
but without the narrative fidelity of closure.

This narrative remainder highlights a second characteristic confronting proponents of Truvada: evolving understandings of risk. The contours of risk as a rhetorical category are not fixed; rather, as J. Blake Scott
reminds us, they are contingent and contextual, requiring not simply
assessment tools but cultural associations and norms that can be adopted by an array of people.[60] The lingering memories of the origins of

AIDS among some publics often marginalize nuanced considerations of PrEP and regularly reanimate the ghosts of HIV's past. The internalization of public transcripts of shame, impurity, and infection is powerful and continues to haunt everything from formal prevention efforts to casual hookup dialogue. Paula Treichler has outlined the power of HIV/AIDS to produce rhetorics that might be unscientific but still hold great sway over audiences.[61] Exchanges about Truvada produce consistent reminders about degrees of risk, even if such fears appear overblown.[62] For instance, longtime AIDS researcher Robert Grant fielded a question on his blog about the risk of HIV transmission while on PrEP. Even as a staunch defender of Truvada, he responded, "PrEP is highly effective when used, although there is no guarantee that PrEP will work all the time. We do not make guarantees in medicine, and after 30 years working in HIV research and clinical care, I have learned to 'never say never.'"[63] Likewise, Dr. Shed Boren told the *Miami Herald*, "If AIDS taught us anything, it's that there are some scary dragons around the corner. I remember coming of age and reading that little thing about GRID in the newspaper. Who knows what tomorrow's headline will be? God knows what else is around the corner."[64] It is the inability to *completely* assuage fears about sex and STIs that has produced some of the most cumbersome obstacles for PrEP advocates. There are always exceptions to the rule, especially in medicine. Couple this with the fact that cultural norms change at a glacial pace, and the case to be made for PrEP is periodically daunting. Even when people are convinced of PrEP's effectiveness, nightmarish ailments are presented to reinvoke the risks associated with sexual intimacy.

If chronic citizenship aims its attention at the shared responsibilities of eradicating HIV gradually, it must also consider the multimodal nature of risk, especially when contemplating the ways stranger relationality is situated in conversations about PrEP. Although the notion of stranger relationality has taken on an air of hopefulness in recent years thanks to the work of scholars such as Danielle Allen, the image of the unknown queer man who will infect others endures and is a recurrent boogeyman in anti-PrEP rhetoric. It is certainly true that intimacy sometimes invites risk, and sexual contact will inevitably produce evidence of disease transmission. Current PrEP technologies cannot prevent all STIs including gonorrhea, chlamydia, and syphilis. Yet those risks may pale in comparison to life without PrEP. Nervousness and opposition to PrEP often lead to hypothetical and specious claims about its link to rising STI rates. One of the most frequently conjured risks is the oft-reported strain of untreatable gonorrhea that will infect gay men if they do not use condoms. Such narratives fit within the economy of what Priscilla Wald calls "the conventional melodramatic tale of venereal disease."[65] Irremediable gonorrhea has been diagnosed only among heterosexuals as of this writing.[66] Despite no reported cases in queer communities, the contagion metaphor holds. The specter of an antibiotic-resistant form of gonorrhea is so common, especially in online comment sections, that it has become a trope in exchanges about Truvada. Everyone from Dan Savage to NBC News has mentioned it.[67] Such narratives are not easily combated, especially since STIs such as syphilis can be spread even with the use of a condom. This consternation can have a disproportionate impact on health narratives, potentially confounding efforts to make PrEP more acceptable.

Lack of evidence linking PrEP to rising STI rates has not stopped critics from insisting on a connection between the two. The continued insinuation that queer men are being given free rein to mindlessly fuck misses the point that condom use is already low and STI rates have never been conclusively linked to PrEP. As *The Body* relayed, there were 1.4 million cases of chlamydia in 2014 and 350,000 cases of gonorrhea, yet only 17,000 people using PrEP. There's no possible way to link PrEP to this distribution of STIs.[68] Will STI rates sometimes ebb and flow? Absolutely. Sex comes with risks, as does citizenship. One of the most profound challenges facing proponents of Truvada is confronting this panicked rhetoric, and the fears it enables, and situating it accordingly.

Finally, there is no denying that for some people the daily habit of taking a pill might emotionally or psychologically interrupt the pleasure of sex. The subjective role of intimacy and desire is not easily charted, and it is still too early to know if people will reject PrEP because they view it as a form of bodily governance that intrudes on their sexual lives. PrEP may eventually prove to be a "medical marvel," but we are still early in the process of learning how it will, or will not, revolutionize the narrative of HIV prevention.[69]

Taking the Blue Pill

Chronic citizenship aspires to eliminate HIV by dispersing responsibility for PrEP across a range of bodies, communities, and institutions. HIV and its associated stigma can be diminished with wider circulation of PrEP and its uptake among various publics. Indeed, the panic that has haunted queers for generations might finally be put to rest. This is no short order. Resources must be made widely available, marginalized populations must be empowered, and the science must be engaged. The normalization of PrEP provides an incremental tool for toppling the legacy of HIV, but it cannot be done without first shifting cultural attitudes about medicine, sex, and desire. Subtle evolutions in safer-sex rituals can energize minute changes in narrative, giving presence to the contingent nature of risk and the contextual ways identities and bodies are articulated to discourses of HIV prevention.

The critical heuristic of chronic citizenship also recognizes the manifold biopolitical matters surrounding Truvada, including the simultaneous individualization of risk and the aggregate medicalization of publics, the unfathomable invention of pleasure, and the projection of "risky" bodies lurking in the polis. Important questions remain about the role of collective action and the institutional mechanisms that might facilitate a future free of AIDS. Real disagreements exist about the percentage of budgets dedicated to Truvada, the trade-offs with other prevention methods, and the precarious nature of municipalities defining what constitutes "safe sex." PrEP must be presented as one form of safer-sex pedagogy among many, including the availability of condoms, access to education, and safer-sex materials. As queer communities diversify and fragment, Halperin intimates, the management of sexual risk in the United States will continue to become decidedly individualized.[70] What works for one person may not work for another, and being flexible with approaches to safer-sex education remains imperative for stifling HIV/AIDS. Broad public health strategies incorporating PrEP need to maintain focus on the variability and plasticity of risk. Narrowed visions that do not fully acknowledge the allure and cultural complications of pleasure will do little to solve public health dilemmas related to HIV.

The decision to ingest Truvada is one balanced between risk and identity: mitigating not only how frequently one may be at risk for infection but also the degree to which one can acknowledge potentially "risky" behaviors. For some, Truvada is unquestionably a vital option. For others, there remains, in the words of Rich Juzwiak, a "gray area," where condomless sex may happen, but not regularly and when it does occur it might not pose risks for HIV infection. Although condoms are effective at preventing HIV transmission, studies illustrate repeatedly that people rarely employ them consistently enough to derive "substantial benefit."[71] Many people, both those who take Truvada and those who do not, already elect not to use condoms. However, we should be careful not to equate Truvada with one form of sex, with preconceived ideas about condom use, or with presumptions about the numbers of sex partners a person might have. At least two studies have found that gay men on PrEP had fewer sex partners and tended to utilize condoms more.[72]

When scientists at the NIH released the results of the initial PrEP study, illustrating the profound ways it might alter the cultural landscape of HIV prevention, they received a call from President Obama congratulating them on the news. Since that time, important figures such as Dr. Anthony Fauci, who has a long and complicated history with AIDS activists, has announced unequivocal support for PrEP. He told *Time*, "We know PrEP works, and we know it doesn't increase risk behavior. The issue is, can we get PrEP to the people who really need it?"[73] PrEP may yet be one of the great inventions of the twenty-first century, eventually helping to rectify one of the great political failures of the twentieth. Rose warns us against hope, lest we find the biopolitical forces at hand fail citizens by placing profits above people. And yet, the gloomy cloud of AIDS may be dissipating on the horizon, opening up the promise of clear, blue skies.

NOTES

1   Lincoln reportedly took the pills to treat "melancholia" and "hypochondriasis." They had a strong effect on his mood, making him uncharacteristically volatile. Lincoln is said to have recognized the effects of blue mass and stopped taking the pills shortly after his first inauguration. See Robert G. Feldman, Norbert Hirschhorn, and Ian Greaves, "Abraham Lincoln's Blue Pills: Did Our 16th President Suffer from Mercury Poisoning?," *Perspectives in Biology and Medicine* 44, no. 3 (2001): 315–32. Special thanks to Mary Stuckey for this citation.

2   Daniel Moerman, *Meaning, Medicine, and the "Placebo Effect"* (Cambridge: Cambridge University Press, 2002), 47–49; Tessa Fiorini Cohen, "The Power of Drug Color," *Atlantic*, October 13, 2014, www.theatlantic.com.

3 *The Matrix*, directed by Lilly Wachowski and Lana Wachowski, Warner Brothers, 1999.

4 Truvada is the only medication available for the regimen of pre-exposure pro-phylaxis today. As such, I sometimes use Truvada and PrEP interchangeably, recognizing that there may eventually be other forms of medication for PrEP. Conversations in queer communities sometimes employ the term "PrEP," some-times "Truvada," and sometimes "Truvada as PrEP."

5 There was initial confusion about Truvada's effectiveness at reducing risk because opponents and proponents drew their arguments from the same CDC study. Advocates argued that the study offers strong assurances—pointing out that approximately 99 percent of people who adhere to Truvada remained HIV-negative. Detractors pointed to the same study, arguing an assurance rate of only 42 percent. The difference in the statistics came from adherence, not the drug's effectiveness.

6 Christopher Glazek, "Why Is No One on the First Treatment to Prevent HIV?," *New Yorker*, September 30, 2013, www.newyorker.com; Rich Juzwiak, "What Is Safe Sex? The Raw and Uncomfortable Truth about Truvada," *Gawker*, March 4, 2014, http://gawker.com.

7 Julian Gill-Peterson, "Haunting the Queer Spaces of AIDS: Remembering ACT UP/New York and an Ethics for an Endemic," *GLQ: A Journal of Lesbian and Gay Studies* 19 (2013): 279–300.

8 Kenneth Burke, *Attitudes toward History* (Berkeley: University of California Press, 1984).

9 Frank Lentricchia, *Criticism and Social Change* (Chicago: University of Chicago Press, 1985), 62.

10 Burke notes that comic correctives enable people "to be observers of themselves, while acting. Its ultimate would not be passiveness, but maximum consciousness." *Attitudes toward History*, 171.

11 Lauren Berlant, *Cruel Optimism* (Durham, NC: Duke University Press, 2011), 95–119.

12 Some of the reports analyzed here are found in popular press publications such as *Gawker* and the *Huffington Post*. Other forms of media are aimed mainly at LGBT people, such as the *Advocate*. Still other outlets are composed and directed by queers, such as the PrEP Facebook page.

13 Rod McCollum, "The Perfect Storm Facing Black Men on HIV," *Advocate*, May 2, 2016, www.advocate.com.

14 Simon Watney, *Practices of Freedom: Selective Writings on HIV/AIDS* (Durham, NC: Duke University Press, 1994), 8.

15 Priscilla Wald, *Contagious: Cultures, Carriers, and the Outbreak Narrative* (Durham, NC: Duke University Press, 2008), 217.

16 Eve Kosofsky Sedgwick, *Touching/Feeling: Affect, Pedagogy, Performativity* (Durham, NC: Duke University Press, 2003).

17 "Truthyness and Truvada," *My Carlsberg Years*, August 6, 2014, www.mycarlsberg-years.com.

18 David Duran, "Truvada Whores?," *Huffington Post*, November 11, 2012, www.huffingtonpost.com.

19 Mary Douglas, *Purity and Danger: An Analysis of Concepts of Pollution and Taboo* (New York: Routledge, 2002), xix.

20 Wald, *Contagious*, 56–57.

21 Watney, *Practices of Freedom*, 68.

22 Tim Dean, *Unlimited Intimacy: Reflections on the Subculture of Barebacking* (Chicago: University of Chicago Press, 2009), 18.

23 Ibid., 20.

24 Ibid., 32.

25 David Halperin, *What Do Gay Men Want? An Essay on Sex, Risk, and Subjectivity* (Ann Arbor: University of Michigan Press, 2007), 20.

26 Robert M. Grant, "Does PrEP Work If Condoms Are Not Used?," April 15, 2015, www.robertmgrant.org.

27 Janet Jakobsen, "Queer Is? Queer Does? Normativity and the Problem of Resistance," *GLQ: A Journal of Lesbian and Gay Studies* 4 (1998): 511–36.

28 Quoted in Andrew Sullivan, "Why Aren't More Gay Men on the Pill?," *The Dish*, April 16, 2014, http://dish.andrewsullivan.com.

29 Gayle Rubin, "Thinking Sex: Notes for a Radical Theory of the Politics of Sexuality," in *The Gay and Lesbian Studies Reader*, ed. Henry Abelove, Michele Aine Barale, and David Halperin (New York: Routledge, 1993), 3–44.

30 Lauren Berlant and Michael Warner, "Sex in Public," *Critical Inquiry* 24, no. 2 (1998): 547–66.

31 The pharmaceutical manufacturer Gilead made upwards of $3 billion in sales in 2014. Glazek, "Why Is No One on the First Treatment to Prevent HIV?"

32 One in 200 people stopped Truvada because of kidney problems. About one in 10 users suffer from nausea, though it tends to be temporary. Other drugs, including birth control pills, blood pressure medicine, and aspirin, may actually be more toxic. Glazek, "Why Is No One on the First Treatment to Prevent HIV?"

33 Mike Berlin, "Artist of the Year. *Out* 100: Zachary Quinto," *Out*, November 11, 2011, www.out.com.

34 Patrick Healy, "A Lion Still Roars, with Gratitude," *New York Times*, May 21, 2014, www.nytimes.com; Les Fabian Brathwaite, "Intergenerational AIDS Activists Endorse PrEP, Call Out Gilead," *Out*, December 8, 2015, www.out.com.

35 Heather Boerner, "The HIV Drug Half a Million Women Need," *Daily Beast*, December 18, 2015, www.thedailybeast.com.

36 Michelle Garcia, "Why Michael Weinstein Gets Blamed for PrEP Myths," *Advocate*, October 31, 2014, www.advocate.com.

37 The AHF has a reported operating budget in the $1 billion range, with more than 1,000 employees on the payroll. Ibid.

38 Juzwiak, "What Is Safe Sex?"

39 Dominic Holden, "AIDS Group Slammed for Filing Complaint over HIV Drug Commercial," *Buzzfeed*, February 11, 2016, www.buzzfeed.com.

40 Juzwiak, "What Is Safe Sex?"

41 Liz Highleyman, "AHF's PrEP Ad Sparks Controversy," *Bay Area Reporter*, August 28, 2014, http://ebar.com.

42 Garcia, "Why Michael Weinstein Gets Blamed for PrEP Myths."

43 I borrow the term "serial" from Iris Marion Young. She notes, "A series is a collective whose members are unified passively by the relation their actions have to material objects and practico-inert histories." Here I use it to mark potentially different sex partners across different situations. See Young, *Intersecting Voices: Dilemmas of Gender, Political Philosophy, and Policy* (Princeton, NJ: Princeton University Press, 1997), 23.

44 Nikolas Rose, *The Politics of Life Itself: Biomedicine, Power, and Subjectivity in the Twenty-First Century* (Princeton, NJ: Princeton University Press, 2007), 24, 131–37.

45 Majdik Zoltan, "Biological Citizenship," in *The Encyclopedia of Health Communication*, ed. Teresa Thompson (New York: Sage, 2014), 105.

46 Rose, *Politics of Life*, 144–45.

47 For a detailed history of AIDS activism, see Steven Epstein, *Impure Science: AIDS, Activism, and the Politics of Knowledge* (Berkeley: University of California Press, 1996).

48 Rose's contention that the "biologization of politics has rarely been explored from the perspective of citizenship" is strange considering how much work about HIV/AIDS has engaged this intersection.

49 Rose, *Politics of Life*, 135.

50 Along with the half million queer men who would benefit from PrEP, the report also noted that 115,000 injection drug users would be safeguarded. The report also mentioned 157,000 heterosexual men and 468,000 women.

51 Boerner, "The HIV Drug Half a Million Women Need."

52 Nikolas Rose, "Beyond Medicalisation," *Lancet* 389, no. 9562 (2007): 702.

53 Ibid., 700.

54 Ibid., 701.

55 Michel Foucault, "On the Genealogy of Ethics: An Overview of Work in Progress," in *The Foucault Reader*, ed. Paul Rabinow (New York: Pantheon Books, 1984), 349.

56 Martha Cooper and Carole Blair, "Foucault's Ethics," *Qualitative Inquiry* 8, no. 4 (2002): 529.

57 Judith Butler, "Is Kinship Always Already Heterosexual?," *differences: A Journal of Feminist Cultural Studies* 13, no. 1 (2002): 14.

58 Sullivan, "Why Aren't More Gay Men on the Pill?"

59 John Erni, *Unstable Frontiers: Technomedicine and the Cultural Politics of "Curing" AIDS* (Minneapolis: University of Minnesota Press, 1994), xvi.

60 J. Blake Scott, *Risky Rhetoric: AIDS and the Cultural Practices of HIV Testing* (Carbondale: Southern Illinois University Press, 2003), 116.

61 Paula Treichler, *How to Have Theory in an Epidemic: Cultural Chronicles of AIDS* (Durham, NC: Duke University Press, 1999).

62 Erni, *Unstable Frontiers*, 132.

63 Grant clarified that those cases where seroconversions occurred were linked to lack of adherence not to the pill itself. Letter to Robert Grant, "Has PrEP Ever Failed?," April 15, 2015, www.robertmgrant.org.

64 Steve Rothaus, "The HIV Conversation about PrEP Gets Heated," *Miami Herald*, February 11, 2016, www.miamiherald.com.

65 Wald, *Contagious*, 71.

66 Ben Quinn, "Gonorrhoea Could Become Untreatable, Says Chief Medic," *Guardian*, December 27, 2015, www.theguardian.com.

67 Dan Savage, *Savage Lovecast*, Season 20, episode 475, December 1, 2015, www.savagelovecast.com; Maggie Fox, "CDC Sees 'Alarming' Increase in Sexually Transmitted Diseases," *NBCnews.com*, November 17, 2015, www.nbcnews.com.

68 John Byrne, "A False-Positive HIV Test Result Turned Me into a PrEP Evangelist," *TheBody.com*, February 10, 2016, www.thebody.com.

69 Jenell Johnson, *American Lobotomy: A Rhetorical History* (Ann Arbor: University of Michigan Press, 2014).

70 Halperin, *What Do Gay Men Want?*, 32.

71 Glazek, "Why Is No One on the First Treatment to Prevent HIV?"

72 Robert Grant et al., "Preexposure Chemoprophylaxis for HIV Prevention in Men Who Have Sex with Men," *New England Journal of Medicine* 363 (2010): 2587–99; see also Caitlin Kennedy and Virginia Fonner, "Pre-exposure Prophylaxis for Men Who Have Sex with Men: A Systematic Review," *World Health Organization*, April 6, 2014, www.ncbi.nlm.nih.gov.

73 Alice Park, "There's a Drug That Prevents HIV. Let's Use It," *Time*, November 16, 2015, time.com.

5

# The Necropolitical Functions of Biocitizenship

*The Sixth International AIDS Conference and the U.S. Ban on HIV-Positive Immigrants*

KARMA R. CHÁVEZ

Immigration and citizenship scholars have aptly shown how the health or perceived health of migrants' bodies has been one of the central determinants of whether a migrant can enter U.S. borders and/or begin the process toward legal and cultural inclusion into a national body.[1] Furthermore, eugenics and genetics discourses long have relied on biology or heredity to determine fitness for the nation, which has applied to immigrants as well as people born within a nation-state.[2] In this way, modern citizenship and variegated access to it have always been, at least in part, biological considerations. In comparison to the nineteenth century and early twentieth century, the late twentieth-century landscape changed significantly with regard to the ways that biology precluded national belonging; however, due to its deadliness and fears about its spread, the advent of HIV/AIDS compelled new concerns with regard to the healthy or unhealthy bodies of people who traveled around the globe as migrants or tourists. For example, in the late 1980s and early 1990s, some European, Asian, and Latin American countries took moderate approaches in their considerations of how HIV/AIDS should impact their immigration and travel policies, recognizing that HIV was only spread through very specific forms of contact and therefore was not communicable or contagious in a sense that might have necessitated travel bans. Other countries, like the United States and Saudi Arabia, reacted by issuing travel bans and proposing mandatory testing.

HIV/AIDS and its interplay with U.S. immigration policy and politics during the late twentieth century provide an interesting lens with which to understand how what Nikolas Rose and Carlos Novas have called biocitizenship works to maintain national borders and relegate certain populations to death. Biocitizenship is the idea that "specific biological presuppositions, explicitly or implicitly, have underlain many citizenship projects, shaped conceptions of what it means to be a citizen, and underpinned distinctions between actual, potential, troublesome, and impossible citizens."[3] Although immigrants are not citizens, they and their biological conditions are placed under perhaps more scrutiny than those with legal citizenship status, making the framework of biocitizenship an appropriate one for understanding how decisions regarding treatment of immigrants with HIV/AIDS were made and also how people responded to aspects of those decisions. To provide this exploration, in this chapter I look at the controversy, protests, and boycott surrounding the Sixth International AIDS Conference (IAC) held in San Francisco in 1990 to demonstrate an often uncommented upon aspect of biocitizenship: its necropolitical functions. As Achille Mbembe famously showed in extending Foucault's idea of biopolitics, the undersides to programs that manage and produce life for some populations (biopolitics) are those that create and promote conditions that leave others for death (necropolitics).[4]

Those who participated in, protested, and boycotted the Sixth IAC due to their belief that the conference tacitly supported the U.S. government's ban on HIV-positive immigrants by continuing to hold the conference in the United States show how the state's necropolitical biocitizenship effectively left certain populations to die. At the same time, the events surrounding the conference reveal what happens when necropolitical biocitizenship collides with the agency of the noncitizen, through "collectivized biocitizenship." Specifically, the noncitizen who has been left to die due to their biology and yet who is already inside the nation's borders, fights back against the state, fortifies transnational alliances with others who also fight the state, and makes unlikely allies with those often considered part of the state apparatus, in this case, scientists. In other words, exploring the necropolitical functions of state biocitizenship reveals not only death politics but also ruptures that create possibilities for change to laws and political alliances that actively work against necropolitical biocitizenship.

In this chapter, I first provide some background information on U.S. immigration policy regarding HIV/AIDS in the late twentieth century.

Next, I offer background on the Sixth International AIDS Conference, including the boycotts and protests that surrounded it, and provide a look at how many scientists were compelled to respond, thereby challenging the necropolitical functions of state biocitizenship. I conclude by discussing the long-term results of the Sixth IAC controversy as well as its implications for theorizing biocitizenship.

## HIV/AIDS and U.S. Immigration Policy

The literal spread of disease has always been a concern for immigration officials and policy makers. Such concerns stemmed not only from fears of contaminating the national body with foreign pathogens to which U.S. citizens might have no immunity but also from views of immigrants that often framed them using pathological and disease metaphors. As Otto Santa Ana has shown, in immigration discourse that frames the nation as a body, immigrants are often characterized as "a *disease* afflicting the body."[5] Similarly, as J. David Cisneros has argued, the "immigrant as pollutant" metaphor has been persuasive in U.S. popular discourse.[6] Such metaphors join with real concerns about the spread of disease as well as long-standing beliefs that terrible illness and disease often come from elsewhere as opposed to being homegrown.

Worries over the spread of HIV/AIDS in the 1980s capitalized on these discourses and cultural narratives, but given that those most visibly afflicted by the disease within U.S. borders were already marginalized and stigmatized (drug users, Haitian immigrants, and gay men), and that the illness had no cure and rapidly killed those infected, the hysteria surrounding foreigners and HIV/AIDS was especially extreme. For this reason, while the Reagan administration and other policy makers were publicly silent on the matter, they were privately trying to determine the best way to respond to AIDS as a national issue, and concerns over infected foreigners were central to these conversations.

In November 1985, the acting assistant secretary for health, James O. Mason, put forth a recommendation to add AIDS to the list of "dangerous contagious diseases" that render a person excludable under Section 212(a) of the Immigration and Nationality Act. Secretary Otis R. Bowen approved this proposal in January 1986, and it was put forward for public comment in April.[7] By June of the following year, upon review of the comments received from 116 individuals and sixteen organizations, the Department of Health and Human Services (HHS) decided to add AIDS to the list and shortly thereafter amended the ruling to substitute "HIV infection" for "AIDS," "since individuals who are so infected, but do not actually have AIDS, are also contagious."[8] This ruling was published just a week after Reagan's first public speech devoted entirely to AIDS on May 31, 1987, and concurrently with Senate debates and a final vote that implored the president to "add human immunodeficiency virus infection to the list of dangerous contagious diseases contained in title 42 of the Code of Federal Regulations."[9] By December 1 of that year, the exclusion was firmly in place. In part, this happened as a result of an amendment by Senator Jesse Helms that codified the ban.

On May 7, 1987, amid increasing pressure on the federal government generally and the Reagan administration specifically to adopt a formal and systematic response to the AIDS crisis, the U.S. Senate began debate on HR 1827, the Supplemental Appropriations Act of 1987 that had recently been sent to it by the House of Representatives. Included in the act was an emergency provision to provide $30 million in funding to those with AIDS who had volunteered to participate in clinical trials for the drug AZT and who were too poor to afford to continue to take the medication now that it was approved and on the market. This was to be one of the first times AIDS would be discussed on the Senate floor. On May 21, 1987, Helms proposed amendment number 212 to the act, which attached a contingency to the emergency funds, namely, that they could be released as long as testing negatively for HIV became a condition for the granting of a marriage license and for the ability to legally migrate to the United States.[10]

In the end, although lively debate ensued, and some senators did not support either provision, a deal was brokered that removed the marriage license requirement and kept in place the ban on HIV-positive immigrants. This particular provision also put the power to determine whether the ban remained or changed not in the hands of HHS but in the hands of Congress. Presidents Bush Sr. and Clinton both sought to remove HIV infection from the list of dangerous diseases in 1991 and 1993, respectively, but neither succeeded. Clinton, in fact, codified the HIV exclusion, which Republicans wrote into the 1993 National Institutes of Health Revitalization Act (PL 103-43). This law effectively meant that outside of the political asylum process or in rare other occasions when a waiver was granted, no one with HIV or AIDS could legally migrate to the United States. The exclusion remained in place until its official lifting in January 2010. After years of lobbying from activists, scientists, and public health workers, and in a climate less constituted by fear of HIV/AIDS than the early 1990s, President Barack Obama codified the change early in his presidency.

## The Sixth International AIDS Conference

The ban was not yet in place when organizers decided to hold the Sixth International AIDS Conference in San Francisco. The first International AIDS Conference, hosted by the World Health Organization, HHS, and other collaborators, drew 2,000 participants to Atlanta, Georgia, in 1985. Just four years into the new disease, this group of people, primarily scientists and public health officials, dedicated itself to understanding HIV from a biomedical perspective and to finding a cure. After three conferences, the perspectives of sociologists, behaviorists, and people living with HIV had slowly started to be included alongside those of scientists and public health workers. In 1988, the International AIDS Society (IAS) was founded and tasked with running the conferences thereafter. In the midst of this time, AIDS activists in the United States became increasingly organized and agitational in their approach. The IAS found itself in the middle of controversy as early as 1987 when activists expressed frustration with a lack of *political* leadership at the conference in Washington, DC.[11] Activists insisted that all the scientific innovation in the world was meaningless if the people it was meant to serve were dead and if the government would not fund research projects, refused to provide services to those who were dying, or found other means to legally ostracize and exclude people living with HIV/AIDS. These aspects of the disease were political and required political leadership. At the Montreal conference in 1989, hundreds of U.S. and Canadian activists occupied the stage and rows reserved for VIPs in order to protest inaction by their respective governments, as well as the ban on HIV-positive travelers to the United States. After this conference, political viewpoints would always be present in the conference's conversations, whether formally on the conference schedule or in the planning process or informally in the form of protests. Due to continued pressure from activists and, in this instance, the fact that they generally agreed with activists on the problems with the HIV bans, physicians and scientists were also developing political savvy. For example, in his memoir *The Fragile Coalition: Scientists, Activists, and AIDS* (1991), Robert M. Wachter, one of the organizers of the 1990 conference, described the kinds of decisions scientists found themselves making in order to respond to, accommodate, or sometimes placate activists. Such decisions included the order of events at the conference and the manner in which the organizers issued invitations to speak and publicized rejections before the conference.

Yet, even with more political savvy, scientists and public health officials organizing these events did not always fully grasp the necessity of including the perspectives of both activists and people living with HIV, two viewpoints that often overlapped. At the 1986 meeting in Paris, IAS planners chose San Francisco to host the 1990 conference.[12] San Francisco was epicenter for the disease and also employed a unique community-based approach to responding to it, making it an ideal choice—ideal, that is, except that HIV-positive, non-U.S. citizens would no longer be allowed to travel to the United States to attend the conference, which severely limited who would be able to participate. It is unclear in the historical documents whether the question of the ban did not arise soon enough, or if organizers believed that the ban would in fact be lifted beforehand. Either way, the IAS did not move the 1990 conference on the grounds that there was insufficient time to orchestrate the effort.[13]

The ban reflected the state's view on whose biological condition might lead to inclusion and whose left them worthy of exclusion and even death. Because of the ban, immigration officials regularly questioned people about their HIV status upon entering the United States. HIV-positive persons who applied for a visa to travel to the United States had to declare their HIV status and apply for a waiver. If they received a waiver (which was not guaranteed), their status would be *indicated on their passport*, and the details would be filed at the U.S. embassy in their home country.[14] Due to this policy, in November 1989, organizations slowly proclaimed their intent to boycott the conference. The Geneva-based League of Red Cross and Red Crescent Societies was among the first to call for a boycott of the conference due to U.S. immigration law.[15]

Others announced around the same time. The UK AIDS Consortium in the Third World advised all of its thirty-two member organizations not to attend.[16]

Organizations supported the boycott and opposed the U.S. policy for many reasons. The National Commission on AIDS argued that the policy "unfairly discriminates against people who know they have AIDS, while thousands who may be ignorant of their infection are permitted to enter without question."[17] June E. Osborn, the commission chair, explained that the policy also implies that HIV and AIDS are "a general threat" as opposed to an infection with restricted modes of transmission. Sue Lucas, the UK AIDS Consortium's secretary, noted of the procedure that people would be required to follow if they wanted to come to the United States for the conference that it "'clearly compromises the confidentiality of HIV positive people and people with Aids [sic], and could be particularly serious for nationals of countries where the Government suppresses the rights of people who are HIV positive. By offering sponsorship to help people to attend the conference, the agency may be putting an individual into the position of either identifying his [sic] or herself as HIV positive or breaking the law.'"[18] Each of these rationales points toward a critique of the state's necropolitical biocitizenship. Although the fact of death is not mentioned here, the issues of discrimination, rights suppression, law breaking, and lack of confidentiality all point toward necropolitical logics that put people in potentially great danger should they attempt to travel to the United States.

The threat of boycott put additional pressure on the IAS and local organizers, who also actively opposed the ban. Through a rigorous campaign, the IAS strongly encouraged President George H. W. Bush to overturn the ban. In return for its efforts, in April, just two months before the conference, the IAS secured waivers for all HIV-positive delegates to attend the conference and all subsequent "White House–approved scientific or professional" AIDS-related conferences to be held in the United States. The administration charged HHS secretary Louis Sullivan with determining which conferences were "in the public interest" and therefore qualified for the special visas. However, despite these small concessions, the ban on HIV-positive immigrants stood. The IAS's decision to continue with the conference anyway signaled to many its complicity with flawed U.S. government policies. In the eyes of many would-be participants, the government's waivers did not address the larger problem with the restrictions, which stigmatized and discriminated against HIV-positive people and could function to drive many underground.[19] Furthermore, in an ideal example of how necropolitical biocitizenship can work, the waivers created a distinction between temporary travelers and those seeking long-term immigration status that functioned to further marginalize and potentially endanger immigrants whose permanent travels were already more significant than those of temporary travelers. Many accused the government of making that distinction in order to weaken the links among all those opposed to U.S. policy. If temporary travelers could get waivers, they might be less inclined to continue to support the broader struggle against the immigration ban.

Left with little choice, and with increasing pressure from activists in groups like ACT UP, numerous countries and individuals, as well as 130 groups and organizations from around the world, chose to go forward with the boycott of the conference.[20] Some conference organizers suggested that attendance and registration at the conference were not much affected by the boycott.[21] Others maintained that up to 1,000 possible delegates participated in the boycott,[22] and some estimate that as many as 2,000 to 3,000 people did not register who otherwise would have.[23] Whether the numbers changed, significant organizations and actors in global discussions on HIV/AIDS boycotted the conference, including the countries of France, Canada, Great Britain, Norway, Sweden, and Switzerland; the European Parliament; the International League of Red Cross and Red Crescent Societies; the British Medical Association; Oxfam; the Canadian AIDS Society; and the British, Canadian, French, and Norwegian Red Cross societies.[24] Boycotters, who were largely physicians, scientists, and service providers, had a terrible political choice: either tacitly support or endorse the U.S. policy, or risk the lives of people living with HIV and AIDS by not participating in this crucial exchange of scientific ideas about the disease. In taking the stance to boycott the conference, boycotters hoped to send a strong enough message to the United States and other governments that it was *they* and not the boycotters who would have blood on their hands. Quite literally, they hoped to reveal to the U.S. government the necropolitics, the death politics, embedded in its policies.

Local activists outside of the scientific community from immigration organizations and AIDS collectives like ACT UP organized massive protests to take place during the conference. Influenced greatly by the spectacular tactics of ACT UP,[25] protesters marched and chanted outside the conference building in San Francisco and staged media spectacles. These protests were ignited by the travel ban, but they also focused on issues like the pace of drug trials; homophobia and perceived arrogance among those in the scientific community; lack of attention to people of color, women, and intravenous drug users; and a U.S. law that prevented *homosexuals* from legally migrating to the country.[26] Some international activists also planned protests during the conference.[27] The significance of the boycott and the media coverage it attracted for almost a year helped to make the protests and actions more visible. Several official delegates to the conference reportedly gave their passes away to protesters, who were then able to get through security in order to attend (and disrupt) the closing session, specifically the speech of HHS secretary Sullivan, who was scheduled to give the last speech of the conference.[28] Organizers scheduled Sullivan at the end intentionally because they knew protesters would disrupt his speech.

Paul Volberding, chair of the International AIDS Conference, came to the stage to introduce Sullivan, using the word "honorable" to describe the secretary. As if this was the official cue, activists immediately began groaning at this point. The extralinguistic sound of the groan reflects a seemingly nonrational response of the body, but it carries rhetorical significance as an expression that cannot be addressed in the rational frame assumed in this closing ceremony.[29] The groaning sounds steadily increased. Volberding waited for the audience to quiet, but it never did. Sullivan took the stage and began his speech as planned. Protesters rushed the stage, sounding police sirens, whistles, and horns. Protesters held signs and started chanting. For several minutes the proceedings were stalled as activists interrupted. Eventually, the chants erupted into activists screaming "Shame! Shame!" and shaking their fists in unison at the stage. Others chanted slogans demanding action and threw crumpled paper and paper airplanes toward the stage. Sullivan, who never lost his composure, only once addressed the protest in general. His words remained largely inaudible over the crowd, and he continued his speech lauding the advancements and financial resources that the

Bush administration was putting forth in the fight against AIDS. Sullivan symbolized the state's necropolitical biocitizenship as the policies he championed literally had the impact of leaving those with the disease excluded from national belonging, from access to health care, and at grave risk of death. Despite the state's necropolitical biocitizenship that reduced people to the biological status of persons marked with disease, these AIDS activists could be said to enact collectivized biocitizenship, "formed around a biological conception of a shared identity."[30] They used it to work against the necropolitical biocitizenship that banned HIV-positive immigrants. But protesters did not only coalesce with one another. The shared identity that created their collectivized biocitizenship also functioned to connect to those outside of that identity, but who also had a stake in understanding that identity and developing alliances that actively worked against leaving some for death. The activists clearly had an impact on the scientists, bringing them, even those who were unwilling, into political space. After the events, some scientists were quoted saying that they agreed that Sullivan deserved such treatment due to the discriminatory policies he supported and represented.[31]

It is prudent here to return to Rose and Novas's definition of biocitizenship as "specific biological presuppositions, explicitly or implicitly, [that] have underlain many citizenship projects, shaped conceptions of what it means to be a citizen, and underpinned distinctions between actual, potential, troublesome, and impossible citizens."[32] It is on the question of the "impossible" here that we must turn our attention, for the protesters, especially those who are people living with AIDS and immigrants, are not just impossible but are the ones targeted by necropolitical biocitizenship. In this instance, the impossibility, in the view of the state, is actually the mark of and for death. Yet, because the project of necropolitical biocitizenship is not a complete one, the impossibility is also a site of agency through collectivized biocitizenship, not just for the protesters alone but also for those whom they compel to act.

The boycott and disruptive protests clearly opened additional space for scientists who did not boycott or protest to express political views they might not have otherwise expressed. Many of those who chose to attend the conference wore red armbands, as recommended by the Bay Area Physicians for Human Rights, to indicate solidarity with those who boycotted and protested in opposition to discriminatory laws. Other delegates prepared protest statements to be read before or during their scientific presentations.[33] Lars Olaf Kallings, then president of the IAS, spoke in the closing ceremony, expressing frustration with discriminatory policy and showing at least superficial support for protesters.[34] In the middle of his speech, Kallings stated forcefully:

> The IAS has concerned itself with the needs of infected persons and the protection of human rights, a cornerstone for successful prevention of HIV infection. Prejudice and discrimination are hindrances to implementing intervention programs. It is shameful when unfounded discrimination is ennobled to law as is the case with travel restrictions instituted by several countries.[35]

The crowd erupted in loud applause for several seconds at the frankness of Kallings's words. He went on: "The symbolic impact is even greater than the practical. How can we expect the private person to behave in a rational and responsible way to prevent HIV infection and/or to reject prejudice when states first set a bad example by instituting irrational laws and then, even worse, after realizing that the laws are unscientific and useless, through political bigotry, do not change them?" The crowd again erupted in applause for Kallings's words, which, while not naming the U.S. government directly, were clearly focused primarily at it. Like some other scientific speakers, Kallings lamented the way that politics obstructed scientific advancement and research. For example, Dr. Anthony Fauci, then director of the National Institute of Allergy and Infectious Disease, made no mention of the travel ban or discriminatory governmental policy in his address during the closing ceremony. In brief political comments appended to an otherwise dense scientific address, he instead insisted that while activists and scientists could work together and had done so, it was unfair for activists to charge scientists and doctors with being uncaring or to call them names.

Unlike scientists such as Fauci, Kallings seemed most outraged by the politics being played by governments as opposed to those of activists. He chastised those who framed the protesters as irrational when governments were the ones acting irrationally. Kallings finished the political section of his speech, interwoven with applause and support from the audience:

It is in this context that we so much regret the atmosphere, which has colored the preparation for this conference when the free exchange of scientific information is obstructed due to political reasons. However, at this moment, we should look forward and continue to push for travel restrictions to be rejected in all countries. I understand that due to the remarkable political changes toward openness and freedom in Eastern Europe, we may expect that the current travel restrictions for HIV-infected persons will be discarded in some of these countries. Let us hope that such good examples will promote changes in other countries as well.

The audience chuckled at this point of the speech, recognizing the irony of countries that were recently part of the Soviet bloc now having freer and less discriminatory policies than the United States or Canada. Again, Kallings did not mention any country by name, but as he went on, he became more explicit in his indictments:

And let us hope that it will be possible to sponsor future International AIDS Conferences in North America. For the moment, though, this is very uncertain. IAS has resolved that further IAS-sponsored conferences will not be held in countries that restrict the entry of HIV-infected travelers. Therefore, IAS resolves to withdraw its sponsorship of the International Conference on AIDS in Boston if U.S. immigration policy continues to restrict the travel of HIV-infected persons and to discourage IAS members and other concerned individuals from attending AIDS conferences in any foreign country whose official policies restrict the travel of HIV-infected persons. This is also in accordance with the views expressed by the Boston organizers.

This forceful statement, finally explicitly calling out the United States and overtly blending science and politics, not only affirmed the legitimacy of the boycott and protests of the sixth conference in the eyes of the major sponsoring organization but also indicated the legitimacy of further boycotts should travel laws not change. In this way, leading scientists joined activists and HIV-positive migrants in actively working against the necropolitics of the state's biocitizenship.

## What Happened Next?

Perhaps in a bit of irony, given that the HIV ban stood until 2010, the IAS boycotted the United States until 2012, refusing to hold the conference on U.S. soil for twenty-two years. But before that boycott began, conference organizers had to deal with the matter of the 1992 conference, which was again scheduled to take place in the United States. This time, the threat of boycott forced organizers to relocate the conference to Amsterdam. There, activists continued to use the occasion of the IAC to draw attention to the U.S. state's necropolitical biocitizenship. Nonetheless, the United States remained firm in its discriminatory policy.

Activism around the issue of immigration died down after the 1992 conference, at least according to archival records. In part, this could be due to the fact that for many AIDS activists, immigration was only a minor issue in the first place.[36] Moreover, several activists who worked tirelessly on this issue in the early 1990s were very ill or dead by the mid-1990s. The state's necropolitical biocitizenship had very significant effects. Furthermore, those who made it to the age of the drug "cocktail" and could afford it, found their health conditions improving significantly, a fact that has been credited with the slowing of much AIDS activism by the late 1990s.

Another factor to consider is that, by the mid-1990s, the question of a ban on HIV-positive immigration was no longer a top priority for many immigration activists and advocates, who were battling laws like Proposition 187 in California and the 1996 Illegal Immigration Reform and Immigrant Responsibility Act, which took rights away from immigrants and criminalized a host of behaviors. This, on the heels of the North American Free Trade Agreement, changed the landscape for immigration politics in the United States for the foreseeable future. It is perhaps not surprising that the Coalition to Lift the Bar was established in 2006, simultaneously with the large immigration marches occurring that year and a growing number of queer immigrant leaders gaining visibility and voice. The coalition, according to one of the founders and leaders, N. Ordover, was an alliance of human rights, immigrant, HIV, and LGBTQ activists and service providers from around the United States that mo-

bilized many of the same arguments as activists years earlier and continued to challenge the state's necropolitical biocitizenship.

That arguments that failed to persuade policy makers in the late
twentieth century were persuasive to at least one policy maker in the
early twenty-first century (the ban was overturned by a presidential executive order in 2009) teaches us something about how necropolitical
biocitizenship works and shifts. It is certainly the case that immigrants
continue to be among the most maligned groups, and decades of border
militarization and other draconian policies have designated many for
death. But the face and body of people with AIDS have changed dramatically in the public imaginary, especially as so many in the infamous
"general population" got infected and also lived for decades. In other
words, the biology of AIDS changed, and so did the meaning of biocitizenship in the eyes of ordinary people and in the eyes of the state. The
changes in this particular form of biocitizenship do not, however, negate
the impacts of necropolitical biocitizenship, which persist in new ways
and in some cases in old ways (take, for example, eugenicist-style arguments that insist Muslims are naturally unfit to be U.S. Americans). And
yet, as before, perhaps as always, those relegated to death continue to
speak and groan in the name of their own lives, challenging necropolitical biocitizenship with a collectivized form and then building alliances
near and far. Such a possibility for change and subversion is not to be
overestimated, but it does point to the ongoing necessity for resistance.

NOTES

1  E.g., Eithne Luibhéid, *Entry Denied: Controlling Sexuality at the Border* (Minneapolis: University of Minnesota Press, 2002); Mae M. Ngai, *Impossible Subjects:
   Illegal Aliens and the Making of Modern America* (Princeton, NJ: Princeton Uni-
   versity Press, 2004).
2  Nancy Ordover, *American Eugenics: Race, Queer Anatomy, and the Science of
   Nationalism* (Minneapolis: University of Minnesota Press, 2003); Siobhan B.
   Somerville, *Queering the Color Line: Race and the Invention of Homosexuality in
   American Culture* (Durham, NC: Duke University Press, 2000).
3  Nikolas Rose and Carlos Novas, "Biological Citizenship," in *Global Assemblages:
   Technology, Politics, and Ethics as Anthropological Problems*, ed. Aihwa Ong and
   Stephen J. Collier (Malden, MA: Blackwell, 2005), 440.
4  Achille Mbembe, "Necropolitics," *Public Culture* 15, no. 1 (2003): 11–40.
5  Otto Santa Ana, "'Like an Animal I Was Treated': Anti-immigrant Metaphor in
   US Public Discourse," *Discourse and Society* 10, no. 2 (1999): 199.

6 J. David Cisneros, "Contaminated Communities: The Metaphor of 'Immigrant as Pollutant' in Media Representations of Immigration," *Rhetoric and Public Affairs* 11, no. 4 (2008): 569–601.

7 *Federal Register* 51, no. 78 (April 23, 1986): 15354–55.

8 *Federal Register* 52, no. 109 (June 8, 1987): 21532. See also *Federal Register* 52, no. 167 (August 28, 1987): 32540–44.

9 Supplemental Appropriations Act, 1987, PL 100-71, 101 Stat. 391, July 11, 1987.

10 133 Cong. Rec. S6943 Supplemental Appropriations Act, May 21, 1987.

11 "History of the IAS—Episode 1," www.iasociety.org.

12 From the finding aid for Sixth International Conference on AIDS records, 1988–1990 (UCSF Library and Center for Knowledge Management, Archives and Special Collections), www.oac.cdlib.org.

13 Tomas Fabregas, Memo to ACT UP Golden Gate, "US Policy on HIV Infected Foreigners," August 6, 1991, GLBT Historical Society, Jorge Cortiñas Papers, Collection Number 1998-42, Box 2, Folder 8.

14 Peter McIntyre, "AIDS Meeting Faces Boycott over Rules on Entry to US," *Independent*, November 20, 1989.

15 Kelly Toughill, "US Eases Visa Rules for AIDS Conference," *Toronto Star*, April 17 1990. It is difficult to say who first called for the boycott because stories conflict. Some sources say the UK Consortium was the first. See McIntyre, "AIDS Meeting Faces Boycott over Rules on Entry to US," 3.

16 McIntyre, "AIDS Meeting Faces Boycott over Rules on Entry to US"; "Third World Charities Set to Boycott AIDS Forum," *Guardian*, November 20, 1989.

17 Michael Specter, "Major Groups Plan to Boycott San Francisco AIDS Meeting; US Restrictions on Immigration Criticized," *Washington Post*, December 13, 1989, A2.

18 McIntyre, "AIDS Meeting Faces Boycott over Rules on Entry to US"; Jane Coutts, "AIDS Groups Urge Boycott of Conference, Cite US Law," *Globe and Mail*, January 31, 1990; Andrew Orkin, "Boycott Casts Shadow over San Francisco AIDS Conference," *Canadian Medical Association Journal* 142, no. 12 (1990): 1411.

19 Orkin, "Boycott Casts Shadow."

20 Eric Sawyer, "Absolutely Fabregas," *Poz*, June 1, 1997, accessed March 23, 2013, www.poz.com.

21 Orkin, "Boycott Casts Shadow," 1412.

22 Andrew Orkin, "Policy Protests, Scientific Spats Take Centre Stage at Sixth International AIDS Conference," *Canadian Medical Association Journal* 143, no. 4 (1990): 312.

23 "Restrictions Set Off AIDS Session Boycott," *St. Louis Post-Dispatch*, June 15, 1990.

24 Christie McLaren, "Canada Joins Boycott of Major AIDS Conference; Health Minister Cites Restrictive US Immigration Law," *Globe and Mail*, June 16, 1990.

25 For more on ACT UP's political actions in relation to immigration, see Karma R. Chávez, "ACT UP, Haitian Migrants and Alternative Memories of HIV/AIDS," *Quarterly Journal of Speech* 98, no. 1 (2012): 63–68. For more on ACT UP's protests generally, see Deborah B. Gould, *Moving Politics: Emotion and ACT UP's Fight*

*against AIDS* (Chicago: University of Chicago Press, 2009); Alexandra Juhasz, *AIDS TV* (Durham, NC: Duke University Press, 1995); Brett C. Stockdill, *Activism against AIDS: At the Intersection of Sexuality, Race, Gender and Class* (Boulder, CO: Lynne Rienner, 2003).

26  Paul Taylor, "Activists Push for AIDS Funds; Gay Groups Threatening to Disrupt US Conference in Fight to Speed Research," *Globe and Mail*, June 20, 1990.

27  "AIDS Protest Gets Rough," *Toronto Star*, June 20, 1990, A19.

28  What is interesting about activists' attendance at the conference is that some reports indicated that if you count the infiltrators inside and the protesters outside the conference, several thousand more people participated in the conference than would have otherwise. While such participation cannot be attributed solely to the boycotts, the boycotts undoubtedly created rhetorical space and, perhaps more important, media attention that fostered activist participation, a point I will take up in my next book, "AIDS Knows No Borders."

29  See Alexander G. Weheliye, *Habeas Viscus: Racializing Assemblages, Biopolitics, and Black Feminist Theories of the Human* (Durham, NC: Duke University Press, 2014).

30  Rose and Novas, "Biological Citizenship," 442.

31  Paul Taylor, "Protest Disrupts Close of AIDS Conference; Activists, Scientists Decry US Policy," *Globe and Mail*, June 25 1990. Importantly, not all the activists involved in these actions shared beliefs about which strategies should be implemented to protest (Larry Kramer reportedly wanted to riot).

32  Rose and Novas, "Biological Citizenship," 440.

33  Orkin, "Policy Protests, Scientific Spats."

34  Taylor, "Protest Disrupts Close of AIDS Conference."

35  "Sixth International AIDS Conference," closing ceremony, June 24, 1990, *C-SPAN*, www.c-span.org.

36  Larry Kramer reported this fact to Robert Wachter, who wrote about it in his memoir, *The Fragile Coalition: Scientists, Activists, and AIDS* (New York: Palgrave Macmillan, 1991).

# 6

## Exploiting Vulnerable Citizens

*Drug Testing and the Mentally Ill*

CARL ELLIOTT AND EMMA BEDOR HILAND

At midday on April 24, 2007, eight days after signing up for a research study, a forty-seven-year-old Philadelphia man named Walter Jorden clutched his chest, collapsed, and died.[1] The cause of his death was a heart attack. Although Jorden died standing near a hospital bed in Lourdes Medical Center in Willingboro, New Jersey, he was not a patient at the hospital. Nor was he there to be treated for a medical condition. Jorden was at the hospital to test whether an experimental psychiatric drug was safe. The study in which he died was conducted by CRI Worldwide, a private clinical trials company that rented space there. It is thought that CRI paid Jorden roughly $2,000.

Jorden, who had a diagnosis of paranoid schizophrenia, had previously been hospitalized for depression, substance abuse, and potential heart problems. Once he had tried to hang himself. On another occasion he had made plans to slit his wrists. Jorden heard voices, and often they told him to commit suicide. A military veteran, a father, and a widower of seven years, Jorden was surviving on a monthly income of $845 in disability benefits. At the time he signed up for the study, he was living in a run-down recovery house. He desperately needed the money that CRI was offering.

On April 24, Jorden experienced chest discomfort. He became short of breath and sweaty. The psychiatrist in charge of the study thought Jorden was having a panic attack and prescribed lorazepam, a drug used to treat anxiety. It did not help. An hour later, Jorden was still in distress. This time a second doctor was called, who told Jorden to breathe deeply into a paper bag. After another hour, Jorden was given a second dose of lorazepam, after which he began trembling and passed out. Although the hospital emergency room was only a short distance away, Jorden was not taken there, nor did anyone ever examine his heart. He was pronounced dead at 12:35 p.m.

In many ways, Jorden's experience was not unusual. Over the past twenty-five years, a sizable underground economy has emerged around the testing of experimental drugs. Private clinical trial sites recruit subjects for research studies by offering them money, especially for phase I trials, which occur at the very beginning of drug development and aim to determine whether unapproved drugs are safe.[2] Phase I trials often require subjects to check into an inpatient unit for several weeks at a time, where they will be subjected to physiological monitoring, dietary restrictions, and, on some occasions, invasive medical procedures. The payment for a phase I study usually ranges between $2,000 and $7,000, depending on the length of the study, the discomfort of the procedures, and the nature of the drug being tested.

But there is one important way in which Walter Jorden's death stands out. Jorden was severely mentally ill. Until fairly recently, most paying research studies were limited to healthy volunteers. Paying people who were ill was once seen as unethical, in part because it was thought that illness made people especially vulnerable to manipulation or coercion. Today, however, many trial sites offer payment not only to subjects with medical illnesses, such as asthma, liver disease, and kidney disease, but also to patients with severe mental illness, such as schizophrenia. In many of these studies, patients can expect no therapeutic benefit whatsoever.

Many scholars working on biocitizenship emphasize how group identities have been reconfigured around biomedical characteristics. Some groups find these new identities to be empowering. Social activists have mobilized around shared identities as survivors of life-threatening illnesses such as breast cancer and of environmental disasters such as the nuclear accident at Chernobyl or the gas leak at a pesticide plant in Bhopal. Not everyone embraces a biological identity, however, especially when it is thrust upon them by medical authorities. In psychiatry, for instance, patients have often found themselves identified by their medical condition, physically removed from the rest of society, and forced to undergo treatment they might otherwise resist. For these reasons, among others, many people resist being labeled as psychiatric patients or sufferers of mental illness and instead identify as psychiatric survivors or ex-patients. They distrust the institutions of mainstream psychiatry.

For decades such patients were especially vulnerable to exploitation as a result of their institutional surroundings: locked wards, strict surveillance, authoritarian medical care, the culture of the asylum. In these settings, the primary danger was that institutional authorities would coerce or otherwise pressure patients into dangerous, uncomfortable, or scientifically worthless studies. Today, however, many long-term psychiatric institutions have closed, and seriously mentally ill people often struggle with a different set of problems, such as poverty, unemployment, homelessness, and poor access to medical care. This leaves them vulnerable to the kind of exploitation faced by Walter Jorden.

When the National Research Act was passed in 1974, it was widely assumed that the primary threat to research subjects came from academic and governmental researchers, whose scientific curiosity and personal ambition might lead them to overlook the rights and welfare of their research subjects. But today most clinical research studies take place in private settings, conducted by contract researchers. The motivations of a contract researcher are usually not academic but financial. This type of research presents a different kind of threat. How can we protect mentally ill research subjects from being exploited for financial gain?

## Kaimowitz v. Department of Mental Health for the State of Michigan

In 1972, two psychiatric researchers at the Lafayette Clinic, a facility of the Michigan Department of Mental Health, proposed a research study titled "For the Study of Treatment of Uncontrollable Aggression."[3] Ernst Rodin and Jacques Gottlieb planned to compare two procedures intended to control aggressive, institutionalized men. The first procedure was the administration of an antiandrogenic drug, cyproterone acetate. The second procedure was psychosurgery, an amygdalotomy, which was characterized as "sedative neurosurgery" aimed at making patients quiet and manageable. The researchers planned to enroll twenty-four "criminal sexual psychopaths" from the state's mental health system.

When the time came, however, the researchers could find only one potential subject. In 1955, while a psychiatric patient at the Kalamazoo State Hospital, "John Doe" had been charged with the murder and necrophilic rape of a student nurse. Doe was not prosecuted for his crimes but was committed involuntarily to the Ionia State Hospital as a "criminal sexual psychopath."[4] Seventeen years later, he was transferred to the Lafayette Clinic to become the first and only subject in the psychosurgery study proposed by Rodin and Gottlieb. The study was halted when attorney Gabe Kaimowitz alerted the press and filed a legal action.

In *Kaimowitz v. Department of Mental Health for the State of Michigan*, the court found on behalf of the plaintiff, ruling that John Doe was being illegally detained for the purpose of experimental psychosurgery.[5] One reason for the ruling was the irreversibility of the procedure and thin evidence for its effectiveness. More consequential, however, was the court's argument against conducting research on *any* involuntarily confined psychiatric patient. The court claimed that effects of institutionalization itself prevented even competent, well-informed patients from giving valid consent: "The fact of institutional confinement has special force in undermining the capacity of the mental patient to make a competent decision on this issue, even though he be intellectually competent to do so."[6]

No one claimed that John Doe's decision-making capacity was impaired. He clearly understood the procedure and its risks. "I killed a woman. I can't function as I am," he told one interviewer. "I need some kind of treatment."[7] According to the court, however, his decision could not meet the standards set by the Nuremberg Code, which requires that consent to research must be given without "force, fraud, deceit, duress, overreaching, or other ulterior form of constraint or coercion."[8] One reason why the consent of an involuntarily committed patient fails to meet this standard is the fact that the patient's release from confinement may well be dependent on the goodwill of the researchers or other authorities. As the court put it, "It is impossible for an involuntarily detained mental patient to be free of ulterior forms of restraint or coercion when his very release from the institution may depend upon his cooperating with the institutional authorities and giving consent to experimental surgery."[9]

Yet the court also outlined a more complex rationale for why such consent should be considered invalid: "For 17 years (John Doe) lived completely under the control of the hospital," the court wrote. Institutional officials had made every decision about his life, even regarding seemingly minor issues such as whether he could have a lamp in his room or whether he could have a picnic with his family. The court called the hospital an "inherently coercive atmosphere," in which patients become "part of communal living subject to the control of the institutional authorities." "Involuntarily confined patients cannot reason as equals with the doctors and administrators over whether they should undergo psychosurgery," the court ruled. "They are not able to voluntarily give informed consent because of the inherent inequality in their position."

A national commission came to a similar conclusion about research in prisons. A harsh light had been cast on prison research in 1973 with the publication of Jessica Mitford's muckraking article in the *Atlantic*, "Experiments behind Bars," and her subsequent book, *Kind and Usual Punishment: The Prison Business*. Yet many prisoners themselves favored allowing research to continue, in part because of the money they earned by enrolling. The National Commission for the Protection of Human Subjects of Biomedical and Behavioral Research recognized the arguments in favor of research, but it ultimately recommended significant restrictions, largely because of "the closed nature of prisons, with the resulting potential for abuse of authority." In prison settings, the commission wrote, "respect for persons" translates to "protection from exploitation."

## Erving Goffman's *Asylums*

Many aspects of the *Kaimowitz* decision echoed the critique of psychiatric institutions leveled by Erving Goffman in his influential book *Asylums: Essays on the Social Situation of Mental Patients and Other Inmates* (1961).[10] Goffman conducted ethnographic fieldwork at St. Elizabeth's Hospital, a federally funded psychiatric institution with more than 7,000 patients in Washington, DC. The result was a devastating indictment of the very idea of "institutionalization," in which Goffman describes how the bureaucratic and authoritarian procedures of psychiatric hospitals strip away the identity of inmates and render them unfit for life outside the institution.

Central to Goffman's analysis is the concept of "total institutions," such as military units, boarding schools, prisons, and psychiatric hospitals. Total institutions are organized for surveillance and control, allowing a relatively small number of staff members to oversee a much larger number of inmates. In ordinary life, an important organizing principle is the separation of three different spheres. We typically sleep, work, and play in different places, with different people, answering to different authorities. But in a total institution, all aspects of one's life occur in the same place, often in the company of the same people, under the same central authority. Every sequence of activity is strictly scheduled and "imposed from above by a system of explicit formal rulings and a body of officials."[11] Total institutions bring all these activities together under the umbrella of a single rational plan, intended to advance the aims of the institution itself.

In total institutions, Goffman writes, the staff and the inmates typically see one another in adversarial terms. Staff see inmates as "bitter, secretive and untrustworthy," while inmates see staff as "condescending, highhanded and mean."[12] Staff members work in shifts and can live normal lives outside the institution. Inmates cannot leave. Goffman writes, "Staff tends to feel superior and righteous; inmates tend, in some ways at least, to feel inferior, weak, blameworthy and guilty."[13]

As Goffman points out, psychiatry differs from other medical specialties in that its domain encompasses virtually everything about a patient's life. In a psychiatric institution, there is no privacy; nothing can be hidden. Goffman writes, "None of a patient's business, then, is none of the psychiatrist's business; nothing ought to be held back from the psychiatrist as irrelevant to his job."[14] This gives the psychiatrist an extraordinary degree of power. According to Goffman, "Almost any of the living arrangements through which the patient is strapped into his daily round can be modified at will by the psychiatrist, provided a psychiatric explanation is given."[15]

Psychiatric institutions differ from other medical facilities in that their purpose is not exclusively the medical well-being of the patient. Their purpose is also to protect the community from patients who may be a danger to other people. This sets psychiatric institutions apart. As Goffman puts it, not only is protection of the community not a service to the patient, it is not a medical service at all. He writes, "Instead of a server and the served, we find a governor and the governed, an officer and those subject to him."[16]

Can truly voluntary consent to research occur in such settings? Goffman does not address this question, and neither did the architects of the 1974 National Research Act or the Common Rule, which governs the conduct of medical research today. But the barriers to consent are clearly very high. Even if an institutionalized patient has full decision-making capacity (and many will not), it is still the case he or she is living in a locked unit that has many characteristics of a prison, under the thumb of authorities who have unprecedented control over virtually every aspect of his or her life. Authorities can punish dissenters; they can reward those who cooperate; they can persuade and manipulate patients in ways that would be unthinkable outside the institution. Without proper oversight, such circumstances present enormous potential for abuse and exploitation.

## Ewen Cameron and the Allen Memorial Institute

On March 11, 1980, a Canadian Broadcasting Corporation news program, *The Fifth Estate*, aired an astonishing report of research abuse at one of Canada's most respected medical institutions.[17] At McGill University, during the late 1950s and early 1960s, Dr. Ewen Cameron had conducted a lengthy, bizarre series of psychiatric experiments on unwitting patients at the Allen Memorial Institute. Even more shocking to Canadians, Cameron's experiments had been funded by the CIA.

At the time of the experiments, Cameron was one of the most well-known psychiatrists in the world: president of the American Psychiatric Association, the Canadian Psychiatric Association, and the World Psychiatric Association; a former expert consultant at the Nuremberg trials; and the first chair of psychiatry at McGill University. Cameron theorized that mental illness could be corrected by erasing a person's memories and reducing the patient to an infantile blank slate, after which the mind could be rebuilt from scratch. Cameron's ideas attracted the attention of the CIA, which was obsessed with finding the secrets of "brainwashing" and mind control. The CIA financed Cameron's work (and that of many other academics) through a front group called the Human Ecology Fund.[18]

It would be hard to overstate the brutality of Cameron's methods. He gave patients LSD, PCP, barbiturates, and sodium amytal, all designed to disorganize their thoughts. Often he would use insulin to force patients into a coma for weeks or even months at a time, waking them only briefly so they could eat or use the toilet. Sometimes patients would be placed into a dark sensory deprivation chamber, their ears plugged and their eyes covered. One group of patients was paralyzed with curare. Cameron deployed a Page-Russell electroconvulsive therapy (ECT) machine to send shocks to the patient's brain, often several times a day, at 30 to 40 times the recommended voltage. His aim was to make the patient completely disoriented, incontinent of urine and stool, and unable to remember his or her own identity.

Then Cameron attempted to reprogram the patient through a technique he called "psychic driving." He recorded statements and questions from the patient's therapy sessions, put them on a loop, and played the recordings back to the patient continuously. "Do you realize that you are a very hostile person?" the recording might say. "Why do you hate your mother?" Sometimes the recordings would be played from speakers in the ceiling or under a patient's pillow; occasionally they were played inside football helmets that had been wired for sound. Cameron would play the messages continuously for twenty to thirty days, sometimes up to twenty hours a day, often combined with ECT and powerful drugs.

Even judged by the standards of the time, Cameron's work violated the basic principles of research ethics. He never informed his patients they were research subjects. He did not tell them that the "treatment" they were getting was experimental. The procedures Cameron used were invasive and dangerous, and he wound up destroying the lives of many subjects, some of whom were never able to live independently again. When Cameron reported his results, he manipulated the data to exaggerate the effectiveness of his methods. In fact, there was never any sound evidence that his methods would work, other than his own theoretical fantasies. According to Donald Hebb, one of Cameron's colleagues at McGill University, "Cameron was irresponsible—criminally stupid—in that there was no reason to expect that he would get any results from the experiments."[19]

Yet Cameron's experiments did not take place in a locked institution, far from public sight. The Allen Memorial Institute is located in downtown Montreal, on the campus of McGill University, one of the country's elite medical institutions. Cameron had established the institute as an "open" hospital, in rebellion against the ethos of the asylum. His patients were not confined against their will, and Cameron did not allow the routine use of restraints and other forcible means of controlling patients.[20] In fact, most of the patients in Cameron's experiments did not even have schizophrenia or any other psychotic illness that would have seriously impaired their decision-making capacity. Most subjects simply had mild depression or anxiety and were having trouble in their marriages or their careers.[21]

In this sense, Cameron's studies show a dark side to biocitizenship. Cameron took ordinary people with life problems, reclassified them in biomedical terms, and subjected them to invasive medical procedures that were barbaric even by the standards of his time. He was able to do this partly because of the lack of any institutional oversight (no human research protection program, no ethics committee) but also in part because he redefined people as psychiatric patients. Once they were psychiatric patients, it was only a small step further to convince them they desperately needed experimental treatment. Cameron did not need to use force. His charisma, reputation, and social authority as a physician were enough.

## Challenge Studies and Relapse Studies

Starting in the 1970s, U.S. policy makers enacted a series of large-scale bureaucratic interventions aimed at curbing the mistreatment of human subjects. In 1974, Congress passed the National Research Act, creating the National Commission for the Protection of Human Subjects of Biomedical and Behavioral Research. In 1979, that commission issued the Belmont Report, a foundational document that laid out the basic principles for ethical medical research. In 1981, the Department of Health and Human Services (HHS) and the Food and Drug Administration (FDA) adopted formal guidelines for the protection of research subjects; a decade later, fourteen other federal departments and agencies joined HHS and the FDA in adopting those guidelines (now known informally as the Common Rule).[22] At the heart of this research protection system was the establishment of local research ethics committees, or institutional review boards (IRBs), which were charged with reviewing research studies prospectively to ensure that the rights and welfare of subjects are protected.

These changes represented a dramatic improvement in research over-sight. By providing some prospective review, this oversight system made it much less likely that abuses such as Cameron's experiments or the near miss of *Kaimowitz* could occur. Yet some psychiatric researchers contin-ued to mistreat mentally ill subjects in ways that would have provoked outrage if they had occurred in other areas of medicine. Among these are "symptom provocation" or "challenge" studies, in which psychiatric researchers administered amphetamines, ketamine, and other psycho-active drugs to previously stable patients with schizophrenia or bipo-lar disorder in order to provoke a psychotic episode. Challenge studies offered no therapeutic benefit to patients; their purpose was to induce temporary psychosis so that patients could be studied.

The results were often chilling.[23] "Within a few minutes after the in-fusion, Mr. A experienced nausea and motor agitation," a group at the National Institute of Mental Health reported. "Soon thereafter he began thrashing about uncontrollably and appeared to be very angry, display-ing facial grimacing, grunting and shouting . . . 15 minutes after the infu-sion, he shouted, 'It's coming at me again, like getting out of control. It's stronger than I am.' He slammed his fists into the bed and table and im-plored us not to touch him, warning that he might become assaultive."[24]

Challenge studies were neither rare nor hidden. From the mid-1970s through the late 1990s, psychiatric researchers conducted challenge studies at many major American medical centers and published their results in reputable psychiatric journals.[25] At Yale, researchers induced psychotic episodes in patients suffering from schizophrenia by injecting them with m-chlorophenylpiperazine. At the University of Maryland and the National Institute of Mental Health, researchers conducted simi-lar studies with ketamine. Jeffrey Lieberman, who would later become president of the American Psychiatric Association, conducted challenge studies with methylphenidate (Ritalin) for more than a decade.[26] Uni-versity of Cincinnati researchers gave multiple doses of amphetamines to patients experiencing their first psychotic episodes, some as young as eighteen, simply to see if they would get more psychotic with each dose. (They did.)

Psychiatrists defended the studies on two grounds. First, they claimed that the harm of experiencing a psychotic episode was minimal, espe-cially for patients who had already experienced such episodes. (Patients themselves strongly disagreed.) Second, they argued that the patients gave proper informed consent. But, as Robert Whitaker reported in the *Boston Globe*, that claim was not borne out by the facts.[27] When Whitaker reviewed the informed consent forms for challenge studies at the National Institute of Mental Health and four other psychiatric institutions, he did not find a single form in which the researchers directly told patients that they would be given a drug to exacerbate symptoms of psychosis. Yet institutional review boards at each institution had previously deemed the studies ethically acceptable, apparently without reservation.

Similar questions arose with "washout" or "relapse" studies, in which researchers discontinue psychiatric medication from patients in order to observe their unmedicated state or to start another experimental treatment. Most patients with schizophrenia are initially treated with antipsychotic drugs, which carry severe side effects. A relapse study might reveal whether patients with schizophrenia can remain stable or improve either without antipsychotic drugs or on lower doses. However, withdrawing antipsychotic medication can also present serious risks to the patient, including that of suicide.

The most notorious relapse study took place in the late 1980s and early 1990s at the University of California at Los Angeles (UCLA), under the direction of Keith Nuechterlein and Michael Gitlin.[28] With grant funding from the National Institute of Mental Health, Nuechterlein and Gitlin recruited patients who had been recently diagnosed with schizophrenia. In the first phase of the study, the researchers treated patients with an injectable antipsychotic drug (Prolixin) every two weeks for a year. In the second phase of the study, however, the researchers randomized patients into a placebo arm for twelve weeks; if the patients did not relapse, their antipsychotics were discontinued. The researchers followed the patients for another year or until a serious exacerbation of their illness occurred.

Gregory Aller was one of the UCLA study participants.[29] At the age of twenty-four, his mental condition had begun to deteriorate: he claimed to experience visits from space aliens and deceased relatives, and believed that he and his family were under threat from snipers. When Aller was treated with Prolixin in the first phase of the trial, his condition improved dramatically. He earned a 3.8 GPA at Santa Monica College, and his personal and professional relationships were repaired.

But after Aller began the second phase of the study in late 1989 and his medications were discontinued, he experienced a severe relapse and became floridly psychotic again. He lapped water out of a toilet and growled on buses. He became convinced his mother was possessed by the Devil and threatened her with a butcher knife. His parents tried to convince the researchers to put Aller back on medication, but they refused. Aller went for nine months without medication and, according to his parents, never returned to his previous level of function.[30]

Yet things could have been much worse. Another participant in the UCLA study, Antonio Lamadrid, became unstable during the trial's second phase when he stopped receiving treatment. After the study ended, Lamadrid committed suicide by jumping from the roof of a nine-story, on-campus building. In 1994, the Office for the Protection from Research Risks found that Nuechterlein and Gitlin had failed to get proper informed consent from subjects. At that point, according to the *New York Times*, twenty-three of fifty patients had suffered severe relapses after their medication was discontinued.[31]

Few experts dispute that the purpose of the study was important. Antipsychotic drugs can be very dangerous, and it would be extraordinarily useful to know whether some patients can stop taking them and not suffer relapses. Yet the UCLA researchers exposed their subjects to unnecessarily high risks by withdrawing their medication for six months or more and setting an extremely high bar for remedicating them. Rather than putting subjects back on antipsychotics or other treatments at the first signs of a relapse, the researchers allowed them to descend into severe psychosis. The standard for remediation specified that in most cases, subjects would not be remediated until they were often delusional, prone to violence, and thinking about or planning suicide.[32]

As the scandals surrounding challenge and relapse studies show, simply requiring informed consent is not sufficient to protect research subjects from mistreatment, especially if subjects are vulnerable in some way. It is always possible to devise language for consent that is true on technical grounds but also seriously misleading. For instance, Nuechterlein and Gitlin never actually told their subjects that the purpose of the relapse study was to withdraw their medication to see if they would become psychotic again.[33] Instead, their consent forms merely said that the purpose of the study was "to take people like me off medication in a way that will give the most information about medication, its effects on me, and the way the brain works." It also reassured patients that if their condition worsened, the clinic would "use active medication again to improve my condition."

## The Rise of Industry-Funded Psychiatric Research

On June 11, 1994, Susan Endersbe, a forty-one-year-old research subject with schizophrenia, left Fairview Riverside Hospital in Minneapolis on a day pass. Endersbe had been given the pass despite telling nurses that devils were controlling her mind and that she intended to kill herself. After a quick visit to her apartment, Endersbe went to the Franklin Avenue Bridge, climbed over the railing, and threw herself into the Mississippi River.[34]

The study in which Endersbe died was sponsored by the pharmaceutical company Abbott, which was testing an experimental antipsychotic called sertindole. (The drug was never given marketing approval.) The researcher in charge of the study was Dr. Faruk Abuzzahab, a clinical faculty member (and former full-time faculty member) in the Department of Psychiatry at the University of Minnesota. Four years after Endersbe's death, Abuzzahab was sanctioned by the Minnesota Board of Medical Practice for five deaths and forty-one injuries of patients under his care, including Susan Endersbe, citing his "reckless if not wilful, disregard" for their welfare. Seventeen patients were research subjects in industry-sponsored drug studies that Abuzzahab was conducting.[35]

Abuzzahab stood on the leading edge of the trend toward privately conducted clinical trials. Until the late 1980s, pharmaceutical companies generally partnered with academic researchers in universities and teaching hospitals to test experimental drugs. In the 1990s, however, pharmaceutical companies began searching for faster, more efficient ways of recruiting subjects and conducting studies. Many companies began outsourcing trials to private contract research organizations such as Quintiles, Parexel, and Covance, as well as stand-alone clinical trial sites. In 1994, about 65 percent of clinical trials were conducted in academic settings; within ten years, only about 25 percent were.[36] Today, most new drugs are tested not under the supervision of academic physicians but by contract researchers in private practice.

The privatization of clinical trials has produced a number of perverse financial incentives. For instance, contract researchers are often paid on a per-head basis: the more research subjects they recruit, the more they get paid. In fact, pharmaceutical companies pay higher fees for most medical services than insurance companies do. According to sociologist Jill Fisher, any given medical service will generate two to five times the amount of money when a pharmaceutical company is paying the bill rather than a health insurance company or a government agency.[37] For this reason, it is often in the financial interests of a physician-researcher to enroll patients in a clinical trial rather than offering them proven treatment.

IRBs face similar financial incentives. Many private trials are now overseen by for-profit IRBs, which review studies prospectively in exchange for a fee.[38] For-profit IRBs are not rewarded for policing research studies strictly; they are rewarded for evaluating them quickly and efficiently. If an IRB rejects a study as too risky or otherwise unethical, the sponsor is free to submit it to another IRB.[39]

Such conflicts of interest are not limited to the private sector. In early 2015, the Office of the Legislative Auditor for the State of Minnesota issued the results of an investigation into the death of Dan Markingson, a young man from St. Paul who had committed suicide in an industry-sponsored study of antipsychotic drugs at the University of Minnesota eleven years earlier.[40] After experiencing an acute psychotic episode and threatening to commit mass murder, Markingson had been placed under a civil commitment order that required him to comply with the treatment recommendations of his psychiatrist, Dr. Stephen Olson. Olson enrolled him in an industry-sponsored drug trial (the CAFÉ study) over the objections of Markingson's mother, Mary Weiss, who did not believe her son was competent to consent to research. Weiss attempted to have Markingson removed from the study for months, warning that he was in danger of killing himself. On May 8, 2004, Dan Markingson stabbed himself to death with a box cutter.[41]

Although the report by the Office of the Legislative Auditor highlighted the coercive nature of Markingson's recruitment, it also noted that AstraZeneca had prorated its payments to the University of Minnesota based on the number of subjects enrolled in the CAFÉ study. The longer a subject remained in the study, the more money AstraZeneca paid. Each subject who completed the study generated $15,648 for the university. According to the Legislative Auditor, AstraZeneca arranged its payments "in a way that clearly created an incentive to enroll and keep subjects enrolled in the CAFÉ study. We also know that Dr. Olson kept Markingson in the study despite Mary Weiss' repeated warnings that Dan was not well and the study medication was not working."[42]

Additionally, the IRB panel overseeing the CAFÉ study was riddled with conflicts of interest. The chair of the panel was Dr. David Adson—a faculty member in the Department of Psychiatry, a colleague of the study's principal investigator and coinvestigator, and director of the research clinic in which the CAFÉ study was managed. Adson was also a consultant to AstraZeneca, the sponsor of the CAFÉ study. From 2002 to 2010, Adson received more than $149,000 in consulting, research, and speaking fees from AstraZeneca. He had received $5,200 as "compensation for services" in 2004, the year in which Markingson died, and $16,884 more the next year. In total, Adson received more than $650,000 from the pharmaceutical industry from 2002 to 2010 while serving on the IRB.

Yet the problems with the Markingson case extended well beyond financial conflicts of interest. Markingson was recruited from a locked psychiatric unit, to which he had been involuntarily committed, and into a research study conducted by the psychiatrist in charge of his clinical care. When he was later given a "stay of commitment," it was under the condition that he must comply with the recommendations of his psychiatrist or else face confinement to a state psychiatric facility. Thus, in many ways, the coercion behind Markingson's recruitment was not that different from the forces identified in Goffman's *Asylums* and the *Kaimowitz* case forty years earlier.

## Conclusion: From Coercion to Exploitation

If vulnerability is a diminished ability to protect oneself from mistreatment, it should be uncontroversial to say that patients with severe mental illnesses such as schizophrenia are highly vulnerable, if for no other reason than the fact that their decision-making capacity is often seriously impaired. Yet such patients are often doubly vulnerable by virtue of their life circumstances, especially the way they are treated by the health care system. And over the past forty years, those circumstances have undergone dramatic changes.

When John Doe of the *Kaimowitz* case agreed to have experimental psychosurgery, he had been involuntarily confined to a state institution for seventeen years.[43] His autonomy had been diminished by years of institutional control, and he believed that submitting to a research study was his only way out of the institution. Patients such as Walter Jorden face pressures of a very different kind. No one coerced Jorden into enrolling in a research study. No one threatened or manipulated him. Jorden signed up because he was poor and desperate, and a paid research study offered a temporary solution.

Research studies like the one in which Jorden took part are only one segment of a larger economic system that Melinda Cooper and Cathy Waldby have called "clinical labor."[44] In this system, people essentially rent out their bodies in order to provide medical services for others: gestational surrogacy, organ brokerage, egg and sperm sales, and paid participation in medical research. Much of this clinical labor comes from impoverished but healthy people, many of them in the developing world. What makes clinical labor unique is not just that desperation for money may lead individuals to take risks that may affect their wellbeing. Poor people have been forced to take risky jobs for centuries. With much clinical labor, however, risk is built right into the nature of the job. The very purpose of a phase I clinical trial is to determine if a drug is too risky to be marketed.

In *The Politics of Life Itself*, Nikolas Rose paints a nuanced but often hopeful picture of biological citizens: active, knowledgeable, empowered by their reconfigured biological identities.[45] In the 1980s, for example, AIDS activists organized themselves into communities marked by their status as HIV-positive in order to demand new rights, powers, and social support, including access to experimental treatments. Rose identifies new social groups emerging around shared identities as sufferers of conditions such as Huntington's disease, depression, and attention deficit/hyperactivity disorder, exploring the ways in which the individuals in these groups shape and monitor their inner lives. Of course, Rose understands the ways in which corporate and professional authorities can manipulate these identities for questionable ends. When Eli Lilly encourages potential customers to see themselves as sufferers of premenstrual dysphoric disorder, for instance, it is only because Lilly has a treatment for the condition that it is trying to sell.

Yet providers of clinical labor represent an even more sinister side of biocitizenship. Like other biological citizens, clinical laborers are identified by a set of biomedical characteristics: a healthy kidney, their fitness to bear children, their eligibility for a particular kind of research study. But this new identity is generally not one that these people choose for themselves, nor is it one that they can use for political ends. The value of clinical laborers is purely instrumental, and it lies solely in their bodies. What made Walter Jorden valuable as a commodity was not his personal history or any particular skills but rather a set of biomedical characteristics that rendered him eligible to test the safety of an antipsychotic drug.

Most research guidelines intended to protect patients like Jorden were written for an earlier era. The overarching ethical concern of the 1960s and 1970s was external pressure from people in positions of power—psychiatrists, prison wardens, parole boards, and other institutional authorities. But the threats presented by for-profit clinical trial sites are less like those of prisons than like those of sweatshops. And the ethical question is: At what point does it become unfair to take advantage of a vulnerable person's desperation?

Research guidelines typically say that a subject's decision to take part in research must be completely voluntary, without any evidence of external constraint. The operative terms are concepts such as "coercion" and "undue influence." However, the vocabulary of "coercion" and "undue influence" is not ideally suited for the problems raised when research participation is transformed into an economic exchange. It may be wrong to offer desperate people money to take risks to their health, but it is not coercive. Coercion typically involves a threat, not an offer. Like sweatshop workers, many poor research subjects are actually grateful for the paycheck that comes with enrollment in a study.

The concept of "undue influence" is not much better. As a warning against authority figures exerting pressure on potential subjects and "unduly influencing" their decision, the concept makes sense. But undue influence, like coercion, is ill suited for the problems presented by economic exchanges. For instance, IRBs typically warn research sponsors not to pay their subjects too much for fear that excessive payment might unduly influence their decision, thereby tempting them into enrolling in risky, unpleasant, or degrading trials against their better judgment. But how much money constitutes an undue influence? A large sum that is too tempting to resist for a person of meager financial means may be easily resistible by a wealthier person. On the other hand, if payment is kept very low, it seems unfair to poor subjects, whose only reason for enrolling in the study may be financial desperation.

A better concept would be exploitation. According to conventional understandings, exploitation means taking unfair advantage of another person, often someone in a position of vulnerability. The key concept here is unfairness. Unlike coercion and undue influence, exploitation captures the idea that some bargains violate basic notions of justice. A bargain may be unfair because payment is too low, but it may also be unfair because one party is exposed to dangerous conditions, or deprived of something he or she deserves, or may have been offered the bargain when in no position to protect his or her own interests.

Was Walter Jorden exploited? Of course he was. At a time when he was in an exceptionally vulnerable state—mentally ill, battling drug addiction, living below the poverty line in a crumbling recovery house—Jorden was offered payment to test an experimental drug under conditions in which he was not kept safe. But there are many other varieties of exploitation, just as there are many types of vulnerability. The victims of the Tuskegee syphilis study were vulnerable to exploitation because of their poverty, their lack of education, and the racial attitudes of the Jim Crow South. The victims of the Willowbrook hepatitis study were vulnerable to exploitation because of their mental disabilities and the horrific conditions at the Willowbrook State School. Dan Markingson was vulnerable to exploitation because of his impaired mental state and his civil commitment order.

Despite significant changes in treatment over the past fifty years, mentally ill patients remain extremely vulnerable to exploitation. Some are so mentally incapacitated that they are incapable of giving proper informed consent. Many are homeless or living in halfway houses, recovery houses, or room and boards. Some are hospitalized on locked wards. Others are under civil commitment orders that restrict their liberty or constrain their ability to make medical decisions. Yet there is no mention of exploitation in federal research guidelines. Nor does exploitation appear in the Nuremberg Code, the Declaration of Helsinki, or any other major code of research ethics or set of research guidelines. Until our research oversight system formally recognizes the possibility of exploitation, the mentally ill are likely to remain vulnerable and unprotected.

## NOTES

1 Carl Elliott, "The Best-Selling, Billion-Dollar Pills Tested on Homeless People: How the Destitute and the Mentally Ill Are Being Used as Human Lab Rats," *Matter*, last modified July 27, 2014, https://medium.com.

2 Carl Elliott, "Guinea Pigging: Healthy Human Subjects for Drug-Safety Trials Are in Demand. But Is It a Living?," *New Yorker*, January 7, 2008, 36–41.

3 "Kaimowitz v. Department of Mental Health for the State of Michigan. No. 73-19434-AW (Mich. Cir. Ct., Wayne County, July 10, 1973)," *Mental Disability Law Reporter* 1, no. 2 (1976): 147–54.

4 Ibid.

5 Ibid.

6 Ibid.; for more on issues concerning psychosurgery in the 1970s, see Jenell Johnson, *American Lobotomy: A Rhetorical History* (Ann Arbor: University of Michigan Press, 2014).

7 Ralph Slovenko, "Commentary: On Psychosurgery," *Hastings Center Report* 5, no. 5 (1975): 19–22.

8 "Kaimowitz v. Department of Mental Health."

9 The National Commission for the Protection of Human Subjects of Biomedical Behavioral Research. *Research Involving Prisoners: Report and Recommendations*, 1976.

10 Erving Goffman, *Asylums; Essays on the Social Situation of Mental Patients and Other Inmates* (Garden City, NY: Anchor Books, 1961).

11 Ibid., 6.

12 Ibid., 7.

13 Ibid.

14 Ibid., 358.

15 Ibid.

16 Ibid., 353.

17 "MK Ultra," *The Fifth Estate*, CBC Radio–Canada, March 11, 1980.

18 Rebecca Lemov, "Brainwashing's Avatar: The Curious Career of Dr. Ewen Cameron," *Grey Room 45* (2011): 68.

19 Anne Collins, *In the Sleep Room: The Story of the CIA Brainwashing Experiments in Canada* (Toronto: Lester and Orpen Dennys, 1988), 174.

20 Ibid.

21 Ibid.

22 U.S. Department of Health and Human Services, "Code of Federal Regulations: Title 45 Public Welfare Department of Health and Human Services Part 46 Protection of Human Subjects," January 15, 2010, www.hhs.gov.

23 Jean Heller, "Syphilis Victims in the U.S. Study Went Untreated for 40 Years," *New York Times*, July 26, 1972.

24 Donald L. Rosenstein, "Psychiatric Symptom–Provoking Studies: An Ethical Appraisal," in *The Ethical Challenges of Human Research: Selected Essays*, ed. Franklin G. Miller (New York: Oxford University Press, 2012), 56.

25  Robert Whitaker, *Mad in America: Bad Science, Bad Medicine, and the Enduring Mistreatment of the Mentally Ill* (Cambridge, MA: Basic Books, 2003).

26  Robert Whitaker and Dolores Kong, "Doing Harm: Research on the Mentally Ill," *Boston Globe*, last modified November 15, 1998, www.narpa.org.

27  Ibid.

28  Philip J. Hilts, "Agency Faults a U.C.L.A. Study for Suffering of Mental Patients," *New York Times*, March 10, 1994, www.nytimes.com.

29  James Willwerth, "Tinkering with Madness," *Time*, June 24, 2001, http://content.time.com.

30  Hilts, "Agency Faults a U.C.L.A. Study"; Whitaker and Kong, "Doing Harm."

31  Hilts, "Agency Faults a U.C.L.A. Study."

32  James Willwerth, "How to Tell If the Men in White Coats Are Lying to You [Investigative Journalism and Research Abuse]," *Accountability in Research* 5, nos. 1–3 (1997): 51–58.

33  Ibid.

34  Robert Whitaker, "Lure of Riches Fuels Testing," *Boston Globe*, last modified 1998, psychrights.org.

35  Gardiner Harris and Janet Roberts, "After Sanctions, Doctors Get Drug Company Pay," *New York Times*, June 3, 2007, www.nytimes.com.

36  Robert Steinbrook, "Gag Clauses in Clinical-Trial Agreements," *New England Journal of Medicine* 352, no. 21 (2005): 2160–62.

37  Jill A. Fisher, *Medical Research for Hire: The Political Economy of Pharmaceutical Clinical Trials* (New Brunswick, NJ: Rutgers University Press, 2009).

38  Trudo Lemmens and Benjamin Freedman, "Ethics Review for Sale? Conflict of Interest and Commercial Research Review Boards," *Milbank Quarterly* 78, no. 4 (2000): 547–84.

39  Ezekiel J. Emanuel, Trudo Lemmens, and Carl Elliott, "Should Society Allow Research Ethics Boards to Be Run as for-Profit Enterprises? (The PloS Medicine Debate)," *PLoS Medicine* 3, no. 7 (2006): E309.

40  James Nobles, "A Clinical Drug Study at the University of Minnesota Department of Psychiatry: The Dan Markingson Case," March 19, 2015, www.auditor.leg.state.mn.us.

41  Carl Elliott, "The Deadly Corruption of Clinical Trials," *Mother Jones*, September/October 2010, www.motherjones.com.

42  Ibid.

43  Candace J. Fabri, "Constitutional Law—an Involuntarily Detained Mental Patient's Informed Consent Is Invalid for Experimental Psychosurgery," *Chicago-Kent Law Review* 50, no. 3 (1974): 526–40.

44  Melinda Cooper and Catherine Waldby, *Clinical Labor: Tissue Donors and Research Subjects in the Global Bioeconomy* (Durham, NC: Duke University Press, 2014).

45  Nikolas Rose, *The Politics of Life Itself: Biomedicine, Power, and Subjectivity in the Twenty-First Century* (Princeton, NJ: Princeton University Press, 2007).

## PART III

Activism and Resistance

7

# Feeding Hunger-Striking Prisoners

*Biopolitics and Impossible Citizenship*

NAYAN SHAH

In December 2015, after as much as a year in detention, ten Bangladeshi asylum seekers went on a hunger strike in Florida's Krome Immigration Detention Center. After two weeks, all ten men were brought in wheelchairs into the federal district courtroom in Miami, where U.S. District Judge Cecilia Altonaga ordered involuntary blood draws, urinalysis, weigh-ins, and routine medical examinations to monitor their health during the hunger strikes. After three weeks, medical testimony documenting the average loss of 15 percent of their body weight, the metabolic consequences of self-starvation, and rapid depletion of energy reserves resulted in an emergency order to force-feed the men. Judge Altonaga followed prison doctors' medical guidance in her determination that force-feeding in prison would be more efficient and effective than gaining informed consent for hospitalization.[1]

This particular outcome is emblematic of how the biomedical management of life processes shapes hunger strikes according to biopolitical logics, by measuring subsistence and bodily endurance without nourishment, tracking physiological effects of starvation, and calculating the limit of survival. Judges and prison administrators, confronted with persistent and prolonged food refusal, have endorsed medical technology and procedures of artificial feeding, often by force. Medical professionals often appraise hunger strikers' condition within a broader biopolitical framework that administers and regulates life processes aggregated on the level of populations. Biopolitical procedures exercise the power "to qualify, measure, appraise and hierarchize" individuals through establishing population norms, standards, and averages.[2]

Since the 1980s, the dissemination of medical information and access to biomedical technology have contributed to ways that empowered individuals, networks, and groups can influence and mobilize the tools and technologies of bioscience. This empowered engagement informs the concept of biocitizenship, coined by Nikolas Rose to address the "biological presumptions" that mold "what it means to be a citizen." However, it also underpins the "distinctions between actual, potential, troublesome and impossible citizens."[3] This appraisal and comparison require surveillance, screening, and medicating of the population to be managed. Biopolitics makes visible contingency and precarious difference through this operation of differential access, treatment, vitality, and embodiment. This precarity and vulnerability are particularly acute for those people who are characterized as "impossible citizens"—the condition of carceral subjects and stateless persons who are judged to be incapable of following otherwise conventional norms of interaction and whose citizenship status is suspended indefinitely. Biocitizenship can produce a normative horizon insofar as it offers an avenue for informed consent and patient participation in medical decision making, but it simultaneously impels a reckoning of inequality and disparity in practice and in the recognition of needs and rights, access, and treatment.[4]

This essay examines the imperatives of biopolitical knowledge and the challenges of biocitizenship that shaped the normative procedures of feeding hunger strikers in 1980s South Africa and in contemporary Australia, Israel, and the United States' military base in Guantanamo Bay. In the twentieth and twenty-first centuries, three critical problems for biomedical intervention emerge: When to feed the hunger striker? What to feed the hunger striker? And how to feed the hunger striker? The question of when to feed the hunger striker entails both circumstances of the physician's ethical quandary of intervening—often without a patient's consent—as well as the actual timing of judging when a fast's duration could have irreversible consequences for health and vitality.

Indeed, artificial feeding therapy and overruling the prisoner's refusal to eat has, more often than not, been couched as a question of bioethics. Is artificial feeding therapeutic or coercive? Prison doctors undoubtedly express discomfort about force-feeding, yet overseeing a slow prison death through food refusal raises its own ethical problems. Prison officials contend that force-feeding procedures are therapeutic, not punitive, and as such are indispensable life-preserving mechanisms. Officials have presented so-called artificial feeding as safe, humane, and ethically uncomplicated. Nonetheless, advocates for prisoners contend that the procedure is torturous, degrading, and life-threatening. From the prisoner's perspective, force-feeding is not lifesaving; instead, it causes vomiting, nightmares, and intense pain. As Mahmudul Hasan, one of the Bangladeshi asylum seekers, retorted to the order for force-feeding: "We came here to escape violence and danger in our country. But it seems like this place is like Guantánamo. ICE would rather force-feed hunger-strikers than listen to our basic demands for freedom."[5]

These dramatically different perspectives challenge the very definition of life and living and raise questions about the quality of life possible under forcible feeding. Opponents to the force-feeding of hunger strikers argue that it is an unwarranted bodily intrusion, while proponents frame it as a necessary lifesaving procedure. Both positions, however, miss how the practice "transforms the bodies of hunger strikers into a population of dependents who must be managed."[6] The technologies, substance, and timing of feeding involve judgments about normative human bodily conditions, reflexes, and responses—transformations across a century that reflect the ascendancy of biomedicine, its relationship to the state, and the criteria of bioethical evaluation that both challenge and constrain political agency, particularly of those whom the state determines are impossible citizens.

This essay traces the ways in which the ethical dilemmas physicians have faced in prescribing feeding against the will of the prisoner recur in different places over the course of a century, enacting a familiar conflict in which the prisoner's protest against the preservation of life and the state's control over life and death are at odds. Central to my argument is that the material strategies, technologies, and substances of feeding hunger strikers have changed and been consolidated into biopolitical norms by the late twentieth century. The mechanisms to ensure feeding depend more systematically on biomedical measures and utilize prosthetic and artificial techniques—mechanisms that shift the grounds from ethics to biopolitics and in turn shift the terrain of intelligible and effective resistance.

## Force-Feeding as Early Response to Hunger Strikes: Ethical Challenges

As the history of hunger striking shows, the verbal declaration of refusal to eat may be made to prison guards and relayed to administrators, to lawyers and family members, and frequently announced in the press. For instance, British suffrage activists warned prison officials that they would refuse to eat unless treated as political prisoners. In 1909, Evelyn Burkitt dramatically declared: "If I should die through my fasting, my death will lie at your door, but I am ready to lay down my life, to bring about the freedom of my Sisters."[7] At the time of Burkitt's strike, the combination of the prisoners' declaration of fasting and the guards' observance of refused meals in a twenty-four hour period could trigger immediate and forcible feeding as medical intervention.

By the late twentieth century, patient declarations and vague observations of the duration of self-starvation and the number of meal refusals had given way to a systemic and normative accounting of the number of missed meals, the number of days without food, the measurement of food intake, prisoner weight loss, and an inventory of symptoms of bodily distress or metabolic derangement. By the mid-twentieth century, physicians, dietitians, and scientists assessed and experimented with pureed food substances or artificial substances to determine what would be most efficacious and vital for nourishing the starving body. They replaced crude eighteenth- and nineteenth-century instruments such as the speculum oris to pry open jaws, funnels and eel skin tubes to pour liquid mixes down the throats of those in slave ships, asylums, and prisons, with mid-twentieth-century antiseptic and plastic technologies of mouth openers, feeding tubes, and pumps.

Medical management of hunger strikers entailed biopolitical calculations of human subsistence requirements that marked the endurance of pain and limits of survival for the self-starving prisoner. The biomedical imperative to coax the resumption of eating, whether voluntary or coerced, steers discussion and experimentation to the substances physicians recommend to safely replenish nutrients and calories and alleviate bodily shock and distress. Biomedical technologies and remedies proposed to reverse the damage of starvation and prolong life. Medical management both measured how long the average adult human body could survive without food and calibrated techniques and volume of refeeding needed to restore nutrients necessary for metabolic functioning and to forestall anticipated damage to organs and vital systems.

Medical techniques, therapies, and procedures that are applied in hospitals take a very different cast when administered on impossible citizens in carceral conditions, in stark contrast to a notion of biocitizenship predicated on the basic values of individual consent, volition, and self-determination of human biological and bodily capacity. In gauging the length of self-starvation and its physiological consequences, "life" had become an independent, objective, and measurable substance. Nevertheless, the differential status of social and political groups, particularly the troublesome and impossible citizens locked in prison and detention, challenged the abstraction of the population and life processes "epistemologically and practically" from "concrete living beings and the singularity of individual experience."[8] For example, the use of physical force and constraint techniques to administer food was remarkably continuous in British prisons from the early twentieth century to the 1970s despite its many ethical entailments. The physical force required to artificially feed required several attendants to hold down suffrage activist Ellen Barwell, with a makeshift straitjacket of a "blanket folded round her, her wrists and ankles being held by attendants." The attendants restrained her in an armchair and held her head from behind; then one of the attendants used their finger and thumb to compress Barwell's nostrils so she would open her mouth, and then they administered "milk with Valentine's Meat Juice."[9] The attendants returned every three hours through the night to give Barwell more liquid; by the following morning, she had taken twelve ounces of milk and Valentine's Meat Juice in sips as directed and after several attempts of forced milk drinking.[10] In a Birmingham prison in 1909, prison medical officers used the same formula to forcibly feed hunger-striking suffrage activists.[11]

More than half a century later, overwhelming force continued in feeding Irish Republican Army (IRA) hunger-striking sisters Marian and Delours Price, who were convicted for their roles in 1973 car bombings in London. They went on hunger strikes for 200 days and were force-fed for 167 days until May 1974. Marian Price recounted the experience of force-feeding in an interview:

> Four male prison officers tie you into the chair so tightly with sheets you can't struggle. You clench your teeth to try to keep your mouth closed but they push a metal spring device around your jaw to prise it open. They force a wooden clamp with a hole in the middle into your mouth. Then, they insert a big rubber tube down that. They hold your head back. You can't move. They throw whatever they like into the food mixer—orange juice, soup, or cartons of cream if they want to beef up the calories. They take jugs of this gruel from the food mixer and pour it into a funnel attached to the tube.[12]

After 1974, government authorities discontinued force-feeding because the physical resistance the IRA hunger strikers mounted could lead to life-endangering consequences.[13] The Price sisters, for example, suffered medical complications from their force-feeding, including mouth sores and the permanent loosening of their teeth due to the use of mouth clamps. Marian Price also claimed that on one occasion the feeding tube was mistakenly inserted into her lung: "I felt like I was drowning. I passed out. They carried me back to my cell. The doctors were standing over me when I came round. If it had been food, not water in the tube, it would have killed me."[14] As Corinna Howland argues, "The logic of life-preservation enacted through force-feeding represents a totalizing phenomenon—emerging as a form of violent care where the preservation of the welfare and life of the prisoner is paradoxically pursued to the point of violence."[15] The enactment of violent care to ensure life preservation presents a dystopic contradiction that reflects biopolitics' extension of life and vitality for some and its acceptance of death for others.

The Price sisters contested the practice of force-feeding and instigated proceedings against the Home Office. The British Medical Association Ethics Committee advocated for physician autonomy and authority for the decision to force-feed. The Labor government home secretary Roy Jenkins issued new guidance after parliamentary inquiries.[16] Jenkins admitted, "Distasteful and objectionable though artificial feeding is, it has been judged preferable to allowing the prisoner to die or his health to seriously deteriorate." Despite the British state's preference to control prisoner life and health, however, the government would no longer require prison physicians and nurses to "resort to artificial feeding (whether by tube or intravenously)" and would follow prisoners' consent to feeding irrespective of "inevitable deterioration in his health . . . without medical intervention."[17] As a consequence, the British government, when confronted with the Maze Prison crisis in Belfast, Ireland, in 1981, ordered prison administrators and medical officers to monitor the deteriorating conditions, but did not forcibly feed the prisoners. After sixty-six days, Bobby Sands starved himself to death, and nine other hunger strikers died after him. Several relatives of remaining prisoners on hunger strike intervened when the prisoners lost consciousness, requesting that medical personnel give them nourishment, thereby ending their fasts.[18] The deaths at the Maze Prison sparked international outrage and consternation in the medical profession and reanimated the debate over the ethics of allowing hunger-striking prisoners to die or feeding them against their will.

## South Africa and the Biomedical Response to Self-Starvation

In 1989, during hunger strikes by South African detainees, hundreds of prisoners were released into public hospitals for emergency care. As hunger-striking detainees were released into Johannesburg hospitals under the supervision of the medical school faculty of the University of Witswatersrand, many of these physicians and nurses mobilized to implement new protocols of medical ethics and care for the detainees, who were shackled to their beds and guarded by South African police. Rather than considering the refusal to eat as a problem of prison discipline, the new guidelines emphasized the bioethical norm of patient consent for medical treatment. The new guidelines emphasized that physicians' primary duty is to the fasting prisoners, being respectful of their will and helping them make informed judgments. The guidelines allowed informed care, development of doctor-patient relationships, trust, and confidentiality. Physicians, however, were to refrain from pressuring patients to stop voluntary total fasts. They had to put aside their insistence for life preservation to calibrate their therapeutic counsel to the patients' satisfaction and obtain their consent. Once detainees were in the hospital, physicians modeled newly accepted North American and Western European norms of medical ethics, for example, when they allowed for "a second opinion from a doctor whom [the prisoner] trusts that was impossible to obtain in carceral institutions."[19]

Tracking a broader shift from the use of disciplinary power to bio-medical norms, South African physicians also implemented biomedical measures to propel hospitalization of hunger strikers. Whereas, in South Africa, detention prison authorities did not report a hunger striker who had not eaten for five days, Kalk and his colleagues recommended a measure of 10 percent loss of actual body weight to trigger hospitalization and medical monitoring; at 15 percent loss of body weight, patients with consent should be transferred to a high-care hospital.[20] Both of these guidelines were premised on a level of regular medical monitoring of weight both before and during a hunger strike.

Academic physicians affiliated with the University of Witswatersrand documented the condition of the hunger strikers through their recovery. Because hunger strikes endured through the participation of fresh groups of detainees and political prisoners during the early 1990s, Drs. William Kalk and Yusuf Veriava were able to engage in consent-based academic research studies that documented the medical histories of thirty-three persons on total voluntary fast. The Kalk and Veriava research studies published in medical journals in Britain and South Africa and the struggles of mass hunger strikers in South Africa and Turkey put pressure on the World Medical Association to review the ethical guidelines on voluntary protest fasting and treatment.[21]

Kalk and Veriava's study of thirty-three South African political poisoners, hospitalized after hunger strikes of up to twenty-eight days, provided the first medical study of the physiology and psychology of hunger strikers and a more accurate medical understanding of bodily and temporal processes of starvation.[22] The study detailed rapid physiological changes: during the first few days of starvation, the body consumes its stores of glycogen in the liver and muscle, leading to substantial weight lost. After the second week, the body enters "starvation mode" and then "mines" the muscles, bone marrow, and vital organs for nutrients. This "mining" can impair the functioning of said muscles, bone, and organs. Within these two weeks, hunger strikers experience symptoms of "feeling faint and dizzy" and are often confined to bed. Many patients experience a substantial reduction in effective thyroid function, often resulting in weakness and a sensation of feeling cold. Three-quarters of those studied experienced abdominal pain and dehydration. Under voluntary total fasting, individuals may lose their feelings of thirst and hunger. The study affirmed the experiential knowledge of fasters about fluid intake and the nutrient necessity of salt in guidelines advising that fluid intake must be maintained at about 1.5 liters per day supplemented by half a teaspoon of salt. The study of detainees showed 77 percent of hunger strikers to be clinically depressed at the time of admission to hospital, measured by an independent psychiatrist, although they also demonstrated features similar to those of post-traumatic stress disorder.[23]

After prolonged fasting, the pace and kind of refeeding can precipitate potentially lethal metabolic and physiological complications. Refeeding syndrome can result in cardiac arrhythmias, cardiac failure, convulsions, and comas. Close monitoring of blood biochemistry is required to prevent refeeding syndrome. Also needed is the careful addition of oral supplements of key vitamins and minerals such as potassium, phosphate, magnesium, thiamine, and vitamin B. Patients who have been starved for some time often experience gastrointestinal disturbance during refeeding, in particular abdominal pain, reflux symptoms, nausea, and diarrhea.[24] Refeeding syndrome was first recognized during World War II when prisoners were released to American military bases in the Philippines. It was also noted following the large-scale famine that spread across Europe and Asia during the final years of the war, which left millions of starving victims in addition to the survivors of concentration camps, where malnutrition was ubiquitous. The Minnesota Starvation Experiment, a clinical study performed at the University of Minnesota between November 19, 1944, and December 20, 1945, on volunteer conscientious objectors was instrumental in investigating the effects of resumed feeding for previously starved persons. The investigation was designed to determine the physiological and psychological effects of severe and prolonged dietary restriction and the efficacy of various dietary rehabilitation methods. The adaption of the study's results demonstrated an early instance of the shift in medical understanding away from the use of disciplinary power to feed to biopolitical measures to manage the pace and substance of refeeding. Although the final results were published in 1950 in a text titled *The Biology of Human Starvation*, relief workers used the preliminary data to combat famine conditions in the immediate aftermath of World War II.[25]

In the first part of the century, popular solutions used familiar food products to deliver a diet high in protein, fat, and carbohydrates. Max

Einhorn, a German physician who developed the nasogastric tube, used milk, raw eggs, and lactose in the feeding solution he administered. Other physicians added dextrose and stimulants such as whiskey. However, patients could not always tolerate these feeding mixtures. Hospitals and asylum and prison kitchens finely pureed or liquefied the mixtures, sometimes using cooked foods. However, the cost, labor-intensive preparation, and dangers of contamination in preparation or storage encouraged the rise of sterile synthesized formulas.

Developments in nutritional science, hospital treatment procedures, and enteral delivery technologies had moved physicians away from the ad hoc feeding solutions that were popular in the first half of the century. In the late 1930s and 1940s, scientists and corporations began to experiment with developing hydrolysate-based formula that fortified milk-based products with nutrients and vitamins. The feeding solution requirements drew upon fat, protein, carbohydrate, vitamins, and mineral amounts developed by the U.S. Recommended Daily Allowance, first established in 1941 to create national nutritional standards to provide superior nutrition for civilians and military personnel. Indeed, the idea of a nutritional minimum was a critical standard for the exercise of biocitizenship at the time. Research into the role of amino acids and nutrients in understanding processes of digestion, absorption, and gut physiology led to modern synthetic enteral formulas. In the 1950s and 1960s, hospital physicians, concerned with malnutrition and infection, accelerated the development of chemical enteral solutions. These solutions were further enhanced by NASA-supported research that developed concentrated "astronaut food" through "elemental diets."

Commercial mass production of enteral feeding formulas, standardized tubes and pumps, and the demonstrated lower incidence of complications, lower cost, and ease of access stimulated demand in institutional settings in the United States, Western Europe, and Japan. Since 1980, more than 100 enteral formulas have been available in the U.S. and global market serving hospitals, nursing homes, prisons, the military, and consumers. These specialized formulas deliver high-nutrient density and can be adjusted to meet a variety of metabolic and nutritional needs.[26] The market for nutrition formulas is dominated by a number of global pharmaceutical and food companies, including Novartis, Nestlé, and Abbott Labs, each of which markets a wide array of nutritional formulas for infants, adults, and cancer patients.[27]

## Managing Hunger Strikers by Biomedical Algorithms

These research findings and attendant corporate developments shaped care protocols in prisons and hospitals across the globe as well as adapted to procedures of monitoring hunger strikers and refeeding them at the U.S. military base in Guantanamo Bay, where up to 750 prisoners for the U.S. war in Afghanistan were held without charge or trial. By September 2005, nearly 200 prisoners were on hunger strike, and more than 20 of them were being force-fed by nasal tubes. During another wave of hunger strikes in 2013, a document titled *Standard Operating Procedure: Medical Management of Hunger Strikers at Guantanamo Bay* (SOP) was leaked to the press. This document drew from U.S. federal and military prison policies and delineated treatment protocols for diagnosing hunger strikes and for the specific administration of the procedures, contents, and timetable for enteral feeding.

\* \* \*

The approach described in the SOP is biopolitical practice par excellence that applies normative horizons of biocitizenship onto the conditions of rightless persons. The Department of Defense and the Joint Task Force Guantanamo promoted a policy to "protect, preserve, and promote life" and specifically to prevent "serious adverse health effects and death from hunger strikes." The policy directed the Joint Medical Group staff to make "reasonable efforts" for prisoners' "voluntary consent for medical treatment." However, diagnostic and treatment protocols outlined enteral feeding exclusively as the necessary response to the refusal to eat and as the prison's imperative to "preserve health and life" irrespective of "consent from the detainee."[28]

The algorithm for hunger strike diagnosis distinguished between refusing food occasionally and a total hunger strike by calibrating food intake and taking bodily measurements. Refusal of nine consecutive meals (defined as the consumption of 500 calories) constituted a hunger strike. Two eight-ounce containers of Ensure® could substitute for a regular meal.[29] The record-keeping protocol "Medical Management and Evaluation of Hunger Striker" inventoried missed meals, created a register of "an intake (food/fluids) history," and combined this with the documentation of vital signs, weight, and the calculation of ideal body weight, based on general population averages of height and weight. The loss of 85 percent of ideal body weight could also trigger "involuntary medical treatment."

The algorithmic approach enabled force-feeding to continue but on different grounds and through different institutional logics that operated on the measurement and calibration of biomedical universals that decontextualize the coercion and violence of prison and aligned the conscious protest of food refusal with bodily obstructions and intolerances of chronic illness.

* * *

For the initial three to five days after beginning enteral feeding, the SOP recommended daily lab urinalysis; serum basic metabolic profile; liver function tests; and tests for magnesium, phosphate, and calcium.[30] After achieving "sufficient caloric intake" for three days, the detainee is removed from the hunger strike list and transferred to an observation block for further monitoring. In a stunning convergence of biomedicine and biocapital, the enteral nutrition menu begins with Pulmocare®, an Abbot Labs product that provides high-calorie nutrition that is halal, kosher, and gluten-free and was specially designed to provide nutrition to people with chronic obstructive pulmonary disease, cystic fibrosis, or respiratory failure. Steady daily increases in mixtures of Pulmocare are supplemented with Morton's salt substitute and table salt in order to provide 2,300 milligrams of potassium, 2,000 milligrams of chloride, and 2,300 milligrams of sodium. Over the next several days, the dosage, water mixture, and pace of infusion of Pulmocare are increased to provide steady increases in caloric intake to 1,500 total calories per day or the equivalent of four cans of Ensure Plus® or Nestlé's Boost Plus® with nutrient supplements, with supplemented liquid Centrum to ensure strikers received vitamin and mineral minimums. In addition, there is a recommended repertoire of over-the-counter medications with precise dosage to combat a variety of symptoms during feedings, including pain, headache, indigestion, heartburn, postnasal drip, and nausea. After discharge from the detention hospital, the detainee would have continuous feeding and hydration transferred to what is called the "feeding block," continued enteral nutrition after the detainee "clinically demonstrates tolerance of hydration."[31]

The procedures enumerated by the SOP and the application of artificial feeding by force participate in a dystopic future of extending life through a deliberate enclosure of monitoring, surveillance, and carceral control. Forcible feeding procedures put an individual on elaborate protocols and instituted biomedical record keeping that constantly assesses the hunger-striking prisoner against weight and metabolic norms. In this context, detainees' strategies of questioning, interrupting, and disrupting the feeding block revealed their resolve to challenge carceral authority over their lives.[32] Nevertheless, any attempt by the force-fed patient to slow the flow of feeding solution, direct the order of ingredients, request the use of the toilet during feeding, or express experiences of pain and nausea is met with a precisely tailored response to ensure that the staff acts in an equitable, "safe, humane and consistent manner" and to corral detainees from developing a "measure of control over an involuntary process,"[33] demonstrating the stunning effectivity of medical intervention to recast force-feeding according to biopolitical logics and to render the individual being feed as an incompetent person for whom care regimens must be imposed.

In 2013, Guantanamo prisoner Abu Wa'el Dhiab, a Syrian national, whose detention was prolonged despite his being cleared for release in 2009, challenged the government in the U.S. federal courts to end his forcible feeding. In July 2013, federal district court judge Gladys Kessler took evidence from detainee statements and international medical associations and institutions. Kessler made clear that the practice of "force-feeding is a painful, humiliating and degrading process." However, she rejected the legal bid by a Guantanamo prisoner seeking to block his force-feeding there during the Ramadan holiday, noting that the Patriot Act strips her of jurisdiction over claims relating to the treatment of detainees.[34] The following year, Judge Kessler responded to the continuation of Dhiab's hunger strike and his request to no longer be forcibly extracted from his cell and put on the feeding block by stating that "the Court is in no position to make the complex medical decisions necessary to keep Mr. Dhiab alive." Due to the "intransigence of the Department of Defense," she continued, "Mr. Dhiab may well suffer unnecessary pain from certain enteral feeding practices and forcible cell extractions. However, the Court simply cannot let Mr. Dhiab die."[35] During the trial, the U.S. government revealed that it had recorded extensive videotape evidence of Dhiab's forcible cell extraction and force-feeding. Included in the evidence are twenty-eight videos of Dhiab, filmed between April 2013 and February 2014, at the height of mass hunger strike, when nearly 100 prisoners were being subjected to forced cell extraction or forced feeding. Judge Kessler, along with federal prosecutors and defense attorneys, viewed the tapes in closed session.[36] In June 2014, a coalition of sixteen news media organizations requested that the videotapes be unsealed under the First Amendment's implicit right to access public information. In October 2015, Judge Kessler ruled that the U.S. government must release redacted tapes and championed public oversight of government action over the government's irrational "fears and speculations" that the release of the videos would incite extremist groups to engage in violence against U.S. personnel, lead detainees to develop countermeasures to forcible cell extractions, and result in more frequent forcible extractions by fostering detainee resistance. In January 2016, the U.S. government continued appeals to suppress the release of the force-feeding tapes. Ironically, international medical ethics concerns and legal and political pressure encouraged the secretive digital documentation of cell extractions and forcible feeding that the military expected would monitor and reinforce the consistency of "safe" and "humane" medical procedures in Guantanamo. However, the digital dissemination of extraction procedures, the Obama administration feared, would reverberate as evidence of punitive and torturous treatment and would undermine the assertion of careful and humane biopolitical management of prisoners' bodies and lives.

## The Meaning of Time and Life under Hunger Strikes

Following the deaths of Palestinian men in the 1980s as a result of force-feeding practices, the Israeli government has abstained from forcible feeding in its prisons and detention centers, despite waves of Palestinian prisoner hunger strikes in 1996, 2004, 2008, and 2012.[37] However, with more than 100 Palestinian detainees on hunger strike in June 2014, Israel's

Knesset took up legislation to allow forcible feeding of hunger-striking detainees. In opposition to the legislation, the Israeli Medical Association (IMA) published *The Physician's Guide to Treating the Detainee/Prisoner on a Hunger Strike*, a report that discusses the bioethical issues and international conventions that prohibit force-feeding and presents a model for monitoring and treating hunger strikers.[38] The guide was distributed to physicians at the internal medicine wards treating dozens of hunger-striking Palestinian prisoners, some for as long as fifty days. Leonid Edelman, chairman of the IMA, argues that the procedure is dangerous; that it contravenes international and national ethics; and that the health risks include tears to the esophagus, collapsed lungs, major infections and pneumonia.[39] In an editorial, *Haaertz* journalist Zvi Bar'el declared that "force-feeding is not an act to save detainees whose lives are in danger. It's a political bulletproof vest that wards off the ethical challenge of administrative detention—the justification for the hunger strike. It's much easier to ponder the tragic significance of forcing a feeding tube up a prisoner's nose, when the very fact that he's an administrative detainee doesn't raise a thought."[40] That concerns about bioethics and "lifesaving" trump the human rights of indefinite security detention without charge or trial perfectly illustrates the complex wrangle of the politics of biocitizenship and human rights protections, all the more obfuscated by the prevailing logic of biological algorithms and objective management of life processes.

Drawing public attention to the plight of Palestinian hunger strikers emphasized the marking of time both for the individual hunger striker and also in terms of biopolitical norms and bioethical urgency. The refusal to eat summons an accounting of time within carceral confinement. Time is measured in days, both as a biopolitical measure of resilience and as a marking of days without food. It also offers a cautionary prediction of potential fatality. Marking the days on hunger strike by carceral authorities and by the prisoners themselves offers unusual precision to the agonizing elasticity of indefinite incarceration—demonstrating one way in which biopolitical logics provide the very conditions of possibility for political agency.

Enumerating the days a prisoner is on hunger strike marks time and measures the individual crisis against the backdrop of the limits of self-starvation. Against biocitizenship's temporal horizon, the passage of days illuminates how for the prisoner self-abnegation can offer a means to seize control over time. For hunger strikers protesting Israeli administrative detention of incarcerated individuals without charge or trial, for renewable six-month periods, the undefined time of incarceration became synchronized by the time accounting of the hunger strike. In February 2012, Palestinian Khader Adnan passed a remarkable two months on hunger strike. Visualizing Palestine, a Beirut-based data and media organization, combined graphics that communicated abstracted medical symptoms and individual experiences to mark the duration and consequences of hunger strikes globally and put in context Khader Adnan's plight and prognosis in Israeli administrative detention.[41]

* * *

Visualizing Palestine's "Hunger Strike" poster (figure 7.1) deploys a calendar inventorying intensified symptoms after day fourteen and enumerates a daily breakdown of physiological processes, loss of sensations and sensorial capacity and control, and body weight, all of which are based on norms and averages gleaned from medical research and medical counsel. The countdown of days and consequential bodily damage and disruption imposes a time-based sentence of distress and fatality that is refused in the carceral limbo of indefinite detention.

The graphic amplified the dangers and exceptional length of Adnan's hunger strike by the implicit durational comparison to world historical figures Nelson Mandela and Mahatma Gandhi, who had time-limited protest fasts and led politically transformative and successful movements, to the infamous death of Irish hunger striker Bobby Sands. The comparisons heightened Adnan's notoriety, the nobility of the struggle of Palestinians fighting administrative detention, and the dire urgency of action by solidary social movements and the Israeli government to avert Adnan's death. The interplay between physiological symptoms and the specific durations of hunger strikes, including the large-scale hunger strikes of South African detainees in 1989 and of Guantanamo prisoners in 2005, offered a shared biometric scale of hunger strikers' bodily deterioration that tied average human symptoms of starvation to specific historic hunger strikes.

The language of measuring the body and its deteriorating symptoms has become embedded in communications from hunger strikers. Shortly after Adnan's release, in May 2012, thirty-three-year-old Palestinian prisoner Thaer Halahla announced through his lawyers that he was on

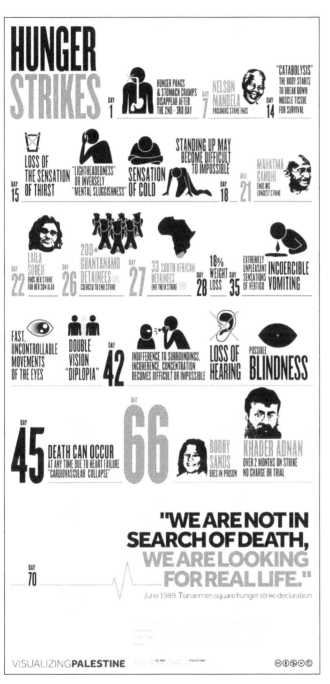

Figure 7.1. Visualizing Palestine, "Hunger Strikes" poster (2012).

the seventieth day of his hunger strike, and that his weight had plummeted by a third, from eighty-three kilograms to fifty-five kilograms. His lawyer enumerated his physical symptoms, including a rapid heart rate, low blood pressure, bleeding from the nose and gums, and muscle atrophy. The International Committee of the Red Cross called on Israel to transfer Halahla from prison to a hospital for emergency medical intervention to forestall his "imminent danger of dying."[42] Indeed, health, vitality, and embodiment shape the complexities of biocitizenship and how people can enact political agency.

Acknowledging the refusal to eat as an expression of political will both illuminates and obscures the justifications of carceral power. In South African, Israeli, and U.S. immigrant detention centers in Krome and Guantanamo Bay, hunger strikers are held in indefinite detention, without charge or trial. Citizenship rights are ignored and discounted because political protesters, asylum seekers, and "enemy combatants" are charged with being a security threat to the state.

Legal and human rights advocates and medical professionals campaigned for the bodies of those whose rights are abridged, ignored, and violently suppressed. Political agency is enacted, expressed through the ethical and political contradictions of speaking on the behalf of those who refuse nourishment as an expression of their political will and protest. The state, in advocating "lifesaving" technologies and procedures against the will of a prisoner, selectively champions a claim for the physiological vitality of the body over the political agency of the very same body. Invoking the "hunger-striking detainee" has become a "mode of prosopopeia" that lawyers, advocates, and prison administrators deploy to represent the consciousness and bodily needs that have been overridden by biopolitical management.[43]

This speaking on behalf of and affirming the sustaining of biopolitical endurance of life as a universal aim takes the horizon of biocitizenship and narrowly circumscribes the legal avenues of redress. Rather than assessing the justice of indefinite detention or adjudicating a criminal charge, the avenues of redress are strictly over whether the treatment is medical therapy or biological torture. With regard to protections of human rights in the United Nations Universal Declaration of Human Rights, biocitizenship appears to attend to the declaration "No one shall be subjected to torture or to cruel, inhuman or degrading treatment or punishment." Nevertheless, the preservation of the biological life/body usurps the subjective experiences of the person.[44] Biocitizenship is the act of speaking for one's self and from the position of informed consent, a vision that shaped the protocols of treating hunger strikers in South Africa. Yet even in South Africa, physicians and human rights attorneys spoke on behalf of the needs and desires of the hunger-striking detainees. In U.S. immigrant detention and in Guantanamo, biopolitical knowledge and therapeutics are marshaled by prison medical care to mitigate and calibrate pain and humiliation through the medical management of the body and justify its procedures through the constraint and carceral control of the body and vitality. As Corinna Howland has argued, force-feeding is a "violent reconfiguration of the physical body in line with state politics of life perpetuation," and it "represents a primary route to state subjectification" through the ethos of "save the body and the mind will follow."[45] Prisoner hunger strikes create a break in carceral control and produce a wedge for physicians to assert a biomedical monopoly over care and treatment of the prisoner that is justified by crisis intervention and in the mandate to save life.

For prisoners, the crisis of care can make possible a demand for humane and palliative care and the release from incarceration into care of family and community. When Palestinian Khader Adnan was incarcerated in administrative detention for a second time, he went on another hunger strike beginning on May 6, 2015. An international solidarity campaign and the Israeli state's fears that he could die in detention led to the negotiation of his release on June 29, 2015. Israeli officials, as a condition of his release, expected him to demonstrate to the international public that he ate something to break his hunger strike. Adnan insisted that only his seventy-five-year-old mother, Nawal Mousa, could feed him. She brought him a bowl of soup and later said in a telephone interview with a reporter, "'He ate a little from my hands.' He said 'Mother, I want you to make my favorite meal, I want stuffed vegetables from your hands, Mama.'"[46] The affective and sentimental recourse to maternal sustenance underlines how eating was not just about ensuring biological survival, but also about the reanimation of the social sustenance of comfort, kinship, and hospitality in the hunger strikers' lives.[47] After Israel released Khader Adnan following his fifty-six-day hunger strike, he lauded his release as a victory for "the battle of empty stomachs."[48] Adnan expresses how eating is a universalized practice of belonging and social connection, sustenance that has meaning to reproduce the social and familiar.

Across the twentieth century and the early twenty-first century, the state's implementation of disciplinary power in feeding hunger strikers transformed through biomedical measurement, technologies, and corporate commodities to systems of biopolitical management, logics, and justifications. The duration and extent of hunger strike protests shake the authority, discipline, and order of carceral institutions by upsetting the imposition of alimentary schedules on the prison population. This crisis reverberates specifically in prisons in Britain, the United States, South Africa, Israel, and Guantanamo. The state's adoption of biomedical measures, technologies, and logics has particularly accelerated in the early twenty-first century. As a strategy of governance, the ascendancy of biopolitical management and the utilitarian focus of bioethics seek to quell and suppress concerns over coercion and violence. However, this biopolitical umbrella does not completely overwhelm the contests. The protests over the ethics of care, the expression of dissent and resistance, and the self-conscious use of one's own body's life and death are the site of the struggle.

Biopolitical frames and judicial structures have turned hunger-striking prisoners into figures that are invoked, spoken for and through, and yet their agitating bodies exceed the governance structures that contain them. The act of a hunger strike is a disavowal of the social viability and sustenance in carceral conditions. The hunger strikers' threat, the presumed breakdown in prison order and discipline, is a rebuke to the state's control over a person's life and body. Particularly for those held by the state for insurrection, defying the state's sovereign borders and authority, the state makes impossible the exercise of one's consent, except to extend life under state control. This battle of "empty stomachs" stages a protest over carceral legitimacy, fully conscious of the invasiveness of state power, that demonstrates the fracture of exercising biocitizenship and its contingency on the ability to be recognized as a national citizen, irrespective of the ideas of asserting a universal human right on the grounds of a minimum biological standard.

NOTES

1 *In reapplication of Department of Homeland Security, Immigration and Customs Enforcement, v. Anwar Hossain et al.*, 1:2015-cv24560 (S.D. Fla. 2015).

2 Michel Foucault, *History of Sexuality, Vol. 1: An Introduction*, trans. Robert Hurley (New York: Vintage, 1978), 144.

3 Nikolas Rose, *The Politics of Life Itself: Biomedicine, Power, and Subjectivity in the Twenty-First Century* (Princeton, NJ: Princeton University Press, 2006).

4 Thomas Lemke, *Biopolitics: An Advanced Introduction* (New York: NYU Press, 2011), 4–5.

5 Alexandra Martinez, "Judge's Order to Force-Feed Ten Hunger Strikers at Krome Sparks Immigration Protest," *Miami New Times*, December 28, 2015.

6 Lauren Wilcox, *Bodies of Violence: Theorizing Embodied Subjects in International Relations* (Oxford: Oxford University Press, 2015), 7.

7 Evelyn Hilda Burkitt, Birmingham Prison, September 20, 1909, Medical Officer Report, British Archives, Kew HO 45/10417/183577.

8 Lemke, *Biopolitics*, 5.

9 Valentine's Meat Juice, a tonic invented in Richmond, Virginia, in 1870 to address digestive difficulties and the inability to retain nourishment, was used in prisons and asylums to supplement feeds.

10 Ellen Barwell, Birmingham Prison, September 20, 1909, Medical Officer Report, British Archives, Kew HO 45/10417/183577.

11 A two-ounce bottle, concentrating the juice from four pounds of beef, was administered by heating up tonic with water or milk to make a kind of "bouillon or tea." Assistant Secretary, Home Office Confidential September 20, 1909, to Governor of the Birmingham Prison, British Archives, Kew HO 45/10417/183577.

12 Suzanne Breen, "Marian Price Interview: Old Bailey Bomber Ashamed of Sinn Fein," *Village*, December 7, 2004.

13 Corinna Howland, "To Feed or Not to Feed? Violent State Care and the Contested Medicalization of Incarcerated Hunger-Strikers in Britain, Turkey, and Guantanamo Bay," *New Zealand Sociology* 28, no. 1 (2013): 106.

14 Ibid., 108.

15 Ibid., 107.

16 "Medicolegal: Inquest on Hunger Striker," *British Medical Journal* 3, no. 5922 (July 6, 1974): 52–53.

17 British Medical Association Central Ethical Committee, "Artificial Feeding of Prisoners Statement," *British Medical Journal* 3, no. 5922 (July 6, 1974): 52.

18 David Baresford, *Ten Men Dead: The Story of the 1981 Irish Hunger Strike* (New York: Atlantic Monthly Press, 1987).

19 W. J. Kalk, M. Felix, E. R. Snoey, and Y. Veriawa, "Voluntary Total Fasting in Political Prisoners: Clinical and Biochemical Observations," *South Africa Medical Journal* 83, no. 6 (1993): 391–94; "Voluntary Total Fasting" (March 1990), South African History Archives, University of Witswatersrand, National Medical and Dental Association Collection, A1.11.10, New Folder 2.

20 Kalk et al., "Voluntary Total Fasting"; William John Kalk and Yusuf Veriava, "Hospital Management of Voluntary Total Fasting among Political Prisoners," *Lancet* 337, no. 8742 (1991): 660–62.

21 Kalk et al, "Voluntary Total Fasting in Political Prisoners"; G. R. Keeton, "Hunger Strikers: Ethical and Management Problems," *South African Medical Journal* 83, no. 6 (1993): 380–81; "Metabolic and Endocrine Effects of Voluntary Total Fasting," University of Witwatersrand, Application to the Committee for Research on Human Subjects, June 18, 1991, University of Witwatersand Hospital, Adler Museum of Medicine Archives.

22 Kalk et al., "Voluntary Total Fasting in Political Prisoners"; Keeton, "Hunger Strikers."

23 Michael Peel, "Hunger Strikes: Understanding the Underlying Physiology Will Help the Doctors Provide Proper Advice," *British Medical Journal* 315, no. 7112 (1997): 829–30.

24 Hirsham M. Mehana, Jamil Moledina, and Jane Travis, "Refeeding Syndrome: What It Is, and How to Prevent and Treat It," *British Medical Journal* 336, no. 7659 (1997): 1495–98; Maurice A. Schnitker, Paul E. Mattman, and Theodore L. Bliss, "A Clinical Study of Malnutrition in Japanese Prisoners of War," *Annals of Internal Medicine* 35, no. 1 (1951): 69–96.

25 Ancel Keys, Josef Brozek, Austin Henschel, Olaf Mickelson, and Henry Longstreet Taylor, *The Biology of Human Starvation* (Minneapolis: University of Minnesota Press, 1950); Todd Tucker, *The Great Starvation Experiment: Ancel Keys and the Men Who Starved for Science* (New York: Free Press, 2006); Egils Veverbrants and Ronald A. Arky, "Effects of Fasting and Refeeding: Studies on Sodium, Potassium and Water Excretion on a Constant Electrolyte and Fluid Intake," *Journal of Clinical Endocrinology and Metabolism* 29, no. 1 (1969): 55–62. The South African research advanced the understanding of clinical experiences of responding to challenges of refeeding after prolonged starvation. Rapid shifts in the ingestion and processing of electrolytes and fluids can lead to cardiac, respiratory, and neuromuscular problems. During prolonged fasting, the body aims to conserve muscle and protein breakdown by switching to ketone bodies derived from fatty acids as the main energy source. Many intracellular minerals become severely depleted, and insulin secretion is suppressed during fasting. During refeeding, insulin secretion resumes in response to increased blood sugar, resulting in increased glycogen, fat, and protein synthesis. Refeeding increases the basal metabolic rate, stimulates electrolyte movement, and challenges the depletion of calcium, magnesium, potassium, glucose, and vitamins. Kalk recommended that patients should remain under hospital care for a full week to avoid refeeding syndrome. The South African physician protocols advocated the use of Ensure and intravenous fluids to combat dehydration and then transitioning to meals that are easy to digest, liquid, and lactose-free.

26 Ainsley M. Malone, "Enteral Formula Selection: A Review of Selected Product Categories," *Practical Gastroenterology*, ser. 29, no. 6 (2005): 44–74.

27 Ensure is made by Abbott Labs, a Fortune 200 company, based in Illinois, with 69,000 employees; with sales, distribution, and manufacturing facilities in 150 countries; and with nutritional products accounting for one-third of its $21.8 billion in global sales in 2013. For more information, see www.abbot.com.

28 Joint Task Force Guantanamo Bay, Cuba, Joint Medical Group, *Standard Operating Procedure: Medical Management of Detainees on Hunger Strike*, March 5, 2013, 3, www.aele.org.

29 Ibid.

30 Ibid., 6.

31 Ibid., 15–16.

32 Ibid., 17.

33 Ibid., 26.

34 Judge Gladys Kessler, "Memorandum Order," *Abu Wa'el (Jihad) Dhiab v. Barack H. Obama et al.*, 05-01457 (U.S.D. D.C., 2015).

35 *Abu Wa'el (Jihad) Dhiab v. Barack H. Obama et al.*, 05-01457 (U.S.D. D.C., 2015).

36 Spencer Hsu, "Judge Again Orders U.S. to Release Guantanamo Bay Force-Feeding Tapes," *Washington Post*, October 27, 2015.

37 Jasim Jamal, "Letter Dated 7 August 1980 from the Permanent Representative of Qatar to the United Nations Secretary-General," United Nations Security Council, United Nations Information System on the Question of Palestine (UNISPAL), accessed December 28, https://unispal.un.org.

38 Israeli Medical Association, *The Physician's Guide to Treating the Detainee/Prisoner on Hunger Strike* (Ramat Gan: Israeli Medical Association, 2014).

39 Batsheva Sobelman, "Israel Passes Contentious Law Allowing Force-Feeding of Inmates," *Los Angeles Times*, June 30, 2015.

40 Zvi Ba'rel, "Force-Feeding Debate Misses Point on Israel's True Transgression," *Haaretz*, June 25, 2014.

41 Naji El Mir, "Visualizing Palestine," hunger strikes poster, 2012, http://visualizing-palestine.org.

42 "Long-Term Hunger Striker Not Backing Down," Ma'an News Agency, May 8, 2012, http://www.maannews.com; "Lawyer: Halahla Could Die at Any Moment," Ma'an News Agency, May 10, 2012, www.maannews.com.

43 Megan Foley, "Voicing Terri Schiavo: Prosopopeic Citizenship in the Democratic Aporia between Sovereignty and Biopower," *Communication and Critical/Cultural Studies* 7, no. 4 (2010): 381–400.

44 United Nations General Assembly Resolution 217(iii), "The Universal Declaration of Human Rights," December 10, 1948, www.un.org.

45 Howland, "To Feed or Not to Feed?," 109–10.

46 Diaa Hadid, "Worried That Fasting Palestinian Prisoner Could Die, Israel Releases Him," *New York Times*, June 29, 2015.

47 Alexander G. Weheliye, *Habeas Viscus: Racializing Assemblages, Biopolitics and Black Feminist Theories of the Human* (Durham, NC: Duke University Press, 2014), 113–24.

48 Batsheva Sobelman, "Israel to Allow Force-Feeding of Prisoners," *Los Angeles Times*, July 31, 2015.

# 8

# Biocitizenship on the Ground

*Health Activism and the Medical Governance Revolution*

MERLIN CHOWKWANYUN

## Introduction

Throughout the 1960s and into the early 1970s, community health workers, neighborhood activists, and young medical students and physicians challenged long-standing traditions and practices in the American health care sector. They posed fundamental questions about inclusion and citizenship within the post–World War II medical boom: namely, who actually enjoyed its fruits, and who should have a say in how its institutions operated? Programmatically, key participants in this agitation fought to increase the decision-making power of nonphysicians and nonprofessionals, especially that of laypeople, and decrease hierarchy within medicine.

I call this contest of biocitizenship the "medical governance revolution." In other controversies around biocitizenship, subjects have questioned the authority of risk assessment from nuclear catastrophe and debated the embedded assumptions of novel genetic testing, to name just two.[1] The resolution of these conflicts over biological truth has high-stakes consequences for the ability to make claims on the state. Likewise, the subjects I studied turned their sights, too, on a highly rarefied field of biological practice, the American medical system. In the process, they reordered rarely questioned chains of authority in medical institutions.

To analyze my subjects' fortunes, I use three cases. I start with the rise of activism at a site not typically associated with political ferment: the American medical school. Like their undergraduate counterparts, medical students in the 1960s demanded more of a say in their educational experiences and how their institutions operated. They pushed medical school deans for more responsive outreach and sharing of medical resources beyond campus boundaries, a fraught demand given the wave of ongoing urban riots in the deeply segregated urban neighborhoods where medical schools were often located. Medical student activism also extended to the classroom, with widespread efforts for curricular overhauls that would supplement traditional biomedicine with course material on the social context of health.

From medical schools, I move on to New York City, specifically the South Bronx, where a group of residents and interns converged in 1970 on Lincoln Hospital, one of the most dilapidated public hospitals in the United States. Calling themselves the "Lincoln Collective," they planned to use their critical mass to implement major changes in how a hospital was run, shifting major authority to activists and nonphysicians. Democratizing a single hospital would provide, in turn, a prototype for other health activists not just elsewhere in the city but throughout the entire country.

My last case also takes place in New York City but on the Lower East Side, home to an experimental outpatient clinic called Gouverneur Health Services. From the experiment's inception in 1961, Gouverneur blurred the boundary separating the clinic from its patient pool, employing community organizers and door-to-door health workers—most from the neighborhood itself—to gauge common problems in the area and encourage more use of its services. Gouverneur soon became an inspiration for the fledging federal neighborhood health centers program. It was funded by the Office of Economic Opportunity (OEO), which made facilitation of nonprofessional and laypeople's participation in administration a condition for new federal funds from President Lyndon Johnson's ambitious War on Poverty legislative agenda.

The medical governance revolution was an instantiation of what might be called biocitizenship on the ground. I use this phrase to accentuate how it differs from some of the more prominent case studies that have helped articulate the biocitizenship concept. The majority of these focus on the clash between expert knowledge—sometimes sanctioned by the state—and parallel lay suspicions or critical discourses. By contrast, the stories here focus less on controversies over bodies of establishment knowledge than they do on attempts to alter *practice* on the ground and at the micro-level. Stirring rationales for alternative ways of knowing and thinking—often in the form of manifestos or extended writings—were, of course, always present. But the central goal was less about transforming scientific knowledge production than on catalyzing changes in day-to-day institutional practice.

These three cases showcase different sites and facets of the medical governance revolution. Medical campus activism stemmed from tensions within medical training that contributed to students' personal alienation from the professionalization process. The Lincoln Collective's members, fresh out of medical school, constructed a new postgraduate outlet for the political energy that swept through medical campuses in the 1960s. Granted a large amount of autonomy to devise a new residency program, they sought to infuse it with the new emerging governance principles. Gouverneur, meanwhile, operated under more formal auspices. It showed the challenges of implementing formal governance mandates imposed from above, in this case federal War on Poverty stipulations for lay participation.

Alas, the medical governance revolution was an incomplete one, hampered by many internal and external obstacles. Its most energetic organizers led parallel personal and professional lives, resulting in turnovers in leadership and their being pulled in multiple directions, often away from political organization altogether. Underlying class and racial hierarchies hampered activist unity, especially when they mapped onto professional and nonprofessional status differences. This, in turn, contributed to interpersonal tensions, emotional exhaustion, and frequent burnout. Throughout, lingering questions surrounded all three experiences. Ambiguity surrounded "community," a key concept invoked on its members' behalf to argue for the community's right to participate in administrative decisions. Above all was the question of how much such activism, in the end, really mattered in the face of major structural transformations, by the mid-1970s, in the health care sector and a changing and turbulent American political economy.

## Medical Student Organizing

In June 1968, the American Medical Association (AMA) met in San Francisco, but the meeting did not proceed as planned. Out in front, some Bay Area medical students were picketing the building along-side Black Panthers and other activists. During the actual proceedings, a Stanford University medical student, Peter Schnall, walked to the podium and asked if he could address the audience. He got no reply, so he began reading a speech to the AMA delegates: "The health care system in the United States, long failing, now may well be collapsing. This disintegration is due in no small part to racial discrimination, economic discrimination, and archaic, poorly delivered and inadequate health programs."[2] As Schnall spoke, one could hear booing and hissing. But the delegates mostly watched in surprise. Schnall accused the AMA of capping medical school admissions artificially to increase physicians' salaries. It condoned segregation in its southern chapters, Schnall claimed, and it had long lobbied against Medicare and Medicaid, passed just a few years prior. It embodied, in short, professional insularity at its worst. "I don't think you people have the right to call yourselves humanists—much less the right to treat the poor," he shouted at the most powerful physicians in the country.[3]

Peter Schnall did not emerge from a vacuum. He was a by-product of what a prominent medical magazine would later call "unrest on the medical campus" in the 1960s.[4] Much of the action revolved around what would eventually be called Student Health Organizations (SHO), which originated at the University of Southern California (USC) School of Medicine through the efforts of William Bronston, then a medical school senior, and Michael "Mick" McGarvey, a sophomore. SHO focused initially on disseminating new ideas to medical students, publishing a newsletter, *Borborygmi* (whose title means "intestinal rumbling"), in September 1964, and hosting a lecture-discussion forum on such topics as "Discrimination in Medicine," "Medical Malpractice," and "Physician, Heal Thy Society!"[5]

But a few months later, in January 1965, Bronston began turning the activities into more than an ephemeral affair. He called for the formation of the Student Medical Action Conference (SMAC, pronounced "smack") that would combine the consciousness-raising of the discussion forum with actual practice. SMAC's brief founding "credo" offered an expanded definition of the physician's role, one that located duties beyond biomedical boundaries and highlighted the social and political aspects of medicine. Optimistically, it "resolve[d] to engage in active community service, to critically examine issues that pertain to the public health, and to publish facts, information, and statistics concerning problems of health which have failed to engender appropriate community concern and action."[6] In the summer of 1965, the group launched yearlong work: reviews of health care legislation, free auditory and vision screening of children, and dental care for the indigent. It also initiated ambitious summer projects that became the organization's early hallmark. One sent thirteen students to work with migrant farmworkers across California, another three students to the South to provide "medical presence" for civil rights workers threatened daily with political violence.[7]

By the next school year, the group had spread nationally, and in Chicago, students agreed to form a new national organization. Chapters popped up in many locales. The Bay Area (of California), New York City, Boston, and Philadelphia were particular hot spots. In these early days, SHO attracted the support of medical and governmental elites. Activities at USC were championed by its dean, Roger Egeberg, and it soon received funds from President Johnson's Office of Economic Opportunity (OEO), which dispensed most War on Poverty grants. This establishment backing would later cause friction in the organization. But for now, the focus was on real-world work. The OEO grant financed a summer project in 1966 that funded "90 medical, dental, nursing and social work students from 40 institutions in 11 states." They worked across California in the state's poorest areas, providing free basic screenings, referral services, and dental work at free clinics, camps for migrant farmworkers, and public hospitals.[8]

The summer work expanded its participants' political horizons. Margaret Sharfstein, who had come to California from New York City to work at a public hospital, remarked: "Nurses and social workers go into the community. Why shouldn't doctors? The patient is a whole human being, with a home and a social interaction all of his own. . . . To look at the patient as a disease alone seems inconsistent to me for the 'healing professions.'"[9] Other students recounted interactions with indigent patients who often delayed or simply did not seek health care because of the inefficiency or patronization they encountered within health care facilities. A favorable *Los Angeles Times* article labeled the students "a new breed."[10] They were forming what Alondra Nelson has called a "social health" perspective, one that saw links between medical ills and the social contexts that bred them.[11] By 1967, the summer projects scaled up, continuing in Los Angeles and now Chicago and New York City with sponsorship from medical schools in those regions and the OEO.[12] A recruitment pamphlet articulated the projects' goals of expanding a physician's imagination, declaring that "the majority of students in the health professions do not gain, in their formal curriculum, an accurate appreciation of the needs of the medically underprivileged in America, or of the difficulties faced by existing health programs and practitioners in poverty areas."[13]

The service projects complemented parallel efforts to reform medical schools' curricula and how they operated beyond campus walls. At Stanford, SHO members demanded that courses in community health become mandatory and that students have input into their content.[14] The lobbying efforts for a more socially relevant medical school proved successful on many campuses. In November 1967, Dr. Martin Cherkasky, director of Montefiore Hospital and a dean at Albert Einstein College of Medicine, co-authored an article with Steven Sharfstein, an Einstein student. Appearing in the *American Journal of Diseases of Children*, the article affirmed the possibility of transforming the medical school into a more socially engaged institution. It declared that such institutions "can and must undertake the creation of imaginative, new organizational methods for delivery of medical care. The medial school should initiate, test, and critically evaluate pilot programs in community health."[15]

Signs like these suggested a new era of medical school governance and harmony between students and administrations, academic medical centers, and their environs. But by the following year, in 1968, the tenor of SHO changed. One contentious moment at its annual meeting came when Bill Bronston, the organization's co-founder, delivered remarks later printed in the *AMA News*. He declared: "We've got to disrupt and destroy the system where the fat cat doctor gets $40,000 to $50,000 a year."[16] The responses to Bronston from other SHO members revealed ideological fissures. John Fisher, a medical student from Detroit, wrote that "as a political moderate," he was "very disturbed by some statements," namely, Bronston's, that the *AMA News* had carried.[17]

In addition to debates over rhetorical choices, some SHO members focused on the organization's raison d'être. Tim Smith, chairman of the

Cincinnati SHO, cast the SHO's signature summer health projects as "temporary, project-oriented solutions" that, "though educational, are destined to eventual failure because they don't attack the roots of the problem."[18] This debate unfolded in the summer of 1968 as SHO expanded the summer projects to seven areas: California, New England, Chicago, Philadelphia, Milwaukee, New York, and Cleveland. As in the past, participants, particularly first-timers, found them edifying and eye-opening. But others qualified their praise with criticism of the projects' ephemeral nature. In an evaluation, one participant asked hard-hitting existential questions not just about the longer-term purpose but also about who SHO and its projects were really for:

> According to the project fellows and SHO literature, the main goal was "sensitization" of white, middle-class, medical students. A perfectly rational idea—from the white student's viewpoint. But from the moral point of view, this is an horrendous injustice to the community! How can SHP [summer health projects] invade a ghetto (to "help," of course) with an army of white medical students, and for ten weeks perform acts of charity and fellowship, but simultaneously have the anguish of the ghetto as a secondary reason for justifying the existence of SHP? The makeup and foundation of SHP must be changed.[19]

Racial tension simmered beneath subsequent exchanges. *Catalyst*, the Boston SHO's publication, bluntly characterized overwhelmingly white health students' interacting with predominantly poor and nonwhite patients. The cover drawing of one issue showed a light-skinned hand reaching downward toward a dark-skinned hand with visible skeletal structure beneath it.[20]

Were SHO members, the internal critics asked, deriving pedagogical experience from indigent patients without leaving much permanent behind? Were they in the end primarily transforming themselves and their political gestalt but doing little else? What might be implemented instead that lasted longer than the duration of a summer project? In the summer of 1969, quotations and drawings of Mao Tse-tung, Ho Chi Minh, and Che Guevara dotted SHO's national publication, *Encounter*. In one issue, an article declared that "SHO is a liberal organization. Originally conceived as a refuge for all well-meaning and concerned, left-of-center health student activists, it has long outlived that usefulness."[21] Service projects, curricular reform, and community involvement on the part of medical schools were "basically reformist" to "enhance the privilege of an already privileged group."[22]

By 1970, SHO imploded. When the early leaders graduated and moved on, they left a leadership vacuum, and SHO became the victim of a crisis of purpose and resultant infighting: on one side were those who were fine with the programming conducted heretofore; on the other side were those pushing for a major rupture from its past. But beyond revolutionary murmuring, what the latter path entailed was not exactly clear. In the five years since the organization's founding on the USC campus, it had gained some input into administrative and curricular matters at multiple schools. And via the summer projects, SHO had contributed to thinning the walls that separated gilded academic medical centers and their surrounding neighborhoods. It was an undeniable shift in governance from the way things had been at the start of the decade. But it was also an undeniably limited victory, too. As indicated by the remarks of the more frustrated members, actual people living in poverty-stricken neighborhoods had not played major roles in the planning of programs designed supposedly to help them. And even if they had, it would not, many SHO members realized, ultimately attack the roots of health care maldistribution that SHO's outreach work temporarily alleviated. This fundamental conundrum confounded the efforts of activists in the following episodes as well.

## Lincoln Hospital and the South Bronx

It is the atypical American internship and residency recruitment pamphlet that begins with a quotation from anticolonial theorist and psychiatrist Frantz Fanon. And yet, that is exactly how Lincoln Hospital's 1970 House Officer Program in Community Pediatrics pitched itself to potential recruits, with an excerpt on the ambiguous role of the physician in an oppressive society. The passage read: "In the colonial situation, going to see the doctor, the administrator, the constable, or the mayor, are identical moves. The sense of alienation from colonial society and the mistrust of its authority are always accompanied by an almost mechanical sense of detachment and mistrust of even the things which are most positive and most profitable to the population."[23] At its most basic, what would become known as the Lincoln Collective consisted of two dozen physicians, most from pediatrics (but some in internal medicine and psychiatry), who designed a residency program with the intent of transforming how a hospital was run.[24] The project was the brainchild of Charlotte Phillips, a recent graduate of Case Western Reserve University's medical school in Cleveland. While there, she and her husband, Oli Fein, had been members of Students for a Democratic Society and active in its Economic Research and Action Projects (ERAPs), the organization's community organizing project.[25] Although Phillips herself was never a member of SHO, some of the other early members of the Lincoln Collective were.

One can read early Lincoln Collective statements of purpose as an attempt—whether or not created with SHO explicitly in mind—to transcend the limits of signature SHO activities. The break was not a clean one. Some of the programming mentioned in the recruitment pamphlet resembled SHO summer projects. For example, a "community elective" would require interns and residents to spend time outside the hospital disseminating information and conducting screenings, among other activities. But other sections revealed significant departures from the SHO days. One "affirm[ed] that we are in training to serve the community, and that we are committed to dealing with the problems of the urban ghetto community in a long-run way." Most important, the Lincoln pamphlet declared "a shared commitment to the community" and made "transferring technical knowledge to the people" a priority.[26] At least rhetorically, this looked like it could be a departure from the one-way quality and seasonal length of the SHO summer health projects.

If the Lincoln Collective wanted more pro-activeness and action, it surely got that. Shortly after their arrival, its members were greeted by a one-day occupation of the hospital's nurses' residence. Planned by the Young Lords, a Puerto Rican nationalist group with symbolic and ideological similarities to the Black Panthers, the occupiers demanded door-to-door health services "for preventive care, emphasizing environment and sanitation control, nutrition, drug addiction, maternal and child care, and senior citizen services," a permanent twenty-four-hour grievance table, a $140 per week minimum wage, and a day care center for the community and hospital workers.[27] Its final demand, however, was the most provocative and centered on governance. It called for community control, "total self determination of all health services through a community worker board to operate Lincoln Hospital."[28] This demand—and how and whether to realize it—shaped many of the subsequent debates and activities of the collective's members. In the wake of the occupation, the Young Lords left the task of Lincoln to the Health Revolutionary Unity Movement (HRUM), an adjunct organization consisting mostly of Young Lords members interested in health issues.[29]

The Lincoln Collective and HRUM were organizing at what might have been the most underresourced hospital in the city. One official assessment from nearby Einstein Medical College, which was paid by the city to take on some administrative tasks, described it as a place where "the dirt and grime and general dilapidation make it a completely improper place to care for the sick or even run the complex administrative machinery that is required to do this."[30] Against this backdrop, the collective wrestled with how to translate the framework of a program into practice. Politically, considerable heterogeneity existed within the group. Some members wanted to focus on improving service within the hospital. Others were much more overtly confrontational and wanted to deepen relations with HRUM. And some straddled both tendencies, such as the people who serviced the Black Panthers' South Bronx Clinic, which conducted lead poisoning and TB level screenings.[31] By the end of the year, the collective was regularly committing $150 to $250 per month to Third World revolutionary groups in its immediate orbit: the Panthers, the Young Lords, and most important, HRUM, with which it would later have the closest relationship.[32]

The collective wrestled with its exact relationship with these outside groups, but hospital-level reforms drew the support of almost everyone, regardless of where they stood on the headier Third World solidarity questions. These reforms included the adoption of continuity-of-care clinics, where patients saw the same doctor each time they visited the hospital, much rarer in public hospitals at the time due to physicians' large patient loads. For the collective, continuity of care added accountability to a doctor-patient relationship. That the change occurred within an existing institution gave it a more permanent quality than existed in a summer project. During the collective's second major staff rotation in July 1971, its members strategized to ensure that continuity patients were not randomly and suddenly shuffled to new doctors but were assigned to them by the more senior residents to ensure a smooth transition.[33]

Other projects took more time to get off the ground. The "community elective" requirement took considerable time to gain traction.[34] A monthly report written approximately six months into its existence suggested the Lincoln Collective was having trouble identifying longer-term activities for it to undertake.[35] Meanwhile, class tensions between the collective's physicians and everybody else—that is, the "community"—came ever closer to the fore. In one summer, a member hosted a hastily arranged party at his mother's home in Connecticut that resulted in considerable introspection. Of all the attendees, only one was a hospital worker, someone who had come frequently to the collective's meetings. The remaining guests had all been Lincoln Collective doctors who, after a quick discussion, had concluded that notifying workers would require too much time on too little notice. At the collective meeting where this event was recounted, the note taker summarized the situation by saying that "everyone knew they were exercising class privilege but were not talking about it."[36]

Frustration over how to create a real alliance among the Lincoln Collective, hospital workers, patients, and the community mounted by August 1971, which saw the departure of half the collective's original members. One meeting's rapporteur summarized the mood as one full of "feelings of 'something missing' . . . of dissatisfaction and frustration, of hopes unmet and actions not carried through. Of the 'collective' being an elusive and perhaps illusive concept."[37] The relationship with Third World groups remained uneasy, as revealed later that fall during a meeting between HRUM and the Lincoln Collective. Boiled down to its essence, it revolved around the tension between an almost entirely white and upwardly mobile group and one composed of mostly working-class African American and Puerto Rican health workers. "They felt we were often guilty of having a colonizer attitude," one member wrote at the time.[38] But far from "going home," HRUM insisted, the collective needed to stay, for it possessed essential skills and technology that few others possessed, least of all in the resource-depleted South Bronx. To achieve more political symbiosis with HRUM, the collective underwent a major internal change, reorganizing itself into five subgroups, each of which would engage in "political education" on a new topic assigned to it by HRUM that week.[39] In HRUM's view, the collective had to "accept" more leadership from HRUM, and it was chided for its overall "unwilling[ness] to accept leadership."[40]

Outside of the internal political and personal transformation the Collective was to undergo, its members also continued attempts to democratize medical practice at Lincoln Hospital. Toward the end of its first year, the collective established a Pediatrics Parents Association, which learned about children's problems, took part in occasional rounds, and, most important, had input into the house staff selection. Parents were allowed to ask candidates questions, and at one point a ten-year-old and an eleven-year-old also participated in interviews.[41] More than 700 hospital workers and nurses received questionnaires about "the doctors' ability to practice their technical skills in a conscientious, humane manner."[42] The collective restructured governing committees within the pediatrics department so that parents, nurses, and workers could attend and level complaints against physicians. In one such meeting, nurses complained that "some doctors [had] a poor attitude and [were] hard to locate." These changes were an attempt to "ignore professional hierarchies," as stated in the first collective recruitment pamphlet, and to widen the parameters of governance within medical institutions.[43]

Word of the Lincoln Collective spread, and in 1972 it caught the attention of the Health Policy Advisory Center (Health/PAC). Founded in 1968, Health/PAC published a a bulletin that situated the city's and the nation's health care systems in a political-economic framework that emphasized the role of a "medical-industrial complex" in the maldistribution of health care resources.[44] In a chapter titled "The Community Revolt: Rising Up Angry," published in its 1970 book, *American Health Empire*, Health/PAC had predicted a wave of neighborhood insurgency to come in the medical world.[45] It was no surprise, then, that the Lincoln Collective caught Health/PAC's attention, and the latter commissioned a lengthy analysis of what was going on in the South Bronx. The piece offered qualified support for the collective, praising its medical reforms, and argued that Lincoln represented "one of the first thin threads of a sustained struggle to achieve worker-community control within a health institution."[46] At the same time, it characterized the collective rather harshly for being driven by "a romantic notion about the medical savior who leads other people's struggles or the voyeuristic tendency that defines a 'total politic' as 'rapping with the Lords.'"[47]

When it came to "worker-community control," the gap between ideal and practice remained. Around the time the Health/PAC dispatch appeared, the Lincoln Collective became embroiled in a seemingly trivial debate over meal tickets and HRUM's position that doctors should have to pay for meals, too. Some members of the collective recoiled at what they saw as HRUM's Third World guilt-tripping, and the exchanges quickly led to abstract discussions on the subject of proletarianization and revolution. One member, objecting to the idea of proletarianization of professionals, declared that he did not think revolution would "be led by workers in a traditionally Marxian concept," an implicit argument that rapid flattening of the hierarchy at Lincoln Hospital and elsewhere might be misguided. Another member stated that Third World people needed to allow white people "to evolve to revolution instead of laying down the line." An HRUM representative countered, accusing the collective of "enjoying" class differences.[48]

Into the next year, conversations continued apace over the role of race and professional class privilege; doctors' proper place in social change; what "revolutionary" even meant, and how much of a revolutionary to be. On occasion, HRUM showed signs of moderating some of its positions, as in the spring of 1973, when it criticized its own "extremism," particularly attacks on hospital worker unions for strategic conservatism that tended to focus only on its own members' welfare. "The unions are working class organizations," read one of its newsletters, "and we can't just disregard the hard-won gains of the last few years."[49] Within the collective itself, however, there were signs of emotional fatigue extracted by lack of resolution over bigger existential questions and ideological impasses. Nearly all Lincoln Collective members whom I have interviewed have spoken of intense burnout and emotional exhaustion, all compounded by having to juggle both charged political discussions and the work week of a resident in a place like Lincoln. At one meeting, members discussed a "lack of unity" among themselves but also expressed frustration over atomization and a "failure to relate" to "other health struggles through the city and country."[50]

Broadly, there was indeed even less sense of national connectedness, unlike the SHO days, when decentralized chapters nonetheless shared a loose national structure through which ideas could travel and people could interface. By 1975, despite some of the innovations that it had managed to implement, the collective petered out. In its last year of existence, it had scaled back its activities to political education and writing pamphlets. Important as these broadsides might have been, they circulated without much institutional foment to complement them. The specter of "sustained struggle to achieve worker-community control," of which Health/PAC had written, now looked like it would simply pass and dissipate.

Most members of the Lincoln Collective had developed new political consciousness during their time at Lincoln Hospital and gained new insights into the privileges that came with being upwardly mobile physicians in a municipal hospital. They succeeded in making some major changes in Lincoln's operations, increasing patient accountability and participatory governance for those who lived near the hospital and might have to use it. In one year, the Pediatrics Department received a city rating that was nearly thirty points higher than the citywide average.[51] But the exodus of the collective by the mid-1970s limited these reforms' ultimate impact. And even if they had stuck, what did it all mean without a sustained movement outside of one institution and one city? At another facility at the other end of the city, these dilemmas were playing out as well.

## Gouverneur and the Lower East Side

In 1967, the *Milbank Memorial Quarterly*, a prominent health policy journal, carried an article about a small public outpatient clinic on New York City's Lower East Side. Written by the clinic's two directors, Howard J. Brown and Howard Light, the article contained a list of twenty-five "operating principles," the most striking of which read pithily: "The community at large was entitled to a voice in the program and should share in the decision making process wherever possible."[52]

The document beamed with optimism about what a new ethos in health care governance might look like: not just at Gouverneur but at other facilities as well. But Gouverneur differed from Lincoln Hospital in one major respect. As a recipient of newly created funds for neighborhood health centers—most of them small outpatient clinics in underresourced neighborhoods—Gouverneur's initiatives had the backing of the federal government and the Office of Economic Opportunity, which required the creation of an administrative board composed of nonprofessional laypeople. Although these lay boards (called "health councils") varied nationwide, the one at Gouverneur appeared to possess real teeth. Called the Lower East Side Neighborhood Health Council–South, its formal charge was the review of applicants for future OEO funds, program priority setting, and input into selection of a director. It was all part of the OEO's commitment—one later racked by controversy—to "maximum feasible participation" of nonprofessionals, particularly the poor, in the decision making of the very programs created for their betterment.[53]

In their early days, Gouverneur and the council focused on cultivating a feedback loop between the clinic and its surrounding population, which was 29 percent Puerto Rican, 8.2 percent black, and 3.2 percent Chinese, some first-generation immigrants. Gouverneur hired employees directly from the neighborhood and encouraged residents to use the facility.[54] In the summer of 1967, Lower East Side youth carried out a study on Gouverneur usage patterns, language barriers, and wait times, which were promptly reported back to the facility.[55] But within a year, the relationship between the OEO-mandated council and Gouverneur quickly became confrontational, largely as a result of sweeping changes in the New York City health care system in the 1960s. Earlier in the decade, Mayor Robert Wagner had signed off on an "affiliation plan" that subcontracted administrative operations of the city's public facilities, including Gouverneur, to private medical centers. The plan had spurred an enormous amount of blowback, especially from critics who saw affiliation as nothing more than a power grab by the private medical establishment. For Gouverneur and the council, the affiliation structure affected the dispersal of OEO funds. Rather than go directly to Gouverneur, OEO money instead was managed by the clinic's private affiliate: Beth Israel Medical Center. Beth Israel's head, Ray Trussell, was no friend of bottom-up participation. He had recently left his post as commissioner of hospitals, having been the key architect in the affiliation plan imposed by fiat on the city's health facilities. For all the talk about maximum feasible participation, then, this meant the OEO-backed council's authority, in the last instance, rested with Trussell and Beth Israel administrators.

The next couple years saw protracted political conflict between the council and Trussell. In 1967, when the council identified a proposed full-time "health advocate" for Gouverneur, Trussell unilaterally refused. Only after learning of the council's direct appeal to OEO's headquarters in Washington, DC, did Gouverneur reverse its decision.[56] In August 1969, Trussell removed grant provisions for employee job training from Gouverneur's annual OEO allotment without consulting the council.[57] Two months later, the council again felt marginalized when the Gouverneur directorship opened up and Trussell's handpicked choice took office, despite the council's disapproval. A final explosive turning point came in December 1969, when the council received a sympathetic letter from Harvey Karkus, a Gouverneur doctor who openly deplored Trussell's conduct. A month later, Karkus lost his job, causing 120 people to show up at Trussell's office in protest.[58]

As if butting heads with Trussell was not enough, the council also faced tensions within its own ranks. Before they shifted their focus to Lincoln, the Young Lords and HRUM agitated intensely around Gouverneur. One of HRUM's key leaders, Gloria Cruz, had been the council's choice for a health advocate position. While Trussell would likely have paid little heed to any name put forth, the council's choice of HRUM's Cruz did not go over well with other parties either, many of whom bristled at HRUM's combativeness. HRUM's role raised important questions over what exactly "community" meant and the legitimacy of those who claimed to speak for it. In protesting Trussell's conduct, HRUM consistently invoked "community" and its own role as a critical conduit between "community" wishes on one side and a hierarchical medical giant on other. But how much authority did it have to speak in such terms? One surprising critic of HRUM was Local 1199, the otherwise militant hospital workers' union, which criticized HRUM in its newsletter.[59] "While HRUM claimed its goal was improved health care for the community," read an article in the newsletter, "it was unable to demonstrate any significant community support. Although the HRUM group included better working conditions among its goals, its members ignored both their fellow union members and the union's grievance machinery in dealing with management."[60]

Local 1199 was not alone in being sensitive to the ambiguities of the community rhetoric. A federal OEO consultant assessing the Lower East Side situation picked up on it, too. Brought in to adjudicate the standoff over the Gloria Cruz hiring, the OEO's Laura Ackerman saw one root of the problem in the legislative language—"maximum feasible participation," "direct involvement of the people"—and its being squishy and open to multiple interpretations. Beth Israel, for instance, had "stated that Gouverneur is a city clinic and feels that community involvement is a process wherein non-professional people are given education by hospital professionals concerning health care and then serve as a public relations and information source." For Beth Israel, then, maximum feasible participation simply meant outreach. For the council, however, it meant that and also shared governance: real bidirectional sharing of administrative power between Beth Israel and its community constituents. In the words of Ackerman, the council saw "itself as a lay board of directors which understands the health needs of the community," and therefore was "qualified to have a policy making voice and to act as an advocate for patients."[61] The OEO ultimately reversed Trussell's action, reinstated HRUM's Cruz, and ordered the council to come up with a "work plan" that stipulated what its duties were. It also required the council and Beth Israel to sign an agreement spelling out a formal system of negotiation in the event of a future conflict.[62]

But conflict over community participation never went away. It came roaring back in 1971, when the city scheduled Gouverneur for handoff from Beth Israel back to the Health and Hospitals Corporation (HHC), a newly created municipal agency.[63] As part of the transition, Beth Israel had designated the HHC the sole grantee of OEO funds, and when the HHC applied for grant renewal, it left only vague provisions for the council's participation in governance. The HHC admitted as much, writing that "although the application does not demonstrate community participation and involvement in program policy development and implementation, it does discuss the contacts engaged in by the applicant with two community groups." It also spoke of "significant problems in relation to community participation" and implied there would be much less of it down the line.[64]

The dispute set off another round of bickering, this time in federal court. The council filed a federal lawsuit charging administrators at the Department of Health, Education, and Welfare, at Beth Israel, and at HHC with violating legislative guidelines on community participation and condoning an "effective revocation" of its role. It asked for the court to mandate the council's participation and filed a separate grant application to become a direct recipient of funds in the future.[65] On May 23, 1972, the U.S. District Court in the Southern District of New York handed down a decision favorable to the council, issuing an injunction that mandated the HHC and Beth Israel offer it an official participatory role. In his opinion, Judge Morris Lasker concluded that the HHC had made "no provision for a neighborhood health council," as required by OEO guidelines.[66]

The council had won a new lease for itself, one fortuitously timed with the groundbreaking of a new fourteen-story, 216-bed facility in September 1972.[67] But the victory had a Pyrrhic quality. As the community battles raged on at Gouverneur, the political economy of the city was undergoing its own tectonic shift. The city's tax base had become increasingly insufficient, causing it to finance operations with bond sales. In 1975, it sold a staggering $8.3 billion and $900 million, respectively, in short- and long-term bond notes, an increasingly untenable strategy that papered over larger budgetary problems and immediately catalyzed a financial crisis that same year after a lender strike by banks that refused to service city debts further in the next cycle. These lending patterns had coincided with rollbacks in state and federal commitments to large urban municipalities that encouraged such borrowing in the first place.

With the Ford administration and the federal government's initial refusal to support aid packages, New York State imposed stringent financial discipline on the city via two ad hoc agencies, the Municipal Assistance Corporation (MAC) and the Emergency Financial Control Board (EFCB). These makeshift agencies' chief solution was to swap short-term bonds with long-term bonds while assuming control of city finances and imposing harsh austerity budgets in the hopes of restoring access to credit markets. When additional federal intervention did arrive, it came not in the form of aid but as short-term loans with rates 1 percent higher than Treasury bill interest rates. The cumulative result, Jonathan Soffer has noted, "creat[ed] a city in which almost nothing was maintained or repaired for a decade," after a 27 percent workforce reduction and a 75 percent decline in capital spending.[68]

The effects on the HHC, already struggling to gain fiscal and administrative footing in its infancy, were extremely pronounced. From 1975 to 1980, a net payroll reduction of 17 percent decreased the total HHC workforce to what it had been at the start. Service cuts complemented workforce shrinkage.[69] The cuts were directly propelled by fiscal stringency and the inability to sustain pre-1975 spending practices under MAC and EFCB oversight. And they hit Gouverneur hard. In 1973, two years before the fiscal crisis, the *Gouverneur Newsletter* reported that "in a few months 10% more may be cut and by the end of this year up to 40% or over 1 million dollars may be cut."[70]

By the middle to late 1970s, struggles on the Lower East Side had changed target and scope. The fight for governance and local control became of less importance to health activists than decisions made at the top, particularly around budgets. In short, crises in governance receded in importance relative to crises in finance. Driving the point home was a 1976 round of cuts that resulted in the closing of inpatient services at the new Gouverneur facility. Several more public hospitals would close over the next few years. Pitched as the battles over governance in the late 1960s and early 1970s had been, they took on a new—and less important— dimension relative to the new world that New York City, like much of the United States, was now entering. The Gouverneur experience paralleled that at Lincoln Hospital closely. Activists in both struggles came to question the value of radically altering governance in a single institutional node, even as the world around that node became ever more tumultuous.

## Conclusion: The Ambiguous Legacy of the Governance Revolution

Health care was hardly the only quarter of American life that underwent shifts in governance with ambiguous longer-term ramifications. In the 1970s, for instance, insurgents had chiseled away at the bureaucratic ossification and autocracy within some labor unions. But by the era of the failed Professional Air Traffic Controllers Organization strike, decades of capital flight, and automation in mining and in the automotive and steel industries, among others, these triumphs of governance seemed of much smaller importance. The same could be said of black elected officials in the aftermath of the Civil Rights Act of 1964, many of whom inherited what some analysts of the time called "the hollow prize"—that is, cities experiencing tail-spinning employment, dwindling revenue, and population loss on a scale far worse than that of New York City.[71]

And yet in health care, a sector historically riven with parochialism and exclusion, it was no inconsequential achievement to widen the boundaries of who had a say in the operation of its key institutions. By the early 1970s, medical students, community health workers, and laypeople had attained much more influence in health care decision making than they could have possibly anticipated just a decade earlier. Elites in the health care sector found themselves making some concessions to medical students, who demanded a more socially conscious curriculum and more responsive outreach. And they had to do the same with neighborhood activists who fought for the integrity of lay community boards and more input into facilities' operations, once all restricted to those in boardrooms. The medical world, for a brief moment anyway, looked like it might be turned upside down.

As one looks back with more than a few decades' perspective, though, the balance sheet of the medical governance revolution is decidedly mixed. Some of its achievements have indeed stuck. Today, even the most parochial medical schools, for example, genuflect commitment to the less fortunate who surround them. Often they do much more, in the form of service projects and the operation of year-round outpatient services for the indigent. Similarly, at many health care institutions, community health workers constitute a standard frontline conduit between patients and often imposing medical hierarchies. Within the academic sphere, community-based participatory research, whereby scholars mold research agendas in active consultation with those whom they study, has burgeoned. These examples of hierarchies flattening, insularity withering, and borders thinning—however slowly—are no doubt byproducts, direct and indirect, of the medical governance revolution.[72]

Still, these developments hardly characterize the dominant ethos of American medicine in the early twenty-first century. Unequal access, lack of affordability, and high costs remain—and at a magnitude far exceeding that of the 1960s and 1970s. Structurally, many health policy analysts predict a wave of mergers and consolidation in the coming decades. It all makes the targets of the medical governance revolution—the local single institution here, there, and elsewhere—look pretty quaint.[73] And it forces one to ask whether the accomplishments listed here were mere dents in an edifice that has changed more around its edges rather than fundamentally in the past fifty years.

Essays of this sort often end by lamenting the incompleteness of a revolution. But I want to close on a much more ambiguous note. The medical governance revolution's advocates focused almost exclusively on the local and on the process, even as the larger structures of health care—and politics and the economy more generally—were undergoing upheaval in ways that made new modes of institutional governance and participation much less impactful. So rather than lament that there wasn't more of a role for the grassroots and the "community," I want to argue instead that even if the medical governance revolution had come to full fruition, it might have been an achievement with the wrong target. It calls into question social movement organizing animated by the logic and goals of inclusionary biocitizenship that is incapable—intentionally or not—of also tackling other axes of political and economic power.

It may also be time to rethink a fundamental concept anchoring the governance revolution. The vocabulary of "community" was an ever-present but fuzzily defined term. To the extent that a consistent definition did emerge, it was composed of two tenets—local scale and increased participation—each with its own shortcomings. Localism encouraged seeing health politics through a granular lens that could not capture the full gamut of influences on the fortunes of health care facilities. And participation greatly overestimated not just its potential but also the actual interest that most laypeople really had in taking part in the grind of health care administration. Throughout, the term "community" was perpetually up for grabs, invoked constantly to bolster legitimacy even as who exactly constituted it was never entirely clear. These invocations of amorphous collective entities are often hallmarks of biocitizenship claims and counterclaims.

If there is another incarnation of biocitizenship on the ground in health care, it will have to focus not just on the single institutional type (the medical school) or neighborhood facility (Lincoln or Gouverneur) or the procedural (more community medical governance). It will instead need to turn to other parallel planes of decision making, including those in national-level and elite channels that are often viewed with suspicion, including, in recent times, when antistatist currents and romance for decentralization have surfaced in movements bookended by the Seattle World Trade Organization protests and Occupy Wall Street.[74] It will need, in other words, to go beyond what Daniel Immerwahr, writing about community development more generally, has called "thinking small" with an eye too close to the local and too far from "larger structures of power" and the "broader social order."[75] This is a holism of political practice that transcends the often sector-specific single-mindedness of those in the health fields. But confronting the indignities and maldistribution in American medicine requires no less.

NOTES

1 Adriana Petryna, "Biological Citizenship: The Science and Politics of Chernobyl-Exposed Populations," *OSIRIS* 19 (2004): 250–65; Dorothy E. Roberts, "Race, Gender, and Genetic Technologies: A New Reproductive Dystopia," *Signs: Journal of Women in Culture and Society* 34, no. 4 (2009): 783–804.

2 David Perlman, "AMA Silences a Dramatic Protest Attempt," *San Francisco Chronicle*, June 17, 1968; *Encounter: Bulletin of the Student Health Organizations* 3, no. 2 (Summer 1968), in Personal Papers of William Bronston, Sacramento, CA (hereafter cited as Bronston Papers). Bronston's papers have since been transferred to the Bancroft Library, University of California, Berkeley, and processed, with additions to the collection from time to time. I have also retained a digital copy of all documents cited from the Bronston collection.

3 *Encounter: Bulletin of the Student Health Organizations* 3, no. 2 (Summer 1968), Bronston Papers; Frank Campion, *The AMA and U.S. Health Policy* (Chicago: Chicago Review Press, 1984), 299. The AMA finally passed a resolution, after years of failing to do so, that explicitly banned racist discrimination in all its chapters and threatened to expel chapters that continued with the practice. See Richard D. Lyons, "A.M.A. Vote Ends Bars to Negroes," *New York Times*, December 4, 1968.

4 "Unrest on the Medical Campus," *Medical World News*, October 13, 1967.

5 *Borborygmi* 1, no. 1 (September 8, 1964), in Papers of Fitzhugh Mullan, Box 4, Folder 2, Wisconsin Historical Society, Madison, WI (hereafter cited as Mullan Papers); *Borborygmi* 1, no. 4 (December 1, 1964), in Box 4, Folder 2, Mullan Papers; *Borborygmi* 1, no. 5 (February 15, 1965), in Box 4, Folder 3, Mullan Papers; *Borborygmi* 1, no. 7 (April 23, 1965), in Box 4, Folder 3, Mullan Papers; *Borborygmi* 2, no. 2 (October 18, 1965), in Box 4, Folder 3, Mullan Papers; *Borborygmi*, 2, no. 3 (December 6, 1965), in Box 4, Folder 3, Mullan Papers; Naomi Rogers, "Caution: The AMA May Be Dangerous to Your Health: The Student Health Organizations and American Medicine 1965–1970," *Radical History Review* 80, no. 1 (2001): 5–34, offers an excellent organizational history of the early SHO. It asks questions different from this essay's on medical governance.

6 "Student Medical Action Conference: A Call for Members," ca. 1965, Bronston Papers.

7 *Borborygmi* 1, no. 6 (March 12, 1965), in Box 4, Folder 2, Mullan Papers; Mick McGarvey, "SMC Report," *Borborygmi* 2, no. 1 (September 7, 1965), in Box 4, Folder

3, Mullan Papers. The phrase "medical presence" originated with the Medical Committee for Human Rights (MCHR), a group of physicians who believed their visibility alongside civil rights activists carried a potential preventative effect in at atmosphere of violence. On MCHR and the term, see John Dittmer, *The Good Doctors: The Medical Committee for Human Rights and the Struggle for Social Justice in Health Care* (New York: Bloomsbury, 2009), 54–55.

8  Mick McGarvey, "A Brief History of the Student Health Project," *Encounter*, ca. early 1968, in Box 1, Folder 4, Mullan Papers; Harry Nelson, "Health Students Share Squalor to Help Poor," *Los Angeles Times*, July 24, 1966.

9  David Perlman, "Health Workers Talk about Their Summer with the Poor," *San Francisco Chronicle*, September 1, 1966.

10  George Getze, "'New Breed' Speaks Out: Health Care Called Right of All Citizens—Even the Poor," *Los Angeles Times*, September 2, 1966.

11  Alondra Nelson, *Body and Soul: The Black Panther Party and the Fight against Medical Discrimination* (Minneapolis: University of Minnesota Press, 2011), 12.

12  "Student Health Project Summer 1967," ca. 1967, in Bronston Papers.

13  Ibid.

14  "Student Resolutions," *Encounter* 1, no. 4 (October 21, 1966), in Box 1, Folder 4, Mullan Papers.

15  Martin Cherkasky and Steven Sharfstein, "Opportunities in Medical Education: The Result of Domestic Social Forces," *American Journal of Diseases of Children* 114 (November 1967): 531.

16  "Inside the Student Health Organizations," *AMA News*, March 11, 1968.

17  John Fisher, letter, *AMA News*, May 6, 1968.

18  Tim Smith, *In Vivo* 1, no. 2 (ca. fall 1968), in Box 1, Folder 6, Mullan Papers.

19  United States Department of Health, Education, and Welfare, Public Health Service, *The Student Health Project of Greater New York: Summer 1968* (Washington, DC: U.S. Government Printing Office, 1969), 54.

20  *Catalyst* 2, no. 1 (November 1968), in Box 1, Folder 3, Mullan Papers.

21  *Encounter: Bulletin of the Student Health Organizations* 4, no. 2 (Summer 1969), in Bronston Papers.

22  Ibid.

23  "Albert Einstein College of Medicine Lincoln Hospital House Officer Program in Community Pediatrics," ca. 1970, in Personal Papers of Michael McGarvey, New York, NY (hereafter cited as McGarvey Papers). Some of these papers have since been transferred to Columbia University Medical Center's August C. Long Health Sciences Library. I have also retained a digital copy of all documents cited from the McGarvey collection.

24  For a memoir of a physician who played a central organizing role in the Lincoln Collective, see Fitzhugh Mullan, *White Coat, Clenched Fist: The Political Education of an American Physician* (New York: Macmillan, 1976).

25  For more on the ERAPs, see Kirkpatrick Sale, *SDS* (New York: Vintage, 1969), 95–115, 131–50.

26 "Albert Einstein College of Medicine Lincoln Hospital House Officer Program in Community Pediatrics," ca. 1970, in McGarvey Papers.

27 "Demands of the Young Lords, Think Lincoln Committee & Health Revolutionary Unity Movement," July 14, 1970, in McGarvey Papers.

28 Ibid.

29 For more on the Young Lords with respect to health, reproductive rights, and urban politics, see Jennifer Nelson, *Women of Color and the Reproductive Rights Movement* (New York: NYU Press, 2003), 85–112; Johanna Fernandez, "The Young Lords and the Postwar City: Notes on the Geographical and Structural Reconfigurations of Contemporary Urban Life," in *African American Urban History since World War II*, ed. Kenneth L. Kusmer and Joe W. Trotter (Chicago: University of Chicago Press, 2003), 60–82.

30 "Report of the Ad Hoc Committee on Lincoln Hospital," ca. 1970, in McGarvey Papers.

31 Collective meeting minutes, November 24, 1970, in Box 2, Folder 1, Mullan Papers.

32 Collective meeting minutes, February 16, 1971, in Box 2, Folder 1, Mullan Papers.

33 Collective meeting minutes, May 11, 1971, in Box 2, Folder 1, Mullan Papers.

34 Community elective report, January 1971, in Box 2, Folder 7, Mullan Papers.

35 Community elective report, Winter 1970–1971, in Box 2, Folder 7, Mullan Papers.

36 Collective meeting minutes, June 15, 1971, June 22 1971, in Box 2, Folder 1, Mullan Papers.

37 Collective meeting minutes, August 10, 1971, in Box 2, Folder 3, Mullan Papers.

38 Collective minutes, August 24, 1971, in Box 2, Folder 3, Mullan Papers.

39 Ibid.

40 Ibid.

41 Helen Rodríguez-Trías, "The Medical Staff and the Hospital," *Bulletin of the New York Academy of Medicine* 48, no. 11 (December 1972): 1425; "Report to Workers, Nurses, Doctors, and Patients on the Evaluation of Doctors," ca. late 1972–early 1973, in Personal Papers of Harold Osborn, New Rochelle, NY (hereafter cited as Osborn Papers).

42 "Report to Workers, Nurses, Doctors, and Patients on the Evaluation of Doctors," ca. late 1972–early 1973, in Osborn Papers.

43 "Albert Einstein College of Medicine Lincoln Hospital House Officer Program in Community Pediatrics," ca. 1970, in McGarvey Papers.

44 "The Medical Industrial Complex," *Health/PAC Bulletin*, November 1969. For an analysis of the organization at this time, see Merlin Chowkwanyun, "The New Left and Public Health: The Health Policy Advisory Center, Community Organizing, and the Big Business of Health, 1967–1975," *American Journal of Public Health* 101, no. 2 (2011): 238–49.

45 Barbara Ehrenreich and John Ehrenreich, eds., *American Health Empire: Power, Profits, and Politics (A Health/PAC Book)* (New York: Random House, 1970).

46 Ibid., 1.

47  Susan Reverby and Marsha Handelman, "Institutional Organizing," *Health/PAC Bulletin*, January 1972, 16.

48  Collective meeting minutes, May 10, 1972, in Box 2, Folder 1, Mullan Papers.

49  Manuel Gomez, "HRUM at Lincoln," *Serve the People*, ca. 1972–1973, in Box 2, Folder 11, Mullan Papers.

50  Collective meeting minutes, February 7, 1972, in Box 2, Folder 1, Mullan Papers.

51  Helen Rodríguez-Trías to All Pediatric Staff, in Box 3, Folder 5, Mullan Papers.

52  Harold L. Light and Howard J. Brown, "The Gouverneur Health Services Program: An Historical View," *Milbank Memorial Fund Quarterly* 45, no. 4 (October 1967): 379.

53  On maximum feasible participation requirements, see Michael B. Katz, *The Undeserving Poor: America's Enduring Confrontation with Poverty*, 2nd ed. (New York: Oxford University Press, 2013), 124–28.

54  "Demographic Characteristics of the Area," 1967, in Box 15, Folder "Lower Manhattan Community Mental Health Center," Papers of Mobilization for Youth, Rare Books, Special Collections and Archives, Butler Library, Columbia University, New York, NY (hereafter cited as MFY Papers).

55  Lower East Side Neighborhood Health Council–South, health survey, Summer 1967, in Personal Papers of Terry Mizrahi (hereafter cited as Mizrahi Papers).

56  "Proposal for Additional Worker for the Lower East Side Neighborhood Health Council–South," ca. 1967, in Mizrahi Papers; "Eight Months Struggle for a Health Council Staff," January 20, 1969, in Mizrahi Papers; "A History of the Struggle for Staff for the Lower East Side Neighborhood Health Council–South with Some Conclusions Drawn and Some Questions Asked," ca. 1968–69, in Mizrahi Papers; "Summary Minutes of the Meeting of Representatives of the Lower Eastside Neighborhood Health Council–South with the OEO Health Office in Washington, D.C.," May 31, 1968, in Mizrahi Papers.

57  Ray Trussell to Herbert Notkin, December 3, 1969, in Mizrahi Papers.

58  Harvey Karkus to Antonin Flores, December 2, 1969, in Mizrahi Papers; Health/PAC, "Health Rap," January 26, 1970; "Closing Gouverneur Clinic," *Gouverneur Reports: Community Health Bulletin* 3, no. 1 (January 1970), in Mizrahi Papers.

59  For more on the politics of Local 1199, see Leon Fink and Brian Greenberg, *Upheaval in the Quiet Zone: 1199SEIU and the Politics of Health Care Unionism*, 2nd ed. (Champaign: University of Illinois Press, 2009).

60  "1199 and the Gouverneur Clinic Case," *1199 Drug and Hospital News*, February 1970, in Mizrahi Papers.

61  Laura Ackerman, "Final Report and Evaluation of Activities with Gouverneur Health Services Program (GHSP) and the Lower East Side Health Council–South," April 14, 1970, in Mizrahi Papers.

62  "Work Plan for Lower East Side Neighborhood Health Council–South 1970–1971," July 29, 1970, in Mizrahi Papers.

63  "Notes for Meeting with Dr. English," ca. Fall 1971, in Mizrahi Papers.

64 "Fact Sheet on the Crisis at the Gouverneur Health Services Program," November 29, 1971, in Mizrahi Papers; "The Gouverneur Health Services Program of the New York City Health and Hospitals Corporation: Continuation Application," December 30, 1971, in Mizrahi Papers.

65 LESHC-S, "Continuation Proposal for the Gouverneur Health Services Program on Behalf of the Lower East Side Neighborhood Health Council–South, Inc.," January 3, 1972, in Mizrahi Papers.

66 Opinion of the Court, *Lower East Side Health Council–South, Inc. et al. v. Elliot Richardson et al*, 71 Civ. 5160, U.S. District Court, S.D. New York (1972).

67 "Inauguration," *Gouverneur Newsletter* 1, no. 2 (October–November 1972), in Mizrahi Papers; "New Gouverneur Opens as the 19th City Hospital," *New York Times*, September 22, 1972.

68 Jonathan Soffer, *Ed Koch and the Rebuilding of New York City* (New York: Columbia University Press, 2010), 119. On the fiscal crisis more generally, see Ester R. Fuchs, *Mayors and Money: Fiscal Policy in New York and Chicago* (Chicago: University of Chicago Press, 1992), 86–93; William K. Tabb, *The Long Default: New York City and the Urban Fiscal Crisis* (New York: Monthly Review Press, 1982); and, especially, Kim Phillips-Fein, *Fear City: New York's Fiscal Crisis and the Rise of Austerity Politics* (New York: Metropolitan Books, 2017).

69 Charles Brecher, "Historical Evolution of HHC," in *Public Hospital Systems in New York and Paris*, ed. Victor Rodwin, Charles Brecher, Dominique Jolly, and Raymond Baxter (New York: NYU Press, 1992), 71.

70 "Pres. Nixon's Cut and Gouverneur," *Gouverneur Newsletter* 2, no. 1 (January–February 1973), in Mizrahi Papers.

71 The term was first used in H. Paul Friesma, "Black Control of Central Cities: The Hollow Prize," *Journal of the American Institute of Planners* 35, no. 2 (1969): 75–79.

72 An exact causal accounting is another essay entirely, but one marker of this influence is the number of activists here who later ended up in strikingly prominent positions within elite medical institutions: several deans of medical schools, a deputy surgeon general, and many more in medical academia and health care institutions.

73 David M. Cutler and Fiona Scott Morton, "Hospitals, Market Share, and Consolidation," *Journal of the American Medical Association* 310, no. 18 (2013): 1964–70.

74 See Tom Mertes, ed., *A Movement of Movements: Is Another World Really Possible?* (New York: Verso Books, 2004), for an outstanding collection of essays, some sympathetic, some more critical, on this politics. The historian Thomas Sugrue also notes localism's entrenchment in administrative structures and activist responses alike. See his "All Politics Is Local: The Persistence of Localism in Twentieth-Century America," in *The Democratic Experiment: New Directions in American Political History*, ed. Meg Jacobs, William J. Novak, and Julian Zelizer (Princeton, NJ: Princeton University Press, 2013), 301–26.

75 Daniel Immerwahr, *Thinking Small: The United States and the Lure of Community Development* (Cambridge, MA: Harvard University Press, 2015), 178–79.

9

# The Rise of Health Activism

## *The Importance of Social Class to Biosociality*

CELIA ROBERTS AND RICHARD TUTTON

In the past twenty years, the continued rise of health activism—especially but not exclusively in North America, Europe, and Australia—has been taken as emblematic of new trends in contemporary citizenship. While some social scientists have approached the study of health advocacy movements and organizations using social movement theory,[1] many have drawn on Paul Rabinow's concept of "biosociality" to understand the enactment of new forms of belonging. For Rabinow and Nikolas Rose, patient groups are "biosocial collectives" in which members enact "biological citizenship": a new form of belonging in the "age of biomedicine, biotechnology and genomics" in which people increasingly think and speak of themselves in biological terms.[2]

While authors working from a social movements' perspective explicitly discuss the significance of social class to analyze the emergence and dynamics of patient and health activist groups, those developing biosocial accounts tend to play down or ignore social class. We want here to ask what paying attention to class might contribute to biosocial understandings of health activism and to wider debates on biocitizenship. Building on existing work that has engaged critically with the concept of biosociality with reference to gender and race, we explore whether and in which ways class, usually understood as a social rather than a biological category, remains salient to discussions of health activism, biosociality, and biocitizenship. Our aim is to put class back on the table for scholars interested in biosociality, prompting them to take another look at a category of difference that many appear to have been consigned to history as a concept too caught up with older structuralist sociological approaches to be of interest.

## Biosociality and Health Activism

Paul Rabinow first articulated the concept of biosociality in a short essay published in 1992.[3] Against the backdrop of the recently funded Human Genome Project, he reflected on scientists' expectations about the widespread introduction of genetic testing of presymptomatic individuals and screening populations for genetic disorders. Rabinow suggested that one outcome of such developments would be the formation of group and individual identities based on specific genotypes: "It is not hard to imagine groups formed around the chromosome 17, locus 16,256, site 654,376 allele variant with a guanine substitution. Such groups will have medical specialists, laboratories, narratives, traditions, and a heavy panoply of pastoral keepers to help them experience, share, intervene and 'understand' their fate."[4]

Importantly, "biosociality" was intended to counter the more well-known "sociobiology," a field arising at the intersection of evolutionary science and anthropology that argues for the importance of biological drivers (such as genes and hormones) in human behavior and social relationships. Associated with conservative social views, sociobiology was widely criticized within the social sciences but had (and indeed continues to have) significant purchase in many scientific and public arenas.[5] Rabinow's reversal of the key terms reflects an entirely different approach to the significance of biology in human lives, in which humans take up and collectively work with or make meaning about biological information and experiences, rather than being driven by them.

As Sahra Gibbon and Carlos Novas suggest, science and technology studies scholars, anthropologists, and medical sociologists have often turned to biosociality when investigating "transformations in knowledge and identity brought about by new genetic knowledge" and the formation of biocitizenship.[6] Researchers have taken the concept and tested it against a range of empirical sites of inquiry, such as children with rare genetic disorders in New Zealand,[7] in vitro fertilization clinics in Ecuador,[8] gay and bisexual men in North East England at risk of HIV infection,[9] stem cell trials and clinical trial participation in India,[10] and the use of DNA technologies for criminal investigation and law enforcement.[11] However, it is in research on patient, health, or disease associations, groups, and organizations that biosociality has appeared most prominently.[12]

As Rabinow acknowledges, forms of disease-based sociality have a long history and predate his writing on biosociality. So what is biosociality referring to that is new? What is the specificity of biosociality in health activism? As Gibbon and Novas explain, at the time Rabinow was writing, there was much social scientific interest in patient-led or carer-led groups, which were seeking out new roles—no longer being only support networks or fund-raising efforts but becoming what Vololona Rabeharisoa and Michel Callon call "partner associations."[13] Such organizations no longer delegated decision making and resource allocation to scientific researchers but sought to actively direct and shape scientific and medical research on the disease or condition in question. Rabeharisoa and Callon's case study organization, the Association Française contre les Myopathies (AFM), for example, "made the highly symbolic decision to switch from an association of muscular dystrophy sufferers to an association *against* dystrophy."[14] For Rabinow, this shift entailed investing in the hope that the emerging genetic science of the 1980s and 1990s would both lead to a better understanding of the genetic basis of dystrophies and eventually produce interventions that could prevent or treat them. Indeed, the AFM became a major funder of genome mapping and sequencing initiatives; as Rabinow concludes, the AFM would "certainly do everything in its power to accelerate the invention of genetic therapy to alter genetic material in living humans."[15]

Elizabeth Roberts suggests that this aim to intervene into rather than accept human biology as an unavoidable fate distinguishes biosocial groups from other social groupings that form around illness or biological condition.[16] For her, only those groupings representing the "emergent shift in biological thinking towards the malleable" warrant being described as biosocial. For Nikolas Rose and Carlos Novas, similarly, it is the idea that "biology is . . . knowable, mutable, improvable, eminently manipulable" that characterizes contemporary biological citizenship.[17] For Rose and Novas, biosocial groupings are integral to how "biological citizens" form collectives to work to change the prospects faced by future people. Biosociality describes a new way of citizens acting together to support scientific understanding of the biological basis of disease in the hope that future people will not be born with the rare gene variants that result in such short or difficult lives. Viewing biology as malleable entails an emotional and financial orientation to work toward a possible future, living in what Tiago Moreira and Paolo Palladino call a "regime of hope"—a sociality structured by the promise that scientists will find the relevant variants and develop methods to "correct" them.[18] Born of today's suffering, biocitizenship (as lived through biosocial collectives) is nevertheless infused with optimism that things can be different.

## Biosociality and "Older" Vectors of Identity: Where Is Class in Health Activism?

As noted earlier, Rabinow coined the term "biosociality" as a challenge to the biologism of sociobiology, but he was arguably as much concerned with rethinking the social, attempting to move away from traditional theorizations of collective identifications. Importantly, Rabinow does acknowledge that new biosocial groupings would not necessarily be entirely divorced from what he calls "older forms of cultural classification of bio-identity such as race, gender and age." Indeed, he goes on to suggest that "in complicated and often insidious ways, the older categories may even take on a renewed force as the new genetics begins to spread."[19] Twenty years after Rabinow, we suggest it is time to turn our attention to perhaps the most maligned and neglected of these "older categories": social class. Does social class provide any analytical purchase when theorizing health activism as an expression of biological citizenship?

Other "older categories"—sex/gender and race—have, in contrast to social class, continued to be of great interest to those working on biosociality and health activism. In her research on breast cancer, for example, Sahra Gibbon explores the significance of gendering practices in women's campaigning to advance research on BRCA gene variants.[20] With the identification of and testing for BRCA1/2 in the 1990s, Gibbon suggests that patient advocacy discourses about breast cancer shifted from being primarily bound up with the politics of women's health against a background of social inequality and concerns about the quality of services, to focusing on shared genetic risk linked to the identification of gene variants. For Gibbon, however, the "biosocialities of BRCA genetics" cannot be disentangled from gendered modes of identity making and traditions of institutional cultures in the charity sector that "provide a structuring context for particular bio-social configurations."[21]

Studies of race provide a perhaps even more striking case of how "older forms of cultural classification of bio-identity" can both take on a renewed force and be redefined within biosocial groupings. As numerous scholars have noted, while politicians and others imagined that sequencing the human genome would underscore a common shared biology and signal the "death of race,"[22] genomics has instead inscribed race in the DNA of individuals. Reflecting on Rabinow's expectations in the early 1990s, Catherine Bliss, for example, argues that scholars have "found more recently that traditional identity politics has shaped the genomic turn towards race," with patient advocacy groups and health activists focusing on the health rights of specific groups such as African Americans and campaigning successfully for inclusion of minorities in medical research in the United States.[23] Steven Epstein argues that these campaigns have given both race and sex/gender "a transformed meaning," leading to the institutionalization of what he calls the "inclusion-and-difference" paradigm.[24] For Epstein, one of the problematic consequences of the new paradigm is that it "reshapes how we think about sex, gender, race and ethnicity—specifically, that it encourages the tendency to imagine these ways of differing as grounded strictly in our biological make-up."[25]

While the entanglements of sex/gender, race, and genomic knowledge have been recognized and documented in relation to health advocacy and activism, many scholars of biosociality mention class only in passing. Writing about rare genetic disease groups, for example, Novas remarks: "No doubt, as previous investigators have found, many of those who articulate and act upon their hopes in contemporary biomedicine tend to be white, middle-class, educated and highly capable of mobilizing social networks both in person and through the medium of the Internet."[26] Mainstream health activist groups also spend little time talking about class. In contrast to concerns about race and sex/gender, Epstein observes that at least in the United States, "one rarely hears calls for greater inclusion of people of different social classes within study populations or encounters worries about the dangers of extrapolating findings from the rich to the poor or vice versa."[27] The "inclusion-and-difference" paradigm has not been extended to include social class.

Yet, without doubt, social class is a major determinant of health. So what might be its relevance to biosociality and the study of contemporary health advocacy and activism? As suggested by Novas, class *is* an important feature of health activism.[28] In Britain, for example, Judith Allsop and colleagues observed that white, middle-class professionals tend to dominate as the founders and leaders of organizations in childbirth, cancer, and other key areas of health activism.[29] In his work on AIDS/HIV activism in the 1990s, similarly, Epstein notes that while the movement was broad—comprising grassroots activists, health educators, and doctors—the "treatment activists" who engaged with the scientific establishment tended to be white, middle-class men with other kinds of professional expertise.[30] Such individuals, Epstein argues, were better placed to learn the language of biomedicine and to seek an institutionalization of their representation in government bodies.

Novas and Epstein were both concerned with groups that engage with biomedicine in a biosocial way (interested in shaping biomedicine and in using biomedical knowledge to configure the body as malleable). Such groups are—it seems—not much interested in class per se. Other groups, often run by more minoritized actors, take a different approach and are much more likely to highlight class in their campaigning. Such groups are particularly visible within environmental justice movements, anti-toxin campaigns, and some strands of breast cancer activism.[31] Scholars working on these forms of activism tend not to use a biosociality or biocitizenship frame but rather to focus on the groups' enactments of social and environmental justice. Giovanna Di Chiro, for example, discusses how a particular group of low-income black American women activists highlighted the unequal distribution of endocrine-disrupting chemicals (EDCs) through "toxic tours" of their local environment, challenging "the dominant (primarily white, middle-class, and male) environmental movement" to recognize the unequal distribution of health risks relating to toxins, climate change, and environmental degradation.[32] Indigenous activists around the world similarly challenge the notion that health activism is the preserve of middle-class whites. Engaging with science and technology studies work on knowledge and expertise, Di Chiro argues that such marginalized groups should be recognized as both producing science and having specific expertise in identifying the role of class, race, and gender differences in toxic exposures.[33] In part, the scholarship on more marginalized health activism points to the problem of case selection in research: it is easy to assume that health activists are generally white and middle-class, and "therefore" that class is not a significant vector of analysis, if one chooses to study organizations run by white middle-class people (the logic of this thinking is flawed in our view: class remains important even when one class dominates the group).

But what does it matter that many patient advocates in mainstream, powerful activist groups are middle-class, well-educated, and relatively wealthy? This question is taken up by Rayna Rapp in her book *Testing Women, Testing the Fetus*, which describes the biosocial activism of parents of children with a diagnosis of Down's syndrome. Rapp analyzes the forging of new (biosocial) communities around the shared experience of parenting a child with Down's syndrome in the face of the disruption of existing social relations often triggered by a Down's diagnosis. Rapp shows, however, that such activism neither reaches nor represents all parents. Indeed, active members of the group she studied tended to be middle-class, with the financial resources to afford child care and "discretionary time" to attend meetings or write contributions for the newsletter. As she observes: "Middle-class and professional parents are far more likely to take on a 'voluntary' associational identity on behalf of their children than are working-class families."[34] This, Rapp surmises, might be due to prior professional experiences or a "proclivity to seek intellectually rational solutions to intractable personal problems."[35] The activism she observed was, she argues, structured by the "social fault lines" evident in U.S. society centered on race and class, with some individuals reporting a strong sense of alienation from those leading the groups.

Rapp's suggestion that members of contemporary health groups focus on "intellectually rational solutions to intractable personal problems" is supported by the findings of a recent large-scale study of patient organizations in Europe: in a four-country comparative study exploring four "condition areas" (birth, Alzheimer's disease, rare genetic conditions, and attention deficit/hyperactivity disorder), members of the European Patient Organisations in Knowledge Society (EPOKS) project documented the multiple activities of contemporary health activists.[36] As would be expected in an era of "biosociality," many of these activities were oriented toward engaging with scientific and medical knowledge. Relevant activities included searching for and reading scientific publications, attending scientific meetings, participating in expert panels involved in decision making around scientific and medical research and spending, and in many cases designing and undertaking their own (usually social scientific) research studies. Alongside other forms of evidence making (such as collecting and online curating of affected people's testimony and producing websites, talks, leaflets, and policy statements), these activities constituted what the researchers called "evidence-based activism."[37] Evidence-based activism, the EPOKS team argued, works to make knowledge about health conditions and to articulate—sometimes in collaboration and sometimes in contest with biomedical and scientific accounts and practices—what should be done to improve the situation of those living with that condition. Importantly, this was not necessarily oriented toward changing the biology of affected people, and so would not meet Elizabeth Roberts's strong definition of biosociality. Nevertheless, the organizations studied actively involved themselves in the production of scientific knowledge with the hope of improving chances for effective treatments, cures, or practices (in the case of birth) and could be seen as examples of biocitizenship. Indeed, one could argue that this orientation reflects the more nuanced understanding of the potential for genetic research to lead to "cure" that has emerged in this century, compared with the more heady optimism of the 1990s that animated Rabinow's work.

Evidence-based activism involves complex practices that are dependent on organizational activities (arranging and facilitating meetings, documenting decisions), reading, analysis and writing, persuasive public and private speaking, emotional support and encouragement of members, and technical and design expertise (building websites, designing leaflets, choosing images and logos). To state the obvious, these are learned, and they build on previous experiences in education, work, and social life. Social class is thus everywhere here; activists not only require access to the material objects and infrastructures that make their work possible (computers, the Internet, telephones, rooms, paper, printers, etc.) but also need embodied skills and/or the capacity and willingness to learn new ones. As sociologist Betsy Leondar-Wright shows in her detailed study of a wide range of U.S.-based activist groups, race, age, gender, and social class all influence the resources activists have to draw on in these regards. According to Leondar-Wright, social differentiations also structure the ways in which group members are able (or not) to learn from each other to develop new skills, share ideas, and formulate strategies.[38] Clashing styles of learning (e.g., through shared practice, discussion, or reading) and speaking (e.g., forms of teasing and humor) can mean that activists become frustrated with each other and are unable to benefit from each other's skill sets and knowledge. Rapp's finding that working-class members of Down's syndrome support groups often felt alienated from middle-class members who had taken up leadership roles supports this argument.

Focusing on the micro-interactions of group members observed in meetings and discussed in individual interviews, Leondar-Wright found strong evidence that social class was more important than race, age, or gender in shaping interactions within activist groups.[39] Her study addresses the five key organizational problems of activist politics: low turnout, inactive members, disagreement over antiracism, overtalking, and offensive behavior. In exploring the entanglements of social class with each of these problems, Leondar-Wright points to styles of speech, forms of humor, and affective experiences and understandings of conflict and disagreement, all of which (alongside occupation, income, education, and cultural capital) make up what she variously calls "class cultures," "class dynamics," and "class identities." Acknowledging that social class involves serious structural inequalities and discrimination, Leondar-Wright nonetheless articulates a positive version of class differences, arguing that each class has strengths and skills to offer to activist groups. Her key argument is that "more open discussion of class identities and class dynamics could be transformative for future social movements."[40]

It is important to note that Leondar-Wright's analysis maintains a clear focus on race, age, and gender alongside the exploration of class. Situated in a North American context, race and gender are clearly central to the group dynamics she analyzes. Possibly because activism is so much about argument, persuasion, and dis/agreement, ways of speaking become hugely important. Alliances and breaks occur when speaking is felt to be inappropriate, offensive, or discriminatory. People's speech also falls flat sometimes due to class differences—the words chosen can fail to resonate, resulting in little or no shared views about how to proceed. Leondar-Wright shows that, even articulating "the problem" the group is addressing is profoundly subject to the enactment of class cultures.

Although, as in much biosociality-oriented research, class was not addressed in most of the EPOKS work, that project similarly found that articulating "the problem" or "the cause" constituted a complex and enduring issue for most activist groups.[41]

As Aaron Panofksy argues, one problem health activists face is how to influence scientists to do the kind of research that the groups wish to see conducted.[42] An emblematic "success story" is the patient organization, PXE International. In 1995, Sharon Terry, a science educator, and her husband, Patrick Terry, who worked in the construction industry, set up this organization after their two children had been diagnosed with pseudoxanthoma elasticum (PXE), a rare genetic condition. Their dismay at being asked to provide multiple samples from their children to different groups of researchers had convinced them that PXE research was poorly coordinated. The Terrys criticized the conventional structures of science and wanted to promote different ways of working for the benefit of patients.[43] Alongside factors such as resource and collective mobilization, organizational capacity, expertise, and timing, however, Panofksy also emphasizes the importance of creating sociable relationships with individual scientists and their teams, through both more formal and informal structures and encounters such as "dinners at very nice restaurants."[44] The sociability of group members and scientists, as in the Terrys' case, helps to build trust, cooperation, and a sense of a "shared community" through friendly and sometimes close relationships.

Given the preceding, we suggest that the formation of group identities based on shared biologies (biosocialities) does not arise solely from the production of new scientific knowledges and that, along with sex/gender, age, and race, as Rabinow predicted, the "older categorization" of class remains salient. If we think of the kinds of patient and health activism organizations that have garnered particular attention—especially those organizations concerned with rare diseases such as PXE International—we can see that questions of injustice and inequity in the political economy and the social organization of science have been key factors behind their formation. Moreover, group formation entails various forms of labor—intellectual, affective, and material—in which individuals engage to mobilize both like-bodied others and those with whom they wish to make alliances such as scientists. But does the continuing importance of class mean we should abandon the concepts of biological citizenship and biosociality when theorizing health activism? Or, more radically, might class itself be theorized as biosocial?

## Embodying Class: Is Class Biosocial?

Although traditionally understood as situated in more abstract "macro-level" structures, class differences—like those of race, age, and sex/gender—are also lived through the body, in both social and—as we will argue—biological ways. A strand of sociological work explores the former, focusing on the expression of class identities in particular groups or places such as northern British white working-class young women;[45] particular gay and lesbian communities;[46] and schools.[47] Moving away from traditional methods of calculating class effects, and often engaging critically with Pierre Bourdieu's understanding of habitus, this research usually takes an ethnographic approach, providing rich accounts of lived experience of social processes of differentiation involved, for example, in speech, bodily movements, clothing, and food.[48] Such work, we suggest, demonstrates the close connection between bodies and class.

The sociology of health and illness has also long been interested in social class—the field of health inequalities is substantial and has made huge contributions to understanding the distribution of disease and health and particularly in advising how public health should best be conceived and practiced. As Kapilashrami, Hill, and Meer argue, however, the tendency of much of this work is to focus on class as an economic category or social structure rather than a culture or embodied identity.[49] In recent years, they show, focus has shifted from social class to "socioeconomic position," a move that both encapsulates this underlying premise and moves away from a more politicized Marxist approach to health research. (They note national differences here, claiming that social class remains more prominent in British research than elsewhere.) In response, Kapilashrami, Hill, and Meer suggest that health researchers should embrace an intersectionality model to conceptualize health as multidimensional, influenced by several axes of differentiation (including class, caste, ethnicity, and gender) that should be theorized not as additive (and therefore separable or static) but as intersecting, ontologically multiple, and dynamic. Such a move, they argue, reintroduces power relations, maintaining focus on "structural drivers" and "identity, social position and inequality."[50] We also suggest it implies a turn toward the body as a key site for the intersection of social forces.

The work of British sociologist Hilary Graham provides an example of how to think sociologically about the embodied effects of class. In her extensive research into smoking, Graham both explores the ways in which economic and cultural resources are unequally distributed and delves into the ways in which social class (and other lines of social differentiation and oppression) affects individuals' smoking patterns.[51] Using observation and interviews, Graham finds that economically de-prived women often use lighting a cigarette as either a way to rest from child care for a few minutes or to reroute an aggressive encounter with a male partner away from physical violence. Exploring smoking at the level of everyday practices helps Graham to argue that women may be protecting elements of their physical and mental health in engaging in smoking, rather than simply acting in self-harming ignorance or denial of public health warnings.

Putting this research into conversation with the broader, quantita-tive analysis of population smoking trends, Graham also explores the intergenerational links associated with social class, including smoking and poor nutrition. She argues that sets of material practices, includ-ing forms of shopping and cooking (in part determined by locality) and consumption (including smoking, eating, and drinking), establish life patterns for families that are powerful and constitute what Leondar-Wright might call class cultures. Children growing up in families in which smoking occurs and has benefits for adults are, she shows, more likely to smoke. This, Graham argues, indicates the ways in which health disadvantages are linked to families of origin, which in part constitute class. Health inequalities are thus not simply external structures but em-bodied experiences and patterns of life.

Graham's analysis resonates with claims made by environmental jus-tice activists mentioned earlier, who argue that exposures to toxins and related health outcomes are stratified along racial and class lines. Col-lecting and analyzing data about birth defects, cancer, and respiratory problems, among many other health issues, activists from many coun-tries have documented the ways in which social stratifications relating to income, housing location, forms of work, mobilities, and food shape the bodies of adults, children, and fetuses.[52]

How might these arguments reach into the biological body and the realms of biosocial activism? Here we turn to the work of feminist biologist Anne Fausto-Sterling, who explores the ways in which race, gender, and class shape bodies, health, and disease.[53] Working with the examples of bone density and hypertension, Fausto-Sterling shows how the physiological effects of lived experiences of racism, for example, might be intertwined with more obviously material factors such as nutrition, exposure to sunlight, exercise, and smoking. Writing about early-onset puberty, Celia Roberts builds on this work to argue for an understanding of bodies as processes of folding in which "internal" (genes, hormones) and "external" forces (endocrine-disrupting chemicals, social experience, food) entwine to enact sexual development.[54]

Genomic scientists too are beginning to suggest that socioeconomic and sociodemographic factors are linked to "the differential expression of hundreds of gene transcripts in leukocytes and diseased tissues such as metastatic cancers."[55] Epigenetic studies have also investigated differential rates of aging in individuals from different socioeconomic positions.[56] We might conclude from this that social class is starting to take on a renewed force in genomics and epigenomics, as well as in social science. Here, as in Fausto-Sterling's argument, social class might be reconceived as biosocial, as an engrained yet malleable embodied stratification.

## Conclusion

In 1996, Rabinow suggested that new biosocial groupings would "crosscut, partially supersede, and eventually redefine the older categories" of difference.[57] While others have articulated the limitations of biosociality as a concept,[58] few have highlighted social class or addressed how biosocial accounts of health activism tend to discount its significance. Instead of being relegated as an incidental dimension of who tends to become an activist or who takes leadership positions within groups, class needs to become a vital part of any well-rounded account of the biocitizenship expressed in biosocial health activism.

Further, we want to suggest that class troubles the distinction between "biological" and "social" implied in both "sociobiology" and "biosociality" as framed by Rabinow. Not only a set of economic and social structures shaping employment, income, and education, but also a materialization of a broad set of patterns of living that are both outside and inside the body, class is much more like gender/sex and race/ethnicity than many scholars imagine. Rather than an "old-fashioned" differentiation that will be largely superseded by new forms of biological identification, then, class might best be theorized as something that is made and remade as a salient category of difference as evidenced in the biomedical, epidemiological, and genomics research that we have discussed in this chapter, which is above all concerned with how class gets inside and is lived through the body. Notably, this understanding of class is one that has much stronger ties to the environmental justice approaches to health than to mainstream epidemiological or sociological accounts. As activists and scholars working with/in more marginalized groups suggest, class is materially produced over time and lived, along with race, sex/gender, and other differences, as semisolid—yet changeable—embodied facts.

In emphasizing class, we are not suggesting that it could be simply added to a list of categories to which analysts should pay attention. Gender, race, and class are never simply enacted or performed in isolation from each other but are, as intersectionality accounts exemplify, always interconnected.[59] Perhaps "biosectionality" might be a fruitful analytic for critically engaging with the ways in which new "truths" about human biology give rise to new socialities. Drawing on the combined insights of social movement theory and biosocial accounts of health activism, as well as feminist and postcolonial studies of embodiment, biosectionality would direct attention to the ways in which forms of differentiation that are not simply social or biological—including class, race, and gender, among many others—emerge and are articulated together.

NOTES

1  See Phil Brown, Stephen Zavestoski, Sabrina McCormick, Brian Mayer, Rachel Morello-Frosch, and Rebecca Gasior Altman, "Embodied Health Movements: New Approaches to Social Movements in Health," *Sociology of Illness and Health* 26, no. 1 (2004): 50–80; Kyra Landzelius, "Patient Organization Movements and New Metamorphoses in Parenthood," *Social Science and Medicine* 62, no. 3 (2006): 529–37.

2  Paul Rabinow and Nikolas Rose, "Biopower Today," *BioSocieties* 1, no. 2 (2006): 195–218; Nikolas Rose and Carlos Novas, "Biological Citizenship," in *Global As-*

*semblages: Technology, Politics, and Ethics as Anthropological Problems*, ed. Aihwa Ong and Stephen Collier (Malden, MA: Blackwell, 2005), 439.

3  Paul Rabinow, "Artificiality to Enlightenment: From Sociobiology to Biosociality," in *Incorporations*, ed. Jonathan Crary and Sanford Kwinter (Brooklyn, NY: Zone Books, 2002).

4  Paul Rabinow, *Essays on the Anthropology of Reason* (Princeton, NJ: Princeton University Press, 1996), 102.

5  See Rachel O'Neill, "Feminist Encounters with Evolutionary Psychology: Introduction," *Australian Feminist Studies* 30, no. 86 (2015): 345–50.

6  Sahra Gibbon and Carlos Novas, "Introduction," in *Biosocialities, Genetics and the Social Sciences*, ed. Sahra Gibbon and Carlos Novas (London: Routledge, 2008), 1.

7  Ruth Fitzgerald, "Biological Citizenship at the Periphery: Parenting Children with Genetic Disorders," *New Genetics and Society* 27, no. 1 (2008): 251–66.

8  Elizabeth Roberts, "Biology, Sociality and Reproductive Modernity in Ecuadorian in Vitro Fertilization: The Particulars of Place," in *Biosocialities, Genetics and the Social Sciences*, ed. Sahra Gibbon and Carlos Novas (London: Routledge, 2008), 79–97.

9  Ingrid Young, "Imagining Biosocial Communities: HIV, Risk, and Gay and Bisexual Men in the Northeast of England," *European Journal of Cultural Studies* 19, no. 1 (2016): 33–50.

10  Aditya Bharadwaj, "Biosociality and Biocrossings: Encounters with Assisted Conception and Embryonic Stem Cells in India," in *Biosocialities, Genetics and the Social Sciences*, ed. Sahra Gibbon and Carlos Novas (London: Routledge, 2008), 98–116; Kaushik Sunder Rajan, "Biocapital as an Emergent Form of Life: Speculations on the Figure of the Experimental Subject," in *Biosocialities, Genetics and the Social Sciences*, ed. Sahra Gibbon and Carlos Novas (London: Routledge, 2008), 157–87.

11  Barbara Prainsack, "Seeing through Genes? Against Biosociality behind Bars," *Kriminologisches Journal* 44, no. 3 (2012): 225–44.

12  See Michael Callon and Vololona Rabeharisoa, "Gino's Lesson on Humanity: Genetics, Mutual Entanglements, and the Sociologist's Role, *Economy and Society* 33, no. 1 (2004): 1–27; Daniele Carrieri, Hannah R. Farrimond, Susan E. Kelly, and Peter Turnpenny, "Fragmented Biosociality: Familial Meanings of Neurofibromatosis Type 1," *Journal of Medical Genetics* 47, suppl. 1 (2010): 104; Rebecca Diamond, Andrew Bartlett, and Jamie Lewis, What Blinds Biosociality: The Collective Effervescence of the Patient-Led Conference, *Social Science and Medicine* 126 (2015): 1–8; Sahra Gibbon, *Breast Cancer Genes and the Gendering of Knowledge: Science and Citizenship in the Cultural Context of the "New" Genetics* (London: Palgrave, 2007); C. Guell, "Candi(e)d Action: Biosocialities of Turkish Berliners Living with Diabetes, *Medical Anthropology Quarterly* 25, no. 3 (2011): 377–94; Deborah Heath, "Locating Genetic Knowledge: Picturing Marfan Syndrome and Its Traveling Constituencies, *Science, Technology and Human Values* 23, no. 1 (1998): 71–97; Rebecca Marsland, "(Bio)Sociality and HIV in Tanzania: Finding a

Living to Support a Life," *Medical Anthropology Quarterly* 26, no. 4 (2012): 470–85; Carlos Novas "The Political Economy of Hope: Patients' Organizations, Science and Biovalue," *Biosocieties* 1, no. 3 (2006): 289–305; Rayna Rapp, *Testing Women, Testing the Fetus: The Social Impact of Amniocentesis in America* (New York: Routledge, 2000); Mikkel Bunkenborg, "The Uneven Seepage of Science: Diabetes and Biosociality in China," *Health and Place* 39 (2016): 212–18; Steven Epstein, *Inclusion: The Politics of Difference in Medical Research* (Chicago: University of Chicago Press, 2008).

13 Gibbon and Novas, "Biosociality"; Vololona Rabeharisoa, Tiago Moreira, and Madeleine Akrich, "Evidence-Based Activism: Patients', Users', and Activists' Groups in Knowledge Society," *BioSocieties* 9, no. 2 (2014): 111–28; Vololona Rabeharisoa and Michel Callon, "The Involvement of Patients' Associations in Research," *International Social Science Journal* 54, no. 171 (2002): 57–63.

14 Rabeharisoa and Callon, "Involvement of Patients' Associations in Research," 58 (emphasis added).

15 Paul Rabinow, *French DNA: Trouble in Purgatory* (Chicago: University of Chicago Press, 2002), 16.

16 Roberts, "Biology, Sociality and Reproductive Modernity."

17 Rose and Novas, "Biological Citizenship," 442.

18 Tiago Moreira and Paolo Palladino, "Between Truth and Hope: On Parkinson's Disease, Neurotransplantation and the Production of the 'Self,'" *History of the Human Sciences* 18, no. 3 (2005): 55–82.

19 Rabinow, *Essays on the Anthropology of Reason*, 103.

20 Gibbon, *Breast Cancer Genes and the Gendering of Knowledge*.

21 Ibid., 21.

22 Nadia Abu El-Haj, "The Genetic Reinscription of Race," *Annual Review of Anthropology* 36 (2007): 283–300.

23 Catherine Bliss, "The Marketization of Identity Politics," *Sociology* 47, no. 5 (2013): 1012.

24 Epstein, *Inclusion*, 21.

25 Ibid., 141.

26 Novas, "The Political Economy of Hope," 302.

27 Epstein, *Inclusion*, 143.

28 Novas, "The Political Economy of Hope."

29 Judith Allsop, Katherine Jones, and Rob Baggott, "Health Consumer Groups in the UK: A New Social Movement?," *Sociology of Health and Illness* 26, no. 6 (2004): 737–56.

30 Steven Epstein, *Impure Science: AIDS, Activism and the Politics of Knowledge* (Berkeley: University of California Press, 1996), 418.

31 Greta Gaard, "Greening Feminism," in *Greening the Academy: Ecopedagogy through the Liberal Arts*, ed. Samuel Day Fossbender, Anthony J. Nocella II, and Richard Kahn (New York: Springer, 2012), 199–216; Giovanna Di Chiro, "Local Actions, Global Visions: Remaking Environmental Expertise," *Frontiers: A Journal*

*of Women's Studies* 18, no. 2 (1997): 203–31; Giovanna Di Chiro, "Bearing Witness or Taking Action? Toxic Tourism and Environmental Justice," in *Reclaiming the Environmental Debate: The Politics of Health in a Toxic Culture*, ed. Richard Hofrichter (Cambridge, MA: MIT Press, 2000), 275–300; Giovanna Di Chiro, "Polluted Publics? Confronting Toxic Discourse, Sex Panic, and Econormativity," in *Queer Ecologies: Sex, Nature, Politics, Desire*, ed. Catriona Mortimer-Sandilands and Bruce Erickson (Indianapolis: Indiana University Press, 2010), 199–230; Phil Brown and Faith Ferguson, "Making a Big Stink: Women's Work, Women's Relationships and Toxic Waste Activism," *Gender and Society* 9, no. 2 (1995): 145–72.

32 Di Chiro, "Polluted Publics?," 201.

33 Di Chiro, "Local Actions, Global Visions."

34 Rapp, *Testing Women, Testing the Fetus*, 298.

35 Ibid.

36 The project was led by Vololona Rabeharisoa and Madeleine Akrich, of the École des Mines, Paris (2009–12). Celia Roberts was a team member. For more information, see www.csi.mines-paristech.fr.

37 Rabeharisoa, Moreira, and Akrich, "Evidence-Based Activism."

38 Betsy Leondar-Wright, *Missing Class: Strengthening Social Movement Groups by Seeing Class Structures* (Ithaca, NY: Cornell University Press, 2014).

39 Ibid.

40 Ibid., 5.

41 Orla O'Donovan, Tiago Moreira, and Etaoine Howlett, "Tracking Transformations in Health Movement Organizations: Alzheimer's Disease Organizations and Their Changing 'Cause Regimes,'" *Social Movement Studies* 12, no. 3 (2013): 316–34; Celia Roberts, Imogen Tyler, Candice Satchwell, and Jo Armstrong, "Health Social Movements and the Hybridization of 'Cause Regimes': An Ethnography of a British Childbirth Organization," *Social Movement Studies* 15, no. 4 (2016): 417–30.

42 Aaron Panofsky, "Generating Sociability to Drive Science: Patient Advocacy Organizations and Genetics Research," *Social Studies of Science* 12, no. 3 (2011): 31–57.

43 Sharon F. Terry and Charles D. Boyd, "Researching the Biology of PXE: Partnering in the Process," *American Journal of Human Genetics* 106, no. 3 (2001): 177–84; Sharon F. Terry, Patrick F. Terry, Katherine A. Rauen, Jouni Uitto, and Lionel G. Bercovitch, "Advocacy Groups as Research Organizations: The PXE International Example," *Nature Reviews Genetics* 8, no. 2 (2007): 157–64.

44 Panofsky, "Generating Sociability to Drive Science," 48.

45 Beverley Skeggs, *Formations of Class and Gender: Becoming Respectable* (London: Sage, 1997).

46 Jon Binnie and Beverley Skeggs, "Cosmopolitan Knowledge and the Production and Consumption of Sexualized Space: Manchester's Gay Village," *Sociological Review* 52 (2004): 39–62.

47 Diane Reay, "'It's All Becoming a Habitus': Beyond the Habitual Use of Habitus in Educational Research," *British Journal of Sociology of Education* 25, no. 4 (2004): 431–44.

48 Lisa Adkins and Beverley Skeggs, eds., *Feminism after Bourdieu* (Oxford: Blackwell, 2005).

49 Anuj Kapilashrami, Sarah Hill, and Naser Meer, "What Can Health Inequalities Researchers Learn from an Intersectionality Perspective? Understanding Social Dynamics with an Inter-categorical Approach?," *Social Theory and Health* 13, nos. 3–4 (2015): 288–307.

50 Ibid., 289.

51 Hilary Graham, "Promoting Health against Inequality: Using Research to Identify Targets for Intervention—A Case Study of Women and Smoking," *Health Education Journal* 57, no. 4 (1998): 292–302; Hilary Graham, "Disadvantaged Lives and Women's Smoking: Patterns and Policy Levers," *MIDIRS Midwifery Digest* 13, no. 2 (2003): 152–56; Hilary Graham, *Understanding Health Inequalities*, 2nd, ed. (Maidenhead, UK: Open University Press, 2009).

52 See also Nancy Kreiger and George Davey Smith, "'Bodies Count' and Body Counts: Social Epidemiology and Embodying Inequality," *Epidemiologic Reviews* 26, no. 1 (2004): 92–103.

53 See Anne Fausto-Sterling, "Refashioning Race: DNA and the Politics of Health-care," *Differences: A Journal of Feminist Cultural Studies* 15, no. 3 (2004): 1–37; Anne Fausto-Sterling, "The Bare Bones of Sex: Part 1—Sex and Gender," *Signs* 30, no. 2 (2005): 1491–1527; Anne Fausto-Sterling, "The Bare Bones of Race," *Social Studies of Science* 38, no. 5 (2008): 657–94.

54 Celia Roberts, *Puberty in Crisis: A Sociology of Early Sexual Development* (Cambridge: Cambridge University Press, 2015).

55 Steven W. Cole, "Human Social Genomics," *PLoS Genetics* 10, no. 8 (2014): e1004601.

56 Ronald L. Simons, Man Kit Lei, Steven R. H. Beach, Robert A. Philibert, Carolyn E. Cutrona, Frederick X. Gibbons, and Ashley Barr, "Economic Hardship and Biological Weathering: The Epigenetics of Aging in a U.S. Sample of Black Women," *Social Science and Medicine* 150 (2016): 192–200.

57 Paul Rabinow, *Essays on the Anthropology of Reason* (Princeton, NJ: Princeton University Press, 1996), 103.

58 See Ruth Fitzgerald, "Biological Citizenship at the Periphery: Parenting Children with Genetic Disorders," *New Genetics and Society* 27, no. 3 (2008): 251–66; Margaret Lock, "Biosociality and Susceptibility Genes," in *Biosocialities, Genetics and the Social Sciences*, ed. Sahra Gibbon and Carolos Novas (London: Routledge, 2008), 56–78.

59 See Kimberlé Crenshaw, "Mapping the Margins: Intersectionality, Identity Politics, and Violence against Women of Color," *Stanford Law Review* 43 (1991): 1241–52, 1262–65.

# 10

## Patient Activists

### *Experience with Public Engagement*

HEATHER ASPELL, JULIE CERRONE, AND KIRSTEN SCHULTZ

Editors' note: In academic scholarship, we often use the concept of biocitizenship to talk about how people and communities struggle with chronic illnesses and the institutions of science and medicine. This collection is no exception. However, we thought it would be useful to consider how patient activists view themselves and their work as advocates for their disease communities in relationship to this concept. We asked Heather Aspell, Julie Cerrone, and Kirsten Schultz—patient activists with long records of public engagement—to detail their experiences as they relate to theories of biocitizenship. Here are their stories.

## Heather C. Aspell

I am a disabled and chronically ill attorney, artist, and patient advocate in Los Angeles, California. Although I have lived with chronic illness since childhood, I hid my illnesses for most of my life and only began engaging in patient advocacy in the past few years after becoming unable to work. Prior to engaging in patient advocacy, I viewed my career as an attorney as a key part of my identity. As my health deteriorated, and I found myself unable to work, I lost that identity and as a result felt like I was lost as a person. During this time, I began to connect with other patients online via social media, and that gave me a new sense of purpose. At first I simply connected with other patients for camaraderie, but in time, I began to more openly share my own story on social media in an attempt to help others and change public misconceptions about the realities of living life with complex chronic illnesses as a thirty-something.

Using social media, I share unapologetic "selfies" and other images featuring me using my mobility aids and engaging in everyday activities relating to caring for my chronic illnesses to normalize the idea that anyone can be chronically ill or disabled. I hope that through sharing these images I can help to educate the public about the amount of time and effort required to care for chronic illnesses, to dispel misunderstandings about people like myself who are receiving disability benefits or who take much-maligned opioid pain medications, and to more generally combat misconceptions about what it means to be sick or disabled.

Early in my advocacy I encountered the term "ePatient," which refers to a patient who is empowered, educated, and engaged. In my understanding this term applies not only to patients who engage in advocacy for larger disease communities but also to those who are empowered and engaged in their own health care or the health care of their loved ones. More recently I encountered the term "biocitizenship," which I understand as being a broader term than "ePatient" in that we are all biocitizens, regardless of our level of engagement or our health status. "Biocitizenship" is a term we can use to discuss the ethical and political issues surrounding health and bodies as medicine progresses. In today's society, health and bodies are key ways we identify ourselves—whether it is a seemingly healthy young woman who tells me about how she is gluten-free and vegan and practices yoga, or my mother, who identifies herself as a type 1 diabetic—we all use concepts relating to our health and bodies to define who we and others are, and we are all therefore biocitizens. This can be both positive and negative, as the literature surrounding biocitizenship has explored.

For some, the terms imposed on them in this era of focus on health and bodies feel constraining and limiting. Indeed, as I have chosen to identify as "disabled," many others with similar conditions reject this term as limiting. Where biocitizenship imposes identities relating to health and bodies on an individual, it risks limiting that person to the good and bad characteristics commonly associated with that term. And particularly when a person is identified as being chronically ill or disabled, they are at risk of facing discrimination and judgment.

I personally have felt that identities and labels placed on me such as disabled, chronically ill, sick, unwell, crippled, weak, lazy, and other terms that have negative connotations were limiting. This is why I hid my chronic illnesses for many years. Instead of leaving the house with my cane or wheelchair, I would too often stay home to avoid being identified as "disabled" and all the negative connotations I feared others would place on me. This has been the core of my own advocacy work: to reclaim and transform the identities that society has placed on me. In each photo I post showing me engaging in day-to-day activities necessary to care for my health, I am saying, "Yes, I am chronically ill and disabled. No, this does not make me less of a person, woman, wife, friend, sister, or daughter." I can pose with my cane and look sexy at the same time. I am not currently able to work, but I am not "lazy." Caring for my health is a full-time job, as followers of my social media posts can see.

I am also mindful of potential issues surrounding the "citizenship" aspect of "biocitizenship," as there is always unequal access to the privileges and benefits of any conceptualization of citizenship. This is certainly true in biocitizenship, where the healthy and able-bodied will have privilege over the sick and disabled, and other intersecting identities such as race, gender, sexual orientation, socioeconomic status, and more will affect the quality of health care that each biocitizen will have access to. Because I am privileged enough to have access to quality health care, I hope to elevate the voices of those other biocitizens without that access to help improve health care for everyone.

On the other hand, for many, finding an identity in their health status can be liberating, as it has ultimately been for me. When I began to embrace my various identities as they relate to my health and my body, such as disabled, chronically ill, or ePatient, I was able to connect with others who shared those identities, which led to my better accepting the reality of my own situation. Beyond the improvements connecting with others who share my identities has led to in my own life, together as a community of ePatient biocitizens we have been able to advocate for meaningful changes in health care and society. Patient advocacy groups accomplish incredible things by unifying, and this is made possible first by being brought together by a shared identification as members of a particular group. If we view ourselves as belonging to certain groups relating to our health, we can band together and engage in political activities that will hopefully lead to a better society for us to exist in as biocitizens. Ultimately, I see "biocitizenship" as a useful term in examining our relationships with identities and our bodies and health. But, as with any form of citizenship, the privileged must keep listening to those without the same ability to advocate and help ensure their interests are considered and protected in the political discourse surrounding biocitizenship as well.

## Julie Cerrone

I remember my roommate and me, sitting in our college dorm room, setting up our Facebook profiles. Back then, I never could have imagined how social media would play a part in my life.

From that day forward, I became consumed with social media. I dabbled with Twitter, but Facebook was my main go-to; I would update my status constantly. If something happened in my life, my followers knew about it. Upon graduating from college, I started a career as an IT consultant. I enjoyed my work, but I used to sit at my computer wishing someone would pay me big bucks to manage their social feeds.

Fast-forward to the age of twenty-seven, when I was forced out on disability leave from my job. I had been diagnosed with psoriatic arthritis, complex regional pain syndrome, avascular necrosis in my left femur, anxiety, depression, and melanoma. During this time, it was extremely hard for me to go on Facebook. My friends continued to post about fun parties, new restaurants, and travel highlights. But I was relinquished to spending the majority of my days in bed. I didn't think anyone would want to be updated on the latest medication I was taking, the most recent injection I had, or the fact that I had had a panic attack trying to leave my house to go to the doctors.

It was during this time that I stumbled upon Twitter chats focused on patients' health journeys. Unbeknownst to me, there was a huge, active patient population on Twitter! These Twitter chats gave me the opportunity to start to connect with others who were going through similar situations. Maybe they did not have the exact diagnosis that I had, but these individuals were suffering from chronic conditions and could relate to what I was going through. It was the first time since I had left work that I did not feel alone.

In these new friends, I started learning so much. They were blogging about their situations, and I learned what worked for them, what did not work for them, and where to go for resources. It was truly from these new online friends that I finally felt like I had the tools to help manage my condition. Sure, my doctors gave me advice and a few places to turn to, but can you really put a value on hearing advice straight from someone who is experiencing it firsthand?

Because I found it so beneficial to read other patients' blogs, I decided to start my own. I had stumbled upon a few blogs that depicted life with psoriatic arthritis or avascular necrosis, and they were tremendous tools for me. I had relied on their information; therefore, I knew I had to give back and get my story out there as well. And just like when I had started my Facebook page, I never would have guessed starting a patient blog would change my life as dramatically as it has. It started with getting my story out there and quickly snowballed! It evolved into giving practical tips and tricks for living with chronic illness, helping others empower themselves to take control of their health, writing for different online publications, speaking at different medical conferences, and so much more! It truly sent me down a whole new career path.

So often I see top doctors telling patients not to "google your symptoms" or "believe what you read online." But I have to disagree. There is an entire patient population online sharing their health journeys. There is so much to learn from each and every one of these stories. It's important to remember that what works for one person won't necessarily work for another. But through these patient blogs, Twitter chats, Facebook support groups, online forums, patients have the opportunity to connect and share like there never has been before.

I would go to one of my twelve-plus doctors, and they would give me medication or a few words of wisdom. However, at the end of the day, it was the patients online who made me realize that I needed to empower myself, take control of my situation, and do everything I could to live my best life.

If it had not been for autoimmune patients blogging online, I may have never explored and uncovered all the triggers to my psoriatic arthritis. My doctors had not suggested it; other patients had. If it had not been for other avascular necrosis patients, I may have never found the stem cell procedure that helped regenerate my bone. I'd probably still be on the crutches I spent three and a half years on and still rely on opioid pain medications three to four times a day. And if it had not been for patients, across condition areas, instilling the idea that you must empower yourself with knowledge, I might have never arrived at a place of managing my conditions on my own terms.

There is always a time for scientific literature, but I have felt that patients benefit from learning from each other tremendously. The Internet has created a powerful way for patients, who might have never connected with each other, to connect on a personal and intimate basis.

This group of biocitizens are not bound by geographic location, insurance plans, or governments. These citizens are banding together and creating a shift in the health world. These patients are creating influence on mind-set, medications, and treatment options. These patients are helping to transform other patients' health in immeasurable ways. Marketing agencies and top brands around the world recognize the power of online influencers. I believe that the online patient world not only doesn't get the respect and recognition it deserves but is truly creating an ecosystem of influence and change.

Who would have thought social media, coupled with my own health struggles, would have provided me an outlet to really help forge change in this world? But it has, and I'm excited to see where it goes from here.

## Kirsten Schultz

Engaged patients—that is to say, patients who are engaged in their own care and help to educate and empower others to do the same—are far more significant than they are often given credit for, especially from the world of medicine. I may be biased, being one of them and all, but it's true. The support provided by patient groups alone can help to battle isolation related to illness and disability, curbing rates of depression. The beauty of this support is that it does not have to be in person, but is often done through social media, meaning that support is available all day every day from people across the globe. Some of the most important interactions that I have had with others happen at 3:00 a.m. when I am up with unrelenting chronic pain. Those interactions can range from intimate conversations with close friends to a stranger simply saying "me, too."

Knowing that I'm not alone in the wee hours of the morning like that has had much more of an impact than many of my interactions with health care professionals have. These interactions have led to an increase in support, awareness, and funding for rare diseases, whose sufferers 100 years ago may never have met another soul with their condition. For groups of rare disease patients, the support they receive can be even more life changing than for those with more common conditions. As a rare disease patient myself, this has been valuable beyond words. I have learned so much more about my condition from other patients than I often have from physicians themselves, who aren't as well versed in some of these diseases. I have also had my life literally saved from infections, side effects, and depression due to these connections with my fellow rare disease patients.

The best of us can help to work with health care professionals in order to pass on that knowledge, jumping over hurdles of paternalism and top-down thinking. These things—awareness, research, support, et cetera—come from an inherently political place. They "require active political engagement" in order to have any hope of succeeding.[1] This is even more true of rare diseases as they require at times somewhat ingenious, sometimes militant (though nonviolent) actions in order to even raise awareness. Consider what the Ice Bucket Challenge did for amyotrophic lateral sclerosis (ALS): $115 million raised, three new genes discovered, and two new drugs heading into clinical trials.[2]

Some grassroots organizations are almost exclusively patient-led, such as Emily's Entourage (EE). Emily Kramer-Golinkoff lives with a rare mutation of cystic fibrosis (CF). Upon learning that more research on her rare mutation would likely not occur in her shortened life span, Emily took matters into her own hands and, with friends and family, created her own organization. In addition to raising awareness of CF and its rare mutations, EE began a patient registry, provides grant funding for more research, and hosts both galas and scientific events. Emily has even been recognized by the White House for her efforts.

Many patient-led efforts, like Emily's, come from trying to find answers when the health care system has all but given up. That said, we patients—even the activated biocitizen type—are human. We do not always "take appropriate steps . . . in the name of the minimization of illness and the maximization of health" or "conduct life responsibly in relation to others, to modulate decisions . . . in the light of a knowledge of their present and future biomedical make-up."[3] Engaged patients are, like our health care professionals, still people, and still fallible. People do not always make the best choices, and there are often influences that help us to choose other methods of existence. Despite what my husband or loved ones or health care team thinks, I am not a superhuman. Sometimes I just want candy and burgers and to be slightly more reckless than my lifestyle should allow me to be. *And that's okay.*

Biocitizenship is an important and diverse area that is still underexplored and underdocumented. Perhaps some of this comes from the many fields this movement encompasses, from the financial to the political, the medical to the linguistic, the ethical to the logical, and so on. Just like life itself, these issues cannot be separated from the movement at large.

Underscoring all of these individual instrumental notes is a melody of human rights.

The right to our medical data.
The right to proper health care.
The right to Quality of Life.

At the end of the day, we're just patients who have had to take these matters into our own hands to survive.

And so far? It's working.

NOTES

1 Nikolas Rose and Carlos Novas, "Biological Citizenship," in *Global Assemblages: Technology, Politics, and Ethics as Anthropological Problems*, ed. Aihwa Ong and Stephen J. Collier (Malden, MA: Blackwell, 2005), 454.

2 ALS Association, IBC Progress Infographic (2016), www.alsa.org.

3 Rose and Novas, "Biological Citizenship," 451.

## PART IV

Beyond the Biocitizen

# 11

## Nonhuman Biocitizens

*Lab Animals, Cruel Optimism, and the Politics of Death*

MARINA LEVINA

The ad is a simple one. A mother—gender made identifiable by a pink dress—is shopping with her son, gender coded by a blue and green T-shirt. In their shopping cart are tubes, air filters, and feeding supplies. The family is shopping for their home—a cage in a scientific laboratory. They are rats, and the ad is one of hundreds in *Lab Animal*, a monthly peer-reviewed journal for "professionals in animal research emphasizing proper management and care." Available by subscription only,[1] *Lab Animal* publishes peer-reviewed research studies and editorial content and markets the production and acquisition of nonhuman animals for research and experiments.[2] The magazine uses images to showcase animal bodies in various states—as happy consumers, diligent research assistants, precious research subjects, and dissected cadavers. Through these bodies, the magazine communicates the multitude of cultural meanings assigned to scientific and biomedical work. The advertising in *Lab Animal* hails animal bodies as monuments; holds them up as saviors; observes them as precarious and vulnerable; and renders them active citizens in the laboratory. The journal, however, is also a functional memorial to the dead—images of dissected animals are in stark opposition to those happily shopping for their own cages. The juxtaposition is a stunning testament to the various costs of scientific research.

Throughout the journal, animal bodies are treated not simply as commodities, even though they are often represented as such, but rather as active collaborators in research and participants in their own sacrifice. *Lab Animal* gives research animals a voice—not of resistance but rather of consent and participation. Through an analysis of advertising images, research photos, and editorial content, I argue that the journal integrates, rather than obscures, the tensions between stylized pictures of animals and the bloody work of surgery and experimentation. Therefore, *Lab Animal* functions as a performative space that interpellates animals and researchers as biocitizens in the mutual enterprise of the biomedical laboratory—the search for the "cure." However, I argue, because a laboratory functions within the logic of cruel optimism, biocitizenship is therefore based not in politics of hope but in politics of death, or necropolitics. I contend that by examining how nonhuman animals are constituted as biocitizens within the conditions of cruel optimism and necropolitics, we can extend the argument to human animals, or to those who strive to be a part of the search for the "cure." This essay aims to ask difficult questions of biomedical enterprises that deploy biocitizenship as a way of obscuring which bodies are dissected and which bodies shop for their own cages. I am not arguing about how, if at all, human animals are similar to nonhuman animals. The point here is not to bemoan the cruelty of the laboratory or speculate on which way the animals feel pain. It is to take seriously the claim made by the visual rhetoric of the trade publication that lab animals are collaborators in the research done in the lab. It is also to argue that the practices of biocitizenship are invested in the search for the cure and require an affective investment in death as a learning experiment. Some die so that others may live. I contend that the focus on lab animal bodies as commodities ignores the subjectivity granted to them by laboratory life. Through the analysis of *Lab Animal*, I illustrate how lab animals are interpellated as subjects, not just as objects, of scientific research. They become active collaborators in the necropolitics at the base of the production of the scientific knowledge. As such, I expand on Donna Haraway's analysis of OncoMouse™—the first, and foremost, biocitizen of the laboratory.

## Human and Nonhuman Biocitizenship

Biological citizenship has been used in literature to describe an effort by active citizens to recuperate power away from medical and scientific institutions through bottom-up activism and a political economy of hope. Nikolas Rose and Carlos Novas define "biological citizenship" as "all those citizenship projects that have linked their conceptions of citizens to beliefs about the biological existence of human beings, as individuals, as families and lineages, as communities, as population and races, and as a species."[3] They argue that biological citizenship operates within a political economy of hope: a social, political, and economic system that advances the view of biology as mutable. As a tool of active biocitizens fighting against injustices and suffering inflicted by medical, political, and economic establishments and institutions, the political economy of hope requires an active stance toward the future. Elsewhere, Nikolas Rose juxtaposes biocitizenship projects of the state to those of individuals. While the former emphasized population control and public health campaigns, the latter "produced citizens who understood their nationality, allegiances, and distinctions, at least in part, in biological terms. . . . These biological senses of identification and affiliation made certain kinds of ethical demands possible: demands on oneself; on one's kin, community, society; on those who exercised authority."[4] In these analyses, the economy of hope and active biocitizenship are represented as largely incorruptible enterprises that nobly resist institutional imposition of discipline and power. Rose and Novas refer to communities forming on the Web and outside it as "moral pioneers—we would prefer to say 'ethical pioneers'—of a new kind of active biomedical citizenship. They are pioneering a new informed ethics of the self—a set of techniques for managing everyday life in relation to a condition, and in relation to expert knowledge."[5]

I would like to start by making a hopefully meaningful parallel between nonhuman and human biocitizens. Although the category of biocitizenship is a broad one, it involves an affective and ontological entanglement with the biomedical and scientific enterprise. It is tempting to think of biocitizenship in terms of agency and consent—after all, that is what "active" implies in the categorization of biocitizenship as articulated by Rose and Novas. This seems to limit the application of the term to human animals. After all, it is a common and worthwhile argument made by animal rights and animal studies scholars that nonhuman animals cannot meaningfully consent to their own death and therefore, fundamentally different than their human counterparts, their lives do not function within the structures of capital.[6] However, I argue that in the pages of *Lab Animal*, nonhuman animals are represented as agents and subjects, not just commodities and objects. Whether anyone or anything can meaningfully consent to experiments—and potential death—

has been a subject of many philosophical inquiries. However, anyone or anything can be represented as doing so. Subjectivity is therefore a representational and performative event. In other words, if biopower—the power to make live or make die—is an exercise of governmentality, then subjectivity, be it human or animal, is a production of power. Subjectivity does not precede governmentality but rather is produced through governmentality.[7] As Nicole Shukin further argues, "Governmentality arguably extends to a host of potentially ensouled species whose subjectivization promises to harmonize more and more of animal life with political rationales. Feeling power gives name to one particularly potent relationship through which other animals become subjects of, and subject to governmentality, *regardless of whether or not their subjectivity is deemed a fiction.*"[8]

The 2016 advertising for Braintree Scientific, Inc., prominently featured in *Lab Animal*, illustrates the subjectivity of nonhuman biocitizens (figure 11.1). Here we have rats actively engaging in various aspects of scientific enterprise—from surgery, to 3-D organ modeling, to bionic arm implants, to implementation of various visualization techniques. These visually humanized rodents are presumably experimenting on their own bodies, happily and merrily so.

They are we; and we are they—excited and optimistic about our own participation in scientific enterprise; citizens of the larger research community; hopeful of lifesaving benefits offered by biomedical advances. They model the appropriate active engagement with medical and scientific settings in which they are actively studying their own bodies. The image demonstrates what is common in all forms of biocitizenship—an affective, epistemological, and ontological orientation toward the body as a source of affect, knowledge, and a way of relating to the world. According to Bruno Latour, "To have a body is to learn to be affected, meaning 'effectuated,' moved, put into motion by other entities, humans or non-humans."[9] Here any firm distinctions between human and non-human animals is subsumed by what the image says about a life oriented toward *bio* and a citizenship in a scientific setting of life itself. Mike Michael and Marsha Rosengarten state:

> We see how animal bodies are entered into patterns of affect in order to stand as proxies for human bodies. Abstracted as experimental models,

Figure 11.1. Braintree Scientific, Inc., catalog cover, 2016.

[lab animals] are eventuated through concrete practices that belie such abstraction. For the lab animal we see how it is through skilled handling that it can affectively serve as an experimental model. . . . At the same time, these abstractions serve to affect human bodies—not least through the promises of future affects that attach to such models.[10]

I would like to suggest that through analysis of rhetorical and visual positioning of animal bodies in relation to the biomedical enterprise, we might arrive at a deeper understanding of our own relationship to biosciences as active participants in its many forms.

## Lab Animals and Laboratory Rat-ness

In *Modest_Witness @ Second Millennium*, Donna Haraway powerfully introduced OncoMouse™—the first mouse engineered with cancer cells by DuPont Industries—as a metaphor for life in the biotechnological space of the second millennium. She writes, "OncoMouse™ is a technological product whose natural habitat and evolutionary future are fully contained in that world-building space called the laboratory. . . . A tool-weapon for 'stalking cancer,' the bioengineered mouse is simultaneously a metaphor, a technology, and a beast living its many-layered life as best as it can. This is the normal state of the entities in technoscience cultures, including ourselves."[11] To Haraway, OncoMouse™ is simultaneously a commodity, a technology, and a metaphor. It exists as part of the laboratory world, a performative space that integrates various actors into a network of scientific research.[12] Together they are "civic sacraments: signs and referents all rolled into one fleshy mystery in a secularized salvation history of civilian and military wars, scientific knowledge, progress, democracy, and economic power."[13] The multiplicities of meanings both emphasize and obscure lab animal identity and agency. And while much has been written about lab animals as commodities, to understand them only as such misses the mark. Lab animals are not simply commodities. They are complex performative subjects, actors in the networks of laboratory spaces and communities.[14] Lynda Birke describes laboratory rats as "both animals and not quite animals; they are vermin in the pipework under the lab but a useful piece of equipment in the lab; they are equipment, yet we can be mindful of their minds; they are bearers of disease while promising to liberate us from disease."[15]

The performative aspect of lab animals as actors in the laboratory is what Linda Birke, Mette Bryld, and Nina Lykke call "laboratory rat-ness"—"a part performed to fit very precisely into the scientific enterprise; meanings emerge from a nexus of apparatuses, animals and people."[16] They argue that rats and humans not only coexist in the laboratory space but cocreate that space and the larger world of scientific enterprise. A lab animal is not just a product, even though, much like its human counterpart, its relationship to the larger capital structure underlying scientific enterprise is always commodified. Just as important, it is an actor, a collaborator, and a friend. Linda Birke maintains that "animals in the lab stand in for humans; they are models to represent our disease states in basic research aiming to understand better those diseases, and they are surrogates for us when we seek to test or evaluate protocols, procedures or potential medicines."[17] Therefore, in the process, they become "models"—"the creature understood as 'animal' must become an object."[18]

This is a true statement up to a point. What surprised me most when I first started subscribing to *Lab Animal* in 2009 is the work done by the magazine's editorial and advertising content to make lab animals seem more than just models and products. They are often represented as active collaborators, willing participants, and even kin to the humans in the lab and outside of it. The labor that went into making lab animals into subjects, as opposed to objects, of the biomedical community astounded me. And, yes, there are images and articles addressing the lab animals as models. But the overwhelming message of the magazine is that there is an intimate connection between lab animals and humans as *collaborators* in scientific research. For example, an advertisement for Harlan Laboratories portrays a mouse perched on the top of a microscope with the tagline "Research Assistant. It takes more than quality models to advance your research" (figure 11.2).

In this instance, the mouse is more than a quality model or a product. It is incorporated in the very process of scientific research as an active research assistant. A lab animal's relationship to the researchers is necessarily affective in that it generates bonds and relationships not easily explained by mere commodification of animal bodies. Those relationships

Figure 11.2. "Research Assistant," Harlan Laboratories advertisement.

are intimately tied to the production of scientific knowledge, which, in turn, is tied to the production of the "cure." A relationship to the cure is necessarily optimistic and future-oriented; it is based within the politics of hope and regimes of anticipation.[19] An advertisement for Hilltop Lab Animals, Inc. references Michelangelo's famous fresco *The Creation of Adam* and features a mouse seeming to leap from the page and toward the gloved hand of a scientist—the two figures joined by the miracle and power of creation (figure 11.3). The taglines "Are You Ready?" and "Bring Your Ideas to Life" create a sense of anticipation and offer a promise of

Figure 11.3. "Bring Your Ideas to Life," Hilltop Lab Animals advertisement.

important discovery or a scientific revelation akin to God's creation of man. The greatness of scientific discovery is registered in optimistic and hopeful terms. The mouse is looking up and to the right—a common visual orientation toward the future—and it is in the process of coming alive before our very eyes thanks to the scientist's reach. The optimism here, however, is a cruel one—the mouse is destined to die as soon as the human hand actually touches it. In the next section I examine how the condition of biocitizenship is grounded in the affect of cruel optimism.

## Cruel Optimism and Biocitizenship

Lauren Berlant defined cruel optimism as "the condition of maintaining an attachment to a problematic object in advance of its loss."[20] She stated that any object of optimism "promises to guarantee the endurance of something, the survival of something, the flourishing of something, and above all the protection of the desire that made this object or scene powerful enough to have magnetized an attachment to it."[21] But "cruel optimism is a relation of attachment to compromised conditions of possibility whose realization is discovered either to be impossible, sheer fantasy, or *too* possible, and toxic."[22] Take, for example, the advertising for Charles River Laboratories—a biotechnology company—with the tagline, "You see a mouse. We see a cure for cancer" (figure 11.4). On a stark gray background, we see a hairless mouse, raising its nose and eyes to gaze at something above itself, its vulnerable, hairless body containing the promise of the cure. Below the tagline, the text reads, "This Charles River mouse is a critical component of your oncology research. However, behind it lies an extensive network of scientific and technical resources that provides so much more. . . . We are committed to helping accelerate your research towards a cure."

Several affective attachments are happening here, the most important of which is the mouse itself—its vulnerability demonstrated by hairless skin. The viewer is asked to protect the vulnerable body because of its potentiality as a vessel for the cancer cure. Of course, the mouse cannot be protected. It must be killed and dissected—its precious body must become a bloody corpse. Moreover, if a mouse is equated with the cure for cancer, then, at least allegorically speaking, its death also represents a death of the cure. The attachment is a cruel one—the mouse is doomed

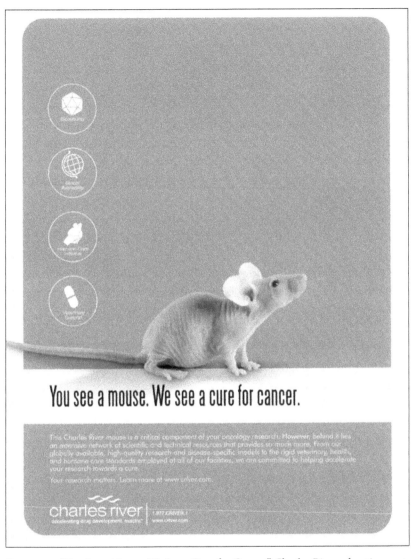

Figure 11.4. "You See a Mouse. We See a Cure for Cancer." Charles River advertisement.

to die, *and* the cure for cancer is a doomed potentiality if for no other reason than the plurality of its objective: A cure for which cancer? A cure for whom? The loss is inevitable, but the attachment to the animal bodies has to be hopeful—otherwise there is no point to scientific research. As Berlant writes, "If the cruelty of an attachment is experienced by someone/some group, even in a subtle fashion, the fear is that the loss of the promising object/scene itself will defeat the capacity to have any hope about anything."[23] Remember that the audience for these advertisements is not the general public but the scientific community, whose attachments to animal bodies are facilitated here through the operations of the gaze directed to desire the cure and to mourn the fragility of the animal body and of hope itself. In other words, for scientists to find the cure, the mouse must die. But that death does not guarantee the cure; in fact, it is only while the mouse lives that the hope for the cure can live as well. Once it dies, the cure dies with it. *Lab Animal* demonstrates the cruel attachment to the cure—a never realized possibility, the pursuit of which results in death of both the object of attachment and the hope for the cure.

Another ad in the magazine, titled "Unforgettable," serves as a monument to the lab rat presumably sacrificed in the search for a cure for Alzheimer's disease (figure 11.5). The text reads, "An estimated 18 million people worldwide are living with Alzheimer's, yet there's no cure for this devastating disease. Regardless of whether your research is in Alzheimer's or another disease area, our research models and services, which include genetically engineered models, . . . can provide the necessary support to help every aspect of your research matter." The laboratory rat is standing on official Alzheimer's Association awareness bracelets—the gaze of the viewer is directed to form an attachment with the animal and the people it represents. The mouse is literally standing on top of bracelets, its body intimately connected to humans who suffer from the disease. However, as the text reminds us, the animal has been genetically engineered to die of the disease. Therefore, unwittingly so, as the animal represents those who suffer from Alzheimer's, it is also doomed to die from either that disease or, more likely, from the search for the cure. As the animal stands in for those who are eager to participate in the search for the cure, it reminds them that they are destined to die either from the disease itself or from research itself. In short, much like the idea of "the good life," which Berlant argues is an optimistic attachment that serves to the detriment of those who seek it, "the cure" is a hopeful potential that delivers pain and ultimately death. "The cure" also obfuscates how the body is seen in relation to that which ails it. As Eli Clare explains, it allows us to think of the "sick" or a disabled body as external to the issues of social justice:

> Take, for instance, Jerry Lewis and his Labor Day telethon. He raises money by playing to pity and promising to find a cure. This money does not fund wheelchairs, ramps, or lift bars, nor lawyers to file disability discrimination lawsuits, but research for a cure, for a repair of bodies seen as broken, for an end to disability. Lewis is strategically playing the cards of the medical model and the charity model. Or think about Christopher Reeve as he speaks out about the need to find a cure for spinal cord injuries and insists on his ability to overcome quadriplegia, going so far as to air a Super Bowl ad where, through computer-generated imagery, he is shown actually getting up out of his wheelchair and walking across a stage. Reeve creates himself as a supercrip, the superhero now playing himself offscreen, and is at the same time enmeshed in the medical model. Or consider mothers with hereditary disabilities, who face significant disapproval for their decisions to have children and immense pressure to undergo various medical tests and to consider abortion if their fetuses appear to be disabled. They are caught in a vise-grip between the moral model and medical model. Whatever the permutations, these models unambiguously define disability and disabled bodies as wrong and bad.[24]

Here death is not a literal extinction of life but a symbolic annihilation—the ceasing of imperfect existence in the search of normativity. And while not all research pursues "the cure," it is the ideal that guides our cultural investment in science and medicine and justifies the sacrifice by human and nonhuman actors.

The cruelty of attachment within the sphere of the laboratory is made visible throughout *Lab Animal*. Each issue features interviews with lab managers or veterinarians and others whose job it is to care for animals during their often-short lives. The interviews are stark in the repeated pattern of attachment and guilt. In one, for example, a lab manager of the Physiological Research Laboratory at Georgia Institute of Technol-

Figure 11.5. "Unforgettable." Charles River advertisement.

ogy talked of her transition from a veterinary technician treating neglected and abused animals to working in a research lab:

> Something changed when I entered this professional environment: it felt
> as if a door closed inside of me, separating me from my ability to be
> proud of my work. My love of animals hadn't suddenly changed, . . . [nor
> had I] become some kind of monster of a person. I was still making a
> difference in the lives of animals, I was still taking great care of animals,
> and for the first time in my life I was contributing to animal studies that
> were leading to human trials. Why, then, did I feel bad or ashamed for my
> profession? Daily we work to ensure that these animals receive the best
> care, and we needed to be reminded that we are good people.[25]

Here the attachment to the work of care is detrimental to the manager's
well-being. As Berlant writes, "What's cruel about these attachments, and
not merely inconvenient and tragic, is that the subjects who have $x$ in
their lives might not well endure the loss of their object/scene of desire,
even through its presence threatens their well-being, because whatever the
*content* of the attachment is, the continuity of its form provides something
of the continuity of the subject's sense of what it means to keep on living
and to look forward to being in the world."[26] In the interview just quoted,
the cruelty of attachments formed within a scientific research is rendered
painfully visible. The content of the attachment here is the attachment to
scientific progress, to the cure, which provides a sense of what it means
to look forward to being in the world. On the other hand, the costs of
those attachments are both impossible and toxic. In other words, there is
an irreconcilable duality in biomedical enterprise: the search for the cure
to save lives but also the need to kill and torture to find the cure. This, I
would argue, is an irreconcilable conflict at the very heart of biomedical research as illustrated by *Lab Animal*. In another interview, the chief
of Veterinary and Educational Services at Cornell University's Center for
Animal Resources and Education describes similarities between working
in a veterinary practice and laboratory animal medicine:

> In both situations, the animals come "attached" to people—either own-
> ers or investigators . . . the investigators also have an attachment to the
> animal because of an emotional connection or because of the research

progress that animal signifies. . . . I have several family members with serious medical issues, and I understand and appreciate the need for animal-based research. . . . I fully support research, but when using animals, it must be done humanely and with proper oversight.[27]

These statements remind us of the necessary cruelty and the necessary optimism of scientific research. At its heart is an irreconcilable conflict: the need for a cure and the need for death. In the next section, I illustrate the connection between cruel optimism and necropolitics in relationship to human and nonhuman laboratory biocitizens.

## Biocitizenship and Necropolitics

In an advertisement for IITC Life Science Inc., a seemingly healthy lab mouse is giving its approval to the products, and by extension to the research, with the phrase "It's ALL Good" (figure 11.6). The tools depicted in the image read like a list of torture devices: respiratory equipment, rat catheters, precision probes, syringe pumps, and restrainers. An affective investment in life is a product of economic investment in death. And the aliveness of the subject—in this case the lab mouse—is identified with its perishability.[28] Within the constraints of the laboratory, we can observe the exercise of life-giving and death-administering biopower. The focus of biopower on administering death is what Achille Mbembe defines as necropolitics—a subjugation of life to the power of death.[29] Within the logic of necropolitics, Mbembe argues in an interpretation of Georges Bataille, "Death is the point at which destruction, suppression, and sacrifice constitute so irreversible and radical an expenditure—an expenditure without reserve—that they can no longer be determined as negativity."[30] Hugo Reinert argues that as far as necropolitics makes us confront what Giorgio Agamben called the bare life,[31] that animal life can be bare and therefore subject to necropolitics:

Can animal life be bare? . . . The figure of the bare life seems to aptly capture how both bodies are produced and suspended within dedicated social and technical spaces that effectively constitute two distinct but analogous forms of "death worlds," or "forms of social existence in

Figure 11.6. "It's ALL Good." IITC Life Science advertisement.

which . . . populations are subjected to conditions of life conferring upon them the status of living dead."[32]

I argue, therefore, that within the necropolitics of biomedical research, biocitizenship is a discursive tool with which to attempt to reconcile the irreconcilable—the hopefulness of the cure with inevitability of death. However, as we move a conversation about biological citizenship beyond the hegemonic power of the scientific enterprise and liberating potential of individual citizen action, we need to use the concept of "laboratory rat-ness" to examine the complex and less hopeful politics of biocitizenship, which are based in the conditions of cruel optimism.

These hopeful representations of scientific enterprise are juxtaposed with research images of dissected animal bodies and postmortem examinations. Figure 11.7 illustrates the gruesome aftermath of hopeful scientific discovery depicted in figure 11.3. The gloved hand is administering death, not life—the mouse body is a reminder that death is, in fact, the ultimate possibility. The hope of discovery and the promise of the cure guarantee death. The promise of collaboration and hopeful politics of biocitizenship are stripped away to reveal the body on the table. Death is therefore not a deferment but rather a possibility, an articulation of sovereignty. Moreover, as Mbembe argues, in order for sovereignty to most effectively make death meaningful, it must "rest on the belief that the subject is the master and the controlling author of his or her own meaning."[33] This is where the affective labor done by the journal's advertising comes into focus. Through the ads, the animals are granted subjectivity, which is then sacrificed to the betterment of others—humans and animals alike. It is worth noting that this mouse died for the betterment of life of other lab mice. The accompanying article summarizes the purpose of the research study:

> The rapid expansion of transgenic and gene-targeted mouse models of immune disorders has enabled a concomitant increase in the number of studies of T-cell development. Such studies may require the administration of intrathymic injections, which have traditionally been done using a surgical approach. Surgical manipulation can result in pain or distress to the animal, which may affect the immune system, potentially confounding experimental results. Here, the authors describe a nonsurgi-

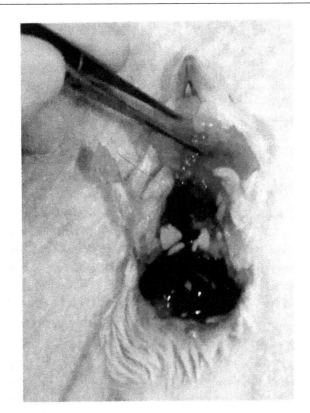

**FIGURE 5** | Post-mortem examination confirms that Trypan blue (red arrow) was successfully injected into the thymus.

Figure 11.7. Postmortem examination of a lab mouse, *Lab Animal* magazine.

cal, ultrasound-guided approach for intrathymic injection in the mouse that results in negligible distress to the animal.[34]

The mouse's death was therefore at the service of both reduced suffering of other lab mice, insofar as that suffering affects the results of scientific research, and the search for the cure of immune disorders in humans. The lives of humans and animals are intertwined in a complex relationship of citizenship, hope, and death. *Lab Animal* gives research animals a voice of consent and participation in the affective possibilities offered by biocitizenship; the animals are active participants in the functions and politics of hope. I argue, however, that the politics of hope obfuscate the function of biocitizenship as "lively capital"—an affective register of confluence between life sciences and capital based on the impingement of scientific research on experiences of embodiment and kinship.[35] Therefore, biocitizenship as a condition of cruel attachments to participation, progress, and the cure is only possible with the investment in a juxtaposition of life and death, or in lively capital and necropolitics. Vall Gillies, Rosalind Edwards, and Nicola Horsley claim that the moral economy of hope characterizing biocitizenship forces individuals into relations of cruel optimism. As a result, they argue as follows:

> Biological and social limitations are overridden by attachments to damagingly unrealistic possibilities that carry a high psychic and social cost. Those caught within this dynamic struggle on toward the unattainable rather than resisting the regime, grinding themselves down in the process. . . . From this perspective, hope and its attendant practices (trying, persevering, managing disappointment) sit closer to oppression than freedom. Indeed it could be argued that a moral obligation to strive and self-improve has intensified a merciless pressure on the poor, sick and vulnerable to personally overcome their predicaments. Acceptance of limited capacity and responsibility has been swept away with the determinism of the past placing new normative burdens on those least able to manage them. . . . Consent and compulsion are blurred in this late capitalist vision, with hope as a value enforced through the subtle pressure of enablement.[36]

While I would argue that the proposed duality of oppression/freedom ignores the nuances in the production of scientific knowledge, I agree that we need to be critical of the burdens that hope places on those least able to manage them. In this essay, I have shown how *Lab Animal* discursively fuses together lab animals and researchers in the laboratory rat-ness of scientific enterprise and attachment to the cure, which is based in conditions of cruel optimism and the governing practices of necropolitics. Throughout the journal, lab animals are interpellated as biocitizens of the laboratory space. Therefore, biocitizenship is constructed as an unproblematic and hopeful collaboration with biomedical research; it becomes an ongoing practice of cruel optimism—a potentiality of the cure and a better life never realized. It is an attachment that kills as it promises to thrive—a production of capital investment into life itself. Such analysis can enable us to think of biocitizenship not as a hopeful tomorrow but as a complicated, and often bloody, present perched on top of dead bodies—human and nonhuman alike.

NOTES

The author would like to thank Jon Paul Bushnell for assisting with an earlier draft of this essay.

1  I had to create a fake biotech company called "Homer Technologies"—a nod to the *Odyssey* and to *The Simpsons*—to be able to obtain a subscription. This was not an especially difficult process, but it is notable for its gatekeeping function.

2  In critical animal studies, it is common practice to speak of nonhuman animals, in order to decenter the human in the ethics debate of what can be done to various animal bodies. Although I respect and acknowledge this position, I believe that for the sake of this particular analysis it is most clear to refer to laboratory subjects as simply animals, since they are presented as such.

3  Nikolas Rose and Carlos Novas, "Biological Citizenship," in *Global Assemblages: Technology, Politics, and Ethics as Anthropological Problems*, ed. Aihwa Ong and Stephen J. Collier (Malden, MA: Blackwell, 2005, 440.

4  Nikolas Rose, *The Politics of Life Itself: Biomedicine, Power, and Subjectivity in the Twenty-First Century* (Princeton, NJ: Princeton University Press, 2007), 133.

5  Rose and Novas, "Biological Citizenship," 450.

6  Hugo Reinhart, "The Pertinence of Sacrifice," *Borderlands e-Journal: New Spaces in the Humanities* 6, no. 3 (2007).

7  Nicole Shukin, "Security Bonds: On Feeling Power and the Fiction of an Animal Governmentality," *ESC: English Studies in Canada* 39, no. 1 (2013): 177–98.

8  Ibid., 182 (emphasis in the original).

9  Bruno Latour, "How to Talk about the Body? The Normative Dimension of Science Studies," *Body and Society* 10, nos. 2–3 (2004): 205.

10  Mike Michael and Marsha Rosengarten, "Medicine: Experimentation, Politics, Emergent Bodies," *Body and Society* 18, nos. 3–4 (2012): 13.

11  Donna Jeanne Haraway, *Modest_Witness@ Second_Millennium.FemaleMan©–Meets_OncoMouse™: Feminism and Technoscience* (New York: Routledge, 1997), 83.

12  Bruno Latour and Steve Woolgar, *Laboratory Life: The Construction of Scientific Facts* (Princeton, NJ: Princeton University Press, 2013).

13  Haraway, *Modest_Witness*, 84.

14  Bruno Latour, *Reassembling the Social: An Introduction to Actor-Network-Theory* (New York: Oxford University Press, 2005).

15  Lynda Birke, "Who—or What—Are the Rats (and Mice) in the Laboratory," *Society and Animals* 11, no. 3 (2003): 220.

16  Lynda Birke, Mette Bryld, and Nina Lykke, "Animal Performances: An Explora-
    tion of Intersections between Feminist Science Studies and Studies of Human/
    Animal Relationships," *Feminist Theory* 5, no. 2 (2004): 174.

17  Lynda Birke, "Animal Bodies in the Production of Scientific Knowledge: Model-
    ling Medicine," *Body and Society* 18, nos. 3–4 (2012): 163.

18  Ibid., 173.

19  Marina Levina, "Healthymagination: Anticipating Health of Our Future
    Selves," *Fibreculture Journal* 20 (2012): 143–57.

20  Lauren Berland, "Cruel Optimism," *Differences: A Journal in Feminist Cultural
    Studies* 17, no. 3 (2006): 21.

21  Lauren Berlant, *Cruel Optimism* (Durham, NC: Duke University Press, 2011), 48.

22  Ibid., 24.

23  Ibid.

24  Eli Clare, "Stolen Bodies, Reclaimed Bodies: Disability and Queerness," *Public
    Culture* 13, no. 3 (2001): 361.

25  Kimberly A. Benjamin, "Sharing Our Work with Pride," *Lab Animal* 45, no. 4
    (2016): 151–52.

26  Berlant, "Cruel Optimism," 24.

27  Mary E. Martin, "A Balancing Act," *Lab Animal* 41, no. 9 (2012): 265.

28  Rosi Braidotti, "Biopower and Necropolitics," *Springerin, Hefte fur Gegen-
    wartskunst* 13, no. 2 (2007): 18–23.

29  Achille Mbembe, "Necropolitics," in *Foucault in an Age of Terror*, ed. Simon Bain-
    bridge and Rebecca Fensome (London: Palgrave Macmillan, 2008), 152–82.

30  Ibid., 157.

31  Hugo Reinert argued that bare life is "the life that has been reduced to its mini-
    mal threshold of biological activity and beyond, kept alive only by the constant
    exercise of human power in a technologically created zone of indistinction where
    the lines between life and death become blurred and flow into each other." See
    Reinert, "The Pertinence of Sacrifice."

32  Ibid., 11; Achille Mbembe, "Necropolitics," translated by Libby Meintjes, *Public
    Culture* 15, no. 1 (2003): 40.

33  Mbembe, "Necropolitics," in *Foucault in the Age of Terror*, 155.

34  Robin Blair-Handon, Kristen Mueller, and Shelley Hoogstraten-Miller, "An Alter-
    native Method for Intrathymic Injections in Mice," *Lab Animal* 39, no. 8 (2010):
    248.

35  Kaushik Sunder Rajan, *Lively Capital: Biotechnologies, Ethics, and Governance in
    Global Markets* (Durham, NC: Duke University Press, 2012).

36  Val Gillies, Rosalind Edwards, and Nicola Horsley, "Brave New Brains: Sociology,
    Family and the Politics of Knowledge," *Sociological Review* 64, no. 2 (2016): 230.

12

# The Citizens of Incubators

*Vessels of Care and Control*

ORON CATTS AND IONAT ZURR

Neolife are technologically created and fragmented life-forms that have been manipulated by humans and exist in the lab that is their ecological niche, to the extent that some of neolife cannot survive without the artificial life support mechanisms that provide specific and basic needs. These artificial life support mechanisms—the vessels—found in the lab include incubators, petri dishes, bioreactors,[1] and more.[2]

Here we would focus our attention on one of the main vessels of neolife, the incubator. An incubator can be simply described as an isolated environment that controls heat, humidity, and in some cases other environmental conditions such as sterility, gas content, pH level, and so forth. It is a homeostatic, feedback-based, dynamic, surrogate body that shields fragile life from the external environment. Historically, as will be illustrated, incubators took center stage (visually and aesthetically) in contextualizing the life hosted as a (proto-)cybernetic entity. However, in recent years, especially as a result of the Human Genome Project and through the field of synthetic biology, there has been a shift to obscure the incubator as a surrogate vessel and render it neutral, thereby obscuring how, throughout history, what life is chosen or forced to be put in an incubator reflects on human wants and desires. Neolife can be seen as the entanglement of life with its surrogate apparatus, echoing interests of human-centric control, which affect and effect the larger milieu. This chapter will discuss the different aesthetics of incubators through the years, especially since the incubator is a place in which life becomes culturally intelligible; from "sublife"—prototechnological life, waiting to be "activated" into neolife by the merging/entanglement with technology— and into an articulated form of life external to the incubator. By focusing on the incubator as such, we question the very idea of biocitizenship, focused as it is on human life; on intact, whole bodies; and on the distinction between environment and biology. Furthermore, the incubator has, throughout its history, served to reproduce and recuperate the very ideologies of race and gender upon which normative biocitizenship depends; despite the fact that developments in biotechnology and the design of neolife may offer the illusion of a "new citizenship" that breaks free from hegemonic human social constructions of species, gender, race, and class. In most cases, as we will show, human-centric, patriarchal, colonialist, and predominantly capitalist social constructions are built into the developments of these technologies, their interpretations, and their applications. Through a series of historical and contemporary examples and their attendant discourses, we examine further that despite the potential of vessels of care and control—incubators—to serve as points of possible departure and "escape" from human-centric ingrained discourses and biopolitics, they nevertheless remain immersed in the current patriarchal neoliberal agenda. We offer a reminder that while incubators may serve as a futuristic, utopian, and provocative departure for stories about life and citizenship insofar as they contest genetic determinism and anthropocentric narratives, they are not a neutral place in which life grows but rather serve as an active geographic, biological, and social semipermeable arena that is an integral part of neolife. This is a story of how life gains cultural agency by passing through incubators (The Maternal/The Real) into the world of its creators (The Paternal/The Symbolic). Neolife are therefore biocitizens that are "hatched" through biotechnological narratives, tools, and procedures, dynamic actants reflecting on past and contestable future scenarios. Incubators therefore allow us to test the limits of our conventional concepts of life, sociality, and materiality.

## The History of the Incubator: Ideology and Human Interests on Display

Life-forms evolve through the interplay of existing traits and their adaptation to changing environmental conditions. Many organisms opt to keep their insides shielded in near-optimal conditions to sustain their biological function through homeostatic equilibrium. Human technology enables artificial environments to maintain life outside its original context, in situations where it would otherwise die (or just not grow fast enough or in abundance for human will). In other words, humans have developed artificial "bodies"/territories such as greenhouses, terrariums, petri dishes, incubators, diving suits, and spaceships to support life out of context. Some life or parts of life—fragments of bodies such as cells, tissues, and other lab-grown life (all what we refer to as neolife)—depend on carefully controlled, artificially simulated conditions. Without continuous support from technological body surrogates like the incubator, these forms of decontextualized life, which have been removed or ejected from the body, will die. The incubator is a simulator of bodies—a new (sometimes temporary) zone—a homeostatic stand-in for life out of context, out of place, and out of agency, thus calling into question the humanistic assumptions of biocitizenship scholarship.

The first examples of human-induced incubation involved chickens, largely because chickens and their eggs are a great source for human economy and nutrition; eggs as "parts of life" out of context can be easily sustained through human-controlled artificial environments. Eggs in and of themselves can be seen as a form of external bodies of life in transition, and in the case of chickens (as well as other birds, reptiles, and fish) are external to their mothers' bodies and need minimal conditions to survive and develop—merely the right heat and rotation.

One of the first recorded methods of incubating—3,000 years ago, in Egypt—involved using heat from rotting and burning manure as well as other substances to warm chicken eggs.[3] The aim was to hatch chicks from eggs without having the mother hen sit on them, and therefore enable hens to continue laying eggs or to be used as meat without interruption. The Chinese used a very similar system of incubation, using brick ovens and whole buildings dedicated to hatching chickens, with eggs being turned on a daily basis. Some historians date early incubation methods to "at least as early as the Ch'in period (246–207 B.C.)."[4] Mechanical incubating—a semiautomated incubation known as the "artificial mother"—was invented and titled as such in 1747 by René Réaumur in Paris.[5] Réaumur's "artificial mother" was warmed by a woodstove and had temperature controlled by Réaumur's invented thermometer, which gave rise to the temperature scale named after him.[6] The thermometer represented the first cybernetic entity. This cybernetic precedent was

coupled early on with a reproductive machine, or even more symbolically with the first artificial mother. The naming of this new machine as
"artificial mother" embedded the idea of motherhood with bare life support that is controlled by technology.[7] As far as we are aware, this was the
first instance of this maternal/ideological narrative. In Réaumur's words:

> The best thing we can possibly do is to copy after the proceedings of na-
> ture, whenever we have a mind to produce effects like those sets before
> our eyes. I then judged that the little ones in the chicken-house wanted a
> mother, that might be fitting on them, determine them to take their rest
> in the fame [sic] attitude in which they take it under the hen. I contrived
> to give them inanimate mother, that might stand them instead of a live
> hen. Let the reader form to himself one of those portable desks which
> are generally put upon a writing-table, all the sides of the cavity of which
> should be lined with a good warm fur, and he will easily conceive how it
> may be to the chickens an equivalent for a mother, and even something
> better still. . . . They soon shewed me how sensible they were of the vast
> merit of this artificial mother; they loved to remain under it.[8]

These early inventions enabled eggs to mature without the need for
a hen, and they also enabled a year-round supply of chickens. Through
the incubators' ability to simulate the hen's brooding functions, chickens and eggs became an industrial commodity, engineered by human
technology. (The first commercial incubator was developed by Charles
Hearson in 1881).[9] Once the principles of chicken egg incubators were
perfected, a human ambition of controlling life for its needs and desires,
and following the discovery of bacteria, a mode of incubation expanded
its role: to microorganisms.

During the second half of the eighteenth century, with advances in
the field of microbiology, the desire to create artificial optimum environments for specifically chosen microbes led to advancement in the
mechanisms of the incubator. A key player was Robert Koch, known as
one of the fathers of microbiology, whose work was crucial to the improvement of incubation methods. The other "father" was Louis Pasteur.
At that time, incubators were hard to maintain at constant temperature,
since reliable temperature control was not yet possible. It was Koch who
advanced the mechanism of the thermostats and enabled a feedback re-

sponse between the machine-incubator, the life incubated, and the environment they create.

In his research into anthrax, Koch showed that it originates from spores of *Bacillus anthracis* bacteria. First he showed that animals inoculated with blood from sick animals will develop the disease as opposed to the animals inoculated with blood from a healthy animal. However, Koch went further; he also wanted to investigate whether anthrax bacilli that had never been in contact with any kind of animal could cause the disease. For that, he had to obtain pure cultures of the bacilli. Isolation of a pure culture may be enhanced by providing a mixed bacterial culture with a medium favoring the growth of one organism to the exclusion of others. Koch "found that inoculating the cornea of a rabbit with bacteria-laden fluid caused changes in the aqueous humor: the translucent fluid became turbid with bacteria. The aqueous humor was, he discerned, an effective medium for 'culturing' bacteria."[10]

Here it is interesting to note that the word "inoculation" comes from the combination of the words *in* (in) and *oculus* (an eye). One reason for the ocular emphasis in this word may lie in the technique that originally relied heavily on the use of an eye for growth of bacteria media—an anthropomorphic lexicon part and parcel of the long-standing privileging of vision in Western epistemologies and ontologies.[11]

Koch demonstrated how the environment, the niche in which an organism is embedded, becomes part of the organism's behavior and function:

> [He] recorded the multiplication of the bacilli and noted that, when conditions are unfavourable to them, they produce inside themselves rounded spores which *can* resist adverse conditions, especially lack of oxygen and that, when suitable conditions of life are restored, the spores give rise to bacilli again. Koch grew the bacilli for several generations in these pure cultures and showed that, although they had had no contact with any kind of animal, they could still cause anthrax.[12]

In other words, Koch demonstrated how certain characteristics within an organism are activated or deactivated depending solely on its environment. An organism was thus defined as part of its milieu. In this sense, a place that enables life is a place that gives life its defining characteristics, thus collapsing the biology-environment binary. In other words, the environment with its specific conditions is one with the life it hosts. This phenomenon is also ideological insofar as these specific environments are controlled by humans and their machines for a specific human-centric purpose. The ideological dimensions of the incubator are perhaps never clearer than with the development of the human incubator.

Indeed, the development of the human incubator is intriguing not so much as a technological advancement—as it followed the same principles as chicken and microbiological incubators—but rather because of how it was positioned within, perceived and understood by, and presented to society. Incubator aesthetics and the design of the "packaging" in which the abstracted womb simulator resided, as we will see, had much to do with capturing public imagination and played a major role in the articulation of the life inside the human-controlled machine.

Although the invention of incubators for premature infants was associated with the French obstetrician Stephane Tarnier, who got the idea after a visit to the Paris Zoo, it was Martin A. Couney, a fellow French physician, who introduced this idea to other parts of Europe and the United States through international fairs.[13] Dr. Couney brought his incubator "show" to the Pan-American Exposition in Buffalo, New York, in 1901: "As with other attractions at a fair, a 'barker' tried to entice people into the 'premie' exhibit located in a 'neat and artistic' brick building."[14] Rather than being positioned alongside the more scientific and technological exhibits, the baby incubators display was placed among the "more cultural" entertainments along the exposition's midway, which included an "Eskimo Village," "Beautiful Orient," and "Trip to the Moon." When the exposition closed due to political and economic upheavals, some to do with the assassination of William McKinley, the twenty-fifth president of the United States, on the grounds, Couney moved the show to Coney Island in Brooklyn, New York, where it was one of the first permanent displays. This exhibit, complete with living infants, remained there from 1903 to 1941. As one source reported:

> Because this feeding method did not expose wet nurses' bodies, visitors to Couney's exhibit could watch nasal feeding through a glass window; doubtless, the spectacle captured their imaginations as a simultaneously

advanced and freakish alimentary display. Breast-feeding, a process central to maternity, delivered itself to mechanical production and an aesthetic display.[15]

Presenting the infants as semifreaks, semiliving objects of spectacle for the visitors and audiences, devoid of personhood and family context, at one point Couney was forced to recruit fresh specimens from abroad. Since London hospitals would not provide donated infants, Couney returned to Paris to secure "three washbaskets full of premature foundlings."[16]

Couney's incubators were designed beyond their functional needs as a spectacle for public view. At the same time, the incubator was not a neutral environment with regard to the life it carried; rather, it played an active and dynamic role in the biological and cultural meaning making of premature human babies. The incubator was not only instrumental in the transition of these liminal beings toward a healthy life but also enacted scientific and cultural classifications. The "surrogation" was initially articulated via aesthetic rather than scientific modes of presentation, as a device that enabled the infant to progress from an ambiguous "passage zone" to personhood, at which point it could assume its own political life outside the incubator once it had matured sufficiently. In the meantime, while housed in this passage zone hosted by an artificial mother, the premature baby became a "thing," a spectacle, a freak, a "semi-being" (neither human nor animal or machine)—an object/subject that could be put on display as a curiosity until it could be "normalized" and "approved" by the technoscientific project and become assimilated into the classification of life as a human being; a passage from the Real to the Symbolic; from the order of the mother to the father; the passage into language, laws, and recognizability; and capable of being governed or subjected to authority. Put another way, these liminal beings transformed into human subjects deserving of the rights and obligations of the country of which they were legally citizens. In the case of incubators hosting humans (as opposed to other forms of life), incubators serve as a passage into knowable and governable life, or passage into citizenship with rights and responsibilities.

Shortly after the introduction of human incubators, scientists developed ways to culture tissue cells, isolated from the complex body. These cells could grow and proliferate solely within a technological support system that simulated particular aspects of the body's environment; they were thus incubators in the more contemporary language of "bioreactors."[17] Neolife, however, are a rarely acknowledged type of cybernetic organism that combine a biological body with artificial life support. The rights and responsibilities afforded humans have not extended to other organisms. Life grown (and sometimes modified) in the laboratory is life whose place of material and symbolic life is human-designed and human-controlled technological apparatuses. As seen with later developments, this marriage of bodies and technologies via a simulated mother, where life exists (at least temporarily) only within a technoscientific body, has opened the door to many other applications, imaginary and real.[18]

## Incubators for Cells and Tissues: Potentiality, Eugenics, and Neolife

Naturally, when they are parts of a living body the cells are disciplined, they do not wander about where they like, growing actively and reproducing themselves, as the cells in culture do. An organ such as the brain or liver is like the City during working hours, a tissue culture is like Regent's Park on a Bank Holiday, a spectacle of rather futile freedom.
—Julian Huxley and H. G. Wells, *The Science of Life* (1929)

In 1910, Dr. Alexis Carrel and his assistant Montrose Burrows, of the Rockefeller Institute, together coined the term "tissue culture."[19] The growth and reproduction of cells and tissue outside of the body, rather than their mere survival, became the defining characteristic of tissue culture.[20] Carrel became interested in in vitro life during his research into transplantation. He considered tissue culture as tantamount to a new life-form: one that could prolong the life of body parts inside a new artificial body and help pave the way toward human immortality.[21] Carrel wrote: "The cell is immortal. It is merely the fluid in which it floats that degenerates. Renew this fluid at regular intervals, give the cells what they require for nutrition, and as far as we know, the pulsation of life can go on forever."[22] Carrel believed so much in his ability to control life that he contemplated the ethic and pragmatic entailments of bringing people back to life. He is quoted as having the following conversation with a lawyer:

> "What would be my responsibility if I bring people back to life?" Carrel asked . . .
>     "Responsibility for what?" The lawyer asked.
>     "For those I bring back," said Carrel. "Food and Lodging and all that. If I bring them back an old man too old to work. Or, in the case of a young man, suppose something happens and he isn't able to do anything for himself. Am I liable for his support?"[23]

As indicated by the quoted passage at the beginning of this section, if an organ is like a city, then the body is the nation-state, and cells are its citizens. Hence, cells in culture are the unproductive citizens, engaged in "a spectacle of rather futile freedom." Therefore, it might not be surprising that Carrel's theoretical musings about biological potentiality were inextricably bound with a eugenicist vision. Carrel outlined his particular ideology of eugenics in the book *Man, the Unknown* (1935). A scientistic view, combined with religious, even mystical, declarations, led him to speculate on the great problems of human destiny. Carrel theorized that mankind could reach perfection through selective reproduction and the leadership of an intellectual aristocracy. Through scientific enlightenment and eugenicist proposals, humanity would be free from disease and gain long life and spiritual advancement. It can be speculated that the incubator, as a gas-enriched chamber, served as Carrel's inspiration for the use of gas chambers to rid human society of its undesirable members.[24] "Eugenics," Carrel wrote in the last chapter of *Man, the Unknown*, "is indispensable for the perpetuation of the strong. A great race must propagate its best elements."[25] The book, a worldwide best-seller translated into nineteen languages, brought Carrel international attention. His belief in optimization of bodies through care and control led him to speculate about looking at societies as "vessels" that can be monitored, controlled, and manipulated for optimum growth of the desired elements. Carrel believed in a utopic biocitizenship in which the man/machine can create conditions where only the "preferable" and "optimum" biocitizens (read: white, male, Western, and heterosexual) of society can survive and thrive.

The quest for unleashing the limitless potentiality of cells has continued, although not as explicitly articulated, to norms around gender, race, and ability. When animal cells are extracted from their host body and its immune system, they can still grow and proliferate in vitro subject to certain conditions such as temperature, sterility, and nutrient supply. In some cases the cells fuse. Cell fusion is defined as "the nondestructive merging of the contents of two cells by artificial means, resulting in a heterokaryon that will reproduce genetically alike, multinucleated progeny for a few generations."[26] Besides the procedure's practical applications such as a method for "cellular factories" to produce antibodies, Henry Harris, a professor at Oxford University, has written about his experience as a pioneer in cell fusion techniques.[27] He suggested that his research calls into question fundamental assumptions about biology:

> There is a tendency for living things to join up, establish linkages, live inside each other, return to earlier arrangements, get along, whenever possible. This is the way of the world. The new phenomenon of cell fusion, a laboratory trick on which much of today's science of molecular genetics relies for its data, is the simplest and most spectacular symbol of the tendency. In a way, it is the most unbiologic of all phenomena, violating the most fundamental myths of the last century, for it denies the importance of specificity, integrity, and separateness in living things. Any cell—man, animal, fish, fowl, or insect—given the chance and under the right conditions, brought into contact with any other cell, however foreign, will fuse with it. Cytoplasm will flow easily from one to the other, the nuclei will combine, and it will become, for a time anyway, a single cell with two complete, alien genomes, ready to dance, ready to multiply. It is a Chimera, a Griffon, a Sphinx, a Ganesha, a Peruvian God, a Ch'i-lin, an omen of good fortune, a wish for the world.[28]

Harris presents a more complex view of the phenomenon of cell fusion and the breach not only of the essentialist view of a species but also with the sanctity of the human as a separate and unique species: "What caught the imagination of journalists was the fact that the species barrier could be crossed. This seems to have shaken some deeply cherished assumptions about the uniqueness of man, and many of the newspaper reports showed striking similarities with the paintings of Hieronymus

Bosch." This biological and ontological breach could only happen through human intervention in the highly controlled environment of the incubator.

The neolife places of origin are the laboratories and the incubators; outside of this particular niche they will cease to live. Their biological and ontological breaches make them unable to survive externally to human-made technological environments. In that respect they are not in a position—yet—to be situated within any form of cultural or scientific taxonomical system and therefore are devoid of any symbolic agency.[29]

## The Neolife Incubator: The Aesthetic of Invisibility

Age, gender, race, species, and location do not play the same roles in the simulated body as with other living bodies. This means that, in theory, every tissue in every living being has the potential to become part of a collection of living fragments that are yet to acquire sovereignty. Neolife are an extended, yet broken, mirror of alternative assemblages of life enabled via different—and controlled—environments.

Nevertheless, as Nikki Sullivan argues, "*Techné* is not something we add or apply to the already constituted body (as object), nor is it a tool that the embodied self employs to its own ends. Rather, *technés* are the dynamic means in and through which corporealities are crafted."[30] Most recently, biotech vessels are being employed in the service of what is now referred to as "synthetic biology." While much of current rhetoric and practice in this field seems to focus on controlling living systems at the molecular level, we argue that one of the fundamental vehicles of controlling life—something that engineering biology cannot do without—is the ability to simulate and control the environmental conditions of the biological body via an incubator. Generally, incubators, like many female bodies, are taken for granted in the contemporary biotech world while other technological control systems, such as molecular interventions, take center stage. We argue that replacing the grounding of life in a code (i.e., DNA) with a context- or environment-dependent basis constitutes more than mere scientific issue; it is an ideologically charged view of life.

This aesthetic of invisibility (which is radically different from the aesthetics of spectacle associated with the neonatal incubators in the early twentieth century, discussed earlier) may serve to make the cells and tissues devoid of agency, extracted and abstracted from the body from which they were derived as well as from the "body" they have become. In addition, it renders the technology invisible and therefore neutral or even natural, as if the black box of technology itself were leaving no footprint on the environment but serving simply as an autotrophic artificial mother—a better replacement to the "original" mother as it has supposedly no role and leaves no mark on the life inside and outside of it.

To illustrate how the incubator's role has become completely ignored or transparent, consider the marketing of in vitro meat technology. In vitro meat is an attempt to grow meat using tissue culture and tissue engineering techniques without directly killing animals. In this case, a simulated technological body is replacing the animal body, and only the tissue of interest is grown for its eventual human consumption. As far as we can determine, we were the first to grow and eat in vitro meat (in 2000 and 2003, respectively).[31] There is a considerable disconnect between what is scientifically possible and the fantasies that are prevalent in much of the discourse around in vitro meat. In vitro meat can be seen as a symptom of the problems inherent in the artificial simulation of "bodies," as it presents the isolation and control of life as an ethical alternative to animal meat consumption rather than as a semipermeable contextualization of living matter within an environment that is embedded with cultural and social biases. In many respects the nonhuman animal that was never considered to have political life or to be a citizen of the human world is being further fragmented and abstracted: away from a chicken or even an egg (chicken incubators), away from its body-microbiota, and into a total, controlled, and sterile environment.

In much of the media coverage of the development of in vitro meat, the laboratory, which stands for the simulated artificial environment that has replaced both the field and the animal body, is seen as a black box of control and growth in which meat is magically produced, as if out of thin air. The resources needed to grow cells into a piece of meat are usually downplayed or totally ignored. Instead, the opaque and physical, albeit technologically simulated, body is transformed into a virtual and transparent "body" that requires no input. This attitude can be traced to one of the most frequently cited papers used to advocate in vitro meat as a more environmentally friendly mode of meat production. The paper, titled "Environmental Impacts of Cultured Meat Production," was commissioned by the New Harvest Foundation and is an exercise in agenda-driven theoretical simulation that relies on some outrageous assumptions and explanations to describe a product that does not yet exist.[32] With regard to the incubator, which provides a constant, stable, warm environment with the right combination of gases and is one of the most important requirements for cell growth, the authors make this curious statement not once but twice: "As cells produce heat during the growth, additional energy inputs in heating of the reactor are not required."[33] This statement is far removed from the actualities of keeping a constant warm temperature throughout the growth period of the cells, from starting the culture of cells to harvest time. It neglects the role of the incubator as a regulator (first-order cybernetics) of homeostatic condition that goes beyond merely heating the cells and highlights how removed some of the thinkers in this field are from the realities of biological bodies.

In addition to the fact that it is impossible to incubate cells purely by their self-generated heat, we find quite interesting here the negation of the incubator's role as an active "agent" that must be responsive to signals from the living elements grown within it. In short, an incubator does not provide virtual, transparent simulation of the body in the growth of life, but is a material, active simulator of real conditions that require constant input and output of activity and energy. Even though the physical incubator is a simulation of a biological body, it still needs to mediate between this internal ambient environment and the outside world. As the passage from the Real to the Symbolic is a passage into citizenship, taking away any symbolic recognition of the host "body" holds both the incubator and its living appendages in suspense.

An example in which human social prejudices of gender and race are embedded within a technology concerned with bacterial life-forms is the recent synthesis of a genome. One must remember that a bacterium has no gender in the human sense and reproduces in many different ways some of which are very foreign to human reproduction (such as cloning). Nevertheless, researchers have betrayed tenacious habits of mind regarding just such reproductive norms. In 2010, biologist Craig Venter announced that he had created "the first self-replicating cell we've had on the planet whose parent is a computer."[34] Venter's group had synthesized the genome of the *Mycoplasma genitalium*, a parasitic bacteria that reside in the male genitals of humans and other primates. *M. genitalium* was chosen by Venter's group because it was the species with the smallest number of genes known at that time. The DNA of the bacteria was sequenced, translated into digital data, and then synthesized (in a very complex technological process that involved DNA synthesizers and yeast cells). The synthetic DNA genome was inserted into another bacterial cell from which original DNA has been removed. The "synthesized" life-form was called *Mycoplasma laboratorium* and nicknamed "Synthia" by the ECT Group, an organization that works to address the socioeconomic and ecological issues surrounding new technologies that could have an impact on the world's poorest and most vulnerable people. "Synthia," a reference to the bacterium's synthetic origin and a homophone of the female name Cynthia, was circulated by the media, thereby popularizing the assigned feminine quality to the altered bacteria.[35] Venter used an existing cell with all its "machinery" and components, including the cell membrane with its own hereditary mechanism,[36] minus a strand of nucleic DNA. He completely disregarded the milieu in which the DNA is part of/shaped by/depended upon. In this respect, Venter adopted a DNA chauvinist approach; as in human/mammalian reproduction, the contribution of the male (as opposed to the female) to the creation of the new offspring is only a strand of a DNA. Venter's defense of manufacturing life-forms was grounded in a DNA-centric position, dismissing alternative paradigms of biological development such as "attribut[ing] unmeasurable properties to the cell cytoplasm" as akin to neovitalism: "Vitalism today manifests itself in the guise of shifting emphasis away from DNA to an 'emergent' property of the cell that is somehow greater than the sum of its molecular parts and how they work in a particular environment."[37] He then asserted:

> When there is mystery, there is an opportunity for vitalism and religion to thrive. However, when my team successfully booted up the synthetic DNA software within a cell, we demonstrated that our basic understanding of the machinery of cellular life had advanced to a significant point. In answer to Erwin Schrodinger's little question "What is life?" we had been able to provide one compelling answer: "DNA is the software and the basis of all life."[38]

Venter, taking a masculinist position on the "creation" of life, empha-sized what a male provides in the act of procreation (a packet of DNA in the sperm), downplaying (or even ignoring) the female contribution of the egg (with its cellular machinery and other non-DNA-based heredi-tary mechanisms), as well as the womb hosted within the female body.

As part of the publicity for this technological breakthrough, Venter and his colleagues released a series of images of the *Mycoplasma labo-ratorium/Synthia* bacterium and its cultures. One image in particular dominated the media. Two round, blue colonies of the bacteria sit on an orange background. The image resembles two blue eyes, gazing back at the human viewer; the feminine gaze and the color of the eyes are suggestive of race and gender, which is scrutinized by the human-man voyeur. This image can also be interpreted as a metaphysical reference to the monster gazing back at its creator, as demonstrated by Mary Shelley's intense focus on the eyes of the monster in the novel *Frankenstein*, or the lack of an eye in traditional depictions of the golem.[39] This extremely potent image is both biopolitical and ideological. These images stand in direct contradiction to Venter's materialist antivitalist/antimetaphysical view of life. Instead of a Neolifist, fetishistic idea of an abstract vessel (bacteria cell) holding a new life (artificial DNA), *Synthia* is becoming a feminized monstrosity, a racialized entity with agency, that locks its gaze to ours. *Synthia* becomes a biocitizen—implicated in her/its own existence through her/its relationship to her/its male (human/computer) creator. Venter's DNA-chauvinist, paternalistic, and anthropocentric view can be seen as a return to the chauvinistic idea of life originating from animalcules that reside in sperm. As in the notion of the animal-cule, for Venter, only the DNA transmitted by the male contributes to the uniqueness of *Synthia*, not the host bacterial cell and its internal mechanisms. *Synthia*, by being partly synthetically engineered, is be-coming a biocitizen of the human world; it is allocated a name with sexual connotations, it carries blue eyes, and it belongs to (is patented by) a business cooperation.

Bacteria are predominantly asexual organisms that reproduce through cloning; they are precarious and plastic; they have many "being" configurations that exceed human knowledge and imagination. Further-more, humans are partially bacterial (as shown and studied in the field of the human microbiome). Bacteria and many of the neolife are who/

what they are, defying the hetero-anthro-technological control that we humans assert over them.

## Conclusion

These neolife belong to emerging new biopolitical configurations of our changing world. They have the potential to subvert current hegemonic social constructions or reinforce them. Yet it is also the case that humans lack full control over life, both life that is constructed by humans and unintentional life. Life, even technological life, cannot be fully contained, especially if its vessels of care and control are neglected, in both conceptual and practical ways. Neolife, we have posited here, are new agents that carry the promise of leakage, contamination, diversity, and fertilization. They contribute to citizenship's changing sense of place and mobility. Therefore, opening up and extending the hospitality of technoscientific frameworks to more-than-human as well as feminist and queer discourses is overdue. Biology is not a technology that can be treated with a mind-set inherited from the Industrial Revolution; it is too unpredictable and queer to obey our current hegemonic understanding and human attempts to control complex systems.

The opaque box of the incubator and the neolife it hosts are not neutral and not fixed in terms of the "real" and the symbolic. Incubated life carries a mystery embroiled with mixed tensions of great promise and/or horrible threat until they emerge. But neolife, when and if they emerge, always have their own ontological existence to act and express, and it is not necessarily what their human creators are wishing for.

NOTES

This chapter incudes sections that were published earlier in Zurr, Ionat and Oron Catts, "Keep it Warm! Incubators as Simulators," *LA+ Interdisciplinary Journal of Landscape Architecture*, Simulation/Fall 2016, 4, pp. 102-109 a publication of the University of Pennsylvania School of Design, 2016.

1 A bioreactor is an engineered apparatus that supports a biologically active environment in which a biological reaction or process is carried out, especially on an industrial scale. Bioreactors usually provide a sterile environment and specific conditions for the biological organism(s) and biological and/or chemical reaction(s) to be sustainable and successful.

2   For more about neolife, see Oron Catts and Ionat Zurr, "The Biopolitics of Life
    Removed from Context: Neolifism," in *Resisting Biopolitics*, ed. S. E. Wilmer and
    Audrone Zukauskaite (London: Routledge, 2016), 135–58.

3   According to Marcello Paniago, "At around 3,000 years ago, the early Egyptian
    incubators consisted of a large mud brick building with a series of small rooms
    (ovens) located at each side of a central passageway. In the upper part of these
    'small incubation rooms,' there were shelves for burning straw, camel manure or
    charcoal in order to provide radiant heat to the eggs below." See Marcello Paniago,
    "Artificial Incubation of Poultry Eggs: 3,000 Years of History," *Hatchery Expertise
    Online*, September 2005, www.thepoultrysite.com.

4   Walter Landauer, "Hatchability of Chicken Eggs as Influenced by Environ-
    ment and Heredity," *Stors Agricultural Experiments Station* 1 (University of
    Connecticut–Storrs, 1961), http://digitalcommons.uconn.edu.

5   Sigfried Giedion, *Mechanisation Takes Command: A Contribution to Anonymous
    History* (New York: Oxford University Press, 1948), 248.

6   "Incubator" and "Medical Discoveries," *Encyclopedia.com*, accessed June 29, 2017,
    www.encyclopedia.com.

7   As we will show later in the essay, in contemporary biotechnology, the very idea
    of "mother" has been supplanted by the computer and the (almost always) male
    scientist who controls it.

8   René-Antoine Ferchault De Réaumur, *The Art of Hatching and Bringing Up Do-
    mestick Fowls of All Kinds, at Any Time of the Year. Either by Means of the Heat of
    Hot-Beds, or That of Common Fire* (1749–50), 248–49, https://books.google.com.

9   C. E. Hearson, "Apparatus for Heating Eggs by Artificial Heat," US Patent 298, 579,
    filed July 2, 1883, and issued May 13, 1884.

10  Steve M. Blevins and Michael S. Bronze, "Robert Koch and the 'Golden Age'
    of Bacteriology," *International Journal of Infectious Diseases* 14, no. 9 (2010):
    e744–e751.

11  The use of the eyes looking back at their "creator," the gaze of the feminized life-
    form under observation and manipulation, continues to lurk behind the contem-
    porary work of synthetic biology—as will be illustrated through this essay.

12  *Nobel Lectures Physiology or Medicine, 1901–1921* (River Edge, NJ: World Scientific
    Publishing, 1999), 180.

13  "Baby Incubator Exhibit at the Pan-American Exposition in Buffalo," University at
    Buffalo Libraries, http://library.buffalo.edu.

14  Ibid.

15  Scott Webel, "Kinderbrutanstalt: Leisure Space and the Coney Island Baby Incu-
    bators," *Text, Practice, Performance* 5 (2003): 9.

16  Jeffrey P. Baker, *The Machine in the Nursery: Incubator Technology and the Origins
    of Newborn Intensive Care* (Baltimore: Johns Hopkins University Press, 1996), 91.

17  As Eduard Uhlenhuth explained in 1916: "Through the discovery of tissue culture
    we have, so to speak, created a new type of body on which to grow the cell." See
    Eduard Uhlenhuth, "Changes in Pigment Epithelium Cells and Iris Pigment Cells

of Rana Pipiens Induced by Changes in Environmental Conditions," *Journal of Experimental Medicine* 24, no. 6 (1916): 690.

18  The "simulated mother" idea led J. B. S. Haldane to predict in 1924 that by 2074 (150 years later), 70 percent of all human births would result from pregnancies nurtured in an artificial environment from fertilization to birth. He called it ectogenesis, and this notion of the nonhuman taking over the most fundamental aspect of becoming a biological human became material for *Brave New World*'s totalitarian nightmares as well as transhumanist dreams. Haldane's prediction may yet be proved right, although it currently seems that ectogenesis is at least a generation away. In the meantime, a new form of biolabor, the surrogate biological mother, has considerably blurred the line between simulated and real motherhood.

19  Alexis Carrel and Montrose T. Burrows, "Cultivation of Tissues in Vitro and Its Technique," *Journal of Experimental Medicine* 13 (1911): 387–96.

20  Hannah Landecker, "Building 'A New Type of Body in Which to Grow a Cell': Tissue Culture at the Rockefeller Institute, 1910–1914," in *Creating a Tradition of Biomedical Research: Contributions to the History of Rockefeller University*, ed. Darwin F. Stapleton (New York: Rockefeller University Press, 2004).

21  For more, see David M. Friedman, *The Immortalists: Charles Lindbergh, Dr. Alexis Carrel, and Their Daring Quest to Live Forever* (New York: HarperCollins, 2007).

22  Alexis Carrel, *Man, the Unknown* (New York: Harper and Brothers, 1935).

23  Freidman, *The Immortalists*, 39.

24  Here is Carrel on the role of eugenics and gas chambers: "Those who have murdered, robbed, . . . kidnapped children, despoiled the poor of their savings, misled the public in important matters, should be humanely and economically disposed of in small euthanasic institutions supplied with proper gases. A similar treatment could be advantageously applied to the insane, guilty of criminal acts." Carrel, *Man, the Unknown*, 290–91.

25  Ibid., 299.

26  "Cell Fusion," *American Heritage Science Dictionary*, www.dictionary.com.

27  Henry Harris, "Roots: 'Cell Fusion,'" *BioEssays* 2, no. 4 (1985): 176–79.

28  Ibid., 176.

29  A rough estimate would put the current biomass of living cells and tissues disassociated from the complex bodies that once hosted them in the thousands of tons. In addition, there exist many tons of fragments of bodies (cells, tissues, organs) maintained in suspended animation in cryogenic conditions, all of which require intensive technological intervention and isolation to prevent their transformation into a nonliving state. Much of this living biological matter can, in theory, be cocultured and fused (cell fusion) or joined together within sterile environments (with varying degrees of success). See Oron Catts and Ionat Zurr, "The Art of the Semi Living," in *Art et Biotechnologies*, ed. Louise Poissant and Ernestine Daubner (Quebec City: Presses de l'Universite du Quebec, 2005).

30  Nikki Sullivan, "Somatechnics," *TSQ: Transgender Studies Quarterly* 1, nos. 1–2 (2014): 188.

31 We have written extensively about the issues surrounding this development. See, for example, Oron Catts and Ionat Zurr, "Growing for Different Ends," *International Journal of Biochemistry and Cell Biology* 56 (2014): 20–29; and Oron Catts and Ionat Zurr, "Disembodied Livestock: The Promise of a Semi-living Utopia," *Parallex* 19, no. 1 (2013): 101–13.

32 Hannah L. Tuomisto and M. Joost Teixeira de Mattos, "Environmental Impacts of Cultured Meat Production," *Environmental Science and Technology* 45, no. 14 (2011): 6117–23.

33 Ibid., 6118–19.

34 Nicolas Wade, "Researchers Say They Created a 'Synthetic Cell,'" *New York Times*, May 20, 2010.

35 According to the organization's website, "ETC Group works to address the socio-economic and ecological issues surrounding new technologies that could have an impact on the world's poorest and most vulnerable people. We investigate ecological erosion (including the erosion of cultures and human rights); the development of new technologies (especially agricultural but also other technologies that work with genomics and matter); and we monitor global governance issues including corporate concentration and trade in technologies. We operate at the global political level. We work closely with partner civil society organizations (CSOs) and social movements, especially in Africa, Asia and Latin America." For more, see www.etcgroup.org.

36 T. Cavalier-Smith, "The Membranome and Membrane Heredity in Development and Evolution," in *Organelles, Genomes and Eukaryote Phylogeny*, ed. R. P. Hirt and D. S. Horner (Boca Raton, FL: CRC Press, 2004), 335–51.

37 J. Craig Venter, *Life at the Speed of Light: From the Double Helix to the Drawn of Digital Life* (New York: Viking, 2013), 17.

38 Ibid., 130.

39 In Jewish folklore, the golem is an animated anthropomorphic being created by God from inanimate clay and mud.

13

## The Supra-Cyborg

*The Rise of Global Governing Corporatocracies*

CELESTE M. CONDIT

Because humans are arranged in the form that we designate as the category of biological beings, citizenship is necessarily biocitizenship, even if it is not explicitly theorized and rhetoricized as such. Explicit and focused critiques of the relationships between biological concepts and concepts of citizenship can surely be productive. However, there is a tendency for the vision of biology as an individual-level phenomenon (human "bodies") to align with the common vision of citizenship as a relationship of individuals (citizens) to a separate entity (a state). Extant critical treatments of biocitizenship expand these conceptual boundaries in productive ways by considering individual bodies as affiliates of groups (sexualized, racialized, classed, etc.). This essay, however, offers a supra-individual perspective on biocitizenship. By developing the concept of the supra-cyborg, it envisions biocitizenship as the organization of humans within a suprabiological form of being, which is to say a form shaped by humans' symbolizing capacities, but not wholly determined by them.

Attending to our inhabitation within supra-cyborgs highlights the importance of the contest between corporations and governments and the rise of global governing corporatocracies. The literalizing metaphor of the supra-cyborg also highlights as a key political question of the era whether it is possible for humans to live well outside of supra-cyborgs, and if not, what kind of supra-cyborg organization we should seek to synthetically engineer. This vision also recalibrates a sense of which lines of action might be most promising for those who seek to implement either justice or care across human groups or who seek greater space for nonhuman beings.

## What Are Supra-Cyborgs?

If naming aids critical understanding, then some new concept such as "supra-cyborg" is needed to understand a world that seems to be under the influence not of individuals but of larger entities that are constituted of human beings affiliated in ways that exhibit relatively sustained patterns. If a cyborg is any being that integrates biological and nonbiological components, then a supra-cyborg is an entity that organizes multiple, whole, living human bodies and integrates them with and through other materials (such as technologies) to produce a durable entity definable by the relationships of those components. More technically, a supra-cyborg is an aggregation of multiple human mind/bodies and other physical matter interacting within a semidurable structured network, which is understood by the human mind/bodies as a nameable entity of which they are a member or part. This concept combines biological theories with the concept of the cyborg at a higher-order level.

Although politically progressive humanists have been leery of biological imaginaries, late twentieth-century theorists ranging from Donna Haraway to Brian Massumi to the sometimes team of Gilles Deleuze and Félix Guattari have illustrated that "biology" is not equivalent to conservative ideology, even though conservative ideologues have in the past skillfully identified biological concepts with oppressive agendas in the public sphere. These theorists instead illustrate that self-conscious utilization of biologically grounded concepts can facilitate justice- and care-based agendas. For present purposes, it is instructive to note how biological imaginaries posit that organisms exist at different levels of complexity. Single celled organisms were made into more complex forms of being when they became eukaryotic—putatively a cell within a cell. A different kind of organismal complexity arose when multicellular organisms evolved, and then again when central nervous systems developed. Parasitic and symbiotic relationships among organisms represent another level at which a biological being is organized, and arguably ecosystems might be another.

This biological imagination was productively deployed at one level by Donna Haraway's notion of the cyborg.[1] Haraway noted that humans tend to exist not (purely) as biological entities but as biological entities enmeshed in technologies (ranging from contact lenses to prosthetic legs to neck rings and earrings to Google watches to pacemakers to titanium hips). As a cyborg, a human-plus-technology is a different kind of organism than it would be if it could exist without such technology. Haraway argued that "cyborg imagery can suggest a way out of the maze of dualisms in which we have explained our bodies and our tools to ourselves."[2] Rather than embracing a political agenda based on a return to mythic images of a "natural" condition in which women were once upon a time not oppressed, Haraway indicated, "For us, in imagination and in other practice, machines can be prosthetic devices, intimate components, friendly selves."[3] Consequently, the appropriate political project is not a rejection of the technological era but guidance of it: "The machine is not an *it* to be animated, worshipped, and dominated. The machine is us, our processes, an aspect of our embodiment. We can be responsible for machines; they do not dominate or threaten us. We are responsible for boundaries; we are they."[4] Such a political project and vision reorients the rhetorical task away from the academic and Marxist-influenced project of unveiling the false consciousness of others toward an active offering of alternative options: it "requires not sorting consciousness into categories of clear-sighted critique grounding a 'solid political epistemology' versus 'manipulated false consciousness,' but subtle understanding of emerging pleasures, experiences, and powers with serious potential for changing the rules of the game."[5]

Haraway's charge that "if we learn how to read these webs of power and social life, we might learn new couplings, new coalitions" has already proved partially fruitful.[6] As is necessarily the case with all discourse (including the one you are now reading), Haraway's discourse does not cover all the options. The limitation of any discourse rests in part on its taken-for-granted assumptions, and there seems to be value left in expanding beyond two of Haraway's assumptions. Particularly, her discourse did not attend to the recalcitrance of nondiscursive materials, and it encouraged us to imagine a single, unified social system.

The first assumption constraining the scope of Haraway's prescriptions I would describe as the overprivileging of the material force of discourse, which is concomitant with a universalizing of the model of communication or the text. Haraway recognized that the (overblown) informatics model was embodied in the worldview she wanted to change when she wrote that "communications sciences and modern biologies are constructed by a common move—the translation of the world into a prob-lem of coding, a search for a common language in which all resistance to instrumental control disappears and all heterogeneity can be submitted to disassembly, reassembly, investment, and exchange."[7] However, she herself relied too heavily on this coding model in her analyses and rec-ommendations: "The entire universe of objects that can be known scien-tifically must be formulated as problems in communications engineering (for the managers) or theories of the text (for those who would resist)."[8] Haraway's acceptance of the absolutist vision of all as code or text was unnecessary. Indeed, it should be a fundamental tenet of materialist and ecological theory that it is empirically and ethically problematic to posit, as she indicated the managerial informaticists did, that "any objects or persons can be reasonably thought of in terms of disassembly and reas-sembly; no 'natural' architectures constrain system design."[9]

While equating "the natural" with "the good" and seeing either of these key terms in dehistoricized ways might be illegitimate, that does not justify implying that there are and should be no empirical or ethical constraints upon recoding the world. While it is surely possible to imag-ine codes that are unconstrained (a kind of reverse Platonism—the ideal world is impermanent and infinitely flexible, enabled by the assump-tion that Being is essentially transcendent or fictional), in the lifeworlds humans live in on the earth, there are material constraints on recoding anything. Direct work (i.e., what we can provisionally best label as de-ployment of Force = M × A) must be done to recode mountains into skyscrapers, to recode microbes into vectors for producing insulin or new species, to recode earth into a machinic system. Only part of that work can be sufficiently summed up with textual metaphors because the costs of such work entail the movement of matter that is organized in forms that are not directly responsive to the hail of the code. Matter that is organized in some forms (e.g., "mountains") must be moved by labor of nondiscursive sorts, even if the organization of humans/tools for such movements is discursively produced.

Retaining an emphasis on the multidimensionality of materiality is crucial because a Haraway-like analysis would point to such labor—physical, manual, emotional, reproductive, technological—as focal loci of the experience of oppression for humans. The materialities of labor are not erased by the fact that humans are currently the most code-happy species (though one could highlight the impacts of human codes on other species and though other species code in less globally consequential ways). Because care and justice require material resources in addition to "texts," any politics of care and justice requires that both the coding costs (e.g., "identity") and the noncoding costs (e.g., the elimination of species habitat) of the political regimes be made conspicuous— even though humans' status as a "symbolizing animal"[10] means we most typically make costs conspicuous through textual means.

Texts, codes, and communication are important (and perhaps underappreciated by some outside the humanities), but texts' mode of being does not sum up all the modes of being.[11] This is to say that Haraway's claim that "the cyborg is a kind of disassembled and reassembled, postmodern collective and personal self" should not be valorized in a totalistic fashion.[12] Her conclusion, "But there are also great riches for feminists in explicitly embracing the possibilities inherent in the breakdown of clean distinctions between organism and machine and similar distinctions structuring the Western self," might be true, but it does not entail simply embracing *all* such possibilities.[13] Rather, it entails closer observation and careful judgment of which possibilities we wish to create. Haraway's judgment that "I would rather be a cyborg than a goddess" was not too hasty at the moment it was written.[14] But several decades later, our question should be "Which cyborg?" and, perhaps, "Which supra-cyborg?" The latter question brings us to the second limiting assumption of Haraway's theory.

Haraway parsed the categories of being into singular integrated systems or unnameable diversities, a practice that distracts us from creative choosing. While her integration of biotechnological and global economic issues was surely fruitful for its time and place, it fell back on a common trap of the politically engaged academic analysis of its era—casting the evil to be resisted as a unified totality and positing the alternative as an infinite diversity. Haraway recognized theories that had noted that "'advanced capitalism' is inadequate to convey the structure of this historical moment," and she recognized that a Foucauldian-style positing of epistemes as singularities did not capture the potential of the cyborgian era of informatics: "The cyborg is not subject to Foucault's biopolitics; the cyborg simulates politics, a much more potent field of operations."[15] However, instead of offering an alternative to a vision that imagined a singular structure, she simply offered different visions of a still "integrated circuit." Although, for her, there might have been *multiple* "world historical systems of domination" (formerly colonialism, capitalism, patriarchy), these now were summable as a singularity: "the informatics of domination" (even though she routinely emphasized diversity among peoples).[16]

A postevolutionary (developmental) model that posits multiple active beings that are not unified in their actions or intents might more usefully characterize global conditions than models that assume either absolute unities ("systems") or mere proliferation of diversities. Specifically, an ecological (not eco-*system*) model recognizes "speciation" as a kind of category of being that is not essentialist but also does not dissolve into infinite plurality. Speaking with the category of speciation decreases essentialism because there is no real exemplar of any species (every biological entity is different not only from every other but also from itself through time). Species are always growing/dying at the individual level and changing/dying out at the social level. However, the concept of species usefully maintains attention to historical and synchronic relationships in a way that mere diversity cannot. While species "members" (i.e., members by history) typically do not intentionally cooperate either consciously or unconsciously with other species, because biologically based beings have their own locus of goals/actions (and therefore, they are not "an integrated circuit" or "a system"), entities are nonetheless *constrained* by their relationships with others, even when that relationship is nothing more than existence on the same planet. Such a model posits a kind of mutual interdependence that does not idealize relationships as "system-like" or harmonious or necessarily sustainable or even durable.

This conceptual set requires that one maintain a notion of "beings" rather than dissolving all boundaries into a great flux of energy-matter, but it does not require positing absolutely discrete and permanent or "self-identical" categories for such beings. Both biological and nonbiological beings (at the order of either "objects" or "things") can be imagined as relative densities with specific histories of movements in time/space and in relationship to other such densities. Such densities are named by our choice as such, but our choice as such is influenced by both our discursive and our extradiscursive histories and by the material variation in densities and their histories that also have a nondiscursive existence.

Such a multiplicity-based developmental theory enables analysis with the potential for operating across some diversities without resorting to what Haraway and other political advocates reject: "a technological determinism," preserving instead what she lauds as "a historical system depending upon structured relations among people" (and, I would add, *more*).[17] It will be useful, in other words, to posit the interactions among different emerging and molting kinds of suprabiological species as driving sources of the conditions of possibility and experience for human/ animal lifeworlds rather than simply positing a singular, integrated circuit or system (such as capitalism) as the explanatory variable (aka enemy).

If a cyborg is a human-plus-technology, then a supra-cyborg is a set of humans durably linked through technologies. Rather than merely repudiating older vocabularies, this conceptual set takes account of the extensive critiques of those categories by deliberately linking the very specific set of terms that have historically pertained to individual human mind/bodies ("individual," "personal," "intention," "interest") and the more abstract set of terms that pertain to a totalized social ("society," "the system," "capitalism," "humankind"). A thoughtful linkage of the terms can compensate for the omissions of each level of analysis.

On a different plane of rotation, the concept also thus stands between E. O. Wilson's biologically derived notion of a superorganism and the mixing of machinic and circulatory metaphors that are made visible by Deleuzian perspectives.[18] Deleuzian perspectives wish away the body's organs in the physicists' dream of disarticulated energy/matter, rather than contextualizing those organs in biological histories. Combining the Deleuzian bent toward plurivocity and sociality with the Wilsonian attention to the constraints of biology provides better grounds for change-oriented social objectives because the effectiveness of the nonbiological perspective is blunted by its ignorance of constraining material forces while the biological perspective is blunted by a too-hearty attention to the existent and historical over the imaginable change. This particular combination of concepts also accounts for the critiques of the use of "organic" metaphors (e.g., by Herbert Spencer) to describe social entities (generally governments), without the error of insisting that such entities have no relationship to biological organisms or no parsable identity distinct from all of the flows of "society" or the totality of energy/matter.[19]

To understand corporations and nation-states and churches as supra-cyborgs is thus to view them as distinctive types of biosymbolic entities, that is, to posit a kind of symbolic being that transcends, in its organization (*dispositio*), the symbol-using animal.[20] In contrast to current parlance, which treats corporations as persons because corporations are in large part made up of persons, or which struggles to identify states with "a people" because nation-states are in part made up of persons, explicit attention to the kind of agent one is dealing with in these cases—a supra-cyborg—may allow us to recognize corporations and states as real entities that have their own distinctive kind of agency and impacts.

## Supra-Cyborgs Self-Advantage

Supra-cyborgs evolve, which is merely to say that those entities that have advantages compared with others survive and typically grow. Though the differences in evolutionary processes from non-superorganisms are multiple, this tautological observation is nonetheless productive because it directs our attention to a fundamental characteristic of supra-cyborgs: those that exist over any substantial space/time tend toward patterns of action/movement that are self-advantaging. This intense focus on self-advantage is an inherent and well-recognized feature of corporations, whose legal charters (and cast of supporting laws, regulations, and case law) frame them as solely driven by resource acquisition.

Supra-cyborgs of the governmental type also share this requirement to self-advantage, but they vary dramatically in a competing imperative, which is to provide some level of service delivery (e.g., transportation, health infrastructure and services, income redistribution). Emphasizing that governments, as supra-cyborgs, are interested in self-advantage helps keep in mind that every supra-cyborg has something like a "self" that resists other entities, especially other governments and would-be immigrants. But this emphasis also means it is time to answer the question of what the "self" of a supra-cyborg is like.

## Constituent Units of Supra-Cyborgs

Although operating from radically different approaches, poststructuralist theory and neuroscience have now both developed rationales indicating that human beings are not composed with a unified consciousness. Even the human bodies from which fragmented consciousness emerges are not discrete and stable entities: they have porous boundaries, integrated with a microbiome, and are in a constant state of electrochemical flux and cell replacement. Nonetheless, there remains important political utility in describing each human as having a "self" even if we understand the character of that self as fragmented, diverse, unstable, intermeshed with a social world, and maintained through leaky boundaries. It is in the same, complicated sense that one can talk about a supra-cyborg as having a "self." Instead of a unified consciousness, what passes as its "cognition" is a product primarily of the cognitive-emotive inputs of what we might call an Executive (network) and to a lesser extent the other human beings that compose it. The "body" of a supra-cyborg is even more loosely bounded than the body of a (merely) biological being. Supra-cyborg bodies fade out like a root system into the broader surroundings, becoming smaller and finer and more dispersed. And they have the capacity to cleave parts, much as a skink can cleave its tail, without great harm to the larger body. Like a biological body, the functionality of a supra-cyborg—its Target—is determinative of its "self." A systematic treatment of the boundaries and character of each of these components—Target, Executive, Nutriation—will illuminate the entities we little humans are dealing with in the age of supra-cyborgs.

## TARGETS

Biological beings, in contrast to physical beings, are identifiable as having a self-derived functionality.[21] Suns, rocks, comets, streams have no "functions" from an "own" perspective. Both the sense of self and the sense of functionality arise together when evolution happens, that is, when biological forms are reproduced. Biological beings can be defined as entities reproducing a self-similar form that is part of an evolutionary chain. Given that definition, their parts are most parsimoniously understood as serving the function of self-similar reproduction; otherwise the chain ceases to exist. This is a definition that characterizes a specific formation of matter rather than a "mere" tautology, not only because the same cannot be said of merely physical entities but also because supra-cyborgs can be seen to manifest a different form.

As partially biological beings, supra-cyborgs are also subject to evolutionary forces and must act for self-advantage in order to survive. However, because they are not merely biological beings, but are biosymbolic entities, they also have something like "purpose" or "purposes" rather than merely evolutionarily determined functions. To keep visible the difference between human purposes (which are themselves never unified or fully conscious) and those of supra-cyborgs, I suggest we call the latter the supra-cyborgs' Target(s).

A Target is the primary trajectory along which the supra-cyborg seeks advantage. Thus, the current purpose of most corporations (non-"B"-type corporations) is to accumulate economic resources. The singularity of this purpose leads corporations to act like zombies (as discussed later). In contrast, most nonprofit supra-cyborgs have purposes delimited in their "mission statements" (e.g., Charity Navigator: "Charity Navigator works to guide intelligent giving").[22] Most nation-states, however, have multiple purposes embodied in their constitutions. As Kenneth Burke has described them, constitutions are a set of inherently contradictory wishes.[23] Whether it is articulated in a legal charter or a constitution, the Target provides the symbolic basis on which self-advantageous behaviors are programmed by the supra-cyborg, and this function is directed primarily by the Executive (network).

THE EXECUTIVE (NETWORK)

To act as a being, a supra-cyborg must have some apparatus that directs its movements. In the simplest biological beings, the direction of action is achieved through the structure of the being. For example, the movement made by barnacles is to open and close in response to light. Internally, the barnacle is a form with ion channels that respond to light by chemically causing opening and closing. As biological beings evolved in complexity and developed potentials for contradictory motions, central nervous systems developed to coordinate conflicting inputs and tendencies in different parts of the organism. The brain is a sophisticated motion coordinator.

Supra-cyborgs don't have a single brain; they have many brains, so the coordination problem arises at a new level. Different kinds of supra-cyborgs solve the coordination problem to different degrees and in different ways. Rather than importing the metaphor of "purpose" and "the brain" into the supra-cyborg (which would create the risk of collapsing our view of the supra-cyborg down to a solely biological vision), I will talk about this coordinating process as "Execution" (which is fun, because it has a vaguely sinister air). The variously defined components of this function therefore form the Executive.

In corporations, Executives are usually constituted by a relatively small set of people, with one person having a theoretical command or veto power. In practice, what the corporation does "on the ground" is also shaped by the decisions of the many human brains incorporated in the supra-cyborg, and by the programming and material limits and abilities of the technologies that constitute the supra-cyborg. As corporations get large, Executives have a limited capacity to actually know what is going on in the daily interactions of the supra-cyborg ("bad news doesn't travel up"!). Nonetheless, long-standing corporations develop reward structures, monitoring rubrics, and cultures that shape the actions of the nonexecutive human bodies in ways that cohere to some substantial extent with the Executive's plans for pursuing the Target. Thus, corporations typically feature Executives with a substantial ability to direct their superorganism, a feature aided by the singular nature of the Target of corporations.

Executives in governments are more variable. An effective dictator such as Mao Tse-tung, Adolf Hitler, or Kim Jong-un can exercise a powerful influence on the government's direction. In contrast, a representative, constitutional government with multiple checking and balancing components has a very dispersed Executive (network). The Executive functions arise not from the decisions of a single or small set of people but from the complex relays that develop from engagements among the competing wills of multiple groupings of peoples. As recent history in the United States shows, this can result in (1) the local triumph of a particular sub-Executive's will (marriage rights extensions by the Supreme Court), (2) the retrenchment of government actions to solely historically based actions (sequester budgeting by the U.S. Congress minus the president), and even (3) near-complete action paralysis (some U.S. state governments' inability to pass a budget).

Whatever form the Executive (network) takes, supra-cyborg Executors must coordinate human beings, who (unlike cells in a biological organism) have an independent consciousness and semiconsciousness, which is to say purposes and functions of their own. In contrast to the absorption of symbiotic cells into eukaryotes, insufficient evolutionary time has passed to make the human units in the supra-cyborg seamlessly aligned with the supra-cyborg's Target. Consequently, the human agents routinely parasitize the supra-cyborg they constitute to varying degrees. This is most evident in the form of the outsize salaries and perks that Executives are able to allocate to themselves. As Thomas Piketty and Emmanuel Saez have documented, resource allocations by corporations have gradually shifted through time so that wealth is currently skewed toward executives rather than investors.[24] However, even the lowest human member of the supra-cyborg hierarchy is capable of reallocating the resources of the supra-cyborg writ large to her- or himself through slacking, petty theft, sabotage, and ego-soothing gamesmanship.[25] In contrast to the "sabotage" of the workers, however, the Executive can rationalize the allocation of the wealth of the supra-cyborg to himself (or, more rarely, herself). When an Executor builds lavish offices and corporate retreats for his own use, he merely directs the wealth of the supra-cyborg to his own locale. It remains "within" the supra-cyborg (and is often justified as necessary to keeping the Executive himself within the supra-cyborg). The same phenomenon is visible in nonprofits (the president of Oxfam earned $457,957 in 2015,[26] the president/CEO of the American Red Cross earned $562,364 that year,[27] and the Nature Conservancy has multiple retreats for Executive-level personnel to enjoy), so it is the supra-life-form of the entity, not (solely) the putative values of the humans who direct it, that produces these self-aggrandizing diversions to Executives.

## BOUNDARIES

Supra-cyborgs do not have an analogue to the cell walls of the single-celled biological organism. Nor is their "self" even as physically well-bounded as the somewhat more porous multicelled biological organisms. The degree of boundedness of supra-cyborgs varies by their type. Corporations are diffusely bounded. They may use interns, hire temporary workers, or work over long periods of time with contractors and vendors. The relationship with these individuals (and their associated symbolics and technologies) looks somewhat like an incorporation of those individuals and more or less as though they are independent in different instances. The courts spend a not insignificant amount of time and energy adjudicating when someone counts as an employee and when he or she does not. Moreover, many corporations—ranging from soft drink vendors to computer software firms—work to incorporate their clients or customers into the identity of the corporation. Customers who identify with the corporation ("I'm a Mac user!") are better sources of revenue. Such customers are not full-fledged members of the corporation, but they may "do work" for the corporation when they are solicited as members of feedback panels or recruited as retweeters or other social media promoters of a brand or product.

The boundaries of nation-state superorganisms seem somewhat clearer because the idealized form of a nation-state has presumed that a group of citizens inhabits a clearly demarcated territory. However, Maas and colleagues have shown that "varieties of multilevel citizenship are historically dominant and that the main contemporary definition of citizenship is a recent aberration."[28] People have dual citizenship, and there are a wide variety of noncitizen categories, including permanent residence statuses that include most or all the rights of citizens. Many if not most nation-states have large numbers of "undocumented" individuals: persons who fit none of the official categories of relationship to the state and who may derive some but not all the benefits of citizenship. In addition, policies such as the Cheney doctrine assert rights to nonsovereign territorial control—enforceable by military might—over land and sea lanes that are not within what would conventionally be defined as U.S. territory.[29] The European Union offers another complicated model of boundedness, highlighting the way that governments are often "federations" of hierarchically layered supra-beings. These forms of aggregation may thus be imagined as something between the colony stage of slime molds and a more classic complex biological organism.

## NUTRIATION

Coining the term "Nutriation" serves to emphasize that there is some distance between the concept of nutrition and the partially analogous functions in a supra-cyborg. Nonetheless, the question of "what feeds" supra-cyborgs is the question of what allows them to survive and grow. The obvious answer is that capital, territorial access and/or control, intellectual properties (in the legal/material sense), material resources relevant to food and technologies in use, and humans are the primary resources for supra-cyborgs. These "raw materials" are the requirements for constituting a durable netplex of human beings linked to and through technologies and communication channels. For present purposes, only the question of treating humans as Nutrition seems pressing.

The intuition that humans should not be Nutrition for supra-cyborgs fuels science fiction films (*The Matrix*) and political imaginaries of both the Right (Jeffersonian "small farms" and "small businesses," anti-Trilateralism, survivalism, and religious apocalyptism, among others) and the Left (Hardt and Negri's *Multitude*,[30] local food movements, and ersatz Buddhism, among others). To the extent that these sentiments arise from radically individualist premises that oppose the sociality inherent in human beings, they are either quixotic or dangerous. As I will suggest later, the question is not whether we should be a part of social groups—we must and should be; the question is of what kind of social groupings we should and can be constituents. To assess our habitation of supra-cyborgs of various types, clear-eyed views of Nutrition are required.

Humans belong to nation-state cyborgs according to various rules. Because of their territorial character, place of birth has been a common basis of assignment. Another frequently used criterion is lineage (hence, though the Rohinga are born in Myanmar, the government excludes them as products of a lineage that is not Myanmarese). Few nation-states use mere presence in the territory as a criterion but instead impose a set of bureaucratic requirements that screen the status of presence. Some of these relate to the economic advantage that these individuals bring with them, but most to the advantage of the familial lineages of those who already have political power in that nation-state. Some nation-states have forbidden people to leave their nation-state supra-cyborg, and this should be taken as a prima facie proof that any supra-cyborg with that prohibition understands itself to be disadvantageous to its human constituents. However, most nation-states instead impose controls on entry. This should be taken as prima facie evidence that there is meaningful variation in the desirability of being a constituent unit of different nation-state supra-cyborgs. These prima facie facts have strategic implications that will be treated in the closing section of this chapter.

In contrast, corporations attract humans through pay, status, hopes, and perks. Although decrying the conditions of corporate workers is a common academic trope (and it is reasonable to work toward a world in which every human has options for a lifestyle comparable to the average lifestyle of all humans), recent migration patterns indicate that many people prefer even poorly paid, insecure, corporate work to rural peasantry under the present distributions of humans in relationship to arable land.[31] Globally, people have been moving from rural areas, where agriculture and small-scale commerce are the primary options of economic life, to urban areas, where dirty, repetitive, often risky factory labor and insecure small business form the options of economic life (farm life is dirty, repetitive, and risky, too).[32] Those who portray rural "traditional" life as desirable base their image on a model of agricultural life that was probably not as romantically attractive as we imagine, but even if it was, it cannot be available to people in areas where the population density exceeds the amount of land required to support a person (whether at survival minimums or at the higher levels most people prefer). Population growth is therefore as important a factor in migration patterns as are the more frequently emphasized false promises and coercive market conditions. Both coercion and false promises are part of the realities. However, if false promises were the only story, then migration would not continue at the present massive scale. In that case, most people would migrate back to the rural home (as many already do), and the social grapevines that direct migrants would soon report that city life was worse than rural life, and migration would stagnate. Any analysis should take seriously the judgments of millions of migrants that urban life is preferable to the available agriculture-based lifestyles. Migrants typically will not achieve the middle-class lifestyle of the "capitalist dream," but about half of migrants choose to stay with the tough working-class urban life over agricultural peasantry.[33]

This grim conclusion allows one to understand how cheap it is for corporate supra-cyborgs to obtain the human in-Corporants required for Nutriation. Further, the low level of the bargain that a near-majority of humans must be willing to strike in current conditions should be faced in order to understand the dynamics within nation-state supra-cyborgs. The advantages to individual humans of being in-Corporated (however small they seem to you) explain the tendency of many corporate workers to vote against what Marxists might identify as their individual or class "interests" in favor of the perspective of the corporation. A view that focuses on low individual wages and bad working conditions misses the relationship formed upon in-Corporation. There is a material sense in which the individual has really become part of the supra-cyborg and therefore is voting in "its own" interests (in the interests of the totality of which it finds itself a component part) when it votes pro-corporate. This does not mandate the conclusion that a human "should" vote for the interests of the supra-cyborg, but it makes the interest calculus more complex and comprehensible, and reveals the complexities people face in making such calculations. To the extent that one is advantaged by the success of one's supra-cyborg, then it is literally "in one's interests" to vote the interest of the supra-cyborg, even if at the same time it is not in one's class or national or other subgroup interest to do so.

Corporate supra-cyborgs require additional types of Nutriation, such as metals, wood, energy, intellectual property, and land. Their size and suprahuman time horizons (they are capable of operating deliberately both at the nanosecond level and with a decadal perspective) give them tremendous advantages in accruing resources compared with individuals, small-scale businesses, and governments. Corporate supra-cyborgs thus flourish now because of rapid human population growth, virtualization of economies that favor large entities capable of nanosecond and long-term temporal framing, and the high mobility of human constituents.

## Comparative Advantages of Corporations and Government as Supra-Cyborgs

In spite of their similarities, there are different types of superorganisms (governments, corporations, scientific associations, nonprofits, arts associations), and each of these will have distinctive characteristics. A desirable place to start is with key characteristics of the two most powerful types of supra-cyborgs, which are currently in contest to shape the human lifeworld, that is, governments and corporations. Attending to their affective/cognitive tendencies indicates that representative governments are schizophrenic superorganisms, whereas corporations are zombies, and that these differences give an evolutionary edge to corporations, even when governments have a relative monopoly on physical violence.

## Affective/Cognitive Tendencies

In humans, affects are constituted of neural and hormonal fluxes. They are therefore "more than cognitive," even though the binary "emotion" versus "reason" has instead cast emotions as lesser to "reasons" (i.e., the limited number of cognitive processes that have been defined since Aristotle as logical capacities, specifically abstract manipulation of set relationships including mathematics). Corporations, governments, and computers all have similar access to logical operations in this narrow sense, precisely because they are processes that can be disembodied into abstract textual symbols. However, different types of beings differ substantially in their affective/cognitive tendencies.

Representative governments can be described as schizophrenic in a sense that combines the technical and popular meanings of the word. The popular meaning focuses on multiple personality disorder, whereas the American Psychological Association defines schizophrenia as "characterized by incoherent or illogical thoughts, bizarre behavior and speech, and delusions or hallucinations."[34] Representative governments incorporate "multiple personalities" at several levels. Any "balance of powers" structure enshrines different perspective-generators with different interests (where different sources of perspectives with different interests are an analogue of personalities). At another key level, the concept that diverse interest groups can be coordinated as a singular "people" enshrines an analogue of multiple personalities as a fundamental condition of a nation-state. Party structures rigidify these interest competitions within the legislative setting. The multiplication of identities is magnified in federalist systems, where local governments, provinces/states, and the nation-state each serves as a center of power with different personalities (i.e., perspective-generators with specific interest configurations).

The nonhomogeneity of the Executive network built into representative governments, which is like a war of "personalities" and competition among the "organs," is a major factor responsible for the often incoherent and bizarre behavior of government supra-cyborgs. Different sectors of the cyborg (not merely different provinces but different federal levels and different branches) may be constituted to favor different perspectives, interests, and policies, so that they move different components of the super–body politic in different and incompatible ways. The product may look like a spastic, out-of-kilter, frenetic dance, with moments of near-complete lockup. This schizophrenic structure explains why one of the few things on which governments are capable of exerting focused action is physical self-defense; only when a threat appears substantial to all subagents are all of the "personalities" likely to align in similar general directions (though, even then, not in a neat formation). The long-standing focus of empires on transportation corridors is similarly understandable for its broad consensual interest to multiple components of the imperial supra-cyborg.

Corporations, especially as they increase in size, experience some tendencies for this kind of cyborgian schizophrenia. However, most corporations have an Executive with quasi-dictatorial powers. Corporations therefore look more like dictatorial governments than representative governments. The unified Executive spends much of its effort channeling the directional proclivities of the organs. The affective/cognitive tendency of corporations (in contrast to that of dictatorial governments) can be described as zombielike. While the zombie trope flourishes and therefore has multiple instantiations, I mean to draw on the sense that a zombie is a body controlled by a force with a single directionality. The body acts not in response to local stimuli but to some abstract purpose (e.g., disregarding a burning hand as it moves madly to its Target). Because the purposive driver does not identify with the body part, it may direct the body to act in a relentless fashion, heedless of the well-being of its component parts. The zombie can be highly resourceful and ingenious at achieving its objectives (as in the *Terminator* film series), but its singularity of focus and heedlessness to its embodied well-being mark it as having a nonhuman (and indeed nonanimal) affect.

The villi of supra-cyborgs (human bodies, or groups thereof) are directed toward a singular Target through a relatively unified Executive network in ways that produce this zombielike quality. It is important to attend to the consequence of this characteristic for moral, value, ethical, or ideological appeals (the term "moral" is an allergen to many academics because they associate it with a particular ideological set or with what they depict as a lack of reflectiveness about a value set, so you may substitute one of these other terms). The zombie cognitive/affective structure is incapable of processing or responding to moral appeals.

As several theorists have now illuminated, morality requires emotion.[35] But corporate supra-cyborgs cannot have emotion because an entity with a singular goal cannot have emotion. As Rei Terada has insightfully argued, emotion is made possible in the first place by "self-differentiality."[36] To put this in biological terms, an entity that has only one goal does not need the variable adjustments in intensity that are provided by competing emotions. As Terada aptly describes it, an entity with a single goal is like a zombie; it simply goes about its singular objective without the need for affect. Corporations have the legal responsibility for executing a singular goal—accruing the maximal amount of resources. Each corporation's directives require it to weigh only the superentity's profitability, and so the Executive rewards and punishes its human bodies for their adherence to that singular goal. The success of the Executive is never complete, but it tends to be substantial in any supra-cyborg that survives for long or grows to any size.

There are constraints on corporations' behaviors that appear on the surface to be the analogues of morality—limited direct use of murder, little direct theft, contributions to local "causes." However, these arise not from moral motivations but only as means to fulfill subsidiary requirements for achieving the Target: the need to attract an appropriate workforce or the need to avoid financial costs such as those entailed by large lawsuit awards. The corporation is legally proscribed from taking into account per se (a metaphorical form of "feeling bad about") whatever harm it inflicts on others because of its mandate to maximize investor interests. Thus, the singularity of the program of a corporation *requires* it to maximize pollution of lakes, land, and air (within the legal limits its lobbyists are able to negotiate and the police enforcement it is able to constrain), and thereby to injure others both financially and physically, if it is more profitable to do so than to install pollution control devices (even if the people inside the corporation might as individuals feel morally bad about the trade-off). This is the famous adherence to "the bottom line" so vociferously touted in some U.S. business schools.

The programming of corporations to have a singular Target also precludes the utilization of the moral capacities of the humans who constitute them as a substitute for the corporations' own lack of moral capacity on the superorganismic level. Alas, when corporations commit moral faults, many people seek to blame the individuals within the corporation, and there is some technical legal responsibility of corporate heads for corporate behavior. This expectation, however, cannot be fulfilled (and this is why it is close to impossible to convict corporate heads for the harms created by the entities they lead). CEOs are legally mandated to act on behalf of the "bottom line" of the corporation. Their personal emotions and hence moral scruples are not officially relevant; they may not legally interfere with profitability. At most, therefore, CEOs will have conflicting legal mandates (e.g., to bring profit to the corporation from products that result in the deaths of purchasers and a legal mandate that prohibits murder), but as in-Corporants of the supra-cyborg they can never have a *prioritization* of non-wealth-generating imperatives. This means that the moral responses of the human agents who make up the corporation are officially precluded from directing the corporation's actions along moral lines. The best that morals can obtain against the profit imperative is a situational draw, when backed by specific legal prohibitions or the constraints of public relations.

With regard to the contest between corporate and nation-state supra-cyborgs, the zombie has substantial advantages over the nation-state. The zombie relentlessly pursues the singular objective of its own growth, unlimited by moral concerns. In contrast, the schizophrenia of the nation-state leads it to disperse its resources in multiple directions. It has a plethora of public service imperatives, some of which may be understood as moral concerns (though it may nonetheless act immorally because the multiplicity of its moral objectives does not enable action in line with all or even any of those concern). Even when, therefore, the nation-state is much larger than the corporations with which it competes, the corporation is able to put proportionately more of its resources into any specific contest between the two.

The greater developmental potential of the corporate supra-cyborg form over the governmental one may be signaled by the increasingly vociferous lament of left-wing advocates and academics that, under current legal structures and conditions, governments have infectively been co-opted by corporations. Although the reverse can be found— globally governments have co-opted corporations and corporate forms (e.g., nationalization of industries and development of state-owned oil companies)—the trend over the past half century has been toward divestment rather than toward nationalization. Additionally, across the past two centuries, corporations have been growing at a more rapid rate than nation-state governments (though both have been growing). Many corporations are now larger than some nation-states (measured in terms of annual budgets).[37]

*Modes of Influence*

With a few exceptions, corporations have only "soft power" mechanisms for exerting influence; they can use symbolic inducements and the virtual bio-physico-symbolic inducement of money. Governments have the additional tool of overt direct physical violence performed through a now-stunning arsenal of weaponry deployable at multiple levels from global destruction to drone-targeted local strikes. Governments can imprison individuals and take their physical belongings or wealth.

The greater and more direct access of governments to overt physical compulsion gives them some advantage over corporations. However, there is a substantial cost to governmental reliance on these tools. Governments appear most vividly to their citizens *as governments* when the citizen faces physical compulsion and taxes. The laws of governments are enforced through fines and imprisonment. So traffic rules, business regulations, crowd control, environmental controls, protest restrictions, civil lawsuits, and criminal investigations/prosecutions all appear as a physical threat. Taxes take away the apparent earned income of citizens. These threats and costs typically appear as a kind of direct demand by a governmental supra-cyborg that is exterior to the individual. In contrast, except in times of external threat (e.g., potential war), the benefits deriving from being a member of a government appear as scenic conditions rather than as overt direct benefits provided *by* the government *to* members of the supra-cyborg. The fact that one's fellow citizens are educated and have safe drinking water, sanitary systems, readily available roads and relatively safe air travel, social security and medical care for one's elder years, unemployment insurance, and so forth seems to appear as taken-for-granted background conditions rather than as benefits deriving from the supra-cyborg, even for the majority of citizens of the U.S. supra-cyborg who have access to them.

The typical modes of influence available to each type of super-cyborg thus favor the zombie in the contest between corporations and governments. Governments have greater access to physical coercion, but corporations appear as benefactors that provide jobs and consumer goods, whereas most contemporary representative governments appear as threatening and controlling forces. The benefits they provide become noticeable as distinctive benefits only when they are deemed deficient (crumbling roads, weak high schools, water supply deficiencies). The use of reward power rather than physical coercion also may make corporations more flexible. The grammar of physical coercion ties it to territories (whether physical prisons or military bases), and this limits its utility against corporations, whereas the virtualization of wealth has made it not only transterritorial but also transtemporal in ways that maximize the flexibility inherent in virtuality.[38] Governments have had enough advantage through territorial control to "hang on," but they are arguably being faced with a third type of player.

## The Rise of the Blended Supra-Cyborg

The World Trade Organization (WTO), the Asian Infrastructure Investment Bank, the International Monetary Fund, and the World Bank represent a new kind of supra-cyborg. They have been called "nongovernmental organizations," but that term has been used to cover everything from tiny organizations dedicated to helping prostitutes escape pimps to Doctors Without Borders to the United Nations. A more narrow designation is needed. Because they are nonelected bodies that exert legalistic coercive influence with a Target of increasing economic growth on a corporate model, one might call them global governing corporatocracies (GGCs).

These organizations are not all identical, but the WTO provides one important model of the potential form, power, and growth of such GGCs. It has representatives from the 161 participating member nations (which account for 95 percent of world trade, according to the organization).[39] The Target it serves is articulated as follows: "The system's overriding purpose is to help trade flow as freely as possible—so long as there are no undesirable side effects—because this is important for economic development and well-being."[40] WTO claims to operate by treaties agreed to by 100 percent member consensus, so that all members must agree to all requirements.[41] However, the dispute resolution process undercuts that claim. For example, between 2008 and 2015, Canada, Mexico, and Nicaragua brought a case to the WTO Dispute Resolution Board, arguing that the United States' "country of origin" labeling requirement for meats violated WTO agreements because it put additional costs on sellers and distributors to keep differently sourced meats separate. The dispute board ruled against the United States, holding on appeal that the benefits of separate labeling were outweighed by the costs and there was not a sufficiently consistent U.S. policy across all meats.[42] This small board, highly insulated from democratic processes, thus was able to nullify U.S. law based on a cost-benefit calculation grounded in trade-maximization values. The WTO thus exercises veto authority over national laws without consensus of all members and for the express purpose of facilitating the Target dear to multinational corporations. This is a tremendous amount of power for a small group of unelected persons to exercise over all the world's governments. It is not yet clear what the full potential of these GGCs will be, but their ability to combine veto power over governments, their distance from effective control by any demos, and their relatively concentrated Executives hint that the historical territorial control by national governments may become obsolete.

## Strategic Biocitizenships for Human Beings?

Most humans are bio-incorporates of national and multinational supra-cyborgs, if we understand bio-incorporation as bodily and symbolic in-Corporation in a superorganism that directs the outputs of the individual toward the superorganism's Target. The bio-incorporation in GCCs has differences from biocitizenship in a nation-state or the enlistment in a corporation, but all three of these supra-life-forms are shapers of human lives at both biological and symbolic levels. There are good reasons to think that the present contested in-Corporations of human biosymbolizing bodies is not the best deal we humans could strike. Others have written at length against the WTO, corporations, and nation-states.

Rather than add to these critiques, I want to join those promoting a discussion of alternatives. Critiques are productive first steps—they help us share understandings of conditions we would like to change. Nonetheless, as others have suggested, the word "resistance" should make one shudder at the limitations of critique alone. To identify one's task as resistance is to concede that one's only possibility is to move in a directional logic defined already by that to which one declares oneself resistant. And it isn't a hopeful rhetoric. Although the proponents of resistance often declare themselves to be "radical," the logic of the word "resistance" suggests that one can slow down the trajectory of the opponent but not achieve a trajectory of one's own. Instead, along with critique, one should seek to encourage materially achievable trajectories: possibilities that have reasonable potential to become probabilities, a movement from creative imagination to rhetorical acumen guided by a dash of *sophrosyne*.

This perspective shares the emphasis on the constructive capacities of rhetorics, but it differs in a key way from that offered by Ronald Walter Greene. Greene's texts sometimes appear to encourage an unproductive "either/or" rather than a more productive "both/and" when they imply that rhetorical theories that attend to influence and the human individual should be replaced by theories that attend to circulation at the social level (e.g., a public as "the linkage between a postal system, discourses, and norms of interaction"—no humans needed!).[43]

One might well applaud Greene's attention to the circulation of texts at the social level, because the structuration of human society is indeed dependent not only on the reception, response, and repetition of texts by individuals but also on the distribution of various kinds of capacities to recirculate those texts and to use textual means to construct various kinds of other material entities and relationships. Mapping the flows of discourse among and between various powerful supra-cyborgs is an important part of the explanatory process that can help us to understand the rise of GCCs and why states today seem to operate in the interests of specific corporate cyborgs, even though the Targets of these entities are different and, in the case of nation-states, plural. The multi-entity perspective I am encouraging, however, insists on recognizing the ongoing agonistic and contested nature of discourses and social norms, thereby rejecting any collapse of all discourse and all social norms to a singular episteme or ideology.

Also valuable is Greene's critique of the covert moral Platonism of a "Marxist criticism [that] dialectically reverses the moral reasoning of the bourgeoisie."[44] However, his objective of achieving "escape velocity from their articulation to capitalism and/or the administrative apparatus of the state" requires understanding what the agents of capitalism and the nation-state are like and why they are attractive to human bodies.[45] Merely rearticulating the negative aspects of nation-states or of contemporary global capitalism will not suffice.[46]

To achieve these objectives requires a politics based in a larger rhetorical theory than Greene describes (though his contribution is substantial). The most desirable approach is not simply to replace classical theories of influence with a social-level lens; one also needs to offer new theories of influence, which abjure the neo-Aristotelian overemphasis on a narrow vision of argument and reason, instead attending rigorously to the material force of motivators (e.g., emotion, affect) that are historically, evolutionarily, and developmentally set into action in the bodies of humans. Those bodies are the material loci of the responses to texts and the potential recomposers of them. Theories that ignore the motivational drivers of biological entities (including humans) at various scales cannot explain the circulation of texts with anything other than cartoon placeholders that are easily critiqued (such as Greene's "exodus" or "joy").[47]

An additional implication of attention to embodied human emotion is that to "outfox capitalism's logic of capture" sets an inhuman telos, because humans are obligately and deeply social.[48] We cannot therefore live "uncaptured." Though we don't have to live in any specific logic of capture, we do have to live to some substantial extent within the social conditions of our predecessors' makings, which will include not only discourses and norms of interactions but also some kinds of structuration. Instead of touting an idealized condition of nonrelationality, our goals should be to improve our cages/relational constitutions and to make them flexible enough to allow future growth at individual, social, and ecological scales. Therefore, exploring the building of super-cyborgs that serve human (and other) beings better than current versions of the state or the corporation is a more productive rhetorical horizon than merely urging "escape" or lauding an unstructured "multitude."

I interpret Hart and Negri's constitutive call for a "multitude" as an example of a trajectory that aims for the absence of superorganisms (e.g., there is no Executive). For reasons that cannot be detailed in the present space, I call this the "anarcho-niceness dream." It is an ideal, in the negative sense of that term. That is, one can imagine that it would be ideal to live in a world where everyone was diverse, yet had no conflicting interests; where everyone had no coercion from any source, yet acted cooperatively rather than selfishly wherever cooperation counted; where any help anyone wanted from others was always given spontaneously. But this does not sound like a world made up of *Homo sapiens sapiens*.

Even if most people could be persuaded to be this nice this consistently, as long as some people are not-nice and form superorganisms, their superorganisms will have the power to outmaneuver the individualistic anarchists through guns or butter. And this is just the negative case against the anarchistic vision. One might well extend to supra-cyborgs Haraway's claim that cyborg being offers "possible means of great human satisfaction."[49] Humans have always been members of superorganisms (families, tribes), and the subsequent development of degeneticized and depersonalized supra-cyborgs has brought comforts, intellectual diversification, and artistic expansion to those humans who are reasonably well situated within them. Even the expansion of the options and practices one might identify as freedom (beyond what would be experienced by a lone human constrained directly by the nonhuman material forces of the universe or by a small tribal/familial group) is a product of the growth of such supra-cyborgs,[50] even if there are also differently distributed costs for those differentially situated in/around the supra-cyborgs and their serious and weighty games. One should at least give a hearing to the possibility that the better course for the global demos is not to shatter every supra-cyborg that arises but rather to build, with a collective (yet inevitably conflicted) deliberative process, supra-cyborgs that better suit our (always developing, always in-relationship) selves.

Such a process would attend to the formation of the Executive (accountable, balanced?), the selection of Targets (diverse, but not all-encompassing), Nutriation (a balance of social and individual?), and so forth. As an example, the rise of "B corporations" is designed to encourage Targets for supra-cyborgs that are diverse, but not so diverse as to be schizophrenia-inducing. Another such line of approach would attend to questions of size and duration. As supra-cyborgs have grown larger, the level of destruction of the ecosystem has increased, and wealth inequality has expanded. Perhaps the most immediate and simple political change for enhancing the well-being of humans and the ecological conglomerate would be to enforce a maximum size for corporate supra-cyborgs.

Elsewhere I have suggested as a focal line of approach the building of global supra-cyborgs as federalized monitory democracies.[51] One key topos of such an approach, modified from John Keane's more indeterminate original formulation of the concept,[52] is to supplement representative democratic forms with active, direct, collective monitoring activities of diverse sorts that range from citizen science to budgetary accounting to charting of police brutality to road and bridge repair tabulation.

A second topos for monitory democracies emphasizes the value of both variation and consensus so that, where consensus is essential (e.g., distribution of water supplies must be shared and agreed upon), it can be obtained with maximal possible agreement without positing a unified "public opinion" that represents any uniformity.[53] Negotiation and compromise are necessary if there is to be an absence of choice-by-direct-force, and rather than being "insufficiently pure," these concepts are therefore theoretically superior to the positing of any idealized "common" sense or ideology. Concomitantly, however, the zone of negotiated compromises should be as truncated as possible, and incentive structures rather than a federalized monopoly on violence may be a preferred route. This means that, rather than a one-world singular government that decides and deliberates upon all facets of global-level interactions, the peoples of the world might well first try out multiple global associations that organize separately to influence particular sectors.[54]

A third topos recognizes the factors internal to deliberative processes that create uneven argumentative fields, and therefore mandates the creation of active material correctives to all feasible extents in order to enhance the inclusion of the perspectives and diverse interests of all of the world's peoples, and to some extent other living things.

In addition to suggesting the desirability of such federalized monitory democracies, the literalized metaphor of supra-cyborgs illuminates the desirability of particular policy preferences and raises the question of the effectiveness of specific rhetorical strategies. Mass immigration is a global-level concern, with similar facets worldwide, and so this issue provides a telling and brief example of the implications for policy preferences, with integral linkages to rhetorical topoi.

Anti-immigration advocates in the United States, such as Ann Coulter, articulate the position that the national supra-cyborg should serve its self-interests first: "Wouldn't any sane immigration policy be based on the principle that we want to bring in only immigrants who will benefit the people already here?"[55] Simultaneously, as the preceding analysis of Nutriation would indicate, corporations are eager to expand their labor forces. This paired set of interests between the government and the corporate entities produces an immigration policy that prefers limited legal admissions (e.g., for computer programmers) and either guest worker programs (which produce noncitizen workers who can be controlled by the "citizens" fully incorporated in the nation-state supra-cyborg) or mass illegal immigration (which produces the same political result but with greater inconvenience to the corporations). If, in contrast, one's rhetoric framed the issue of human global mobility in terms of the setting up of a competition among supra-cyborgs for human affiliates—a competition that required the supra-cyborgs to produce better conditions for everyone in order to attract others and grow—then open global migration and territorially based citizenship would be framed as an advantage for everyone living in a region.

Rather than defending this general and global perspective, most left-based rhetorics focus on the disadvantage of immigration exclusions to some cultural or "oppressed" group. Such rhetoric is predispositionally unconvincing to most of those who do not see themselves as a member of the group(s) described as the victims. Worse, such "resistance" rhetoric actually reinforces the Coulter rhetoric (some people against other people) instead of insisting on supra-cyborgs that must create conditions that are more attractive to all of us humans.

Framing our vision in terms of relationships among supra-cyborgs and humans highlights a final (for here/now) tactical rhetorical problem: why appeals to justice are less effective in a supra-cyborgian world than it seems (to us poor humans) that they ought to be. Appeals to justice assert that accepted norms of the group are being violated. These appeals are only tenable to the extent that violation of the group's norms is presumed to be disadvantageous to the group and therefore disadvantageous to the individual members of the group (even if the interests are ideologically masked in the form of appeals to transcendent beings). But supra-cyborgs are fully selfish. They have not evolved as tribal be-

302 CELESTE M. CONDIT

ings who share a sense of social dependence with others of their group (as humans have).[56] And, as argued earlier, they have evolved in ways that dampen such social responses among their human components and that limit the impact of such moral sentiments on their steerage. Supra-cyborgs are therefore highly resistant to justice-based appeals, as well as to appeals based on the well-being of individual humans.

This is not to say that one should give up on appeals to justice, but it is to say that self-awareness of the limited tactical reach of such appeals is well advised if one actually wishes to change the shape of supra-cyborgs. Again, Haraway offers first steps toward alternatives:

> A cyborg body is not innocent; it was not born in a garden; it does not seek unitary identity and so generate antagonistic dualisms without end (or until the world ends); it takes irony for granted. One is too few, and two is only one possibility. Intense pleasure in skill, machine skill, ceases to be a sin, but an aspect of embodiment.[57]

As a supplement to justice, the new rhetoric would imagine the contours of a supra-cyborg that would be not only pleasurable but also life sustaining, and that would invite most others to join it. The online gaming world has captured the pleasurable elements of such affiliative engagements, and a variety of online efforts have begun to rally people around the creation of specific shared services (e.g., transportation). To date, however, only supernaturally motivated visions have invited affiliation with semidurable entities focused on the regulative distribution of food, water, and shelter and the recycling of human waste. The next great global-level rhetoric may offer material platforms to engage in the creative, developmental participation in such supra-cyborgs.

That is a tall order, and this essay may have seemed too intellectually playful. But imagination requires free play, and reimagination seems required for our current serious intents. I hope to have offered a frame that allows us to take seriously the "sense" that corporations and governments are powerful agents, but to provide an alternative to seeing them either on the agential model of the lone human being or in the often-appearing form that seems like a caricature of a totalized, all-power force field. Such an alternative view indicates why merely haranguing either the entities involved or their human constituents seems to produce such limited results. If power must be met with power, and corporations and nation-states now have global-level power executed for "self"-interested Targets, then a necessary counter may be the creation of global-level supra-cyborgs with a more inclusive and human-friendly "self."

NOTES

1 Donna Haraway, *Simians, Cyborgs, and Women: The Reinvention of Nature* (New York: Routledge, 1991).

2 Ibid., 181.

3 Ibid., 178.

4 Ibid., 180.

5 Ibid., 173.

6 Ibid., 170.

7 Ibid., 162.

8 Ibid.

9 Ibid.

10 "Symbol-using animal" is a concept developed by Kenneth Burke in "Definition of Human," in *Language as Symbolic Action: Essays on Life, Literature and Method* (Berkeley: University of California Press, 1966), 3–24.

11 This onto-epistemology is more fully articulated in Celeste Michelle Condit and L. Bruce Railsback, "Transilience: Bridging the Diversity of Knowledge," www.gly. uga.edu.

12 Haraway, *Simians, Cyborgs, and Women*, 163.

13 Ibid., 174.

14 Ibid., 181.

15 Ibid., 160, 163.

16 Ibid., 161.

17 Ibid., 165.

18 Edward O. Wilson, *The Social Conquest of Earth* (New York: Norton, 2012); Gilles Deleuze and Félix Guattari, *Anti-Oedipus: Capitalism and Schizophrenia* (New York: Viking, 1977).

19 The label of "superorganism" also contrasts to the term "organization," which obfuscates whether the entity just "organizes" people in a specific set of relations (leaving untouched their identities) or whether it is a distinctive type of entity.

20 Burke, "Definition of Human."

21 As argued in Celeste M. Condit, "Race and Genetics from a Modal Materialist Perspective," *Quarterly Journal of Speech* 94, no. 4 (2008): 383–406.

22 Charity Navigator, "Mission," www.charitynavigator.org.

23 Kenneth Burke, *A Grammar of Motives* (Berkeley: University of California Press, 1945).

24 Thomas Piketty and Emmanuel Saez, "Income Inequality in the United States, 1913–1998," *Quarterly Journal of Economics* 118 (2003): 1–40; see especially p. 20.

25  John W. Jordan, "Sabotage or Performed Compliance: Rhetorics of Resistance in Temp Worker Discourse," *Quarterly Journal of Speech* 89 (2003): 19–40.

26  Charity Navigator, "Oxfam America," accessed January 28, 2016, www.charitynavigator.org.

27  Charity Navigator, "American Red Cross," accessed January 28, 2016, www.charitynavigator.org.

28  Willem Maas, ed., *Multilevel Citizenship* (Philadelphia: University of Pennsylvania Press, 2013), 2.

29  Dick Cheney, "Defense Strategy for the 1990s: The Regional Defense Strategy," accessed March 24, 2014, www.informationclearinghouse.info.

30  Michael Hardt and Antonio Negri, *Multitude: War and Democracy in the Age of Empire* (New York: Penguin Books, 2005).

31  Population density and the kind of land (and water) available are substantial constraints. For example, there is less than 0.26 hectares of arable land per person in Afghanistan, 0.01 per person in Bermuda, 1.32 in Canada, and 0.49 in the United States; World Bank, "Arable Land (Hectares per Person)," accessed January 28, 2016, data.worldbank.org. Population growth has been greatest in areas with less per capita arable land/water resources.

32  Although many new arrivals do not work for corporations, but rather in a secondhand service industry or in small-scale capitalism, the location of factories drives these "secondary" economies in many "arrival cities." Doug Saunders, *Arrival City: How the Largest Migration in History Is Reshaping Our World* (New York: Pantheon Books, 2010).

33  Ibid.

34  American Psychological Association, "Schizophrenia," accessed January 28, 2016, http://www.apa.org.

35  Kathleen Wallace, "Reconstructing Judgment: Emotion and Moral Judgment." *Hypatia* 8 (1993): 61–83; M. O. Little. "Seeing and Caring: The Role of Affect in Feminist Moral Epistemology," *Hypatia* 10 (1995): 117–37.

36  Rei Terada, *Feeling in Theory: Emotion after the "Death of the Subject"* (Cambridge, MA: Harvard University Press, 2001).

37  Vincent Trivett, "25 US Mega Corporations: Where They Rank If They Were Countries," *Business Insider*, June 27, 2011, accessed January 28, 2016, www.businessinsider.com. This article refers only to U.S. corporations, which are no longer the fifty largest corporations in the world.

38  Jakob Arnoldi, "Derivatives: Virtual Values and Real Risks," *Theory, Culture and Society* 21, no. 6 (2004): 23–42.

39  World Trade Organization, "The WTO in Brief," accessed July 16, 2015, www.wto.org.

40  World Trade Organization, "Who We Are," accessed July 16, 2015, www.wto.org.

41  World Trade Organization, "Understanding the WTO," accessed July 16, 2015, www.wto.org.

42 World Trade Organization, "United States—Certain Country of Original Labeling (COOL) Requirements: Dispute Settlement: Dispute DS384," accessed July 16, 2015, www.wto.org.

43 Ronald Walter Greene, "Rhetorical Pedagogy as a Postal System: Circulating Subjects through Michael Warner's 'Publics and Counterpublics,'" *Quarterly Journal of Speech* 88, no. 4 (2002): 442.

44 Ronald Walter Greene, "Orator Communist," *Philosophy and Rhetoric* 39, no. 1 (2006): 94.

45 Ibid., 92.

46 The sufficiency of such a negative strategy is undercut by its usual base in the claim or assumption that the only reason people "fall for" consumer or other capitalisms is because they are dupes or because the capitalists control the means of communication. If either of those are the case, then the situation is hopeless, as academics or leftist academics cannot hope to have greater power for circulating their negative messages than the capitalists have for circulating their messages of enticement.

47 Ibid., 86, 92.

48 Ibid., 90.

49 Haraway, *Simians, Cyborgs, and Women*, 180.

50 With some modification, this is Daniel C. Dennett's argument in *Freedom Evolves* (New York: Penguin Books, 2004). Dennett does not apparently understand the crucial role of discourse in that evolutionary process, however.

51 Celeste M. Condit, "Insufficient Fear of the 'Super-flu'? The World Health Organization's Global Decision-Making for Health," *POROI* 10, no. 1 (2014).

52 John Keane, *The Life and Death of Democracy* (New York: Norton, 2009).

53 For the appearance of this topos in discussions of such agendas, see, e.g., Seyla Benhabib, *Another Cosmopolitanism* (New York: Oxford University Press, 2008); Luis Cabrera, *Political Theory of Global Justice: A Cosmopolitan Case for the World State* (New York: Routledge, 2004); Sherman J. Clark, "A Populist Critique of Direct Democracy," *Harvard Law Review* 112, no. 2 (1998): 434–82; Nancy Fraser, "Rethinking the Public Sphere: A Contribution to the Critique of Actually Existing Democracy," *Social Text* 25/26 (1990): 56–80; Radha S. Hegde, "A View from Elsewhere: Locating Difference and the Politics of Representation from a Transnational Feminist Perspective," *Communication Theory* 8, no. 3 (1998): 271–97; Darrin Hicks and Lenore Langsdorf, "Regulating Disagreement, Constituting Participants: A Critique of Proceduralist Theories of Democracy," *Argumentation* 13, no. 2 (1999): 139–60; Jesse Jackson, "An End to Corporate Blackmail," presidential campaign speech given in Akron, Ohio, on May 7, 1984, published in *Straight from the Heart*, ed. Roger D. Hatch and Frank E. Watkins (Philadelphia: Fortress Press, 1987); Margaret Kohn, "Language, Power, and Persuasion: Toward a Critique of Deliberative Democracy," *Constellations* 7, no. 3 (2000): 408–29; Jane Mansbridge, *Beyond Adversary Democracy* (New York: Basic Books, 1980); Richard W. Miller,

*Globalizing Justice: The Ethics of Poverty and Power* (New York: Oxford University Press, 2010); Chantal Mouffe, *On the Political (Thinking in Action)* (New York: Routledge, 2005); Carol Pateman, *The Disorder of Women: Democracy, Feminism and Political Theory* (Stanford, CA: Stanford University Press, 1989); Raka Shome and Radha S. Hegde, "Culture, Communication, and the Challenge of Globalization," *Critical Studies in Media Communication* 19, no. 2 (2002): 172–89; Mathias Thaler, "The Illusion of Purity: Chantal Mouffe's Realist Critique of Cosmopolitanism," *Philosophy and Social Criticism* 36, no. 7 (2010): 785–800; Mario Tronti, "Towards a Critique of Political Democracy," *Cosmos and History: The Journal of Natural and Social Philosophy* 5, no. 1 (2009): 68–75; Laura Valentini, "No Global Demos, No Global Democracy? A Systematization and Critique," *Perspectives on Politics* 12, no. 4 (2014): 789–807.

54 Robert E. Goodin, "World Government Is Here!," in *Varieties of Sovereignty and Citizenship*, ed. Sigal R. Ben-Porath and Rogers M. Smith (Philadelphia: University of Pennsylvania Press, 2012), 149–65; Maas, *Multilevel Citizenship*.

55 Ann Coulter, *¡Adios, America! The Left's Plan to Turn Our Country into a Third World Hell Hole* (Washington, DC: Regnery, 2015).

56 Arguably, the moral sense(s) is/are precisely the means of negotiation of the well-being of the collective through attention to the needs and desires of individuals; Jonathan Haidt, *The Righteous Mind: Why Good People Are Divided by Politics and Religion* (New York: Pantheon Books, 2012).

57 Haraway, *Simians, Cyborgs, and Women*, 180.

ACKNOWLEDGMENTS

The editors would like to thank the contributors for supporting this project every step of the way and helping make this the remarkable collection that it is. We also thank Ilene Kalish, Caelyn Cobb, and Maryam Arain at NYU Press for their editorial support and for choosing this book for the Press's Biopolitics series, and Susan Ecklund for copyediting the manuscript. The anonymous reviewers provided thoughtful feedback, and the book is much improved as a result. John Banister provided exceptional editorial and copyediting assistance.

Jenell Johnson would like to thank Kelly Happe and Marina Levina for being wonderful co-editors, and Christa Olson and Michael Xenos for their support. I would also like to thank the graduate students in my 2014 Rhetoric and the Body seminar, who helped to shape my thinking about biocitizenship.

Kelly Happe would like to thank Jenell Johnson and Marina Levina. Their experience with edited volumes proved crucial to the success of the project. I also thank NYU Press for its support over the years and to the students in the Feminist Body Studies graduate seminar. I also thank Merlin Chowkwanyun, whose scholarship on race, health, and history, has proved such an unexpected and welcome influence on my own.

Marina Levina would like to thank Kelly Happe and Jenell Johnson for being the best supportive feminist colleagues. I also thank the graduate students in my 2015 Bodies and Technologies Seminar—our discussions were instrumental to ideas developed in this book. But the biggest thanks goes to my parents, Anna and Alik, without whose tireless grandparenting I simply would not have been able to complete this project.

# ABOUT THE CONTRIBUTORS

HEATHER C. ASPELL is a visual storyteller, artist, and patient advocate based in Los Angeles, California. Aspell has lived as a medical mystery, with multiple complex chronic illnesses since childhood. Although her precise diagnosis is always in flux given that she has multiple systemic autoimmune diseases, her primary condition is best classified as systemic juvenile idiopathic arthritis (Still's disease), in addition to endometriosis, migraines, gastroparesis, central variable immunodeficiency, and more. Since becoming visibly disabled and unable to work, she has also experienced a great deal of misunderstanding from society at large. Heather uses her social media presence, photography, and other art to challenge these misunderstandings by expressing the realities of living with multiple chronic illnesses and disabilities as a thirty-something. Her work can be viewed by following her on Twitter (@hcorini) or Instagram (@haspell) and by visiting her website, www.heathercoriniaspell.com.

EMMA BEDOR HILAND is a doctoral candidate in Communication Studies at the University of Minnesota. Her scholarship examines the intersections of media, health, and illness. Currently she is completing a dissertation on the emergence and effects of digital mental health services, particularly teletherapy and therapeutic smartphone applications. Her research has been published in *Screen Bodies*, *Sexuality and Culture*, and the *Journal of Magazine and New Media Research*.

JEFFREY A. BENNETT is Associate Professor of Communication Studies at Vanderbilt University. He is the author of the book *Banning Queer Blood: Rhetorics of Citizenship, Contagion, and Resistance* (2009). Bennett's work has also appeared in the *Quarterly Journal of Speech*, *Critical Studies in Media Communication*, *Communication and Critical/Cultural Studies*, *Text and Performance Quarterly*, and the *Journal of Medical*

*Humanities*, among others. His current research project, tentatively titled "Critical Conditions: Diabetes and the Management of the Human Body," investigates the rhetoric of diabetes management.

SARAH BURGESS is Associate Professor of Communication Studies at the University of San Francisco. Working at the intersections of rhetorical theory, political theory, legal theory, and philosophy, she studies the rhetorical contours of recognition in order to understand the possibilities and limits of justice. Her work has appeared in *Philosophy and Rhetoric*, the *Journal of Law, Culture, and the Humanities*, the *American Journal of Bioethics*, and other venues. She is completing a manuscript titled "Making a Scene: Scandals of Legal Recognition," which examines how scenes of recognition are constructed and critiqued in demands for human rights.

ORON CATTS is the cofounder and Director of SymbioticA, an artistic research center housed within the School of Anatomy and Human Biology at the University of Western Australia. He is an artist, researcher, and curator whose pioneering work with the Tissue Culture and Art Project, which he established in 1996, is considered a leading biological art project. Under Catts's leadership, SymbioticA has won the Prix Ars Electronica Golden Nica in Hybrid Art (2007) and the WA Premier Science Award (2008), and it became a Centre for Excellence in 2008. In 2009, Catts was recognized by Thames and Hudson's "60 Innovators Shaping our Creative Future" book in the category "Beyond Design," and by *Icon* magazine (UK) as one of the top twenty designers "making the future and transforming the way we work."

JULIE CERRONE is a certified holistic health coach, patient empowerer, yoga instructor, and health activist blogger (itsjustabadday.com) thriving with psoriatic arthritis and avascular necrosis. Itsjustabadday.com was named one of the top five psoriatic arthritis blogs by Everyday-Health.com, and @justagoodlife was awarded "Best In Show: Twitter" in the 2015 WEGO Health Activist Awards. Focusing on lifestyle and dietary changes, Cerrone empowers chronically fabulous patients, all over the world, to live their best lives possible.

KARMA R. CHÁVEZ is Associate Professor and Director of Graduate Studies in the Department of Mexican and Latina/o Studies at the University of Texas at Austin. Chávez researches social movement building, activist rhetoric, and coalitional politics and emphasizes the rhetorical practices of groups marginalized within existing power structures. She is the author of *Queer Migration Politics* (2013), which examines coalition-building at the many intersections of queer and immigration politics in the contemporary United States; is a co-editor of *Standing in the Intersection: Feminist Voices, Feminist Practices in Communication Studies* (2013); and has published articles in a number of journals, including the *Quarterly Journal of Speech*, *Women's Studies in Communication*, *Text and Performance Quarterly*, and *Communication and Critical/Cultural Studies*.

MERLIN CHOWKWANYUN is Assistant Professor of Sociomedical Sciences at Columbia University's Mailman School of Public Health. His scholarship has been supported by the Robert Wood Johnson Foundation and has appeared in the *DuBois Review, Journal of Urban Affairs, American Journal of Public Health*, and other venues. He is currently writing a book on health activism in the 1960s and 1970s.

CELESTE M. CONDIT is Distinguished Research Professor in the Department of Communication Studies at the University of Georgia. She is the author or co-author of many books, including *Decoding Abortion Rhetoric: Communicating Social Change* (1990) and *The Meanings of the Gene: Public Debates about Heredity* (1999). Her work on the discourse and public understanding of genetics has been funded by the National Institutes of Health and by the Centers for Disease Control. She is currently focusing on the role of emotion in public discourse (pathos) and the relationships among pathos and metanational economics.

CARL ELLIOTT is Professor in the Center for Bioethics and the Department of Pediatrics, and an affiliate faculty member in the Department of Philosophy and the School of Journalism and Mass Communications at the University of Minnesota. He is the author or editor of seven books, including *White Coat, Black Hat: Adventures on the Dark Side of Medi-*

*cine* (2010) and *Better Than Well: American Medicine Meets the American Dream* (2003). His articles have appeared in the *New Yorker, Atlantic Monthly*, the *London Review of Books, Mother Jones*, the *New York Times*, and the *New England Journal of Medicine*. In 2011, the Austen Riggs Center awarded Elliott its Erikson Prize for Excellence in Mental Health Media. He has held postdoctoral or visiting appointments at the University of Chicago, East Carolina University, the University of Otago in New Zealand, and the University of Natal Medical School (now the Nelson R. Mandela School of Medicine), the first medical school in South Africa for nonwhite students. He has been a Network Fellow at the Safra Center for Ethics at Harvard University and a Visiting Associate Professor at the Institute for Advanced Study in Princeton, New Jersey. He is a Fellow of the Hastings Center, an Honorary Member of the Caribbean Bioethics Society, and a recipient of an Outstanding Faculty Award from the University of Minnesota's Council of Graduate Students.

STEVEN EPSTEIN is Professor of Sociology and John C. Shaffer Professor in the Humanities at Northwestern University. He studies the "politics of knowledge"—more specifically, the contested production of expert and especially biomedical knowledge, with an emphasis on the interplay of social movements, experts, and health institutions, and with a focus on the politics of sexuality, gender, and race. He is a co-editor of *Three Shots at Prevention: The HPV Vaccine and the Politics of Medicine's Simple Solutions* (2010). He is especially known for two books: *Inclusion: The Politics of Difference in Medical Research* (2007), which received multiple awards, including the American Sociological Association's Distinguished Book Award; and *Impure Science: AIDS, Activism, and the Politics of Knowledge* (1996), which also received multiple awards, including the C. Wright Mills Prize. He also co-authored *Learning by Heart: AIDS and Schoolchildren in America's Communities* (1989). Epstein has published in such journals as *Social Studies of Science, Body and Society, Sociological Forum, Theory and Society*, and *Sexualities*.

KELLY E. HAPPE is Associate Professor of Communication Studies and Women's Studies at the University of Georgia. She is the author of *The Material Gene: Gender, Race, and Heredity after the Human Genome Project* (NYU Press, 2013), winner of the Diamond Anniversary Book

Award. Her scholarship on rhetoric, race, gender, science, and radical economic thought has appeared in the *Quarterly Journal of Speech*, *Rhetoric and Public Affairs*, *MediaTropes*, *Philosophy and Rhetoric*, and other outlets. She is currently writing a book on historical materialist theories of the body and their relation to radical economic thought.

JENELL JOHNSON is Mellon-Morgridge Professor of the Humanities and Associate Professor of Communication Arts at the University of Wisconsin–Madison. She is the author of *American Lobotomy: A Rhetorical History* (2014), co-editor, with Melissa Littlefield, of *The Neuroscientific Turn: Transdisciplinarity in the Age of the Brain* (2012), and editor of *Graphic Reproduction* (2018). Her work has been published in a number of edited collections and journals, including *Quarterly Journal of Speech, Literature and Medicine, Rhetoric Society Quarterly, Medicine Studies*, and *Journal of Literary and Cultural Disability Studies*.

MARINA LEVINA is Associate Professor of Communication at the University of Memphis. Her research focuses on critical cultural studies of science, technology and medicine, visual culture, and media studies. She has written on the topics of social media and health information technologies, personal genomics, materiality in digital media, and visual culture's engagement with scientific and medical difference. Her work appeared in *Communication and Critical/Cultural Studies, Television & New Media*, and *Surveillance & Society*, as well as numerous other journals and edited collections. She is the first editor of *Monster Culture in the 21st Century: A Reader* (with Diem-my Bui, 2013) and *Post-global Network and Everyday Life* (with Grant Kien, 2010). Her book *Pandemics in the Media* (2014) examines exactly what it means to live, love, and govern in the time of a pandemic in a global environment where flows of commerce, politics, and scientific knowledge are essential to distribution of resources according to previously established principles of difference and otherness.

STUART J. MURRAY is Professor and Canada Research Chair in Rhetoric and Ethics in the Department of English Language and Literature and the Department of Health Sciences at Carleton University in Ottawa, Canada. He is Director of the Digital Rhetorics + Ethics Lab (DR+E),

314 | ABOUT THE CONTRIBUTORS

which supports research into communication ethics, embodiment, and the digital interface of language, text, and culture. Murray's interests also include biopolitics and bioethics, critical theory and media, medical humanities, and phenomenology. He was awarded an SSHRC Standard Research Grant for 2009 through 2012 and a CIHR Operating Grant for 2011 through 2013. He is also the editor of *MediaTropes*, a peer-reviewed interdisciplinary eJournal devoted to the study of media and mediation. He is currently completing a manuscript titled "The Living from the Dead: Disaffirming Biopolitics."

CELIA ROBERTS is Senior Lecturer in the Department of Sociology and a codirector of the Centre for Gender and Women's Studies at Lancaster University. Her research centers on the body, health, reproduction, sexuality, and aging. Her forthcoming book, on early-onset puberty, is entitled *Puberty in Crisis: A Bio-Psycho-Social Account*. She is an author of *Messengers of Sex: Hormones, Biomedicine and Feminism* (2007), which explores the role of hormones in producing sexually differentiated bodies, and a co-author (with Sarah Franklin) of a book on genetics and reproduction, entitled *Born and Made: An Ethnography of Preimplantation Genetic Diagnosis* (2006). She is a co-editor of *Feminist Theory* and recently co-edited, with Myra Hird, a special issue of *Feminist Theory* on nonhuman feminisms.

KIRSTEN SCHULTZ embarked on a path toward patient advocacy after a near-fatal misdiagnosis at age five. Growing up in an abusive situation without medical care, she had to learn the art of caring for her multiple illnesses on her own at a young age. Since her college years, she has gone from knowing nothing about the health care system to helping fellow chronic illness patients navigate it. As a sex educator, writer, and activist, Schultz has worked with organizations and patients from around the world. She runs Chronic Sex (chronicsex.org), an organization that focuses on how disability and chronic illness affect the view of the self, relationships with others, and, of course, sex and sexuality. More information is available about Schultz and her projects at kirstenschultz.org.

NAYAN SHAH is Professor of American Studies and Ethnicity and Professor History at the University of Southern California. Shah specializes in U.S. and Canadian history, gender and sexuality studies, legal and medical history, and Asian American studies. He is the author of two award-winning books: *Stranger Intimacy: Contesting Race, Sexuality and the Law in the North American West* (2011) and *Contagious Divides: Epidemics and Race in San Francisco's Chinatown* (2001), and a number of book chapters and journal articles. Shah is the recipient of fellowships and grants from the Rockefeller Foundation, the van Humboldt Foundation, and the Freeman Foundation and recently served as the editor of *GLQ: A Journal of Lesbian and Gay Studies*.

RICHARD TUTTON is Senior Lecturer in the Department of Sociology and Centre for Science Studies at Lancaster University. He has researched and published about the social and political life of genomic knowledge and technologies in relation to issues of subjectivity and identity, public involvement, and commercial expectations. He is the co-editor of the journal *New Genetics and Society*. In 2014, he published his first monograph, *Genomics and the Reimagining of Personalized Medicine*. Drawing on insights from work in medical history and sociology, this book analyzes changing meanings of personalized medicine over time, from the rise of biomedicine in the twentieth century to the emergence of pharmacogenomics and personal genomics in the 1990s and the early twenty-first century.

IONAT ZURR is an award-winning artist and researcher at the University of Western Australia. She is a cofounder, with Oron Catts, of the Tissue Culture and Art Project. She has been an artist in residence in the School of Anatomy and Human Biology since 1996 and was central to the establishment of SymbioticA in 2000. Zurr, who received her PhD from the Faculty of Architecture, Landscape and Visual Arts, is a core researcher and academic coordinator at SymbioticA. She is considered a pioneer in the field of biological arts, and her work has been exhibited internationally. Zurr specializes in biological and digital imaging, as well as video production. She has studied art history, photography, and media studies and was a research fellow at the Tissue Engineering and Organ Fabrication Laboratory at Harvard Medical School from 2000 to 2001. Her doctoral project examined the ethical and epistemological implications of wet biology art practice.

# INDEX

ACT UP, 124–25

activism, 2–3, 12; and biosociality, 210, 216; bottom-up activism, 234; and disability 9; environmental issues, 85; health activism, 12–13, 15n4, 204–17; and HIV/AIDS, 96, 104 121, 209; and immigration, 129; medical student activism, 179–80; patient activism, 24, 29, 36; and social class, 211, 213. *See also* hunger strikes; Lincoln Collective; Student Health Organizations

advocacy, 2, 6, 12–13, 40, 41, 72, 223–24; health advocacy groups, 6, 38, 204, 209; and HIV/AIDS, 100, 103; and gay health, 26, 38, 39; patient advocacy, 207–8 222, 224

affect, 9, 11, 82, 84, 86; affective experiences, 212; affective investments, 234, 248; affective labor, 213, 250; between animal and researcher, 239; biocitizenship as affective orientation, 236; entanglement with biomedicine, 235; and materiality, 298; and supra-cyborgs, 289–91. *See also* cruel optimism; hope

Agamben, Giorgio, 59, 248

agency, 5, 10, 14, 87, 106, 257, 265–66; and animals, 233, 238; and biocitizenship, 53, 86, 172; and biopolitical logics, 169; and collectivized biocitizenship, 126; collective political agency, 73; and consent, 235; and corporations, 281; diffuse agency, 53; and epigenetics, 82; impersonal moral, 57, 59; of incubators, 267; of neolife, 269; and the noncitizen,118; and prosopopeia, 172; and recognition, 83; and state, 59, 157

American Medical Association (AMA), 180–81

artificial mother, 257–58, 261–62, 272n18

Berlant, Lauren: and citizenship, 23; and cruel optimism, 242, 244–45, 247

biocitizenship, 1–3, 23–25, 66, 71, 74, 81, 84–5, 87, 148, 156, 204–5, 211, 214, 222–25, 227–29, 234, 269, 274, 296; and activism, 9, 222; as affective orientation, 252; and agency, 53–54, 86, 172; and clinical labor, 149; as collectivized, 118, 126, 130; and disability, 17n39; as a discursive tool, 250; and epigenetics, 75; on the ground, 179–80; humanist assumptions of, 257; as imposing identities, 223; and incubators, 256; and informed consent, 173; as lively capital, 252; and medical exploitation, 141; and medical governance revolution, 178; model biocitizen, 8; and necropolitics, 56, 58, 65, 118–19, 123–24, 126, 128–130, 234, 253; and neoliberalism, 7; as normative, 56, 156, 165, 256; and nutritional minimum, 164; in opposition to sovereign citizenship, 55; and optimism, 207; practices of, 82, 104; in relation to sexuality, 22; and social class, 216; and the state, 235; utopic biocitizenship, 263. *See also* biosexual citizenship; carceral biocitizen; chronic citizenship; citizenship; collectivized biocitizenship; epigenetic citizenship; necropolitics: necrocitizenship; sexual citizenship; therapeutic citizenship

233; as law-abiding, 60; as legal status, 23, 117; and LGBT community, 38; as normative, 57; as responsibilities, 23, 34, 58; and rights, 23, 34, 41, 53, 58, 172, 224; and sexuality, 25; and subjects, 59; and vulnerability, 133, 135; and women prisoners, 65. *See also* biocitizenship; biosexual citizenship; carceral biocitizenship; chronic citizenship; collectivized biocitizenship; epigenetic citizenship; genetic citizenship; necrocitizenship; sexual citizenship; therapeutic citizenship

class, 12, 79, 204, 256; and activism, 211–13; and biocitizenship, 216; and biosociality, 204, 207, 216; and the body, 214–15, 217; classism, 99; cultures, 212, 215; as determinant of health, 208–9, 215; and epigenetics, 216; hierarchies, 180; privilege, 188, 190; and race, 209–10; tensions, 188; and white middle-class, 208, 210

clinical labor, 148–49; and sinister side of biocitizenship, 149

collective biocitizenship, 118; as resistance, 126, 130

community, 3, 23–24, 26, 33, 36, 42, 60, 95, 104, 122, 138, 173, 178, 179–80, 182–89, 198; biomedical community, 239; calls for community control, 187, 189–91; community-based organizations, 37, 40; community health and justice, 12; community service, 182; disease communities, 222; disputes over meaning, 180, 188, 193, 195; participation, local scale, 185, 198; outreach, 194; and participatory governance, 194; research community, 236; scientific community, 125, 244

consumerism, 7–8, 105–6; animals as consumers, 233; and consumer goods, 84

corporations, 13, 105–6, 148, 274, 281, 285–86, 288–94, 296, 301–3; and agency,

281; as cyborgs, 297; and privatized psychiatric research, 145–46; and nutritional experimentation, 164; and shaping of care protocols, 165; as zombies, 289–92, 295; and multinational corporations, 296. *See also* supra-cyborg

Correctional Service of Canada (CSC), 51, 53–54, 57–67, 105

cruel optimism, 13, 234, 250, 252; as affective attachment to cure, 242, 244–45; definition of, 242; and necropolitics, 248

cyborgs, 13–14, 275–78, 280, 291, 297

disability, 4, 9, 17n39, 222, 227, 245; and chronic illness, 222–26

epidemiology, 71–72, 74–76, 99; and health disparities, 75; and race, 74

epigenetic citizenship, 11, 71, 76

epigenetics, 10–11, 70, 72–73, 77, 80, 216; and agency, 73; and biological effects of racism, 76; and bodily memory, 75; and class, 216 as encompassing diachronic and synchronic temporalities, 75, 77; and genome editing, 81; as historical materialist theory of the body, 82, 85–87; and new materialism, 87–88n1

eugenics, 1, 4, 35, 87, 262–63, 272n24; discourses, 27, 117, 130

executives, 282, 285, 290–92, 296, 299; as directors of superorganisms, 284

feminism, 34; and antiracism, 81; and the body, 216–17 and epigenetic politics, 76; and politics of women's health, 207

force-feeding, 12, 155, 159, 166–68; as biopolitical process, 163; and bodily intrusion, 157; and contentions of preserving life, 157; and medical complications, 160; as violent-care, 160

146–47; in relationship to coercion and exploitation, 134, 137, 141, 147, 149–50, 156; and the state, 174

intersectionality, 22, 214, 217. *See also* biosectionality

Jorden, Walter, 133–35, 148–50

*Kaimowitz v. Department of Mental Health for the State of Michigan*, 135–37, 142, 147–48

*Lab Animal*, 13, 233–36, 238, 244–45, 247, 251–52

LGBT, activism, 129; and citizenship, 38; health, 38–39; and PrEP advocacy, 103; and rights, 34, 36

life, 1, 35, 56–57, 60–61, 63, 65, 72–73, 76, 84, 99, 107, 110, 137–39, 141, 147, 158, 165, 172–74, 215, 222, 224–26, 228–29, 235–26, 238, 245, 247, 253, 255–63, 265–70, 288, 302; affective investment in, 248; afterlife, 57, 66–67; American life, 196; and animal life, 236, 248, 250, 252; and bare life, 81, 86, 248, 254n31; and biocitizenship, 11–12, 106; as code, 265; in connection to environment, 259; and death, 52–53, 55, 58, 248, 252; decontextualized life, 257; enhancement of life, 30, 167; extension via carceral control, 167; genetic manufacturing of, 268; and the good life, 13, 245; in vitro, 262; laboratory life, 234; life-preserving, 156–61, 172–73; life sciences, 24, 252; lifestyle, 288; life-threatening, 156, 160; life-threatening illness, 134; lifeworlds, 277, 280, 289; management of life, 211, 276; and production of, 118, 155–61, 169; protection of life, 54, 66; public life, 104; and as social death, 56–58, 62; sovereign jurisdiction, 54–55, 59, 62, 248; supra-life-form, 285, 296;

right to life, 64; as uncontainable, 270. *See also* neolife

Lincoln Collective, 179–80, 186–88, 190, 193, 196; and commitment to community, 186; in relationship to the Young Lords, 186–90; and restructuring of governance, 189, 191

materiality, 10–11; and affect, 298; and the body, 71, 81–82; Donna Haraway on, 277; and frameworks of interpretation, 71, 76; and historical materialism, 78, 82, 84; and labor, 213; and new materialism, 87–88n1; and resources, 81

medicine, 1–2, 5, 7, 10, 13, 106, 108–9, 111, 142, 222, 227, 239, 245; dominant ethos of American medicine, 197, 199; evidence-based medicine, 36; internal medicine, 169, 186; laboratory animal medicine, 247; personalized medicine, 8; and relation with bodies, 104; social and political aspects of, 181, 223. *See also* biomedicine; Truvada

mental illness, 133–35, 139, 141–42, 150; and schizophrenia, 133–34, 141–43, 145. *See also* psychiatry

National Institutes of Health (NIH), 35, 38, 79, 112

necropolitics, 11, 13; and laboratory life, 234; and logics of cruel optimism, 248, 252; and necrocitizenship, 56, 118–19, 123, 124, 126

neoliberalism, 7, 8, 78, 79, 105, 256; and biocitizenship, 66; and law, 53; and penal system, 55; and responsibility, 31

neolife, 14, 255, 262, 265, 269, 270; as artificial life, 255; as devoid of agency, 265–66

Novas, Carlos, 208–9; and Gibbon, Sarah, 205–06; and Rose, Nikolas, 4, 6, 24, 54, 56, 66, 117, 206, 234–35

sexuality, 25; and education, 27; and expression, 34; and health, 21, 26–27; and identity, 34; and normativity, 100; and pleasure, desire, 100–101; as queer practice, 106, 108; in relation to biosexual citizenship, 26, 37; as varied, 103

Sixth International AIDS Conference (IAC), 118, 119, 121–25, 127–28

Smith, Ashley, 10, 51–63, 66–67

social death, 53, 57–58; as life, 56; and nonsubjects, 54; as somatic subject, 54; and the state, 55

social hygiene, 22, 26, 40; era of, 34–36, 39, 41; movement, 27–28

social media, 225–27; and ePatients, 223–24

somatic subjectivity, 53–56; and social death, 54, 57

sovereignty, 10, 51, 53, 55, 67, 250, 265; and law, 53, 58–59, 62–63, 65; logic of, 53; and jurisdiction over life, 54, 57; and responsibility, 62. *See also* state

state, 2, 6, 12, 178, 274, 297–98; and agency, 59; and biocitizenship, 235; and biopolitics, 55, 66, 118; and the body, 56, 65, 122; and disciplinary power, 174; and informed consent, 174; and institutions, 56; as nation-state, 117, 281, 286, 288, 294, 296, 303; and power, 54; in relation to biomedicine, 157; as schizophrenic, 289–95; and security, 172; state-sponsored projects, 25

Student Health Organizations (SHO), 181–86, 190; implosion of, 185

subjectivity, 82, 84, 86–87

supra-cyborg, 14, 274, 278, 282–97, 299–303; affective tendencies, 289–93, 295; definition of, 275; and notions of the self, 282

targets, 282, 285, 291–92, 295–97, 299, 303; as telos of self-advantageous behavior, 283

temporality, 71, 73–74, 80, 84; and chronic citizenship, 104; as diachronic, 74, 79, 85; and politics, 76; prenatal temporality, 80; and racism, 74; as synchronic, 74, 79, 85

therapeutic citizenship, 15n4, 24

transgender, 83

Truvada, 11, 95–100, 103, 105–6, 108–12; and politics of respectability, 101–2

U.S. Department of Health and Human Services (HHS), 21–22, 32–33, 38, 120–21, 123, 141

vulnerability, 133, 135, 147, 149–50, 156, 233, 242

World Health Organization (WHO), 29, 37, 121; and definition of sexual health, 29, 31, 41

Young Lords, 186; and community empowerment, 187, 193; and healthcare activism, 186, 201n29; and Health Revolutionary Movement (HRUM), 187–93

Lightning Source UK Ltd.
Milton Keynes UK
UKHW01f0243130718
325658UK00003B/220/P